Health Technology Development and Use

How does the development and use of new technology relate? How can users contribute to innovation? This volume is the first to study these questions by following particular technologies over several product launches in detail. It examines the emergence of inventive ideas about future technology and uses, how these are developed into products and embedded in health care practices, and how the form and impact of these technologies then evolves through several rounds of design and deployment across different types of organizations.

Examining these processes through three case studies of health care innovations, these studies reveal a blind spot in extant research on development-use relations. The majority of studies have examined shorter 'episodes': moments within particular design projects, implementation processes, usability evaluations, and human-machine interactions. Studies with longer time-frames have resorted to a relatively coarse 'grain-size' of analysis and hence lost sight of how the interchange is actually done. As a result, there are no social science, information systems, or management texts which comprehensively or adequately address:

- how different moments, sites and modes of shaping new technology determine the evolution of new technology;
- the detailed mechanisms of learning, interaction, and domination between different actors and technology during these drawn out processes; and
- the relationship of technology projects and the professional practices and social imaginations that are associated in technology development, evaluation, and usage.

The "biographies of technologies and practices" approach to new technology advanced in this volume offers us an urgent new insight to core empirical and theoretical questions about how and where development projects gain their representations of future use and users. It also illustrates how usage is actually designed, how users' requests and modifications affect designs, and what kind of learning takes place between developers and users in different phases of innovation—all crucial to our understanding and ability to advance new health technology, and innovation more generally.

Routledge Studies in Technology, Work and Organizations

EDITED BY DAVID PREECE, *UNIVERSITY OF TEESIDE, UK*

1. Information Society and the Workplace
Edited by Tuula Heiskanen and Jeff Hearn

2. Technological Change and Organizational Action
Edited by David Preece and Juha Laurila

3. Managing Complex Projects
Networks, Knowledge and Innovation
Neil Alderman, Chris Ivory, Ian McLouglin, Alfred Thwaites and Roger Vaughan

4. Information and Communication Technologies in Rural Society
Being Rural in a Digital Age
Grete Rusten and Sarah Skerratt

5. Software and Organizations
The Biography of the Enterprise-wide System or How SAP Conquered the World
Neil Pollock and Robin Williams

6. Technological Communities and Networks
Triggers and Drivers for Innovation
Dimitris Assimakopoulos

7. Health Technology Development and Use
From Practice-Bound Imagination to Evolving Impacts
Sampsa Hyysalo

Health Technology Development and Use

From Practice-Bound Imagination to Evolving Impacts

Sampsa Hyysalo

Routledge
Taylor & Francis Group
New York   London

First published 2010
by Routledge
270 Madison Avenue, New York, NY 10016

Simultaneously published in the UK
by Routledge
2 Park Square, Milton Park, Abingdon, Oxon OX14 4RN

Routledge is an imprint of the Taylor & Francis Group, an informa business

© 2010 Taylor & Francis

Typeset in Sabon by IBT Global.
Printed and bound in the United States of America on acid-free paper by IBT Global.

Library of Congress Cataloging-in-Publication Data
Hyysalo, Sampsa, 1974–
   Health technology development and use : from practice-bound imagination to evolving impacts / by Sampsa Hyysalo.
      p. cm. — (Routledge studies in technology, work and organizations; 7)
   Includes bibliographical references and index.
   1. Medical technology. I. Title. II. Series: Routledge studies in technology, work and organizations; 7.
      [DNLM: 1. Biomedical Technology. 2. Diffusion of Innovation. W 82 H999h 2010]
      R855.3.H99 2010
      610.28—dc22
      2009051956

ISBN13: 978-0-415-80646-6 (hbk)
ISBN13: 978-0-203-84915-6 (ebk)

for Matti Hyysalo

and in loving memory of Pirkko Karhu

Contents

List of Figures   xi
List of Tables   xv
Preface   xvii
Acknowledgements   xxi
Introduction   xxiii

PART I
Design–Use Relations and Biographies of Technology

1   From Markets to Social Learning: Mapping the Dynamics of
    Design, Use, and Early Evolution of New Technology   3

2   Biography of Technologies and Practices: Studying Technology
    across Time and Space   30

PART II
Grounding and Theorizing

3   The Birth of the User: Community and Imagination   63

4   The Anticipation of Need: Investigations and Intermediaries   95

5   Visions in Matter: Invention and Erosion   109

6   Nurturing Technology: Enactment and Impact   139

7   The Post-Launch Change: Learning and Reconfiguring   163

PART III
Comparisons and Implications

8   Diabetes Databases: Co-Design, Its Evolution, and Power
    Relations   185

9   TeleChemistry: Radical Innovation, Deviance, and Path
    Formation   209

10 Conclusions: Findings and Theorizing   231

11 Implications: Policy, Evaluation, and Development Practice   254

Data Appendix   277
References   283
Notes   307
Index   317

Figures

1.1 User-producer pairing seen as consisting of two dyads A-B and B-C.   7

1.2 To account for the users in innovation we need to clarify how they are positioned between primary supply organizations and primary user organizations of a given technology as well as in regards to developing and using.   20

1.3 Pipeline linear development and diffusion.   21

1.4 Pick and mix model.   22

1.5 User-centred design.   23

1.6 Technology experiment / evolving co-design project.   24

1.7 Innofusion and domestication model.   25

1.8 Learning economy as an attempt to replace the "black box" of markets by identifiable mechanisms of learning.   28

1.9 Processes that are seen to mediate between the domains of supply and use in learning economy and social learning.   29

2.1 MIRP "fireworks" model of innovation.   35

2.2 Stylized research design for a study on biography of technology on safety alarm systems for the elderly.   42

2.3 Strauss and Corbin project matrix.   45

2.4 Clarke's situational matrix.   50

2.5 "Hutchins cube," a representation of how multiple developments and speeds of change (the arrows) are present within a "moment of human practice" (the cube).   51

3.1   A schematic portrayal of the overlapping ICT and elderly
      worlds in early 1990s.   66

3.2   Early visions of Vivago-Wristcare.   69

3.3   While Kuhn sees scientists operating within a paradigm,
      Bijker recognizes that people may be members of more than
      one community (E, E2), and influenced by more than one
      frame (TF, TF2, TF3).   78

3.4   Screenshot of EU partner search announcement in 2006.   81

3.5   The development of Vivago-Wristcare from inception in
      1992–1993 to the post-market-launch period in 1998–2000.   90

5.1   Design setting.   114

5.2   Early drawings and first-generation Vivago-Wristcare as an
      artifact used to envision the push-button functioning and
      shape.   116

5.3   Progression of drawings for the push-button.   120

5.4   Third-generation Vivago in 2009, second generation in
      2002, first-generation device in 1998, and 1995 design sketch. 127

5.5   Different bracelet solutions, tests, and sketches.   129

6.1   Vivago-Wristcare as a new means for the interactions
      between residents and home-care workers.   143

6.2   A nurse making a diagnosis with the help of activity-graph
      monitoring.   146

6.3   A nurse listening to an alarm message through her cell
      phone.   149

6.4   The elements of elderly care in a rest home depicted as an
      activity-system from a nurse's perspective.   152

6.5   The network of activity systems around the rest home in the
      city of Espoo.   154

6.6   The network of activity systems around the rest home in the
      city of Turku.   155

8.1   PDMS diabetes database program in its late second
      generation.   191

8.2   Potential ZPD for the PDMS project in autumn 2000.   203

10.1   Major categories and illustrative subclasses for sources of
       representations of use in technology design.   234

Tables

2.1   Methodological Criteria for Socio-Technical Change in the
early 1990s and Guideposts for Living up to Them Taken
on in the Present Volume   31

2.2   Traditional and More Recent View on Innovation   33

4.1   The Main Conclusion of the Marketing Surveys and User
Interviews and an Evaluation of its Critical Potential for Design 99

4.2   The Main Conclusions of the Design Study, and the
Evaluation of its Critical Potential for Design   101

4.3   The Main Results of the Pilot Use and an Evaluation of its
Critical Potential for Design   102

5.1   Map of Features that Were Recognized to Affect Usage in
the Second-Generation Design Process of Vivago-Wristcare   111

5.2   Origins for the Push-Button Solution, Goals for its Design
and Specific Features Realizing These   124

6.1   Vivago-Wristcare in the Work of Rest-Home Managers   141

6.2   Vivago-Wristcare and Elderly Residents' Lives: Projects and
Purposes   145

6.3   Vivago-Wristcare in the Work of the Nurses and Home-
Care Workers   148

8.1   Reasons Given for Abandoning the Use of Databases   195

8.2   Reasons Given for the Continuation of Use of the Databases   195

9.1   A Shift in Innovative Activity from Oxidizers to the LMP
Project   216

9.2   The Rise of a "Hermetic Pathway"—The Fall of a Product
       Concept   221

9.3   The Characteristics and Development of the
       TeleChemistry System Compared with the
       Characteristics of a Conventional Clinical Testing System   226

11.1   Comparison of Three Micro-Niches for TeleChemistry   273

A.1   Interviews Conducted for the Vivago-Wristcare Study   278

Preface

It would save us much fuss if we could just ask. We could gain a first-hand report on what the defining moments were that led to success and hardships, what lessons had to be learned before any prosperity could follow, and what events rendered all the effort finally obsolete. But technologies cannot tell their own stories. To our good fortune, technologies do not lead Robinson Crusoe lives, and whatever happens to them happens intertwined in the activities of their conception, production, uses, misuses, *et cetera*. In this sense, it is only proper to ask people around a technology about the course of its life. In telling the story about the technology, people employ the object to tell the story about their lives and concerns, and this connection is exactly what we must understand if we are to tell the biography of new technology.

The trouble with just asking, though, is that most accounts on technology rely on strong conventions of how technologies and inventions are talked about. Hagiographies of great inventors and social reformers abound. Perseverance stories of bringing magnificent novelty to the market despite all incredulity are common, as is the storyline of just stumbling across something insanely wonderful. Utopian registers of a new world technology will create have their counterparts in the dystopian anticipations of the "brave new worlds," the stories of disastrous technological failure, and portrayals of technology as yet another useless gizmos.

History and sociology of technology has ample evidence to show how the inventors and scientists learn to tell a polished story of what went on in the discovery and its subsequent refinement. If they go into too much detail, audiences beyond their close colleagues are lost. Should they relate all the great uncertainty, incidents, and drawbacks, their plausibility as business partners and charismatic leaders in their fields could become compromised. Succeeding with new technology requires learning how to tailor its story for many audiences and ironing out the non-fitting elements in the storyline. Indeed, upon encountering a newspaper headline such as "Billion markets in the wrist!" as we did in the course of research reported upon in this book, we could by and large guess the familiar on-the-verge-of-success narrative that indeed followed it. We could equally anticipate how the ingredients in the story had been catered by the president of the start-up company in question, which he later verified, and how he, in turn, had anticipated what the reporter would write and how his story could influence potential investors and clients.

Similar narrating and editing goes on in the stories technology's adopters tell. When a technology represents the latest advances in their field, few wish to appear Luddite or incompetent with it, and so the hardships and helplessness experienced tend to become edited. In such case the potential of new technology is often rescued by blaming insufficient training, hiccups in design, or poor management of implementation. On the other hand, when technologies are more peripheral to people's prime concerns, separating oneself from a technology becomes common by, for instance, parading ones indifference to it or denouncing the value the technology may have. Stories of impoverishment of working life via the introduction of new technology are also a familiar genre relating technology to organizational reforms and management control.

An important feature of all narratives is what sources and stories are made to figure in the story, what is edited and what is let take center stage. It makes a great difference how we tell the biographies of technology, just as it makes a great difference to our understanding of human lives how we tell human biographies. Since human biographies are more familiar to us, let us illustrate the matter with one particularly sober and terse observation about the matter:

> "Once upon a time there lived in Berlin, Germany, a man called Albinus. He was rich, respectable, happy; one day he abandoned his wife for the sake of a youthful mistress; he loved; was not loved; and his life ended in disaster.
>
> This is the whole of the story and we might have left it at that had there not been profit and pleasure in the telling; and although there is plenty of space on a gravestone to contain, bound in moss, the abridged version of a man's life, detail is always welcome."

(Vladimir Nabokov, Laughter in the Dark, *first two paragraphs*)

What Nabokov here pretends to chronicle are the typified features of human lives—what is commonly used to characterize us (social status, economic wealth, comfort in life), what truly drives us (desire and love instead of ease of life), how life evolves (a mix of contingencies and a causally understandable chain of events), and what morals we draw from these (whimsically forsaking a respectable life for one's desire leads to disaster). Nabokov then goes on to spell out the irony he sees in settling with such a portrayal of life in the scope there is available in telling biographies: we truly need not tell more than the moss-covered edition of man's life consisting of a name, two dates, and perhaps a little aphorism; everything beyond this is a matter, as he nicely puts it, of "profit and pleasure," a matter of our choice.

These remarks are particularly poignant with regard to academic portrayals of new technology, for these make no exception in providing highly edited narrations of technology's life. The dominant genre of academic writing on technology closely resembles that "moss-cover edition of man's life"—namely, statistical comparisons between different technologies that tend to reduce technologies to their barest essentials. And in affinity to the presumed core features of human lives, such as those spelled out by Nabokov in regard to Albinus' life above, the biographies of technologies in this book could be condensed as a rather short confirmatory message concerning assumptions in some of the existing research. For instance, "The conception of the three Finnish health care inventions we study owed to historical accumulation of resources, to fortuitously combining mutually complementary resources as well as to contingent events. The projects studied won funding and prizes and showed great promise of economic profits and addressing socially significant problems. But a precondition to gaining markets and usefulness was the drawn-out interchange between developers, users, and third parties. The initial shape of these technologies, their uses, and criteria for what they should do evolved for years, even decades, and over several product launches. Even at the end of our extended study period, their eventual form and manner of success was yet to be seen."

While such distilled findings do reveal important phenomena that characterize the (early) biographies of new health technology, we insist, in affinity with Nabokov above, that to fathom the reality from which such description can be distilled, a far more precise understanding of what went on in these projects is needed.

But, and this is very much the key issue in this book, unlike the novelist who could fill in the colors to the story of Albinus at his will (or, rather, through mastery of literary conventions and the possibilities of language), our academic quest for better conveying the evolvement of new technology and its social effects hinges on whether we can build a research approach that can provide relevant real-life details in the first place. The "biographies of technologies and practices approach" we elaborate in this book is an attempt to do this. It is thus far unique in that it spans both *development and uses of the same technology* and studies them on multiple scales of analysis, *from minute interactions to decades of development*. This approach allows us to foreground the highly consequential but grossly under-studied issue of how social imaginations and routine practices (of both developers and users) intertwine and how they change. This throws new light to questions of agency, learning and designer–user relations in socio-technical change as we do not need to resort to armchair theorizing or "patching together findings" from different studies on different technologies and user practices as has largely been the case to date. The more full bodied studies, and resulting biographies, also help in comparing developer-initiated, user-initiated, and breakthrough innovation projects in greater depth. As these issues we cover in this volume are arguably for both "profit and pleasure" in our understanding of technology, its development and its appropriation, we now invite you to explore with us the biographies of technologies and related practices—as empirical case studies, as a methodological development and as a source for new theoretical insight.

Acknowledgements

Even though half of my case studies have been conducted solo, the research leading to this volume has very much been a group effort. I had the privilege to join and work for years in a research program set up by Reijo Miettinen, Mervi Hasu, and Janne Lehenkari. My later co-research with Maria Höyssä, Nina Janasik, and Leena Gävert has been just as important a learning journey.

I am grateful for the generous and courageous attitude the personnel in start-up firms and in medical settings had to being interviewed, being video-recorded, and having their past documents zealously photocopied without full certainty of what would eventually come of it all. Vivago Oy, ProWellness Ltd., TeleChemistry Oy, and MuodonVuoksi Oy deserve to be remembered as companies that let others see their innovation processes and daily work in a realistic manner without the usual mystifications and polishing.

Over the years, many mentors and colleagues have contributed their insight to the analyses and theorizing in this volume. My warmest thanks go to Geoffrey Bowker, Michel Cole, Yrjö Engeström, Kirsten Foot, Judith Gregory, Mark Hartswood, Eva Heiskanen, Janne Hukkinen, Mikael Johnson, Sirkku Kivisaari, Kari Kuutti, Turo-Kimmo Lehtonen, Markku Nurminen, Mika Pantzar, Neil Pollock, Matt Ratto, Fritjof Sahlström, Jussi Silvonen, Susan Leigh Star, James Stewart, Juha Tuunainen, and Robin Williams.

In practical preparation of the book, my warmest thanks go to Taina Seiro; Anna Shefl; and, in Routledge to series editor David Preece, four anonymous reviewers, Laura Stearns, Stacy Noto and Michael Watters.

I am grateful for permissions to reprint material from the following articles. Some passages in Chapter 1 and 10 have been first published in "Learning for learning economy and social learning". *Research policy 38* (5):726–735 and a part of Chapter 1 in "Intermediaries, users and social learning in technological innovation" in *International Journal of Innovation Management 12* (3): 295–325, the latter of which I wrote together with James Stewart, whom I thank for his permission to reproduce parts of our joint paper. Part of Chapter 3 has appeared as "Representations of use and Practice Bound Imaginaries in Automating the Safety of The Elderly".

Social Studies of Science 36 (4):599–626. Earlier versions of parts in Chapter 4 have appeared in "Some Problems in the Traditional Approaches of Predicting the Use of a Technology-Driven Invention." *Innovation 16* (2):118–137, and in "Users, an emerging human resource for R&D? From preference elicitation towards the joint exploration of users' needs." *International Journal of Human Resouce Development and Management 4* (1):22–38. Earlier versions of parts in Chapter 6 have appeared as "Versions of care technology". *Human Technology 3* (2):228–247 and in "Technology Nurtured—Collectives in maintaining and implementing technology for elderly care." *Science Studies 17* (2):23–43. Earlier version of Chapter 7 has appeared as "The role of learning-by-using in the design of healthcare technologies: A case study". *The Information Society 22* (2):89–100. Some of the text in Chapter 8 has been first published in "Contextualizing Power in Collaborative Design". In *PDC 2002, Participatory Design Conference 23.-25.6.2002*, edited by T. Binder, J. Gregory and I. Wagner. Malmö, Sweden: Computer Professionals for Social Responsibility and in "An Activity-Theoretical Method for Studying User-Participation in IS Design." *Methods of Information in Medicine 42* (4):398–405. Both articles were written together with Janne Lehenkari. Earlier version of Chapter 9 has appeared as "The fog of innovation: Innovativeness and deviance in developing new clinical testing equipment." *Research policy 38* (6):984–993, written together with Maria Höyssä. Short passages of Chapter 10 have appeared in "Figuring technologies, users and designers—Steps towards an adequate vocabulary for design–use relation." In *Use of Science and Technology in Business: Exploring the impact of using activity for systems, organizations and people*, edited by E. Baraldi, H. Håkanson, F. Prenkert and A. Waluschewski. Bingley, UK: Emerald Publishing Group.

Introduction

Technological dreams are persistent. Paperless health care was just around the corner by 1980. The revolutionizing march of the digital appeared inevitable in the information-intensive medical world, and, indeed, 30 years later, the first paperless hospitals have been created and a wide range of e-health is routinely available in most industrialized countries. But what we have at present mocks the initial dreams in many respects. Poor usability and interface design continues to hinder work. Programs and databases do not interoperate sufficiently, and they suffer from frequent slow-downs. The variation in the practices of caregiving, data recording, and client preferences splinters markets, yet the customizations of systems still do not support the work sufficiently. Questions of data protection and confidentiality remain difficult, not to mention those involving varying classifications, recording practices, and metadata. Other hindrances abound, and over the years frustration has been high over what machines (or engineers) still can't (or won't) do, why (medical) practitioners fail to appropriate innovations, and why (health) administrations fail to introduce needed reforms. Yet these difficulties have not spelled an end to financing, development, or procurement of e-health applications. Quite the contrary. And even though many dreams of e-health have not come to full fruition, other, previously unanticipated applications and services have emerged. Digital health care is persistently just around the corner.

If we resist the temptation to isolate the problems in the slow technological transformation of health care with any one group of actors, this transition provides us with particularly fertile ground for learning how technological change takes place. To understand why and how technological dreams persist and how they turn into eventual social effects of new technologies, we need to examine in depth the practices in technology development and use and the concrete processes that transform initial ideas into evolving impacts of new technologies.

This is acute in medical settings presently, but relevant also elswhere. Digitalization is presently seeping through organizations and practices in most walks of life, from grocery stores to libraries and from child care to border controls, and it will continue to do so for some time to come. This will affect our lives profoundly. And as important a transformation as digitalization is, it is not the only major transformation taking place in our infrastructures and instrumentations even presently. Technological change has become a pervasive part of our lives and we are in need of better understanding of how to orient ourselves in the midst of it, regardless of if we have to engage with new technology as citizens, as professionals, or as specialists in technology.

Unfortunately, some of the commonest ideas of how development and utilization of new technology are related are also some of the most misleading. The stories of genius matching technical capabilities with dawning human desires, the market mediating a finite set of economic and technical attributes and consumer preferences, innovations "diffusing" through social systems like sweetener in a glass of water, technology's inherent laws driving development, or science advancing on its endless frontier are all well rehearsed. Yet these narrative registers skip over the typically drawn-out circulation of people, ideas, and technical efforts that goes into factually achieving a match between design and desire (Hennion 1989; Callon et al. 2002). As a part of this, these explanations mask the often dramatic changes taking place in developer organizations in the course of innovation. They also fail to address how new technology enters practices laden with existing instrumentation, routines, and visions of the future, and misrepresent what is involved in attempts to change the technical mediation in such relatively durable social formations. Consequently, these registers leave us high and dry when it comes to understanding technological change, particularly on the scale of our own work and organization.[1]

Handling the relationship between new technologies and their future uses appears to be particularly hard. The failure to respond to the preferences and needs of users has been persistently reported as being the major reason for unsuccessful R&D, particularly in the high-tech and software fields. In the 1970s, a series of studies, most notably "project SAPPHO," compared successful and unsuccessful innovation projects. The (mis)understanding of user needs was one of the very few factors that were statistically significant and consistent (Coombs et al. 1987; Rothwell et al. 1974). In the 1980s, 70 percent of large UK and US information systems were classified as "functional failures," bringing only harm or marginal utility to their customers (Gibbs 1994). In the mid-1990s, product developers' own estimate of the failure rate of software projects was an astonishing 84 percent, with failure to meet user needs featuring again as the most common reason, at 12 percent (Standish Group 1995). More recent updates on these self evaluations feature higher success rates, but it is still by no means a decisive change (there was still a 68 percent failure rate in the 2009 study). More in-depth inquiries on the dynamics of particular R&D processes portray a similar difficulty in dealing with use- and user-related issues in design (Miettinen et al. 2003; Rohracher 2005; Williams et al. 2005). At the same time, the past two decades have also seen a steady increase in management literature stressing users and clients as a key competitive asset (Leonard 1995; Prahalad and Ramaswamy 2004; von Hippel 2005).

This state of affairs has been characterized as the *producer–user paradox* (Miettinen et al. 2003): while both researchers and practitioners have consistently voiced the need to more carefully attend to future usage, changes in technology production seem small in comparison.

In order to throw light on what these problems are composed of and why they persist, the present volume seeks to provide an empirically detailed and theoretically elaborated view of how development and use interrelate in the early years of new technology. To this end, we report on detailed case studies of health technology across several cycles of designing and using— covering the early emergence of these technologies from the technological dreams that preceded them to their embedding in users' practices and the subsequent evolution of their impacts. In doing so, we seek to address the work required to make new technology succeed, regardless of whether this concerns adapting cultural representations, organizational practices, and interactions between people or technical problem-solving and economic calculation.

Unhelpful Compartmentalization of Research

One reason we need better comprehension of the aforementioned themes lies in the difficulty of dealing with the interrelations of the various constituent parts of the development–use nexus. A number of separate and in many respects poorly compatible disciplines (or fields of research) deal with (industrial, software, and systems) design, appropriation, implementation, marketing, post-launch improvements, product development, organizational change, learning, technology management, technology policy, and so on. Each field has its own focal areas of interests, typical research set-ups, preferred types of data and analysis, and questions asked, which makes comparisons and aggregate models hard to achieve (for reviews see, e.g., Russell and Williams 2002; Pollock and Williams 2008; Fagerberg et al. 2005). The academic research is further structured in two distinct ways that hinder the production of adequate insight on the processes that take place in between these areas.

The first division line runs across scales of analysis. The vast majority of research on socio-technical change operates on a single unit of analysis in terms of the time span and granularity of data analyzed.

Research with a coarser granularity of analysis indicates that design and use interrelate but can seldom address how. One gets a deterministic sense that divergent interests, operating logics, work cultures, business models, etc., must result in a certain number of failures (Freeman 1994; Lundvall 1985). While such a view has limited use for people enmeshed in an innovative project, it is also at striking odds with micro-scale studies on methods developed for managing user centered design that emphasize all that can be done (e.g., Beyer and Holtzblatt 1998; Kuniavsky 2003; Bødker et al. 2004). This research on the scale that focuses on relatively short episodes from minutes to months of designing and using excels at showing *how*, but in turn, it faces difficulty in bridging its results on design and use in a sound manner.

This brings us to the second division of research: part of the broad-scale inquiries aside, research focuses either on development or use. As Pollock and Williams (2008) point out, the most common type of studies, the "impact" and "implementation" studies, by default "black-boxes" the development process. It then remains a mystery how cumbersome technology can persist and proliferate despite significant difficulties in particular implementations and how a positively appraised technology does not spread "as it should." Unfortunately (but symmetrically), the studies on design and development tend not to follow the technology into use. They rather assume the negative effects of technologists' practices in "configuring users" (Woolgar 1991) or the positive effects, such as fluent use and happy users, from sales figures (Kotro 2005).

This split in studying *only use* or *only design* has a surprisingly strong hold on research. It crops up even in the most unlikely places, for instance in the studies of co-design between designers and users and the increasing number of studies on innovation by users. These do study designers and users but in point of fact do not study the everyday use of technology. They restrict the analysis to the design and innovation that emerges *from it* (von Hippel 1988; Luethje and Herstatt 2004; Prahalad and Ramaswamy 2004) or study usages only as grounding and inspiration *for* (more accountable) design (Bødker et al. 2004). Neither do they study in detail what happens to co-designs or user-innovations after their initial successes.

Thus, we would argue that most existing studies either are too "short term" in their research design, and thus missing important developments in the lifecycle of new technologies, or resort to too distant an analysis to really address how development and use interrelate in the evolution of new technology. Together these divisions help to foster various kinds of "narrative bias" that easily prevail within given types of study even if they conflict with other, arguably related lines of studies (Stewart and Williams 2005).

In order to go beyond these limitations of previous research, we have developed what we believe is a more adequate type of research design, which we call "biography of technologies and practices" study (see Miettinen et al. 1999, 2003; Pollock and Williams 2008), elaborated on in the course of this volume in terms of theory, methodology, and—most importantly—the kinds of new findings it has provided in our concrete research projects addressing the developer–user nexus.

Biographies of Technologies and Practices

Let us briefly illustrate the kind of issues biographies of technology and practices study tends to raise to the surface by briefly reflecting on some of the key moments of our study of software for diabetes treatment (that we shall examine properly in Chapter 8 of this volume).

A diabetes database project was developed in intense collaboration with groups of users and a software company. After its 2.0 version was launched, it proliferated to most hospital districts in Finland and was expected to conquer the land. Both users and developers were happy, and plans to copy this sort of illness-specific medical database for other chronic diseases were drawn up, as were strategies for how to export it to, for instance, the UK.

After the first couple of months of our research on this project, it appeared as nothing short of a textbook case of the power of user–developer collaboration, and our main research aim was to detail good practices that other companies could use in setting up mutually beneficial user–producer collaboration. But things turned out not to be quite so simple. When both technology development and use are examined on multiple scales of analysis, a mixture of contingencies and patterns tends to come into view. Projects are primed with previous projects in the same class of technology, such as an "organization-wide software package" (Pollock and Williams 2008) or "diabetes database programs," that is advanced (or reinvigorated and re-innovated in a different form). They are also primed by the patterns in the development of users' practices and in the way these have been coupled to date. The "biography approach" does not stop at any one design or appropriation episode and consequently can reveal dynamics in how exactly the changing of technological practices happens over time.

After the fourth of our interviewees had noted in passing that he also had previously tried to build a database for diabetes care, we became suspicious. How many of these projects could there have been in a small Nordic country like Finland!? It was no trivial task to build one, and reasonable technical means had been around only for 15 to 20 years. Our decision to conduct interviews in all major Finnish hospitals revealed that there had been at least 21 of them. Our nickname for the phenomenon—the graveyard of diabetes databases—began as a sort of compelling joke until the data and analysis accumulated. It turned out that these programs had been built largely for the same reasons in data handling, by roughly the same sort of highly specialized people in diabetes care, and had waned because of equally identifiable and common patterns in their design and usage. No joke. Years of specialist time, tens of millions in wasted money.

These findings threw important new light on the design collaboration we were studying up close. They made us understand why the medical practitioners were so proficient in elaborating requirements and providing design ideas—many drew from their personal history in building similar artifacts—but also opened our eyes to the patterns there were in how these systems had been designed and perils this could entail for the present and future projects.

While the program we followed most closely did proliferate to nearly the whole of Finland, it became used only in units specializing in diabetes and not in primary care, where the majority of the diabetics were treated. The interface and architecture of this program could navigate the shortcomings of earlier diabetes programs in specialist hands and with specialist enthusiasm. But when it came to less frequent and less central usages by regular GPs and nurses, it ran into the same types of problems as the programs in the graveyard in not fitting the work and being too complex to use during patient reception. This jeopardized both the supplier's profits and user developers' aspirations of enhancing diabetes care on the whole.

At the same time, the software company became increasingly reluctant to incorporate any more development suggestions from its user-collaborators. Having now accumulated an extensive amount of functionality for its diabetes product, the company moved to more incremental and more in-house-led development. The former partner–user organizations were now charged for using the database. Yet the company's sales in primary care in Finland and its initiatives in the UK did not move forward much for several years.

The understanding we came to develop of the strengths of lead-user–industry collaboration (the project produced a program that was commercially viable and served well in at least specialist diabetes care) as well as its challenges (in, for instance, managing divergent interests and requirements and the co-evolution of product, user-innovation community, and collaborative relations) was richer than would have emerged under a more limited research design using only one granularity of analysis and focal point of inquiry. Indeed, the promise of biographic studies of new technology and related practices lies not only in providing a temporally extended in-depth view of the process of innovation but also in being able to document what issues affect the directions the innovation processes take. In this capacity, the approach of the volume focuses on the following four interrelated themes.

1) How new technologies evolve during their first generations. Particular emphasis here is laid on how initial concepts for new technology emerge and how these ideas and their technical embodiments change over the years, what associated changes take place over the years in the practices of supplier companies and in those of adopters of the technology, and how different ways of organizing the innovation (e.g., "linear development" or "collaborative design") vary in these early years and what effect these have on the project success.

2) How development and user practices interrelate in the various stages of early biography of technology. Key issues include but are not limited to what roles users and intermediary actors play in innovation and how their different involvements affect the emerging technology, what sources of representations of technology and its use there are during the early evolution of new technology, and how their relative levels of importance change.

3) The distribution and kinds of "agency" that developers, users, artifacts, and regulatory bodies come to have in different phases of early development. The key topics here include what constitutes "users" and "developers" and "technology" at different sites and moments of innovation; how previous practices enable and constrain envisioning of desirable future directions; and how the "impact" of technology on user practices changes over the years.

4) Learning that takes place between developers and users. This, includes what issues and contents developers and users must learn about in the course of early evolution of new technology, what forms of learning factually take place in the learning "in the wild" between developers and users, conditions that facilitate or hinder learning in different constellations between development and use, and how various means and methods can facilitate learning.

Readers versed with the literature on technological change recognize these four themes as familiar topics in previous research but recognize equally that the questions clustered under the four themes differ importantly with respect to the questions that have been customarily asked. This is either because they span both development and use and their interrelations over time or because they examine in-depth phenomena that have been taken as an explanans, phenomena used for explaining innovation, rather than something inquired into in-depth. Indeed, mainstream innovation studies have predominantly examined the aforementioned themes by using quantitative materials—usually whole firms and whole innovation projects as minimal units of data—and have demonstrated their wider and aggregated significance to technological and socio-economic change, rather than opening up what these are composed of in actual innovation processes. Increasing our understanding of these underlying key issues offers fresh insight not only for researchers but also for those attempting to foster innovation on the company floor or in user organizations. Similarly, the biographies approach offers integrative insight for researchers in human–computer interaction design and information systems, who predominantly engage in technology projects only during some of the design and implementation episodes and consequently seldom gain an encompassing view of processes that relate different moments and sites in the evolution of new technology and practices. Likewise, practitioners must improvise in their current more or less unique situation and have a limited repertoire from earlier experiences and from other guiding stories in their field. The kind of systematic research pursued in this volume broadens the range of cases practitioners can use in reflecting on their current projects and provides means for better extrapolation between cases, sites, and moments in technology projects.

With these considerations in mind, the present volume is primarily addressed to three audiences.

1. researchers and professionals in interaction design, usability, information systems, and medical informatics whose topical field is human–technology and design–use relations.

2. social and behavioral scientists, who increasingly study technology-intensive settings, work practices, and technological change.
3. policymakers, information systems managers, organization researchers, and business scholars who deal with technological change at a more aggregate level and seek to gain more insight on these processes.

In all, the "biography of technologies and practices" approach is part of the move towards what some have called next- or third-generation technology studies (e.g., Pollock and Williams 2008). Many recent studies in their own ways have given a more nuanced and rounded view of how the construction of technology meanders through society and how the implications of technology shift during this journey (Clarke 2005; de Laet and Mol 2000; Mol 2002; Oudshoorn, 2003; Sorensen and Williams 2002; Williams et al. 2005; Rohracher 2005; Voss et al. 2009a; Bowker and Star 1999). What is at stake is reiteration of the methodological and theoretical repertoires of social studies of technological change.

OUTLINE OF THE BOOK

The book is structured into three parts. The first part, Chapters 1 and 2, introduces the theoretical and methodological underpinnings of the volume. The persistent difficulties researchers and practitioners face when they seek to bridge designing, implementing, using, and managing new technology are partly constituted by a lack of integrative frameworks for the topic. Microeconomic and evolutionary economics frameworks appear to many observers as the natural candidates for such a framework. We argue that these accounts remain too general when addressing the social, cultural, and learning processes involved, hampering their usefulness for researchers and practitioners in areas such as health technology. The "social learning in technological innovation" framework is introduced as a more viable alternative for mapping the different constellations of development and use and for addressing the complex, uncertain, and in many respects unelaborated practices and organizational dynamics of innovation in different innovation contexts.

Chapter 2 lays out a longitudinal "biography of technologies and practices" approach to studying innovation. It discusses its rationale among more temporally and spatially limited mainstream studies and critically evaluates previous longitudinal approaches to the study of technology–society relationships. The elaboration of framework is further structured to address the key questions about how to relate context and change and how collectives and practices have been understood in conjunction with evolution of technology.

The second part of the book, Chapters 3 through 7, grounds these ideas in an empirical study of the Vivago-Wristcare safety-alarm system for the elderly. We open the study by focusing on the question: where do the developers gain their early ideas of the technology and its uses and users? Conceptually Chapter 3 contributes to the research on user-representations and how social imaginations become transformed to materialized characteristics. It critiques notions such as "technological frame" in describing how developers orient to emerging technologies and introduces the core concept of the book, "practice-bound imaginary." We come to examine how practice-bound imagination affects the ways usages were envisioned, purposefully configured, and designed on account of routine procedures, the R&D models used, and messy interactions between people and materials.

In Chapter 4, we take another angle to the interplay of social imaginations and material characteristics, that of emergence of "user needs". We focus on market surveys, user interviews, design study work, and pilot use, which were used to further clarify the needs and requirements for Vivago-Wristcare. The interplay between broad cultural representations about the safety technologies in general and representations of the particular future technology in question takes center stage in the analysis. We also encounter an ecology of actors found to be involved in this interplay (intermediaries conducting the studies, developers, potential investors, and user-representatives) wherein the expected characteristics of technology, use, and users become further constructed.

Having examined the Vivago-Wristcare project on an analytical scale of decades and years, we then zoom in to minutes, days, and weeks of designing usage and follow a series of design meetings where the second generation of the Vivago device was envisioned. Emphasis is put on how the key understandings of "user" entered the design process and on how they were transformed during it and solidified as characteristics of the artifact. We examine four mini-biographies of solidification and erosion of user-representations entering the process and becoming further worked on in the course of the design work. This adds to our critique of too simplistically assuming that artifacts reflect the values and priorities of their developers (rather than those of its future users).

Chapter 6 takes us from development to use. We first observe how the technically unsophisticated elderly users and nurses shaped Wristcare by various mundane acts of adapting it materially, as well as by attributing divergent meanings to it. The enactments and differing "versions" of technology created by the elderly and home-care workers resonate well with research on domestication of new technology. The reliability of the "stand-alone" safety system was factually achieved by intertwining it into biographies of other technologies, of work procedures, inter-organizational arrangements, and the everyday life of elderly residents. However, our follow-up studies four and six years later revealed an "evolution of the impact": work-replacing features of the technology had reappeared once the now more "mature" technology was adopted in a new type of elderly-care facility that sought to transform caregiving practices.

In the final chapter in Part II, we deepen the discussion of the early evolution of new technology. The significant improvements to new technology during their early diffusion are commonly attributed to a process of "learning-by-using." However, the micro-level processes by which learning-by-using is actually achieved remain under-studied. Chapter 7 examines these processes in depth and identifies several processes and preconditions for learning that constituted learning-by-using in the five years following the market launch of Vivago-Wristcare. The results call into question the dominant image of learning-by-using as a harmonious flow of user feedback and show a range of work that needs to go into achieving it.

In all, the Vivago study in Part II of the book elaborates why we indeed are in need for studies that span both development and use and follow the artifacts and peoples in multiple scales of analysis: it allows us to see how significantly the "agency" of different peoples and material artifacts varies from one moment and site to another, as do the developer-user relations and whatever learning there is in between developers and users.

The third part of the volume, Chapters 8 through 11, elaborates on the significant variations and differences in different innovation contexts and different shapes of technology and ends with two synthesis chapters.

In Chapter 8, we turn to user-initiated innovation and focus on periods of collaborative design between producer and users. The project examined here, to build groupware and database application for diabetes care, sheds light on the means, promises, and challenges of participatory design "in the wild." It also provides a rare window to the evolution of such efforts. The project built on the "graveyard of withdrawn diabetes databases" and later veered away from co-design, due in large part to shifts in power relations between the producer and users as well as among the user groups.

Both safety phones and the diabetes database feature a gradual evolution of innovative solutions in design and also in user practices. The TeleChemistry project, which we discuss in Chapter 9, is a more radical project. This potential breakthrough technology is today discontinuous in relation to extant clinical chemistry analyzers, clinical laboratory work, the underlying scientific principles, and market structures, but, interestingly—and this is the focus of the chapter—it was not born so. A 40-year and still ongoing biography of success and failure and the gradual severance of ties with the extant instruments and practices have taken place. The shifting trajectory and the great uncertainty about the innovativeness and deviance of this project provide us with a research window to the dynamics of user involvement as well as stability and novelty in breakthrough innovation.

The synthesis of findings from the three cases follows in Chapter 10. This chapter is oriented to the research community, and we hence also take some time to sketch, in Chapter 11, the key implications of the volume for user-driven innovation policy and health technology evaluation. At the very end, we return to the TeleChemistry project, at the point when it is about to be launched in pilot testing, to elaborate on some of the insights the book provides for practitioners enmeshed in developing new health technology.

Part I

Design–Use Relations and Biographies of Technology

1   From Markets to Social Learning
Mapping the Dynamics of Design, Use, and Early Evolution of New Technology

Several disciplines have generated research and theory that provide insight for managing relations between designers and users in developing new technology. The list grows significantly shorter, however, when the aim is, as for us here in this chapter, to find frameworks that would provide integrative yet also usefully nuanced insight on matters comprising developer–user relations. The inquiry into the integrative theories of developer–user relations is organized as follows. We first examine two long-standing strands of research, which specifically focus on the engagement of users in innovation: "participatory design movement" and "user-innovation research." Both these strands of research are key to understanding the users' direct involvement and innovativeness in technology development, yet they remain somewhat narrow for the scope of issues the present volume is concerned with. We hence turn to B.-Å. Lundvall's "learning economy," which is a commonly used point of departure in innovation studies and policy. While we broadly agree with the learning economy's ideas, we come to find Lundvall's framework paradoxical; it raises interaction and learning between producers and users to the fore, yet fails to address the substantial variations and dynamics in how these play out. To address these key issues we turn to the social learning in technological innovation (SLTI) framework, which addresses these matters more fully. At the end we spell out an agenda how the present volume seeks to take the SLTI further.

PUTTING USERS' INNOVATIVENESS ON THE MAP: PARTICIPATORY DESIGN AND USER-INNOVATION RESEARCH

The participatory design movement (PD) has been in many respects a forerunner in the co-design of novel technologies with end users and implicated users. Emerging out of the realization that workers and trade unions were not able to negotiate good design of work in the way they had been able to negotiate pay bargains, early PD was primarily concerned with satisfactory work life as a source of well-being and productivity. Workers' participation in technology design was seen as a means to counter negative effects (reductions of workforce, de-skilling, and reduction of the quality of working life) that management-deployed technologies could introduce (Bjerknes et al. 1987; Bansler 1989).

The interests of management and different groups of workers were regarded to be adversarial, *per se* (Ehn 1993; Bansler 1989), resulting in an array of measures to balance the situation. Efforts were made to come to an agreement with management about the project, and its objectives and long-term maintenance. Designers aligned themselves purposefully with the users and took it upon themselves to acquire an in-depth understanding of the work practices involved (Bødker et al. 1987; Törpel et al. 2009; Bjerknes and Bratteteig 1987). All the affected worker groups were to be represented in the design process and emphasis was laid on ensuring that all the participants had an opportunity to express their points of view. Specific tools and arrangements were developed to provide the workers with means to understand the design process and have a true impact on it. The idea was that these tools would have to be relevant to workers' actual experiences and allow them to comment on the details of the design and envision how they would influence the work (Ehn 1993; Schuler and Namioka 1993). Implicitly, the emphasis was laid on ensuring democratic processes within the design project, even though the prime threats were seen to arise from the society-wide political asymmetries.

Since the 1970s and 1980s PD has proliferated beyond its original contexts. The borders between participatory and other collaborative design projects (e.g., in open source software development and user-centered design) have become increasingly blurred. Methods and procedures originating from PD have become commonplace tools for the mainstream software design and industry, including major techniques such as collaborative prototyping, use of ethnographic methods for design, prefilled joint inquiry forms, "soft" work and system modeling, *et cetera*. This development coincided with workplace-specific information systems giving way to increasingly generic and packaged products developed for wider clientele, rise of PD-oriented projects done by companies as well as vaning of trade union power and their interest in new technology (Voss et al. 2009a).

In the midst of these changes, the collective resource approach and most of its descendants (for reviews see Bansler 1989; Kensing and Blomberg 1998; Hirschheim and Klein 1989) remained focused on articulating how technology *should* be developed more democratically and how this could be realized in development projects, rather than mapping out all the empirical issues involved in development–use relations. In regards to this latter concern the most formidable integrative frameworks around participatory design movement appear to be those that combine its accumulated insights with research in science and technology studies (e.g., Suchman et al. 1999; Suchman 2002; Voss et al. 2009a; Hartswood et al. 2002). Out of these, we shall discuss in detail in the following the SLTI framework (Sorensen

1996; Williams et al. 2005), which broadens the extant participatory and user-centered design frameworks to better account for the increasingly multifaceted and dynamic constellations and practices that comprise developer–user relations.

The case is somewhat similar with the pioneering line of research on user-innovation led by Eric von Hippel and others. Since the mid-1970s it has focused on verifying the amount of inventions made by users, identifying the users that are likely to innovate, why and where users innovate, and the makeup of user-innovation communities. In striking contrast to the assumptions in the traditional linear model of innovation, 19 to 36 percent of users of industrial products (von Hippel 1988; Herstatt and von Hippel 1992; Morrison et al. 2000; von Hippel 2005) and 10 to 38 percent of consumer products (Luthje and Herstatt 2004; Franke and Shah 2003; Luthje et al. 2005) have been shown to develop or significantly modify products. The approach is best known for its work in identifying and working with lead-users, users that are most likely to be ahead of market trends and innovate products that appeal to the rest of the user-base and their work on open source and other user-innovation communities and various innovation toolkits to facilitate shifting inventive activities to users (Luthje and Herstatt 2004; von Hippel 1988, 2001; von Hippel and Katz 2002; Luthje et al. 2005). In affinity to PD this research has shown that corporate R&D labs are by no means the only, necessary, or in many domains even the primary sources of invention (von Hippel 2005).

This line of research has also examined information asymmetries between developers and users, characteristics of "user-innovation niches" and effects of "sticky information," information that is difficult to detach from its domain of origin, in the interchange and learning between manufacturers and users both after the market launch and in problem identification (Luthje and Herstatt 2004; Tyre and von Hippel 1997; von Hippel 2005; Lettl et al. 2006). In so doing, the research has moved beyond inventions by users, and, as one of the latest steps, inquired into the pathways traversed when user-innovations are transformed into commercial products, and the effects user-innovation has on industry development in the longer haul (Baldwin et al. 2006; Hienerth 2006). However, this research tradition offers an empirical and theoretical framework for studying and understanding user-driven innovation, rather than provides an integrative framework to the range of issues that comprise the relevant behaviors in development–use relations. Put in other words, both PD and "user-innovation research" have focused on perhaps the most interesting and radical forms of user involvement in innovation, rather than seeking to extensively cover the constituents, relations, and dynamic interplay that comprise the developer–user nexus, including the cases where users' influence to development is restricted to phases after the initial market launch of new technology (Voss et al. 2009a).

Where then to turn? We could, of course, ask: isn't the underlying theoretical framework in user-innovation research economics and in the early PD Marxist political economy? In that case, shouldn't economics be regarded as discipline that provides, or at least should provide an encompassing framework for the range of issues in how production and consumption relate? As this position is widely held, particularly among economists, let us move to the debate and frameworks for producer–user relations within economics.

INTEGRATIVE FRAMEWORKS FOR DEVELOPMENT–USE RELATIONS: FROM THE INVISIBLE HAND TO ORGANIZED MARKETS . . .

While economics is the one discipline focused on the question of how supply and demand relate, its traditional means of analysis, data-sets, and models become less obvious when the focus is shifted from relatively stable classes of products and relatively stabilized patterns of consumption to products that are just emerging (Freeman 1994; Rosenberg 1982; Fagerberg 2003). Such products often do not as yet have a clear market or direct competitors, but instead try to establish a new category of goods amongst potential buyers and users and regulators (Green 1993; Callon et al. 2002). When perspective is further shifted from production and purchase to designing and using—elongating both ends of market relation so as to include what gets to be produced and why something gets purchased—the scope of appropriate questions and thus the appropriate framework become further complicated. Indeed, a persisting feature of innovation studies and institutional economics is the critique of neoclassical economics on its difficulties in dealing with technological change and the associated economic growth (Freeman 1994; Fagerberg 2003). Here B.-Å. Lundvall's argumentation largely converges with our view.

Lundvall asserts that in standard microeconomics:

> agents—firms and consumers—are assumed to behave as maximizers of profits and utility. Perfect competition with numerous buyers and sellers, the flow of information connecting them, encompassing nothing but price signals, is the normative and analytical point of reference of the theory . . . In such a market the only information exchanged relates to products already existing in the market and it contains only quantitative information about price and volume. (1988, 349–350)

Both producers and users would thus operate under extreme uncertainty without the qualitative information about the preferences and needs of users or the values that a new product would offer in practice.

For an opportunistic actor involved in an innovative quest it appears rather *post-festum* to accept that demand becomes visible once the new product is in the market, and the good will find its correct price and volume of production. Nonetheless, there is a range of preparations and precautions one meets in standard editions on marketing and entrepreneurship that comply with assuming that only a black box of "markets" exists as a mediating mechanism between actors in the supply and demand side of a given line of products (Proctor 2000; Kotler and Armstrong 2004; Malhotra and Birks 2003). Yet high uncertainty over the fate of novelties would arguably favor incremental product variations as well as favor products that can be scaled to large series in case they meet up with high demand; not least to compensate for the likely array of failures. We can debate if in such a view it makes sense at all to develop products for relatively small niche markets or to complex user practices requiring in-depth qualitative information on user's needs and preferences (which is the case with most health technologies), but it is clear that actors involved with this kind of an innovative quest would receive little support in terms of how to proceed with it.

Indeed, Lundvall's own work on producer–user interaction reveals that in many sectors producers and users do not leave themselves at the mercy of markets, but, instead, develop sustained relations that allow the exchange of qualitative information related to user's needs and technological possibilities. The resultant form of producer–user relation has been characterized as "organized markets," where a producer develops sustained a relationship with one or several selected user organizations and vice versa (Lundvall 1985, 1988). The minimal unit of an organized market can be depicted in a stylized manner as two dyads of producers and users as in Figure 1.1.

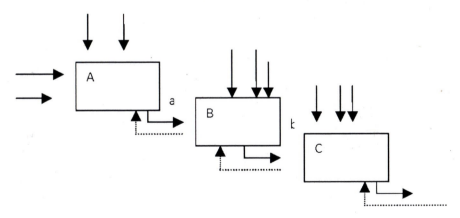

Figure 1.1 A user-producer pairing consisting of two dyads A-B and B-C. The product a of A is a resource for B, which B uses, along with other resources, to create its product b that C in turn uses in his process. B and A need information (dotted lines) about the needs and processes of C (and B respectively) to meet the needs of users.

In such niche markets innovations targeted to external users (product innovations) are frequent (Pavitt 1984), implying that in-depth information sharing does not lead to integrating the user or producer into a hierarchical relationship. Diversification of skills, for instance, to medical electronics and treatment of cardiovascular diseases, is also a substantial reason for nonintegration. Organizations have to make considerable investments to build and sustain competitive skills, knowledge, machinery, marketing, and delivery mechanisms. This reduces their opportunistic desire to expand their business up- or downstream, even in a case when a particular innovation makes such moves potentially profitable (Freeman 1994). Integrating two levels of production would also make the actor compete directly with other users, turning into a less preferable business partner for them (Lundvall 1985). Organized markets also lower producers' marketing costs and, for users, lessen transaction costs in finding suitable and reliable resource providers. They also lessen further agency costs: (a) costs incurred to monitor the agent to ensure that it (or he or she) follows the interests of the principal, (b) the cost incurred by the agent to commit itself not to act against the principal's interest (the "bonding cost"), and (c) costs associated with an outcome that does not fully serve the interests of the user (von Hippel 2005, 6, 46–52). These findings are particularly relevant for health technologies, which tend to be used in highly specialized contexts and by highly specialized people.

The result of these considerations is, in Lundvall's words, a "focus upon a process of *learning*, permanently changing amount and kind of information at the disposal of actors . . . we shall focus upon the systemic interdependence between formally independent economic subjects" (Lundvall 1988, 350; emphasis in original). The most examined kind of learning Lundvall refers to is "learning-by-doing," which was originally offered to explain why the cost of manufactured goods tends to decline significantly due to accumulation of skill in producing them (Wright 1936; Arrow 1962). Similar improvements and cost reductions result from "learning-by-using" capital goods: the users' increasing skill and/or understanding in using the product, leading to, for instance, less maintenance and new uses. The redesign of products due to feedback of users' problems and requests and locally made modifications by the users themselves lead to "embodied" learning-by-using (Rosenberg 1982). To capture the overall thrust of these findings, Lundvall introduces the term "learning-by-interacting" to stress the active engagement between designers and users as a source of new knowledge, technical improvements, and economic growth (Andersen and Lundwall 1988; Lundvall 1988).

This learning by doing, using, and interacting (DUI) is accompanied by learning-by-searching (in education, training, R&D market research), and stressing science–technology interaction (STI) as an important thrust in the horizontal and vertical interchange between and among various producers, users, and regulatory bodies. Various regulatory bodies, multiple horizontal connections of both producers and users, technological trajectories, and broader "technological regimes" set preconditions and limits for what are sensible actions for both producers and users (Nelson and Winter 1982; cf. Hoogma et al. 2002). Lundvall conceptualizes the whole of such relations as a (national, regional) system of innovation (NIS) (Lundvall 1992).

The advice for producers and users involved in innovation is a rich scheme for how to organize producer–user relations. To thrive in this kind of learning economy, actors are encouraged to complement their specialization with active linkages and in-depth, trust-based relations with strategically chosen clients, upstream producers, as well as by engaging in tactical information exchange with universities and other producers. The specific measures include monitoring the innovations and modifications that users may do to existing equipment (cf. von Hippel 1988, 2005) as well as bottlenecks and technological interdependencies that represent potential markets for the innovating producer. Along seeking direct collaboration with some users, producers should estimate their skills and capabilities in adopting new solutions as the basis for their design decisions (Lundvall 1985, 1988). The scope of useful information to be kept on track spans from codified know-what to explanatory know-why to know-who, when, and where and finally to skills and actionable knowledge as know-how. The learning economy concept also recognizes the importance of power and dominance among actors as well as orients to balancing learning new issues and forgetting and remembering issues in regard to the current relevance of knowledge (Lundvall and Johnson 1994; Lundvall and Vinding 2004). In all, in comparison to more orthodox economics, learning economy framework provides substantially more apt insight for policymakers and practitioners developing innovations (also peoples in the lower echelons of organizational hierarchies) that apply to fields such as health technology, where niche products are common.

. . . AND FROM LEARNING ECONOMY TO SOCIAL LEARNING IN TECHNOLOGICAL INNOVATION

While learning economy provides an appealing and accessible way to integrate key facets of producer–user relations, it runs into a quandary. Put sardonically, its appeal lies on how it capitalizes on the potential of learning as an economic explanation, but does so in a manner that economizes on learning as an empirical phenomenon and an object of study. The limits of "learning-by" conceptions have been well characterized by Eric von Hippel and Marcia Tyre:

Although the economic significance of learning by doing and using has been made clear, the *process* by which these gains are achieved is still quite unclear. That is, we do not know the micro-level mechanisms by which learning by doing is actually done. (1995, 1; emphasis in the original)

Miettinen draws the implications further:

Learning still tends to remain an inferred necessity for explaining the economic development. It tends to remain, itself, a black box. To understand the dynamics of interactive learning or knowledge creation, we need to study interaction between people: what was learned, how, by whom and at what level of work and organization. . . . A paradox in Lundvall's theory is that it postulates a central mechanism or phenomenon that cannot be studied with the traditional data and methods used in economics. (Miettinen 2002b, 45)

Likewise, interaction, firm, organization, use, production, and interests of parties are presumed to concur with economic expectations and research affiliated with learning economy typically operates in within-sector or cross-sector levels of analysis.

To gain a more nuanced understanding of the social and cultural processes that remain under the radar in broader-level comparative studies, ethnographic case studies has been an increasingly popular strategy in innovation studies in, for instance, examining routines and capabilities (Narducco et al. 2000), knowledge integration through software (D'Adderio 2001), and in learning-by-doing and "stickiness" of information in dealing with technical problems (von Hippel and Tyre 1995). SLTI framework integrates such in-depth research on development–use relations (Rip et al. 1995; Sorensen 1996; Williams et al. 2005). The approach "seeks to explore empirically and in detail the operation of learning economy . . . as a process of negotiation, subject to conflicts of interests amongst players with rather different capabilities, commitments, cultures and contexts" (Williams et al. 2005, 8).

SLTI is a relatively recent framework, but it developed out of the 30-year or so tradition of the "social shaping of technology" approach (MacKenzie and Wajcman 1998; Williams and Edge 1996) by combining it with insights from other research fields.[1] The development of new technology is characterized as an uncertain process and characterized by complexity, contingency, and choice (Williams and Edge 1996). Innovation is not seen as a one-off act in prior design, but as "part of an iterative series of activities, informed by earlier design practice and feedback from the appropriation and use of other systems (earlier technologies in this application domain; similar technologies in related domains)" (Williams et al. 2005, 110). This focus on multiple, overlapping cycles of development and implementation (Rip et al. 1995) guides attention to the coupling between technological and social change, and the difficult and contested processes of learning that are integral to innovation. The approach is thus socio-technical and studies "the many visible hands" that shape and reshape innovations and (narrowly conceived) markets, accounting for the interactions between the key actors and persisting patterns structuring those interactions, such as institutions, regulations, technological frames, and socio-technical regimes (Rip and Groen 2001; Hoogma et al. 2002). Along processes earlier characterized as learning by DUI, SLTI stresses learning-by-regulating (Sorensen 1996), as particular players attempt to assert their power though nontechnical rules and regulations, shaping the "rules of the game" from everyday use to state policy.[2]

The social learning SLTI refers to is thus not a narrowly cognitive, social, or modeling process, and the term is used in a very different way from its usage in education and social psychology, such as that of Bandura (1977). In the socio-technical usage, social learning denotes the *reflexive* yet often negotiated, complex, and "political" processes in transforming environment, instrumentation, and work that reach beyond single groups of actors. This usage also differs from more generic conceptions of social learning in evolutionary economics (Gertler and Wolfe 2002), where learning tends to be taken as an explanatory term for growth, as in the learning economy concept (Lundvall and Johnson 1994), without its micro-scale mechanisms and social dynamics being examined (von Hippel and Tyre 1995; Miettinen 2002b).

Central to the innovation processes identified in SLTI is the circular movement between *design* (configuration, materialization, inscription), *appropriation* (adaptation, domestication), and *representation* (modeling) that all equally concern *technical configuration, content, usage, users, uses*, and *rules*. Let us next briefly review some of the research in topical areas central to SLTI, grouped under the following headings:

1. *Representation of uses and users*, beginning from concept design and continuing throughout the development.
2. *Translating and inscribing* understandings of use into technical characteristics during design.
3. *Adapting* technology and work at implementation and further appropriation.
4. *Post-launch iteration and improvement* between designers and different user parties beginning at early prototyping and years after launch.
5. The involvement of *innovation intermediaries* in and between supply and user sides.

Representations of Use and Users

Far from being solely an up-front "user needs and requirements capture" process, creation of user-representations continues throughout multiple generations of product development. Social studies of technology production show that technologists are active in prefiguring the use of their technology

(Akrich 1995; Grint and Woolgar 1997; Cooper and Bowers 1995; Agre 1995; Williams et al. 2005). These studies have also generated a family of concepts that try to describe visions and assumptions that designers have of the use of technology, such as "user-representations" (Akrich 1992, 1995), "configuring the user" (Grint and Woolgar 1997; Oudshoorn, 2003), "programmes for action" (Latour 1991), "inscriptions of use" (Akrich 1992), and "representation of user" (Williams et al. 2005). The power of these concepts lies in that they link the multiple modalities a design takes on prior to use: visions, claims, assumptions, ideas, pictures of user practices, sketches, prototypes, the artifact wrapped for sales, and the technology in the hands of users. Thus, it has been seen as convenient to just talk about "user-representations" as if there were a clearly defined linkage from the artifact to design actions and to the various representations that designers in effect have of use while designing.

The social learning framework reveals how representations of use, users, and usages tend to stem from multiple sources, and that there is considerable variation as to which one of these provide the most actionable and adequate understandings of use in each particular case. Explicit requirements-gathering techniques, such as market or customer research, are not the sole or a sufficient source for representing use in design (Akrich 1995; Oudshoorn et al. 2004; Williams et al. 2005). Designers tend to regard information gathered thus as too unspecific for designing the actual details and too sparse to be used as a sole foundation for the overall design (Beyer and Holtzblatt 1998; Cooper 2004). User-centered methods and designers' "emphatic" acquaintance with users' contexts are sometimes used to complement these representations (Beyer and Holtzblatt 1998; Kuniavsky 2003), as are literature searches on previous studies (e.g., evaluation reports) on analogical technologies or user environments.

Another source for designing use is the involvement of some users either as hired in-firm experts or participants in consumer panels and user groups (Leonard 1995; Pollock et al. 2003). Users are sometimes keen enough to act as partners in designing or visioning new products (Bødker et al. 2004; von Hippel 2005) as well as to act as testers of early beta and later pilot versions of the technology (Schrage 2000; von Hippel 2005).

Designers also use their own experiences as representational of the behavior of users. Using oneself as a reference for the user is common practice, and has been labeled as I-methodology or Ego-design (Akrich 1995; Oudshoorn et al. 2004; Russell and Williams 2002). The in-depth personal experience of doing users' activities, such as climbing or sailing while designing for these activities, can be a powerful resource (Kotro 2005). Generic visions about the future (the paperless office, telecommuting) can also function as focusing points and proxies for what users' context will look like by the time the product is launched (Konrad 2006; Lente 2000; Lente and Rip 1998). Some of these visions bundle into sets that form pervasive imaginaries (e.g., Suchman and Bishop 2000; Flichy

2007) and incomplete utopian projects, such as Taylorism in management (Gregory 2000).

Product developers' professional background provides another set of representations of use. R&D professionals tend to have experience of and ample folklore about use-related issues in previous development projects and implementations (Johnson 2007; Hyysalo 2006, 2004b; Woolgar 1991). Notions such as the "average user" can be deployed not only as simplifying gloss (regarded unacceptable in human–computer interaction literature), but also as a category that balances out the demands of louder and better articulated groups of users, whose representations of use otherwise configure the designer too much (Johnson 2007). An important part of recent research has been a more detailed look at technical visions, engineering traditions, and organizational constraints that inform design (Bijker 1995; Lente and Rip 1998; Johnson 2007). Design is conducted with limited resources and heuristics, and pressing schedules, and is affected by organizational divisions of labor, rules, career paths, and hierarchies of decision making (Bucciarelli 1994; Van de Ven et al. 1999). Whilst a look in HCI and interaction design textbooks and courses suggests that principles from cognitive psychology and usability principles should constitute the major grounding for any decision concerning future usage (Dix et al. 2004; Saariluoma 2004), this view appears hopeful at best. In the late 1990s and early 2000s studies of over 30 promising European ICT projects revealed that only in a few were user-centered methods present and, university research projects aside, virtually nowhere were they used as the key input for designing usage (Williams et al. 2005; Hyppönen 2004; Miettinen et al. 2003).

The final key source for representations of use identified thus far is cultural maturation. Technologies build on widespread media and technology genres that are assumed to be familiar to users. Generic genres of prevailing technological culture such as "movie" or "telephone call" elements of WWW-navigation or interface using the Windows–Icons–Menus–Pointing device (WIMP) are powerful conventions in bridging design and use. More restricted are digital artifact genres such as automated tiller machine (ATM), an editing program or an instant messaging application (Löwgren and Stolterman 2004). As generalized appropriation experience, such conventions, images, "grammars," and narrative structures can be trusted by designers to be decoded in fairly nuanced ways by all those people who have basic competency in a given technological culture. While this cultural stabilization of meanings provides safe ground for variation and experimentation it also sets up limits as to how certain solutions can be understood (Haddon 2004; Williams et al. 2005).

The present volume comes to investigate all these sources of user-representation, and stresses the difficulty in making comparisons between the strengths and weaknesses of different approaches based on, for instance, successful or unsuccessful cases: different approaches are related to different ways of organizing the product development process as a whole and also have different epistemological grounds (Leonard 1995; Boland 1978; Ives and Olson 1984; Edström 1977). Moreover, the present volume will emphasize (in Chapter 4) the importance of users' own representations of their needs and preferences, that is, how people grow to have opinions, preferences, and clearly definable "needs" and how they are able to elaborate and articulate them (both for themselves as well as to technology developers or outside investigators using different research setups).

Materializing Representations into Technical Characteristics

Early social studies on technology tended to regard design as a fairly straightforward issue of operationalizing into technical features the perceptions that engineers had of users and usages. The analyst could then read "politics" behind artifacts from the artifacts (Winner 1980; Joerges 1999), emphasizing the impact and immutability of designers' aims as they become delegated to machinery (Noble 1984). Williams (Williams et al. 2005; Pollock and Williams 2008) regards this as a "design fallacy" and goes as far as to describe the ensuing picture of design work as "bizarrely politicized" when it regards design as solely "configuring the user," as Woolgar (1991) does.

This critique towards too simplistically politicized stance towards design has a point. Even the standard product design literature is more nuanced, even if overly rationalist in regards to how designing usage takes place. While it focuses on reaching requirements specification and rationally comparing alternative design solutions until a satisfactory concept can be found (e.g., Ulrich and Eppinger 1995; Cross 2000), the literature recognizes the drifting that occurs during concept design and technical realization of product—hence for instance its emphasis on target and final specifications (Ulrich and Eppinger 1995). Making trade-offs between manifold border conditions, requirements, and properties is everyday work in design. The usability and even functionality can slide significantly off the intended when manufacturability, reliability, component prices, maintenance, and so on, each require their alterations to the concept. This is particularly so in systems where qualitative detail such as look and feel matter and very detailed specification and preemptive thinking through all the nitty-gritty of possible trade-offs is either hard or impractical (Gedenryd 1998; Schon 1983; Simon 1996; Suchman 1987).

SLTI stresses that designing of usages builds on historical accumulation. Solutions found in previous products, design practices, and requirements set by earlier users are relied on as forming the launch-pad for any design efforts (Pollock and Williams 2008). Preformulated solutions and problem-solving strategies comprise much of the often rather unimpressive work of design, and designing use is not a grand exception here. Transferring and accumulating the rationale for design appears just as decisive an issue as any explicit "configuring the user" does. And the former poses just as formidable challenges for several reasons. The gross majority of contextual and qualitative knowing remains poorly elaborated and much of it in the heads of the people most involved. Some of that was always tacit, and much of it decays in the memory during months and years of not being used. Knowing gets further lost when people are promoted or shift projects or workplace. Road maps and the makeup of boards that decide upon what is included in each product release add to the complexity of decision making on how the user, if s/he ever does, gets to be configured along the myriad of other design issues (Johnson 2007). These questions are further elaborated on in Chapter 5 of this volume.

Adapting Technology and Practice

Uses of technology were traditionally assumed to have a fairly clear and straightforward relation to the characteristics of a product. In an economic perspective, products have been seen as bundles of attributes that yield particular benefits. From a symbolic perspective, products have appeared as vessels of meaning that signify similarly across consumers (Holt 1995). Both views assume that users do not significantly alter the material characteristics of technology, but rather employ it in the manner designers have intended, with greater or lesser success.

This understanding of technology use has been contested by an array of studies that have actually gone and looked at what happens in technology use. Ethnographies of work have shown that technology-mediated action usually requires, by its very nature, work-arounds, artful integration of various technologies, and articulation work to keep things on track (Clarke and Star 2003; Karasti 2001; Suchman 2002). While a successful tool results from a gradual convergence between the tool or procedure and the rest of the work practice, such convergence often turns to include struggle or dismay when the technology hinders effective action or induces unwanted changes. Even successful implementation may require significant work from users (Berg 1997; Hasu 2000; Hyysalo 2004a).

Ethnographies of consumption have demonstrated that consuming is an effortful accomplishment, underdetermined by the properties of the product, that varies from person to person (Holt 1995). As Alfred Gell (1986) defines it, "consumption involves the incorporation of the consumed item into the personal and social identity of the consumer," which makes technologies "domesticated in the social and cultural ends" (Strathern 1992). Silverstone et al. (1992) elaborate on four processes that take place in the consumption of technology within a household. The "appropriation" of technology, in the narrow sense of bringing it into one's possession, is followed by its "objectification," adjusting it into the existing environment and imposing on the new technology the values one desires the artifact to represent. In parallel, the technology is "incorporated" into the functional sequencing of life, and "converted" into a means of enhancing one's status in the outside world.[3]

Users may also not wish or may not be able to follow designers' ideas about the proper use of technology. At the most subtle end, usage remains compliant to designers' built-in prefiguration and intention but only in terms of "going through the motions," as in Helgesson's study of randomized clinical trials that showed how clinicians determined by smell which envelopes contained the placebo and which contained the drug to be tested, yet acted towards the testing company as if they did not know this detail (Helgesson and Kjellberg 2006). Usages can also become "compliant but nonaligned" to prefiguration, as in Star's (1991) example of buying a standard hamburger and scraping off the onions that she is allergic to rather than directly demanding alteration, as in ordering an onion-free hamburger that the restaurant would be slower to deliver. Conversely, aligned (to prefiguration) but noncompliant (to intention) would be the case of being a loyal customer but not using the loyalty cards with which a store expects to reward loyalty that many find obtrusive (Helgesson and Kjellberg 2006).

Such subtle cases of ignoring ascription or prescription embedded in products and services are often complemented with more visible changes such as actively working around cumbersome features, complementing technologies with others or with social interactions with peers, repurposing, altering their constitution with self-made hacks, *et cetera*. Highly cumbersome technologies are nurtured and attended to when they serve an important purpose in somebody's life or work, or when an organization has effective regulation in place to enforce certain patterns of use, regardless of their inconvenience (Nurminen et al. 1994; Heikkilä et al. 2003; McLaughlin et al. 1999). Reflecting these kinds of findings, technology adoption has been characterized as "mutual adaptation" of technology and organization (Leonard-Barton 1988) and as "learning by trying" to emphasize the difficulties that often ensue (Fleck 1994).

In Chapter 6 of this volume we examine usage of technology in three time spans. Along with immediate human–technology interaction we examine the socially, spatially, and temporally wider organization among people and technology that creates its meaningfulness and results in significant shifts in the expected and realized "impact" of technology.

Post-Launch Improvement of Technology

In analogue to the traditional view of technology use, mainstream diffusion research has been most concerned with how "potential users become informed about the availability of new technology and are persuaded to adopt, through communication with prior users" (Attewell 1992), resulting in the spread of the innovation (Rogers 1995). But diffusion is not only dependent on the signaling and learning about the availability and potential of the new technology, but also on the learning required to realize the potential in the technology. This was recognized rather late by diffusionists through the notion of re-innovation, by which they denote adjusting the innovation to different audiences and contexts to make it more appealing for the particular (and often subsequent) audiences (Rogers 1995).

Perhaps surprisingly, the importance of modifications-in-use became visible in airplane design as early as the 1930s (Wright 1936), and it was further elaborated by examining the development of successful airplanes such as the DC-3 and Boeing 707. Similar findings then accrued from other industries. These studies showed that innovation typically results from the accretion of multiple, often hundreds, of small improvements and the emergence of associated technologies, services, and organizational rede-signs that significantly enhance its value for the adopters. Even when these improvements may require only routine engineering, they are crucial for the economic value of the innovation for its various users and thus for its prolif-eration. Innovation tends to be continued by both its users and developers over a significant period of time. Correspondingly, the importance of the flow of user-identified problems and solutions to the iteratively improving design has been emphasized (Rosenberg 1979; David 1990; Gardiner and Rothwell 1985). However, many studies have drawn attention to the lack of such interaction in actual corporate environments and the impediments to realizing it (Leonard 1995; Miettinen et al. 2003; Williams et al. 2005).

In Chapter 7 of this volume, we return to von Hippel and Tyre's state-ment: "we do not know the micro-level mechanisms by which learning by doing is actually done" (von Hippel and Tyre 1995, 1), by examining the micro-level mechanisms of learning-by-using between designers and users during a five-year period after the market launch of the Vivago-Wristcare technology. We identify several learning dynamics that sharpen our under-standing of the learning that goes on after the market launch, extending previous research on how situatedness or "stickiness" of knowledge of designers and users affects diagnosing, answering to, and collaborating around solving problems-in-use (von Hippel and Tyre 1995; Tyre and von Hippel, 1997; Orr 1996).

Innovation Intermediaries in and Between Supply and Use

Few of us buy ICT products and services from their original developers; we rely on networks of retailers, banking services, transportation agencies, and service institutions to make them available to us. Likewise, various consultants, distributors, government agencies, etc., routinely play impor-tant roles in setting up and maintaining markets between technology pro-ducers and consumers (Howells 2006). They are key players in what Callon calls an "economy of qualities" by which the needs and desires of consum-ers are shaped and products adjusted (Callon et al. 2002). This shaping— say, from an orange tree in a grove to a branded juice bottle grabbed from the home refrigerator or between the early demos of a pop music artist and the song in the stereos of his eventual audience—in many ways constitutes technology through packaging, distributing, assembling, quality assurance, testing, bundling, and branding it. Likewise, the "consumer" is shaped by intermediary actors involved in segmenting, persuading, selling, advising, studying, and regulating the consumption, and in so doing, creating attachment to consumed items. Together these very tangible networks are able to shape, respond to, and maintain seemingly abstract characteristics such as styles and tastes (Hennion 1989; Callon et al. 2002).

When we move away from rather stabilized markets and products such as orange juice and pop music to studying new types of products and novel uses, the complexity of intermediation in innovation networks tends to be underestimated by both practitioners and socioeconomic research alike. In uncertain markets, intermediaries are just as crucial, but the mechanisms and contexts of their mediation can be fragile and difficult to predict (Williams et al. 2005; Russell and Williams 2002; Stewart and Hyysalo 2008). *Innovation intermediaries* are actors who create spaces and opportunities for appropriation and generation of *emerging* technical or cultural products by others. In the phrasing of James Stewart (Stewart and Hyysalo 2008, 297):

> Innovation intermediaries can be identified by their engagement in activities, in which they gather, develop, control and disseminate knowledge, collect and disseminate financial, technical and institutional resources, such as the support of users and sponsors and attempt to regulate uses, developments, participation and the actions of others in the network. The extent to which they do this depends on their access to resources and their connections in the 'constellation' of actors associated with a particular project or emerging market. . . . They configure the users, the context, the technology and the 'content', *but they do not, and cannot define and control use.*

Research on intermediary organizations in innovation such as consultants and other technology brokers began to grow during the early 1990s (Bessant and Rush 1995; Hargadon and Sutton 1997). At the time, models of innovation were rapidly changing from fairly linear ones to ones emphasizing uncertainty, shifting the character of effort and the complex interactions between multiple actors (Freeman 1979; Kline and Rosenberg 1986; Williams and Edge 1996; Van de Ven et al. 1999). Analyses of the then relatively new and rapidly evolving fields of robotics and computerized manufacturing technology showed that talk of diffusion of generic systems poorly matched the extensive adaptations and further developments done by adopter organizations (Fleck 1988, 1994; Rush and Bessant 1992). In short, when the producer company lost its position as the privileged source of innovation, it became urgent to understand how the knowledge from a range of actors flowed into the innovation process.

The various intermediary organizations (various consultancies, state research centers, etc.) and the roles they play in fostering innovation at the development end and in technology procurement have received attention in various literatures, including innovation management (Hargadon and Sutton 1997; McEvily and Zaheer 1999), literature on innovation systems (Stankiewicz 1995), and science and technology studies (Procter and Williams 1996; Van der Meulen and Rip 1998; Callon et al. 2002). Diffusion studies have stressed the importance of change agents and opinion leaders in the diffusion of innovation (Rogers 1995; Attewell 1992), and particularly after the late 1980s began to emphasize the work these actors do in adjusting the innovation to different audiences (Rogers 1995). From a more generic perspective, social network studies have also begun to show the importance of network "bridgers" in not only transferring knowledge across structural holes in networks, but as important sources of innovation themselves (Burt 2004).

Intermediaries at the supply-side, business-to-business environment tend to be more numerous, visible, and formal than those close to the end users of consumer goods. Interest in their operation has been further spurred by the rise of knowledge-intensive business services (KIBS) in many industries (Howells 2006). While user-side intermediaries enjoy less attention on the whole, those involved in the buying and paying for new technology are relatively more visible than those that help people use, fix, maintain, and update their technologies. The latter may perform their work as peer favors or side jobs to their formal work, and as a consequence, it is particularly these intermediaries that are systematically neglected or underestimated. It is indicative that discussions of such peoples as "local experts" (Stewart 2007), "technology mediators" (Okamura et al. 1994), or "tailors" (Trigg and Bodger 1994) remain absent from technology management volumes that abound with literature on product champions, business angles, etc., at the supply end.[4]

Moreover, there are few studies and frameworks that address in detail the whole range of intermediaries and intermediation that transform technologies, uses, and qualities in both the using and producing side, and explicate the bridges and gaps that exist in different *ecologies of intermediation* between design and uses. Learning economy and national innovation systems literature aims at this (Lundvall and Johnson 1994; Stankiewicz 1995), but only at a fairly coarse granularity. Yet the empirical relevance of this topic is evident. There are high uncertainties and information asymmetries involved in "choosing" or "creating" the right intermediaries for inventive technologies or new groups of users. Many innovations have withered because the established intermediaries turned out not to be up for the tasks required, be these in distributing, adjusting, configuring, helping to maintain, or in gathering feedback to supply-side actors. At the same time there are successes occurring with the establishment of new intermediaries and by the work of informal intermediaries. Intermediaries and their role in design–use interaction are discussed particularly in Chapters 4, 6, and 8 of this volume.

Innovation Contexts: The Range of Different Constellations Use and Development Can Take in Innovation Processes

The above understandings about processes at play within developer-user nexus add important specificity to SLTI framework over for instance the Learning Economy. Perhaps the main critical thrust in the SLTI approach is to incorporate the role of users in innovation in a more nuanced and fruitful way. It highlights that many activities and situations that are not conventionally included in the definition of innovation are in fact important moments in innovation cycles. Moving the focus from the supply side towards the demand side means increased attention to how constellations of players, intermediaries, and intermediate and final users come to constitute the demand side for emerging new technologies. This includes examining how people develop uses for technologies and users' role in feeding back their experience, practice, and innovation to the supply side over multiple long-term innovation cycles.

As already suggested earlier, the "user" is a complex idea: on the one hand, it is a category used by engineers and developers to refer to those who may eventually use their systems; on the other, it can refer to a range of other individuals and institutions, imagined and real, some of which begin to develop various kinds of engagement with a technology over time. There are many different "users": intermediate users, end users, and proxy users, all of which can play more or less active roles in articulating their own requirements and in the creative process (Figure 1.2). The ability and willingness of

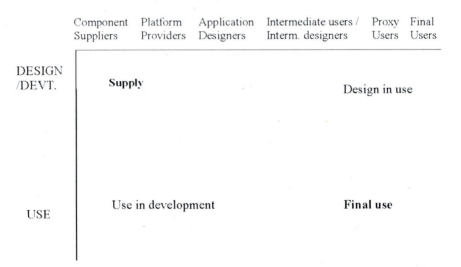

Figure 1.2 To account for the users in innovation we need to clarify how they are positioned between primary supply organizations and primary user organizations of a given technology as well as in regards to developing and using (Stewart and Hyysalo 2008, adapted from Williams et al. 2005).

developers to engage with these users, and for users to engage creatively with developers, is thus central to success, but often extraordinarily difficult.

SLTI uses the term *intermediate users* to refer to a particular sort of *intermediary organizations* that adopt a technology for their customers or employees (but generally involve a relatively few individuals within that organization). Examples are mobile phone operators, banks, retailers who sell a service based on a technological system to end users, and any firm adopting a system to be used by their employees. Subsets of these are innovative "content developers" or content service providers. For example, a service provider such as a broadcaster or publisher offers both a delivery platform and added content for end users. These organizations can be seen as supply side or demand side within an evolving market according to the particular case and particular point in the innovation and implementation process.

There are remarkable differences in the degree of freedom for innovative actors, particularly users, to try out new things, exercise choice, or act reflexively (Rush and Bessant 1992). At one extreme, users remain relatively "passive" with little choice over adoption. This is the much criticized "linear" innovation model, where users appear as consumers of preformed technologies, where their only choice is between use and nonuse of a technology. Coming close to how Lundvall implicitly comes to model producer–user interaction (Figure 1.1), each member of a supply chain can be regarded as an intermediary between the preceding and following player, and end users only have contact with the final player in the chain. Suppliers and end users are separated and user preferences and user-innovations are signaled at arms length through a market back to suppliers. We can display this graphically (Figure 1.3), which also clarifies that such market signals may not be very clear, and certainly not to the whole market, and invisible to firms deep in the supply network (Fleck 1988).

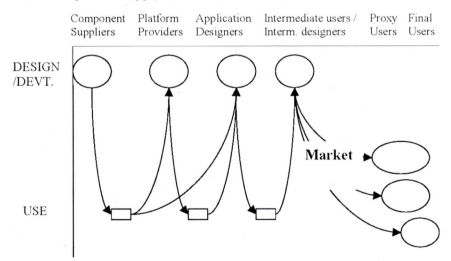

Figure 1.3 Pipeline linear development and diffusion (Stewart and Hyysalo 2008, adapted from Williams et al. 2005).

In the 27 case studies done as part of the European *social learning in multimedia* project in the late 1990s, four other modes of user involvement in innovation became evident: "pick and mix"; user-centered design; co-design and technology experiment; and the "innofusion and appropriation" (Williams et al. 2005). These provide us with useful heuristic models to characterize innovation processes.

The "pick and mix" innovation context is closest to the market model, where intermediate and end users are able to pick from a huge range of available generic technologies and configure them together (Figure 1.4). This model is characteristic of the current home ICT market, where intense competition, flexible standard platforms such as common operating systems and Internet protocols, and open programming interfaces and tools make it relatively easy and very cheap to configure. On the other hand, pick and mix context can create substantial trouble and confusion amongst users over which systems to invest in and how to configure them. This leads to many niches for various intermediaries such as businesses for configuring reliable and consistently working systems, and running locations such as Internet coffee shops.

There are also a number of design and development processes that involve users in more active ways. The first of these is user-centered design (UCD) processes in which end users—or more correctly "proxy users" who represent eventual users—are put at the center of design. Detailed studies of users, along with negotiations with proxy or intermediate users of their "needs and requirements," help those creating new technologies or integrating systems to create products and services that closely match the existing culture and activities of specific users (Norman and Draper 1986). However, the majority of

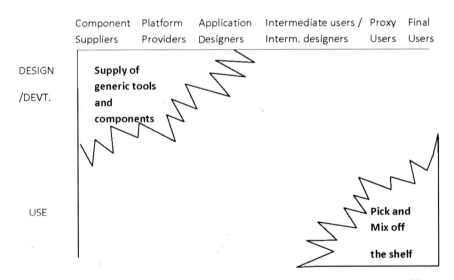

Figure 1.4 Pick and mix model where there are large clusters of generic offers at the supply end and the configuration of off-the-shelf components at local user sites (Stewart and Hyysalo 2008, adapted from Williams et al. 2005).

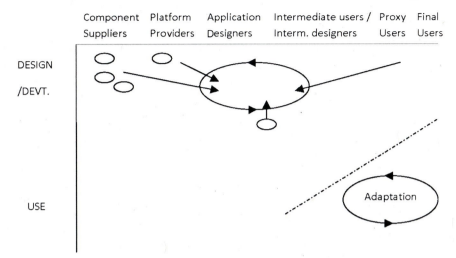

| Component | Platform | Application | Intermediate users / | Proxy | Final |
| Suppliers | Providers | Designers | Interm. designers | Users | Users |

Figure 1.5 User-centered design. A more dedicated application is built with the help of proxy users (Stewart and Hyysalo 2008, adapted from Williams et al. 2005).

user-centered design projects focuses on design work prior to market launch and neglects the activities of a range of users in actually getting the "finished" product to work (Stewart and Williams 2005). It also neglects the processes of "generification" that usually follow specific design, as developers actually try to remove user-specific features to create a generic product suitable for larger markets or adjust it to suit nearby market niches (Pollock et al. 2007). UCD contexts typically feature a strong presence of professional intermediaries such as researchers, usability consultants, or industrial designers for mediating use to design, which is typical to user-centered design, as is organizing it in projects (e.g., in concept design) both in terms of company practice and more academic literature (Dix et al. 2004; Preece et al. 2002; Benyon et al. 2005). Depicted graphically in Figure 1.5, the key issue here is that proxy-user involvement is limited to initial design stages of the innovation and the crossover between developers and users does not continue as strong after the product has been launched.

The Technology Experiment is a mode of collaborative innovation that involves a range of players, such as government agencies, intermediate users, developers, and suppliers (Williams et al. 2005; Brown et al. 2003), often deliberately constructed into a constituency by certain key players to provide a framework of ideas and resources to shape innovation (Molina 1995). Here development of the technology and building the market go hand in hand: these are continuing activities and there is no clear boundary between technology development and diffusion. There can be progressive broadening of the socio-technical constituency of involved players as barriers between technology developers and users are eroded and the boundaries of the project expanded (Williams et al. 2005). Such a process can be based

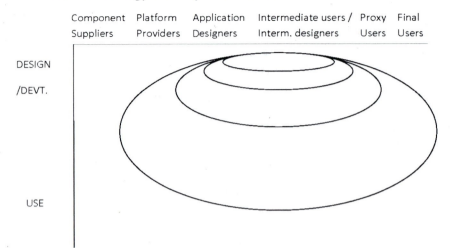

| Component | Platform | Application | Intermediate users / | Proxy | Final |
| Suppliers | Providers | Designers | Interm. designers | Users | Users |

DESIGN

/DEVT.

USE

Figure 1.6 Technology experiment / evolving co-design project (Stewart and Hyysalo 2008, adapted from Williams et al. 2005).

on co-design between designers and users, comprise an open source–type development or at least temporarily involve users fruitfully (Hyysalo and Lehenkari 2003).

Many innovations by users and user-innovation communities as well as many participatory design projects (see beginning of this chapter) map onto this innovation context. However, participatory projects where user involvement remains limited to the initial design phase, however long this then takes, would map onto the UCD context in this view (this, in fact, probably includes most "corporate PD" projects, see Törpel et al. 2009).

A technology experiment can also merely verify the chosen technology model negotiated early on in the process. This partly depends on the degree to which core players are open to innovation by users, and the points at which configurations are locked into place (Van Lieshout et al. 2001; Hoogma et al. 2002). It is also noteworthy that in the evolving co-design, user-representations and intermediation between development and use can differ dramatically from the previously discussed innovation contexts. In Chapter 8 of this volume we shall discuss how a group of lead-users enrolled an IT company to join their effort and in doing so effectively bridged over any ecological niches in designing, marketing, proliferating, or assisting the use of the technology that outside consultants or the like could have inhabited.

The final SLTI model draws on two concepts: domestication and innofusion. *Domestication* (Silverstone et al. 1992; Lie and Sorensen 1996) captures the practical, symbolic, and cognitive dimensions in the selection, deployment, and adaptation of new technologies (see earlier in this chapter). The *innofusion* concept (Fleck 1988) highlights the explicit technological innovation done in these processes, occurring in and being controlled by the user environment. The interactions between networks of users and designers tend not to be continuous or controlled, but are constantly changing, as different sets of actors in the constellation of interested parties are temporarily linked. This innovation context differs from user-centered design in that it is in users' sites, not in prior design, where key user involvement occurs and where their innovative inputs can last for years. Innofusion differs from evolutionary co-design in that the relations between producers and users may not be collaborative, purposefully coordinated, or co-located.

Examples of innofusion and domestication context can be found in various types of technologies. A recent well-documented case comes from enterprise resource planning systems (ERP) in the educational sector (Cornford and Pollock 2003; Pollock and Williams 2008). The developer companies made initial customizations to systems built for other sectors. The early customers were involved in further specification of the modules, contents, and functionality of the system. Their IT staff worked further on the system, including configuring the package in-site within its myriad of built-in parameters, more extensive customization through rewriting of code, selective appropriation of the package as well as integrating add-on, bolt-on, and extension software. Some of these modifications later became incorporated as parts of the supplier's generic package. In contrast, many later adopters were effectively confined to more limited domestication in-site, having little chance to shape the evolution of the generic system more to their liking (Pollock and Williams 2008).

The SLTI innovation contexts were originally distilled from particular innovation projects, and offer a grounded yet generalized typification of long-term unfolding of innovation trajectories. Yet, some projects (for instance, all cases examined in this book) accentuate an even more complex reality where a particular project, technology, or constituency can over time move between different innovation contexts, for example, when

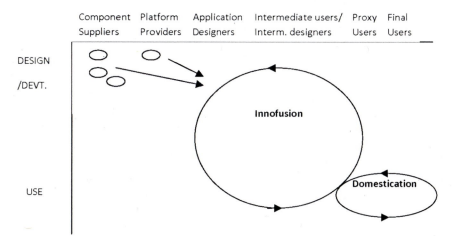

Figure 1.7 Innofusion and domestication model (Stewart and Hyysalo 2008, adapted from Williams et al. 2005).

a technology moves from an exploratory phase to generification for a mass market (Hyysalo and Lehenkari 2003; Hasu 2001a; Hoogma et al. 2002; Williams et al. 2005).

What advantages then does SLTI offer as an integrative framework for developer–user relations over "the learning economy"? Most importantly, in contrast to the stylized treatment of supplier–user information exchange, SLTI innovation contexts provide a generalized yet substantially more accurate description for the significantly different forms by which development–use relations take place. Likewise, it provides means to take into account the form of technology and the differences to supplier and user actions and strategies that are likely to ensue from it. Third, it opens up to closer scrutiny the range of innovation-relevant activities by users, intermediaries, and developers that are relevant to pay heed to in the early evolution of new technology. These are all but glossed over in the DUI model as is the complexity that surrounds "information exchange" between producers and users through the cycles of representation, materialization, and adaptation of both systems and uses. Finally, SLTI guides attention to the specific moments in innovation cycles when development–use relations are likely to be most accentuated, and how this is likely to play out in different contexts. In all, while learning economy and neoclassical economics can provide means for cross-sector and within-sector comparative analysis of firms and their R&D, SLTI excels at integrating research findings on the realities that particular innovation projects face in their developer–user relations.

AGENDA: REFINING THE SOCIAL LEARNING FRAMEWORK IN STUDYING HEALTH ICT INNOVATION

In the mid-1990s when SLTI began to take shape in the UK and mainland Europe, learning related to design and use of technology also began to be studied in Finland. This research—initiated by Professor Reijo Miettinen and Dr. Mervi Hasu—drew from theories within the umbrella of social shaping of technology, but combined it with research on collective learning, especially within the tradition of cultural psychology and activity theory (Engeström 1987; Cole 1996). This book seeks to explicate how research, ideas, and concepts from these Finnish studies further develop some aspects of the SLTI framework.

First, while SLTI researchers argued that biased models of innovation have resulted from snapshot inquiries that separated design, marketing, implementation, appropriation, and domestication of technology (Stewart and Williams 2005; Williams et al. 2005), very few studies actually spanned this range.[5] For instance, in the major international SLTI project *social learning in multimedia* only four out of 27 case studies reached from design to the use of the same technology. The project still bridged several case studies on different moments in the biographies of innovations as well as combined studies with coarser grain size with more narrow but detailed foci of analysis. The Finnish studies covered the entire early histories of health care innovations ranging from MEG-brain imaging technology (Hasu 2001a, 2000), to PET-tracer development (Hyysalo 2000), diabetes management database (Hyysalo and Lehenkari 2003, 2002), WWW-shopping service for the elderly (e.g., Hyppönen 2004), alarm and monitoring technology for the elderly and disabled (Hyysalo 2004c), and novel clinical chemistry analyzers (Höyssä and Hyysalo 2009).

Second, as we shall examine later, the capacity to study these trajectories in depth in the varying sites and times depended on using a more integrated theoretical framework. It has been characteristic of SLTI studies to draw useful concepts from a broad range of studies. While this approach has its merits in terms of having a range of concepts to choose the most apt for the task at hand, it tends to resort to asymmetrical and even altogether different frameworks for studying design and use in terms of sensitizing fieldwork, examining findings, as well as providing theoretical models. This runs a risk of essentializing the characteristics of design and use and explaining, for instance, characteristics of design in recourse to it being design. As such bias is exactly of the kind that SLTI framework would not wish to introduce, we shall seek improved sensitizing theory and methodology from symbolic interactionism and activity theory, which reject artifact-centered accounts of technology and place activity, work, and practice in the middle of analysis, which allows studying the different kinds of collectivities in their own terms and in their distinct relations to the artifacts.

Third, an important facet in studying design-use relations is the ability to focus on events that happen in different time spans and scales. A principled way of relating those different scales of analysis and different granularities of data is needed to inform and juxtapose findings in a meaningful way, that is, for bridging between practitioners' "frog's-eye view" to higher level analysts' and policymakers' "bird's-eye view."

Fourth, studies in social learning in sustainable transport (Hoogma et al. 2002), education (Van Lieshout et al. 2001), and ICT design and uptake (Williams et al. 2005) have focused on organization, conduct, and outcomes of various experiments and trials that bridge designers, users, and other societal actors such as government administrators. Still the *social* and *society-wide* aspects of social learning or "reflexive governance" (cf. Rip et al. 1995) have been explored more thoroughly than the *learning and its relevance for particular innovation*, which will be examined in more detail in the present volume. It may not be coincidental that nearly all SLTI researchers have been social scientists rather than, say, scholars of learning. Also the idea that research should facilitate learning between the participants and not only provide descriptions or theoretical insights has been a central theme in Finnish studies (Miettinen et al. 2003; Miettinen and Hasu 2002). These facets will be discussed at length in the next chapter.

CHAPTER DISCUSSION

This chapter has argued that a useful integrative framework for design–use relations, health technology as its focal point, must be able to provide detailed understanding of how design and use link in different moments, sites, and contexts of innovation. The granularity of explanation and described phenomena are of key importance: it makes a difference in the applicability of a framework whether it aims to account for the workings of economy or chart the exchanges between particular development contexts, innovation processes, and domains of use and the particular dynamics within them. Thus, explained phenomena hark back to primary concerns of theories and the kind of issues that a given framework regards as relevant for the relations between production and uptake of new technology.

From the perspective of Lundvall's learning economy theorizing, assuming that supply and demand are mediated solely through markets turns the identifiable, more in-depth collaborations, qualitative information exchange, and learning into a black box (Lundvall and Johnson 1994). Such black-boxing appears unrealistic and unhelpful particularly with the kind of niche products that most health ICTs are (Figure 1.8).

When we examine learning economy and its key concepts, such as organized markets, learning by DUI, and science–technology interaction, the framework appears geared towards analyses between and within industrial sectors analysis. It provides less insight for people engaged with innovative projects and companies managing these. Playing with the metaphor of the "black box," Lundvall's learning economy appears as "a grey box," in contrast to a more fine-grained description of the mechanisms that mediate between supply- and use-side competences and resources (Figure 1.9). In this capacity, the SLTI framework provides indications of the key variations that exists in these processes from one development project to another and lays the ground for examining the learning challenges involved.

These three positions discussed earlier have different aims and levels of explanation, but the comparison articulates the granularity of analysis, scope of issues, and the degree of attention to empirical realities of

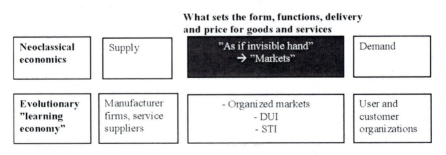

Figure 1.8 Learning economy as an attempt to replace the "black box" of markets by identifiable mechanisms of learning.

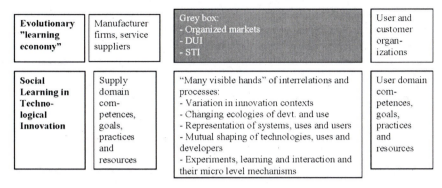

Figure 1.9 Processes that are seen to mediate between the domains of supply and use in learning economy and social learning.

development projects that need to go into an integrative theory to be useful for people engaged in innovation in health technology.

Finally, the quest for an integrative framework for studying, grasping, and managing the issues in developer–user relations fundamentally plays in *spatial register* in trying to explicate the range of actors, processes, and constellations involved (Williams et al. 2005). What is evident, however, is that both learning economy and SLTI are "spatial cuts" to phenomena that are equally temporal by character, as qualitative and quantitative change is fundamentally at stake. We move now into explicating further the theoretical and methodological framework of the present volume, and in doing so, shift to a "temporal cut"—even though it is one that, in turn, aims to retain spatial and contextual elements also in view.

2 Biography of Technologies and Practices
Studying Technology across Time and Space

Research on socio-technical change is fundamentally research on temporal processes. It can take, and has taken, place in a wide range of focal areas and on very different time scales of inquiry. Traditionally this condition has been deemed less consequential than the problems in comparing development projects in different fields, eras, firms, *et cetera*, and the use of altogether different frameworks, methods of inquiry, and kinds of data (Fagerberg et al. 2005; Freeman 1994; Stewart and Williams 2005). The maturing of the "new sociology of technology" has, however, led us to notice that while, for instance, data and the theory used do have significant impact on what kind of findings arise, the research practice is just as importantly affected by seemingly less lofty questions of how research is framed temporally and spatially. When, for instance, design, development, marketing, implementation, and appropriation of technology are studied separately, the other sites and times in the shaping technology become assumed rather than studied in relation to the topic at hand. As a consequence, contradictory findings about technology and its consequences continue to live in different discourses centered on a particular type of study—say, "implementation studies," "impact studies," or "design studies" (Williams et al. 2005; Pollock and Williams 2008). When one actually goes beyond a single focal area and grain size of analysis, as we do in the present volume, the effects of differently framed "snapshots" of technological change become striking.

There have been many labels for attempts to follow the development of new technology and innovation in depth, including "trajectory," "career," "journey," and "biography" of technology—often taken to include (some of) the related biographies of organizations, institutions, and participants. When spanning both development and use, such studies naturally hold promise for gaining a more balanced insight on different moments and sites in socio-technical change. Such studies have emerged, for instance, from innovation studies (Van de Ven et al. 1999), new sociology of technology (Bijker et al. 1987; Miettinen et al. 2003; Pollock and Williams 2008), new history of technology (Hughes 1988a; Kline and Pinch 1996; Fischer 1992), and the "biographies of things" approach in consumption studies (Appadurai 1986; Kopytoff 1986) and deploy different registers to what is by and large the same kind of study.

We shall discuss these under the heading of *biographic studies of technology* while stressing that we could just as well use any of the other terms, too.

The present chapter seeks to advance further the conceptual and methodological issues in studying technology and related human action across time and space. We are less interested in proposing yet another new framework or theory than in bringing to the attention of readers a set of issues we must—as individual researchers and collectively as a field—find plausible solutions for if we are to reach a more adequate understanding of processes of innovation and socio-technical change. To aid a more in-depth reading of the chapter, which on the whole has a somewhat complex line of argument, we shall now present its key argument or "take-home message" as a roughly one-page "advance organizer."

Many relatively recent studies stress methodological issues that could be characterized as the *balance* and *reach* of the study that do not remain confined to a single *scale* of analysis, be that a "frog's-eye view" of practitioners enmeshed in developing and using new technology or a "bird's-eye view" of policymakers and high-level analysts. Many studies also stress more careful attention to what is the actual *shape of technology* in different foci and loci of analysis. For instance, Zimbabwean water pumps, ERP systems, and many health ICTs have more flexible compositions from any one particular instance and time to another than, for instance, pens, bicycles, or electricity grids (e.g., Clarke 2005; de Laet and Mol 2000; Mol 2002; Sorensen and Williams 2002; Williams et al. 2005; Brown and Webster, 2004; Bowker and Star 1999). Taken together, these four guideposts appear not to stand in opposition to earlier programmatic articulations about how socio-technical change should be studied—e.g., Bijker's early

Table 2.1 Methodological Criteria for Socio-Technical Change in the early 1990s (Left Column) and Guideposts for Living up to Them Taken on in the Present Volume (Right Column)

Change / Continuity: the framework should account for change as well as for continuity and stability. **Symmetry:** the useful functioning of a machine should be taken as a result of socio-technical development, not its cause. **Actor / Structure:** the framework should account for actor-oriented and contingent aspects of socio-technical change as well as the structurally constrained ones. **Seamless Web:** no a priori distinctions of what is social, technical, scientific, or political as these shift within the seamless web of socio-technology.	**Reach:** the framework should not rely on or favor "snap-shot" studies but encompass multiple times and loci where technology is shaped. **Scale:** bridge bird's-eye view with frog's-eye view. **Balance:** the framework should attend to the empirical asymmetries between resources, practices, interests, and make-up of different actors, yet not lead to overemphasis on technology and its development or what people do with technology. **Shape of Technology:** the study should not fix the ontology of technology to discreet "artifacts" or systems.

1990s summary (1995, 13; see Table 2.1 left-hand side)—but they do present a challenge in how to live up to the earlier principles in a conceptually and methodologically sound way.

This chapter sets out one way to realize these guideposts through what we call "biographies of technologies and (related) practices" study. Its core ideas can be expressed as follows:

1. Longitudinal analysis of the biography of technology from its inception to at least the early stabilization of uses.
2. Conducting this analysis and related data-gathering with multiple scales of inquiry and granularity of data: development of practices; biography of the technology and related activities; conduct of design and appropriation episodes at monthly, weekly, and minute scales. These are further linked to more obdurate patterns in socio-techno-economic change.
3. The focal points for more close-up inquiries are chosen so that they are likely to be informative with regard to broader scales of change in design–use relationships as indicated by previous studies and/or likely to reveal patterns that are of special interest for the study.
4. Combining a range of complementary data sources and methods and both historiographic and ethnographic inquiries to accomplish the preceding.

To gain a better sense of these methodological premises, and just as importantly to understand why we should bother with such a research setup in the first place, we need to embark on a journey that takes us through various studies on the *biography of technology* to questions of how to handle the interrelation of *change and context* that inevitably arises in such studies, and, further on, how these two questions intertwine with stances of *collectivity and practice*. Rather than just spelling out our own position, we seek to engage in an *appreciative critique* but also hope to avoid the unfortunately common "that's what we have been saying all along" responses to clear points of contestation. To this aim, discussion in each topical area departs from general concerns or well-known approaches to its theme and then examines contributions made in science and technology studies, particularly in social construction of technology (SCOT) and actor-network theory (ANT), before spelling out how the present volume addresses each topical area.

BIOGRAPHY OF TECHNOLOGY

Biography 1: The Innovation Journey and the Biography of Things

Let us depart from the early 1980s, when the Minnesota Innovation Research Program (MIRP) began to conduct 14 longitudinal in-depth case studies of various innovations (Van de Ven et al. 1999). The rich interview, observational, and document data and findings from these studies were radically dissonant with extant, typically more macro and more quantitative inquiries: "Field studies radically altered our initial conceptions of the innovation journey . . . although the left column [in Table 2.2 in this chapter] may appear naïve today, it reflects the mainstream view in academic and professional literature when our MIRP studies began in 1983" (Van de Ven et al. 1999, 7).

MIRP proposes a model of 12 common characteristics for innovation, divided over three sequential periods of initiation, development, and adoption/termination:

Table 2.2 Traditional and More Recent View on Innovation, Adopted from the MIRP Position Statement (in Van de Ven et al. 1999, 8, 5–16)

Aspect of innovation	Traditional assumptions, often implicit in literature	MIRP view to innovation process reflecting the current research
Ideas	One invention, which is then operationalized	Reinvention, proliferation, reimplementation, discarding and termination
People	An entrepreneur with a fixed set of fulltime people	Many entrepreneurs, distracted fluidly engaging and disengaging over time in a variety of roles
Transaction	Fixed network of people/ firms working out details of an idea	Expanding, contracting network of partisan stakeholders who converge and diverge on ideas
Context	Environment provides opportunities and constraints on innovation process	Innovation process creates and is constrained by multiple enacted environments
Outcomes	Final result orientation; a stable new order comes into being	Final result indeterminate; many in-process assessments and spin-offs; Integration of new technical and social order with old
Process	Simple, cumulative sequence of stages and phases	From simple to many divergent parallel and convergent paths; some related others not

Initiation period:

1) *Gestation:* Several years "in which seemingly coincidental events occurred that preceded and set stage for the initiation of the innovation," no purposeful aim towards the particular invention or a central actor machinating the events.
2) *Shock:* In all cases, a shock from inside or outside the organization triggering the concrete actions.
3) *Plans:* Served more as sales vehicles to obtain resources than as realistic scenarios of development.

Development period:

4) *Proliferation:* The initial innovative idea spread to parallel and interdependent ideas and efforts, resulting in "chaos" to be managed.
5) *Mistakes, setbacks, and unanticipated events:* They altered the grounding assumptions of the innovation, pushing back its schedules and costs, and caused interlinked problems in parallel efforts.
6) *Criteria shift:* Criteria about success and failure often changed and were contested by sponsors and developers, often linked and leading to power struggles.
7) *Fluid participation of personnel:* Different personnel were engaged and disengaged in the innovation process during its course, depending on their interests and organizational commitments.
8) *Managers and investors:* They did not appear as a unitary front but played different roles and balanced each other. Vicious cycles common in innovation processes often required intervention from these sponsors.
9) *Expansion and stabilization of the innovation network:* The progression of invention was related to more and more people, units, and organizations getting involved with the development. The dynamics in these networks—collaboration, groupthink, competition, and so on—shaped the process.
10) *Influencing infrastructure:* Inventors sought to enroll, among others, competitors, political actors, and government agencies to create necessary social, organizational, and technical infrastructures for their innovation.

Adoption/termination period:

11) *Implementation and adoption:* New and old technologies often overlapped one another; re-innovations and more or less successful implementation and organizational changes in user practices took place.
12) *Attribution of success and failure:* Innovation processes were terminated because resources ran out, or once the technology became implemented and/or institutionalized. At this point, resource controllers evaluated the innovation.

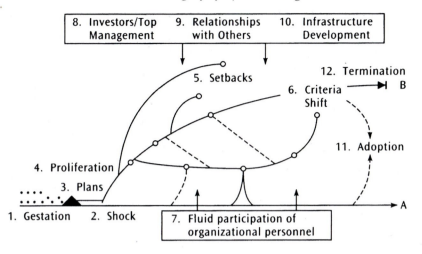

Figure 2.1 MIRP "fireworks" model of innovation (Van de Ven et al. 1999, 25).

The MIRP researchers came to talk about "the innovation journey" to emphasize the complex, nonlinear, and ill-defined paths of the development processes they studied. The choice of wording, along with *the kinds of data* they gathered that led them to discover these qualities, have close affinities to all later studies we regard as "biographic studies of technology" in this book. However, MIRP studies had a limitation: they did not bridge the innovation journey thouroughly enough to its uses and re-innovations.

Even though it never evolved much further than a thought experiment (Graeber 2001, cited in Engeström and Blackler 2005), Igor Kopytoff's concept of "the biographies of things"[1] (Kopytoff 1986, 66–67) illustrates the point. He asks us to consider:

> [t]he biography of a car in Africa . . . the way it was acquired . . . the uses in which the car is regularly put, the identity of its most frequent passengers and of those who borrow it, the frequency of borrowing, the garages to which it is taken . . . and in the end . . . the final disposition of its remains. All of these details would reveal an entirely different biography from that of a middle-class American, of a Navajo, or French peasant car. (1986, 67)

Silverstone interprets this further: "Through those changes and transformations they [artifacts] reveal the changing qualities of the shaping environments through which they pass" (Silverstone et al. 1992, 17). Indeed the biography of innovation does not stop or start at the factory door, but must include development and consumption of technologies and the various loops in between them (Miller and Slater 2007).

Soon after the onset of MIRP studies frameworks in new sociology of technology emerged for the studies on construction of technology and its shaping of society (Bijker et al. 1987; Law and Bijker 1992).

Biography 2: Social Construction of Technology

The idea to follow the development of technology in detail came to the sociology of technology from social constructivist science studies. Historical or genealogical studies were employed to "open the black box of science and technology" and to show the choices and politics involved.[2] A formulation of this early technology studies thinking that has a strong follow-up even today is the SCOT model (e.g., Bijker and Pinch 1984; Bijker et al. 1987; Bijker 1995; Pinch and Oudshoorn 2003b). SCOT stresses that we should not fall victim to the common linear and rational view of the development of technical artifacts. Such "Whig-historical" accounts take the result of socio-technical construction, a working artifact, to explain the process of its construction. This leads to an asymmetrical explanation: a failed artifact has failed because it was bad all along, and a successful one is merited because of its success (Bijker 1995).

Hence, SCOT studies follow the construction of technology from its beginning onwards and treat it impartially regardless of whether the changes in (and the effects of) the technical artifact were technical, economic, social, or political in nature, as these form a "seamless web" in the construction of technology (Bijker 1995; Hughes 1988a; Hughes 1979). The approach aims to account for change and stability, as well as the influence of structure and agency in the socio-technical ensembles (Bijker 1995, 12–16). These are the four principles stated in the opening of this chapter (see Table 2.1).

The SCOT studies came to examine how "interpretative flexibility," regarding the meaning of artifact, and "closure," regarding its accepted form, diminished or grew among the "relevant social groups"—groups of people for whom the artifact has the same meaning. Consequently, the studies examined what are the conceptions about and criteria set for the emerging technology by these groups and how the artifact comes to reflect these meanings in the course of its life. The end point of inquiry would be, for instance, when closure and stabilization have occurred among all relevant social groups and no contest about the artifact persists—that is, no social forces demand significant change in it (Bijker 1995; Bijker and Pinch 2002).

These methodological principles of SCOT have allowed for portraying the contours of the gradual, often decades-long, constructions of technologies and sensitizing the study of transitions and alternatives. SCOT also presented an articulated methodology for such analysis that allows outlining of the shifting of problems, solutions, artifacts, frames, and relevant social groups during these processes. These are achievements that have had a lasting influence on studies of socio-technical change.

However, in doing so, SCOT has introduced—partly due to methodology, partly due to historical materials used in SCOT studies—several unhelpful simplifications about studying socio-technical change. The framework rests on a rather limited set of explanatory principles (social construction, interpretive flexibility, sameness of meaning), is geared towards only one set of relevant influences (those affecting the meaning and form of technology), and appears to presume that there is one clear-cut artifact or technology that is constructed (e.g., a bicycle, Bakelite, or fluorescent lighting device). Following from this, SCOT studies also tend to provide a single-grain-size overview narrative "truth" of the construction process even as they are geared to show considerations of alternative paths. Roughly comparable "unidimensionality" can be found in other early S&TS and history of technology biography approaches, such as Hughes's (early) work on (the growth of) large technological systems (Hughes 1979; Hughes 1988a) and Noble's (1984) study on numerical control process automation.

Most gravely for us here, however, SCOT delineates social groups in their relation to the artifact under construction and, in so doing, discusses their practices and composition in a narrow manner (we shall return to this point when discussing collectivity and practice later). This lack of capacity for duly addressing use and users is a major weakness of SCOT. Our view here is in obvious disagreement with the claims by SCOT proponents about the strength of their framework in addressing use and users (e.g., Pinch and Oudshoorn 2003b).[3]

In sum, SCOT has had a highly important role in setting the right methodological directions (Bijker 1995, 6–15), but its answers leave room for improvement. As many potential improvements are well articulated in actor-network studies, this is the direction in which we turn next.

Biography 3: Actor-Network Theory

The methodological maxim of following the actors and associations without presuming beforehand their character has sensitized actor-network analysts to what scientists and engineers do when they seek to extend, realign, and stabilize the networks that make up technology and science. This has meant close-up interest in what trials, classifications, contests, and claims consisted of in their often hybrid existences and what work went into the processes that allowed them to become purified as "social," "natural," or "technical" (Latour 1983, 1987, 2005).

In terms of actual biography studies, for instance, Latour's study of the ARAMIS personalized mass-transit system (Latour 1996) and Callon and Law's study on the TSR II fighter plane (Law 1988; Law and Callon 1992) spelled out a rich picture of the changing coalitions, materializations, and visions that shaped the path of these large-scale projects that never reached implementation. In this they drew attention—in notable affinity to MIRP innovation journey studies—to the meandering and shifting character of building an innovation after its initial envisioning (Russell and Williams 2002).

However, even more important for us here is Akrich's ethnographic study of an ongoing design and use of electricity technologies in France and in Senegal and the Ivory Coast (Akrich 1992). *Really not knowing* the end result beforehand, and *really attending to what people did* with technology produced an interestingly different portrayal of the biography than, e.g., SCOT studies or historical studies in ANT. Inscriptions of use by designers and the deinscription of technological objects by users drew attention to not only how the technology became shaped but also how the interlacing of technology and previous practices led to a mutual, yet characteristically partial, shaping of the actions of both designers and users. The deinscriptions by users marked dramatic changes to the configuration of the technology and, potentially, to its further design both in user settings and as a generic offering.

ANT studies insist on attending seriously to the changing relations that constitute technology—that is, attending the *shape* of whatever technology is examined (Russell and Williams 2002). In currently fashionable terms, this marks a shift from implicitly proceeding upon the static ontology of "objects" to studying how their ontology shifts and what sort of patterning different shifts form (Fleck 1993a; de Laet and Mol 2000; Law and Singleton 2005; Engeström and Blackler 2005). "Classical" ANT characterized objects and technologies as "immutable mobiles" that can move around but also hold their shape both in terms of the physical and geographical space they occupy and in terms of being composed of a more or less stable network of associations. Such objects allow usage without knowledge and skill to mingle with the interiors and, in so doing, allow long-distance control both in space and in time, and are thus imperative for any understanding of how large collective formations—empires, markets, science—can hold together (Latour 1987; Law and Singleton 2005).

The partial mutability was implied by Akrich's study but became seriously considered as a success criterion for technology in de Laet and Mol's (2000) study of the Zimbabwean bush pump that relied on its "fluid" character: nearly every part of the technology could be replaced by something else, in terms of both its material constitution and its functioning: what counted as its capacity to produce clean drinking water. Law, Singleton, and Mol have also tried to characterize different medical objects as fluids, multiples, or as having characteristics of "fire objects" that are constituted by "present but absent" conditions (Law and Singleton 2005; de Laet and Mol 2000), while Darking and Whitley (2007) observe both "fluid" and "fire" characteristics patterning open source infrastructure development.

This ANT development was anteceded by studies in other branches of technology studies. In his studies on industrial robotics in the 1980s, James Fleck noticed that instead of clear-cut innovation and diffusion, there was a prolonged reconfiguration and particularization of these—assumedly generic and multipurpose—technologies in their industrial contexts of use (Fleck 1988). Such "innofusion and diffusation" drew attention to the differences there are in whether technologies are *discrete objects*, can only function as *component parts* of a larger whole, form a tightly integrated *system* or what Fleck came to term *configuration*, more loosely coupled and locally adjusted technology featuring a degree of variety across sites (Fleck 1993a). Configurationality (or "fluidity" or "plasticity") of technology can take many forms, take place through time, and cover different parts of the architecture of the technology. There is a spectrum of differences in what the technologies can do, are composed of, and invite being shaped into (Lehoux 2006; Tierney and Williams 1990).

In sum, actor-network analyses of the biography of technology provide a unified framework that allowed the networks of development and use to be examined in detail with the same concepts without inherent bias towards one or the other mode of engaging with technology. They further sensitize one to examining the changes in the constitution of technology in detail and move beyond presuming it is a unified "artifact," object, or black box. ANT explicitly focuses on action, practice, and materialities instead of meanings as SCOT does.

However, the ANT take on biographies of technology has programmatically refused to address socio-technical change on multiple time scales of inquiry, so as not to reintroduce the kind of social structures it denies (Latour 1987; Law and Callon 1992; Latour 2005). The side effects of this choice are many; with regard to biographies of technology, the most pertinent ones have very telling names. "Machiavellism" has become the nickname for overemphasizing central actors and/or the emerging artifact. As actor networks expand more or less infinitely, the work of really tracing all relevant associations in a content-specific way becomes insurmountable (Miettinen 1999). Thus, in practice, studies tend to, somewhat arbitrarily, privilege the perspective of some central actor with few guidelines available on how not to overemphasize it. A close companion to Machiavellism is "Sartrean engineering," a tendency to portray the designers as "modern-day princes" or "sartrean characters" (Latour 1988) who are (unrealistically) free of their organizational constraints, professional practices, and other relatively more stabilized sociocultural formations in making their decisions about how to weave further human and nonhuman elements into actor-networks (for this critique see Pollock and Williams 2008; Gingras and Trepanier 1993; Miettinen 1999; Lehenkari 2000). ANT has also been justly criticized for reifying the tactics of technoscience: remaining indifferent to the nature of the entities and borders between different social domains; focusing on tactics and strategic moves, adopting the perspective of the central actors, etc., effectively reproduce the image of reality in managerial regimes that draw from economics and systems theory. Tending to take the technology as the key defining characteristic of the ensembles formed further leans towards the producers' and managers' dominant point of view and leaves weak and marginal actors without due attention (Star 1991; Clarke 1998, 267; Pinch and Oudshoorn 2003ba, 7–12, 17; Miettinen 2000). Finally, ANT's emphasis on examining science and technology as power plays, strategies, circulation, and transactions of materials offers a powerful resource in describing a biography of technology. But it also easily truncates the repertoire with regard to phenomena such as learning, motivation, emotions, and experiences (Lehenkari 2000; Hyysalo and Lehenkari 2005; Miettinen 1999; but see e.g. Hennion 2007 on possibilities ANT holds in these regards). The tendency to resort to a single narrative in describing the complex biographies of technologies adds to this bias, just as in the SCOT case.

The ANT research community has been active in reframing the theory to steer clear of these problems (and others that any theory necessarily introduces; Law and Hassard 1999; Law 2004; Latour 2005). The most interesting development for us here can be found in the methodological turn from "entrepreneurial ANT" to "ecological ANT" (Gherardi and Nicolini 2006) by shifting focus from particular entrepreneurial or technological trajectory and "center–periphery" relations to a more varied interplay of multiple actors and actor-worlds, in effect introducing several scales and focal points of inquiry (Gherardi and Nicolini 2006; Helgesson and Kjellberg 2006). In turn, this has meant drawing insight for ANT development from symbolic interactionist, social shaping of technology, and activity theory studies on science, technology, and society (Gherardi and Nicolini 2006; Pollock and Williams 2008). This is where we turn now in regard to biography yet return to points of contestation with "classical" SCOT and ANT when discussing collectives and practices later.

Biography 4, the Present Book: Intertwining Multiple Time Frames and Focal Points of Analysis

Researchers pursuing the social shaping of technology approach and those working with activity theory began to stress, in the mid-1990s, that the detail and scale of analysis and the length of inquiry made a decisive difference in our portrayals of socio-technical change. By focusing solely on the years and decades of change such as SCOT, one tends to find shifts in the constitution of the *class of technology*, such as the bicycle (Bijker 1995), the telephone (Fischer 1992), or an enterprise planning system (Pollock and Williams 2008). But during such changes the shape of adopter organizations has shifted also, as have the identities of their various users and the practices in which the technologies are being used. The changes in the class of artifacts thus need to be connected to change in the *class of usages and related users' practices* (Miettinen 1993; Hyysalo and Lehenkari 2003; Pollock and Williams 2008; Fischer 1992). Yet focusing solely on the scale of "class of technology and practices" runs a risk of losing the details of negotiation and practical achievements through which the technologies are made to work, both in their design and in their usages—indeed, such events tend to remain as anecdotes from data or are inferred or assumed from the broader-level description. To complicate the matter further, it should by now be clear that the constitution, the ways of designing and appropriating, and the implications of a particular technology can shift significantly in the course of its life span (Fischer 1992).

The "biographies of technology and practices" approach in this book means attending to the intertwinement of multiple ongoing processes through multiple foci and time spans of analysis. Somewhat similar ideas have guided more long-term and less detailed historical studies on technology use and development (Kline and Pinch 1996; Fischer 1992). The closest approaches to our own, and among the ones with the most give and take, are interactionist science, technology, and medicine studies (Star 1989a; Clarke and Star 2003) and the "biography of artifacts" studies by Pollock and Williams (2008) that feature the idea to deploy a number of mutually complementary studies or "studies within a study" on different aspects of the biography of technology and on different time frames of analysis. However, several specific features of our own research setups are worth foregrounding.

First, studying several sites related to the same technology—e.g., developer company, user organizations, and various intermediaries—necessarily depends on the skill and luck in, for instance, gaining access, being able to document the events, and gaining funding for follow-up studies. However, unlike Pollock and Williams (2008), who relied on the empirically resulting "varying research geometry," our studies were more strategically geared to a particular methodology and research setup, partly informed by activity theory and its application in developmental work research (Engeström, Y 1995; Miettinen 1993). This included:

1. We regarded ethnographic field study on both development and use as the best way to get to the intricacies of how the two inter-relate, and acknowledged that such study could not realistically be pursued for more than one to three years within the limits of any initial funding.
2. We took a particular innovation process as an initial focal point, and most often initiated its study at the point when its first generation was already being used, so as to be able to deploy ethnography on both development and user practices.
3. Since the early stages of the technology project (on both developer and user sites) could not in this arrangement be studied by a field study, we reconstructed them from historical materials and interviews.
4. We broadened the inquiry into the more long term development of practices of developers and users in order to understand their evolution in regard to the class of technology and the particular technology project in question.

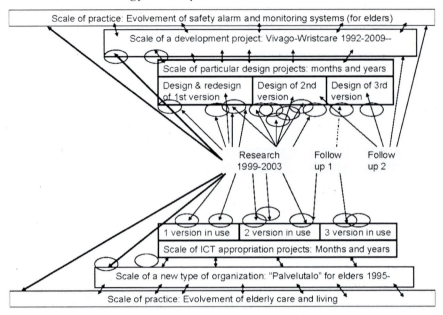

Figure 2.2 Stylized research design for a study on biography of technology on safety-alarm systems for the elderly. Multiple scales of analysis were deployed on both development and use. Arrows represent research activities, circles represent shorter episodes that the informants or the researchers regarded as particularly significant. Different bodies and granularities of data and time frames of analysis were systematically compared. (What this figure misses is, e.g., inferences and interaction that spanned development and use as well as change at each scale.)

5. Whenever sensible, we engaged the research subjects in elaborating their future development, as well as conducted follow-up studies some years after the initial study, to track the further evolution of the particular project and practices relating to it.

The research designs in this approach can be schematically portrayed by looking at the study of safety-alarm technology for elderly people that comprises the second part of this book (see Figure 2.2). The lines in the diagram signify research efforts targeted at different moments, sites, and scales of change in the relevant socio-technical biographies.

This diagram further reveals how this type of study operates in several time frames of analysis within one study. These roughly correspond to three distinct time frames on how technology projects and technological change have been (exclusively) studied in the previous research.

1) *The span of particular design and appropriation episodes.* Development of a technological innovation typically involves a series of shorter and longer design phases ranging from hours to weeks to months (Van de Ven et al. 1999; Schon 1983). Most studies on

design interaction, design decision making, and ethnomethodological studies of technology operate (exclusively) at this level.

2) *The development of a particular innovation and the organizations and people connected to it.* An innovation typically forms a biography or trajectory that lasts from five to 20 years, which has its own transitions and crises (Van de Ven et al. 1999). These events are connected to the trajectories of its producer company (or companies) and those of its key user partners, and the professional careers and life of the individuals participating in them (Miettinen 1998; Miettinen et al. 2003; Hasu 2001a).

3) *The coupling of "class of technology" and related sociocultural practices.* The practices of both the producers and users of technology change with the passing years and decades rather than in the span of any particular event or even that of a particular technology. These practices, such as elderly care or the telecommunications business, have formed relatively stable institutions and organizations of work, including a strong sense of the appropriate logic and path of development. Any new technology faces these preexisting arrangements in the organizations it is designed in (Grudin 1993), as well as in the organizations within which it is used along with other artifacts and tasks (cf. Clarke and Star 2003, 12). Yet transitions do take place both in practices and in the way two or more practices are coupled.

Finally, all of these developments are affected by:

4) *Long-term patterns in how design and use are organized.* Some aspects of design and use have prevailed in the industrial production of consumer goods ever since the rise of mass production (Hyysalo 2009a). In so doing, they have been shaped, but also endured, through "long-waves," significant overall reorganizations of production caused by the emergence of the upsurges of new generic technologies: electrification, motorization, and computerization (Freeman and Louçã 2001, esp. 140–151). Attempts to characterize somewhat more rapidly changing, but still very "obdurate," socio-technical formations include industry sectors, interorganizational fields, and socio-technical regimes (Nelson and Winter 1982; Hoogma et al. 2002).

The key issue here is not to regard the different time spans as somehow ontologically distinct even though studying them means employing an array of different materials and various foci of closer inquiry. An event is not pinned down to a place in the preordered scheme of things but seen as simultaneously constituting and being constituted by broader patterns. Various events can be examined as evidence of these patterns, while the patterns can be constructed from a range of evidence beyond the foci and granularity of a single site under analysis. But we need another detour to theorizing on "change and context" to clarify how the "biographies of technologies and practices" seeks to relate these scales.

UNDERSTANDING CHANGING CONTEXT

Understanding Changing Context 1: That Which Surrounds

If we take seriously that there is dramatic change as well as prevalence and persistence in how design–use relations play out, we are faced with the need to link the broader and more slowly changing, more obdurate, end of socio-technical change to biographies of innovation and episodes within it. This, in turn, takes us to questions of how we should understand "change" and "context" and their interrelation to begin with. Attention to context (some-times dubbed environment, background, or ecology) has gained urgency far beyond the studies of technology, organizations, and society.

Michel Cole (1996) argues cogently that the dominant approach to thinking about context is through distinct levels, such as micro, meso, ekso, and macro level (or system). Seeing context as "that which surrounds" is often expressed by relating "more micro phenomena" within the nested circles (concentric or overlapping) of broader systems or through systemic diagrams where smaller units are enclosed by larger entities (Cole 1996, 131–134; Strauss 1993). Individual action and interpersonal interactions take place at the micro level; this is surrounded by work group, community, and organizational levels, and these are again enveloped in an industry sec-tor, in a cross-sector innovation system, in a nation-state, and so on, all the way to global economy and politics (Cole 1996).

The rationale for seeking contextualization this way is articulated well by Anselm Strauss and Juliet Corbin's (1990) account on what they term conditional matrix and conditional paths. Strauss and Corbin make an astute remark about the vast difference there is in saying that "AIDS is having an effect on hospital work" and showing what this means through tracking the conditional path of this effect in the related conditional matrix—certainly one of the most sophisticated ways to handle context within the "surrounding" metaphor (Strauss and Corbin 1990, 162–171). Let us recount their example:

A physician came into the unit to make rounds, and while doing so she wished to check the colostomy of one of the patients. She asked the team leader, a nurse who was accompanying her on the rounds, for a pair of size six sterile gloves—a relatively small size. The team leader checked in the unit's storage area but the smallest available size was seven. She offered these larger gloves to the physician, who refused them. This posed a problem for the team leader.

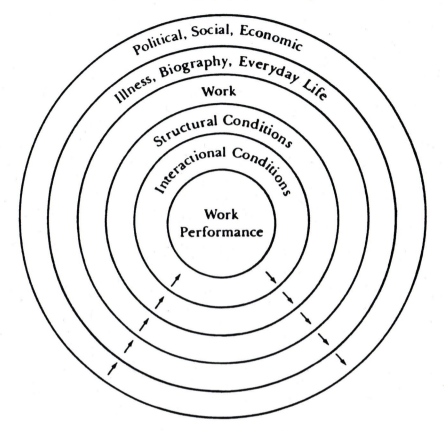

Figure 2.3 Strauss and Corbin project matrix.

Strauss and Corbin then move on to describe their tracking of the conditional path in the following matrix (see Figure 2.3):

(a) We begin with action, which was interrupted because the needed resource was lacking (b) Next . . . move to the interactional level of the conditional matrix. The head nurse had attempted unsuccessfully to persuade the physician to accept the larger gloves. The physician had been adamant in her refusal. The head nurse then contacted central supply; here too she attempted to persuade, but was unsuccessful. Finally, she was able to persuade one of the other units to loan her some gloves. (c) Next . . . move to the individual level of the matrix. Another physician may have accepted the larger gloves, but this one refused. Her hands were small. So physical size plays some part in the refusal. (d) Then . . . the suborganizational level of hospital ward, where the work occurs. Gloves were in short supply on the unit. Only a few limited sizes of sterile gloves were available. Why? Because they were being used so much.

Why? Because of the newly published national guidelines on infectional control. To protect themselves and other patients, health workers were being asked by the National Centre of Communicable Diseases to wear gloves when working on patients in a manner that might involve contact with their body fluids (since the patients might have AIDS) . . . (e) . . . gloves are in short supply within the hospital. To insure that each unit has an adequate supply for its respective type of work . . . gloves are kept under lock and key, and given only according to need. (f) Next . . . the community level . . . the supply of sterile gloves here is also limited, for in this community many hospitals and nursing homes are following the same national guidelines. This brings us to production, distribution, and supply of sterile gloves with the community [where] local suppliers were caught unprepared for the demand. (g) Now . . . move to the national level where the new guidelines originated, and ask "why?" here we can trace the situation back to the current perception of an AIDS epidemic. So, [the researcher] can show a relationship between AIDS and the work on a hospital unit by tracing upward through each of the conditional levels. Each level is more distantly removed from the problem at hand, yet in a wider sense contributes to it.

Such careful tracing combats "the untenable assumption of two contrasting realms of the macroscopic and microscopic," as Strauss (1993, 64) puts it. But this further opens rather than closes the array of related questions. As remarked by Peter Hall (quoted in Clarke 2005, 70), "[T]he imagery of the conditional matrix as a set of concentric circles, while perhaps a heuristic device, conveys an erroneous vision of social topography, one that I would rather leave to empirical examination." At this there is a preset vision of types of actors and actions that are pertinent in each level (e.g., "organizational"- and "institutional"-level actors) that does not do full justice to people's multiple memberships and engagements. It also remains odd to think that, for instance, "economic" or "political" or "illness" would reside only at a greater remove than, say, "work" and in need of somehow being translated into "work performance." They are rather right there, even if they are also elsewhere.

Furthermore, if we follow Strauss's assertion (1993) that conditional paths need to be shown rather than remain assumed, both epistemic and very practical questions arise. As Clarke (2005) questions, what would a grounded *analysis* of the other levels and their bearing upon the situation look like? In concentric circles topology, this would mean a massive enterprise that requires different types and granularities of data even when dealing with relatively straightforward and small events such as the AIDS and sterile gloves example (Strauss 1993, 64). Such analysis would be further complicated by these concerns with different types in the topology: what sorts of data does their adequate analysis require, and how compatible then are the mechanisms of affecting another sphere?

These questions and quandaries of how a given context (or entity) affects and gets affected by more micro and more macro levels equals, quite obviously, the question of change. In the "surrounding" topology, it is hard to handle.[4]

Understanding Changing Context 2: Intertwined Speeds of Change Constituting a Given Present

The problem with change is that it becomes a rather slippery thing when you try to fathom how it happened or, even more so, happens. Most disciplines steer clear of this by working with a sanitized notion of change: you take some unit of measure and measure events at the time t1 and again at t2, t3, t4, and so on. If the measurements differ, then a change has occurred. This is then attributed to endogenous forces in the measured entity or to exogenous ones in its environment, or a mix of both. But in such reasoning there is an assumption that the entity is the same at t1, t2, t3, etc., and so are its contexts and contents. When it comes to human change, particularly socio-technical change, this is seldom the case: humans act reflexively, adapt their actions, and shape their environments. Many actions are non-recursive and close down further sets of potential actions for the actor and others. The event, the entity, the relations, and their setting go through qualitative transformations along with quantitative ones. This is very burdensome, perhaps impossible to duly account for in "context as that which surrounds" view. Attending to such change escapes simple measures.

At this we can learn much from historians, the scholars of change *par excellence*. The one thing historians of almost any creed simply do not do is spend great expanses of time building formal accounts of how changing context and events interrelate and go about straightforwardly *applying* any such template in their craft. They would rather attend in depth the available source materials and build a web of inference from the myriad of direct and indirect evidence, background understandings about the era and place, ethical stances, preferred style of narrating, and so on (Ginzburg 1989). This reasoning, reconsidering, weighing, etc., usually results in a compelling narrative that attends the intertwined contexts and their changes (this is, of course, after historians of, for instance, science and technology gave up heroic and often Whiggish accounts of great minds).[5] Some of the most interesting insights about context and change from historians stem from their interchange with anthropology and sociology in annals (Braudel 1995; Le Goff 1988) and micro-history traditions (Ginzburg 1989; Levi 1988). Some of this thinking has explicitly made a crossover to technology and innovation studies, so let us begin from there.

In his attempt to write what he regarded as total history, historian Ferdinand Braudel distinguished among the slow-time of geographical change—the "longue durée," long-term seeping change of societies and mentalities—and the short-term conjuncture, passing of events that a

journalist or a chronicle might report (Braudel 1995). In more formal terms
later articulated by historians participating in the multilevel perspective
(MLP) on socio-technical change, such differently paced understandings of
change proceeds on a rather reasonable assumption that a broader context
has more inertia and systemic resistance than any of its parts. It consequently changes more slowly and painstakingly (Geels and Schot 2007).

Drawing also from evolutionary economics and science and technology
studies (Hoogma et al. 2002; Elzen et al. 2004; Geels and Schot 2007), MLP
asserts that in terms of heuristic analytical concepts "there are three levels of structures that differently influence local practices where actors (inter)
act" in regard to socio-technical change (Geels and Schot 2007, 404). These
are innovation-niches, socio-technical regime, and socio-technical landscape. The perspective underscores the carelessness in reducing technological
change to overly macro or only local events and stresses a principled way to
link how phenomena on different time scales of change are intertwined and
how they can be regarded as exerting influence on one another.

Geels and Schot (2007) indicate that there is more than an arbitrary
connection between the three levels in MLP and speeds of historical change
examined by Braudel. The three levels in MLP are located towards the
quicker end of Braudel's spectrum: landscape and the most durable aspects
of socio-technical regimes are within longue durée in Braudel's terms, while
niche development and more rapidly changing parts of regimes move within
conjecture.

Yet the greatest affinity between the two approaches lies in their principle of inquiry. Both Braudel and MLP aim to catch the relations between
different time scales of change through covering the entire contextual
range, examining each in different granularity of data, and elaborating
mechanisms of how the different durations interrelate. Rather than posit-
ing stable descriptions of contexts and getting stuck in how those change,
the question of context is itself cast in terms of change: duration, range of
influence, systemic dependencies, and recalcitrance.

But durations and socio-technical reach do not match as neatly as the
structuralist MLP model purports. In the MLP view, habits, customs, and
everyday perceptions among particular peoples, old units of measurement,
architectural rules, tastes, and prohibitions are constitutive of "more rapidly changing niches" as they hinder regimes from prospering uniformly.
But habits *et cetera*, if anything, have proven recalcitrant and durable. That
ladies are let through the doors and escorted on the left-hand side of the
cavalier on the street is regarded as courtesy today, but 700 years ago the
reasons were more pointed: the nobleman needed to have his sword hand
free and was most vulnerable to assassination from the front when passing
through doors. The fossilized habits live on through being interwoven with
new meanings and considerations, and, indeed, present-day guidebooks for
proper conduct feature wonderful turns such as that the gent walking on
the street side does so to protect his lady from car splashes! The cultural

everyday thus seems to reside simultaneously in the macro, the landscape, as well as in the very micro, the niches, and the associated durability complicates how MLP can conceptualize the pace of change. There are fast and slow processes everywhere.

Yet there is something genuinely generative in the idea that some processes form aggregates that indeed do change in slower rhythm, or, put more cautiously, that when one uses a particular grain size of data or time frame of analysis certain patterns of change and some contextual elements come more clearly into view, while others tend to disappear (cf. Boeke 1957; Eames and Eames 1977). However, a structuralist approach to writing a total history or generating a multilevel perspective reintroduces the problem of the amount of work that would actually be needed if all the contextual layers were truly analyzed (and indeed, Braudel's works on Mediterranean and French history are gigantic works).

But attending different paces of change and multiple time frames of analysis can be done without committing to total history or structuralist frameworks.

Understanding Changing Context 3, the Present Book: Context as the Differently Paced Constituents of the Situation

The various sorts of uneasiness that tend to follow when one tries to "place" an event in its "context" have led many researchers in social, cultural, and behavioral sciences into less clear-cut and less grandiose ways of grabbling with context. Cole (1996) perceptively notes that in such accounts there tends to be frequent use of metaphors of strands, threads, ropes, and weaving. Context is examined not as isolated from the situation inquired about but as constituting it and being constituted by it. The context of a situation (structure, economy, politics, illness, microbes) is that which is being woven together into a definition of the situation for the actors as well as for the researcher. Reality and situations are indeed constructed *in situ* (Lave 1993; McDermott 1993), but we are never alone (or) at its (sole) construction site (Latour 1987). The question of context gets transformed into asking how these conditions appear—make themselves felt as consequential—inside the empirical situation under examination (Clarke 2005, 71–72). The conditioning elements and contexts (or structures) do not have relevance in the abstract but insofar as they are *enacted* in a given situation (Lave 1988; Orlikowski 2000; Mol 2002). As illustrated by Jean Lave with regard to a supermarket (1988, 150–151):

> The supermarket, for instance, is in some respects a public and durable entity. It is physically, economically, politically, and socially organized space-in-time. In this respect it may be called an "arena" within which activity takes place. . . . At the same time, for individual shoppers, the supermarket is a repeatedly experienced, personally ordered and edited

version of the arena. In this aspect it may be termed a "setting" for activity. Some aisles do not exist for a given shopper as part of her setting, while other aisles are rich with detailed possibilities.

In acting on their settings, shoppers directly have limited registers to influence the political economy of the supermarket (Engeström 1993), yet it is due to performing as shoppers that people (in the mass) feed into the construction of the arena and versions that are enabled and constrained within it. Graphically such a stance can be illustrated as in Clarke's "situational matrix" (see Figure 2.4).

Lave's emphasis on the durability of the organization of, for instance, the supermarket is well recognized by most (but certainly not all) scholars who deal with context along the lines of the "weaving" metaphor. Hospitals, discourses, and social worlds are analyzed as durable social organizing that

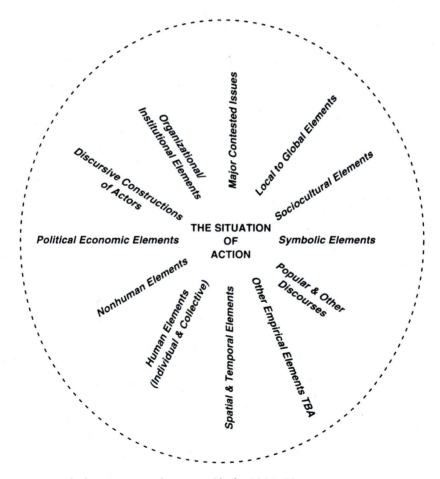

Figure 2.4 Clarke's situational matrix (Clarke 2005, 73).

has a bearing upon situated actions (Star 1989b; Clarke 2005; Engeström et al. 1999b). An event is seen as simultaneously constituting and being constituted by broader patterns.[6] This approach is exemplified by Edwin Hutchins's study of the unfolding of distributed action in navigation. In his analysis, any moment in human conduct is a part of the fairly rapid, some hours, of conduct of an activity such as preparing for and then steering a ship into a harbor. It is simultaneously also a moment in the years of development of the participants (who learn) doing it. The event also contributes to the evolution of practice that takes place slowly over decades and centuries "as partial solutions to frequently encountered problems are crystallized and saved in the material and conceptual tools of the trade and in the social organization of work . . . the microgenesis of the cultural elements that make up the navigation setting is visible in the details of the ongoing practice" (Hutchins 1995, 374). The crux of the matter is that these are not different layers of context, as they all take place in one and the same process (Hutchins 1995, 372–374).

While multiple speeds of change can be seen to be at stake in the ongoing flow of human activity, there are also events and moments in which conduct of action is at a particularly critical juncture in relation to more slowly changing patterns such as the development of a practice. Such instances can emerge because they feature prominent alternatives to choose from, pressure to comply with a tradition even when it is ill suited for the current situation, or simply caused by breakdowns and bottlenecks in the conduct

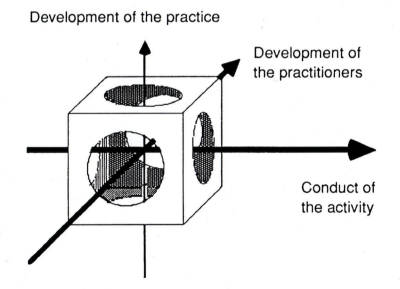

Development of the practice

Development of the practitioners

Conduct of the activity

Figure 2.5 "Hutchins cube," a representation of how multiple developments and speeds of change (the arrows) are present within a "moment of human practice" (the cube) (Hutchins 1995, 372).

of action that call for altering the routine way of conduct. Hutchins's example of a breakdown of electronic navigation systems onboard a battleship entering a harbor is a prime case: the participants are faced with the need to resort to seldom-used skills that had been part of their training a long time ago, articulate their perceptions of proper conduct and risks, and improvise (some of) their arrangements and (partially) redesign their means to get through the tasks at hand (Hutchins 1995). Along with members' categories, previous research may suggest where to look for such critical junctures, moments in which actions are likely to have significant impact, where choices are likely to be become articulated, or where extant research assumes certain behaviors to become enacted. In symbolic interactionism, a similar procedure is called theoretical sampling (Clarke 2005).

Once the events in a particular trajectory are seen as potential expressions and realizations of more long-term dynamics, the contingencies and potential generality of local problems may be assessed and understood in greater depth and more data can be gathered on elements that now appear important to understand. A detailed case analysis, in turn, provides concrete grounds to draw inferences for the general concerns—that is, weak but grounded generalizing in relation to more overarching studies and frameworks (cf. Clarke 2005; Geertz 1973a, 25–30; Flick 1998, 68–73). Thus in the present volume, focus on details of innovation biographies is not to delimit the inquiry to the micro level but to use it to elaborate on patterns that are likely to crop up also in other places and other times in creating and implementing health ICT, even though not in the exact same manner. Furthermore, within the study the multiple time frames of analysis for the processes under study are used to enrich each other and gain a sense of how the evolution of new technology and related practices is simultaneously taking place in multiple processes and at different speeds of change.

COLLECTIVITY AND PRACTICE

Collectivity and Practice 1: Relevant Social Groups and the Social Construction of Technology

Thus far we have outlined how the biography of technology approach tries to account for both emerging and more durable socio-technical organizing, bridge the different granularities in the loci and foci of studies, and reach through multiple cycles of development and use. In Chapter 1 of this volume and in discussing SCOT and ANT, we also suggested that design and use ought to be studied in symmetrical terms and this raises a question about what terms could be adequate for the job. There tend to be vast empirical asymmetries as to how designers and users relate to technology and there is thus a real danger of falling into unhelpfully reductionist registers.

Indeed, developers and users most often have a different social background: class, gender, ethnicity, age, and so on. They have different interests; for instance, producers may aim for a hegemonic global design, users for a working local configuration. Their roles, strategies, means, and access to technology vary greatly. Designers may seek to prefigure use by altering the constitution of the technology and instructions about its use. These strategies are in stark contrast with users' strategies in shaping technology in their everyday practice: work-arounds, neglecting functionalities, redefining it, building add-ons (Suchman et al. 1999; Lie and Sorensen 1996, 254). Yet these asymmetries between design and use are "secondary asymmetries" in that they are not "natural" or necessary characteristics of socio-technology, as is evident in the innofusion and evolutive co-design innovation models outlined in Chapter 1 of this volume. Consequently, these should not displace the requirement to keep the theory symmetrical with regard to success and failure, or for the different ways (technical, social, economic, and cultural) technology is influenced. Nonetheless, various asymmetries between designers and users are so prevalent in our current societies that due attention must be paid to them by any methodology aiming to examine the production and use of technology.

Perhaps a more poignant way of stating the preceding is that theories and methods used to study biography of technology and related practices should be able to study these collectives in their own terms and not fall victim to artifact-centrism. To illustrate this point, let us return to perhaps the greatest weakness of the SCOT framework. SCOT and many other early science and technology studies theories were interested in sketching out the social (or socio-material) construction *of technology* (or a scientific fact in the sociology of scientific knowledge). In explaining how the social affects a technology, the sameness of meaning and, consequently, the actors' interests in and preferences for what the technology is and should be are, of course, critical, since these comprise the social forces that demand change or stability in the artifact (Bijker and Pinch 1984; Pinch and Bijker 1987). But this way of accounting for sociality reveals its problems once the focus is broadened to include how the technical affects the social in a detailed analysis. By using the sameness of meaning with regard to the artifact as the defining criterion for a "relevant social group," Bijker and Pinch buy themselves into what we would call a "marketing man's collectivity." This can result in curious social groups such as "El-Vital shampoo users" that "share meaning" but only in terms of sharing some preferences and potentially some similarity in their income, hair types, and practices of washing.

Put sardonically, "relevant social group" is more prone to delineate a statistical marketing grouping rather than a social group, let alone a more in-depth collectivity. Indeed, it is seldom that the technology (or the sameness of the meaning for technology, for that matter) would be the prime reason for the existence of collectives in which technology is actually used and produced, such as companies, workplaces, science labs, or families (Strathern

1992, vii, vi–xii; Suchman 2002; Klein and Kleinman 2002). Joint action characterizes these collectives and even as effective communication and coordination of action among members does require sufficiently shared meaning of symbols, objects and gestures etc., it clearly does not require the sameness of meaning and is often accomplished precisely because of different starting points, resources, and meanings (Bowker and Star 1999; Star and Griesemer 1989; Miettinen 1999). As a result, SCOT offers little insight into the internal dynamics of such collectives, and fails to provide criteria for delineating any such (at least equally) relevant collectivities.[7]

Collectivity and Practice 2, the Approach of this Book: Activity Theory and Symbolic Interactionism

The shortcomings such as those resulting from SCOT's focus on meaning can be arguably steered clear of by placing doing and practice at center stage. As (Miettinen et al. 2009) observes, the "practice turn" in social and organizational studies (e.g., Schatzki et al. 2001) has been spurred by two partially independent developments. First, the concept of practice has been increasingly used to rephrase questions concerning epistemology and ontology in philosophy as well as problems concerning the nature of social order in social theory. Second, as also argued earlier with regard to biography, there is an increasing interest in studying in depth how the everyday conduct of various people takes place, what it is that people do when they do things. Such focus on professional and leisure practices has provided insight on intricacies of practice-specific cognition and action that tends to fall under the radar by more conventional research designs. In this capacity, studies on practices fill in blanks regarding, for instance, materiality, instruments, habits, and hindrances as well as possibilities for reforms. For instance, the rapid and wide proliferation of ANT owes much to the fact that it explicitly makes these two interests converge. It studies in depth *how* associations are built and maintained in forming hybrid entities, "nature societies," and, in turn, uses this material for reframing grand questions in philosophy and social theory (Callon and Latour 1981; Callon 1998; Latour 1987, 1999, 2005).

The concept of practice, however, is understood very differently, depending on tradition and field, both in terms of what it incorporates and in terms of the extension of "a practice." In some accounts, practice consists solely of talk and/or bodily performance, in others of artifactual yet rather minuscule habitual behaviors such as spreading butter on bread (Schatzki et al. 2001; Bernstein 1999). This book follows cultural psychology in taking practice to entail substantial forms of action, spread over time and place, that have often resulted in relatively durable collectives of various sorts (Chaiklin and Lave 1993; Cole 1996; Lave 1988).

Symbolic interactionism (SI) and activity theory (AT) are practice theories that share a number of features making them particularly sensitive for studying practices of designers and users, and their asymmetric interactions (Star 1996). A number of reviews of SI exist within technology studies (Clarke and Gerson 1990; Clarke 1990; Clarke and Star 2003). Activity-theoretical studies began to appear in the 1990s in technology studies and human–computer interaction (Nardi 1996a; Miettinen 1998; Hasu 2001a; Foot and Schneider 2006). There are several texts that discuss SI in relation to AT, such as those of Engeström (1987), Star (1996), and Miettinen (2002a). Hence, here we introduce only those features that are most pertinent to our present concerns and where we see SI and AT convergent or complementary in a compatible manner.

The first shared characteristic of these two theories is the emphasis on the process of human action, mediated by symbols, other cultural objects, and people. Interpreted action and interaction is one of the primary points of departure for SI. Interactionism sees that without the ongoing process of action, any structure of relations between people would be meaningless (Blumer 1969, 1). Action is seen as situational and taking place in relation to other people. Through symbols, patterns of reciprocal anticipation are formed in the interaction, in the verification of outcomes. It follows that the meaning of knowledge is given in its consequences, in a community of listeners, not in its a priori analytical specification (Joas 1987, 91; Star 1996; Blumer 1969, 61–77). In addition to people, situations are composed of objects, which are seen as human constructs in terms of being defined as well as being materially shaped. Such objects include bodies, artifacts, matter, ideas, infrastructure, and so on, and these interpreted objects comprise the conditions for action (Blumer 1969, 68–69).

This grounding gives rise to the first key point in studying the collectives in design and use: they are approached as work and collective action (Clarke and Gerson 1990, 182) and seen to take place in relation to "going concerns," enterprises, institutions, organizations, associations, and families (Hughes 1971, 54–55). These going concerns allow their participants to take for granted what the important activities are, and commitments related to them (Becker 1960; Clarke 1990, 18). In other words, unlike SCOT, which delineates "relevant social groups" in relation to the technology that is the analyst's interest, SI studies collectives in terms of their reasons for existence, while technology may feature in a variety of roles, from prime going concern to auxiliary means.

Activity theory is a theory about human cognition and action that stems from the work of Russian psychologists Vygotsky, Leontjev, and Lurija starting in the 1920s. It has since been developed further for studying collective work activities, and for studying technology production and implementation (Engeström et al. 1999b; Nardi 1996b).[8] Like interactionism, AT analyzes technology, subjects, and the social as hybrid and intertwined systemic wholes (Engeström 1996b). These "activities" (often "activity systems") are formations of relatively long-lasting "durable" collective action in which members' actions are mediated by tools and signs, rules, other members, and division of labor (Engeström 1987). An activity is seen as animated by their "object" or "objective horizons," the social purpose for the existence of the activity in question (e.g., for a health care center, maintaining the primary health needs of citizens). Such social motives are (partially) shared by the participants (e.g., doctors, nurses, and receptionists) and (partially) materialized in the objects (e.g., illnesses, microbes, and patients' complaints) the activity is transforming into outcomes (e.g., referred and cured patients and treatments administered; Leontjev 1978; Engeström 2001a; Kaptelinin 2005). Hence, in AT reason for existence and activity being conduced are used to define collectives rather than analyst interest or an artifact.

Activity theory places emphasis on changes in mediation, which is seen as *transforming* (not merely augmenting) the structure and content of work, thinking, and learning humans engage in. For instance, the operation of solving the multiplication problem 17 x 15 on paper is not an augmentation of the in-the-head computation but a significant reordering of most of the mediators by which multiplication is carried out. A further transformation of this cognitive action would be using a calculator or asking someone for the answer. In all of these ways to solve the multiplication problem, cognition and action are distributed to intramental and external operations. When signs are used intramentally, they act as "psychological tools" that typically were once encountered as externalized signs and relations. Similarly, the manipulation of signs as external cultural artifacts drawn on paper, in a calculator, or verbalized to a fellow owes to one's capacity to externalize the multiplication problem in question. Signs and tools are seen as cultural products: mediators and outcomes of previous labor done in the same or some other activity. Languages, machines, scientific theories, service models, and buildings are equally such "ideal-material" creations that can feature in multiple roles within an activity system (Engeström 1996b).[9]

The second shared aspect of SI and AT constitutive to the present framework is their shared emphasis on studying work across multiple scales, which is a marked difference from, for instance, ANT. In the most detailed inquiry, SI focuses on tasks, problems, and negotiations that constitute the immediate flow of work (Clarke and Gerson 1990, 180–185, 199; Fujimura 1996; Star 1996). On the scale of work organization, the focus is on the development of conventional procedures and arrangements, commitments, alliances, and going concerns that coordinate and enable the work (Clarke and Gerson 1990, 184–188; Clarke and Star 2003; Star and Griesemer 1989). On the broadest scale of inquiry, "social worlds" and their subworlds are studied. By social worlds, interactionists refer to the way reference groups (such as professions, disciplines, and social movements) organize social life by generating shared perspectives for their actions (Shibutani 1955, 1962; Strauss 1978). "Social worlds are groups with shared commitments to certain activities sharing resources of many kinds to achieve their goals, and building shared ideologies about how to go about their business.

They are interactive units, worlds of discourse, bound not by geography or formal membership 'but by the limits of effective communication'" (Shibutani 1955, 566; cf. Strauss 1978; Clarke and Star 2003). They consist of at least one prime activity, sites on which activities occur, and technological means for carrying out activities (Strauss 1978, 122).

AT shares the premise of analyzing work across multiple scales. Activities are seen as consisting of intentional "actions" directed towards particular conscious goals, carried out by one or more individuals. "Operations" transform actions into actual situation-dependent and embodied realizations of a goal. These aspects of human conduct are mutually dependent. Nothing is left of the motive (activity) other than what is acted out in actions, and we fully know our goals (actions) only after we have acted— that is, we have carried out the situationally adjusted operations (Leontjev 1978, 63–65). Studies of the micro-scale of work and action are thus intrinsically seen as connected to the broader organization of activity. There is a range of processes that take place in between activity and action, variously organized "strings of action" as Yrjö Engeström (1995) characterizes them, an example being the "personal and group projects" of the rest-home staff and residents we examine in Chapter 6 of this volume. We will also "scale up" activity theory to incorporate more than just activity-scale, meso-level, sociocultural formations in Chapter 3 of this volume.

In addition to somewhat more tightly conceptualized relations between scales of action, AT stresses temporality and historicity in all analysis. Things, individuals, cognitions, and collectives are examined in terms of their evolvement. It provides a particular sensitivity to internal tensions and contradictions that drive individuals and activities to transform their existing ways of conduct (Engeström 1987). Activity theory also has an 80-year history and burgeoning present research on the myriad of forms in which *change and learning* take place in various workplace settings, child development, and various leisure and educational activities (Engeström et al. 1999b; Cole 1996).

The third key feature in studying designer–user relations is concepts for studying interaction, exchange, and multiple memberships. SI has been particularly sensitized to such analysis within and across the scales: at the workplace where different peoples meet (Hughes 1971); in the identities and careers of (marginal) people (Star 1991; Becker 1953); in objects and infrastructures, and in the exchange between social worlds (Star and Griesemer 1989; Bowker and Star 1999); and in arenas where issues become debated, negotiated, forced, and manipulated (Strauss 1978, 124). The notion of "implication" is also relevant in examination of implicated work and implicated users who are connected to technology without their own consent, as well as those affected by the technology, often without the possibility to affect it (Clarke 1998, 267).

Multiple memberships has since the beginning been a concern also for AT (Leontjev 1978, 127–130), visible, for instance, in analysis of group perspectives on an activity and in emphasis on multivoicedness as a key feature of activities (Engeström, R 1995; Holland and Reeves 1996; Engeström 2001b; Miettinen 1993). Studies in developmental work research have increasingly focused on two or more interacting activity systems since the early 1990s (Engeström 1996a). Interactions between the members of activity systems have been conceptualized as trying to construct a mutually shared object in their interaction and cross boundaries that prevail between them and on differently stabilized forms of network collaboration (e.g., Engeström et al. 1999a; Toiviainen 2003; Kangasoja 2002). In studies leading to this book, networks of activity systems have been related to a trajectory of technological artifacts and seen as pools of resources and sources of various interests affecting the technology (Miettinen 1998; Miettinen and Hasu 2002; Saari 2003; Miettinen et al. 2003).

In sum, activity theory and symbolic interactionism provide conceptual means to examine the activities of various peoples related to technology projects in terms that do justice to the constitution and reasons of existence of those collectives. They also provide a rich theoretical repertoire for examining the biographies of technologies and practices on multiple scales of analysis and relating those analyses in a principled manner along the weaving metaphor as discussed earlier. Combining these theoretical resources with the integrative and comparative insight SLTI provides (see Chapter 1 of this volume) for findings related to the development–use nexus provides us with a strong basis for examining the early evolution of new technology.

Biographies of Technology and Practice out in the Field: Intertwining Historical and Ethnographic Inquiries

Studies of change that span several practices and scales have been characterized equally aptly as "ethnography of a networked activity" (Saari 2003, 48–51; cf. Toiviainen 2003) as well as "ethnography of change" (Hasu 2001a; Foot 1999). These ethnographies have not limited their analyses to the unfolding of events but used historical analysis to grasp multiple sites and multifaceted change (cf. Engeström 1987; Miettinen 1993; Engeström and Escalante 1996).

Following biographies of technology between networked activity systems makes field observations proliferate into many ongoing streams of action, accompanied by rounds of interviews and document-gathering. Such a form of observation differs from the traditional ethnographic setup in which the ethnographer spends a considerable time immersed in another culture to provide a rich contextual understanding of the culture (Geertz 1973a). It also differs from micro-sociologies, such as conversation analysis, that have solved the reliability problem by resorting to highly detailed analyses of audio-recorded/videotaped data through tedious procedures in interpretation (e.g., Jordan and Henderson 1994). The ethnography of change in biographies of technologies and practices approach navigates its way in the middle between these extremes: it tries to achieve a rich and contextual, yet sufficiently detailed, account of change when combined with historical analysis methods.[10]

In so doing, the reliability of interpretation is partially achieved through the longitudinal scope of study: false interpretations and "shows put on for the ethnographer" are leveled out when one enters the site along a sustained period of time and gathers data from multiple interlinked activities. Ethnographic observation, recorded in field notes and audio and video recordings provided firsthand experience of the realities of design and use of technology. The accounts of technology developers were typically filled with visions and optimism and blurred the actual present-day matters with their potential. Users, in turn, were often not fully aware of what they do with artifacts, or could not quite articulate it. Observation, even on a rather modest scale, helped to open up a deeper and more critical dialogue with the research subjects. It also contextualized and gave more sensitivity in analyzing other sources of data, such as documents and interviews, and provided detailed bodies of data about events that appeared particularly interesting for the research.

The historical analyses in this book built on the author's M.A. and Phil. Lic. education in cultural history, yet the studies also opened up some new questions and possibilities. First, the focus on the very recent past allowed the creation of new detail-rich data through interviews. Second, the ethnography of change offered a good data-gathering method and a way to gain contextual understanding, through the wealth of events and issues that indirectly witnessed the previous events as "tradition sources" (Renvall 1983, 199). Third, being present on many occasions allowed one to ask specific questions and to gather documents that might have been thrown away soon after the occasion. As, importantly, it allowed for the generating of a track of data and participants' interpretations that were not affected by hindsight and the juxtaposing of the then-current views of the participants with their previous accounts and evaluations of events past and future. It thus took the "anti-Whig" program of SCOT (and historiography in general) to the extreme in regard to data-gathering (Fleck 1979; Bijker 1995, 10–17). This ongoing accumulation of data and interpretation was intertwined with principles from historiography such as internal and external source criticism (cf. Renvall 1983), the formation of the explanatory narratives that provide the connections between various documents and bodies of data, and allow for the contextual understanding to fill in the gaps and provide an account of the past event, in contrast to an account of the past documents (White 1973; Ankersmit and Kellner 1995; Pihlainen 1999). Also the methodological maxim to gain and analyze data on multiple time scales of analysis proved productive here, as the work proceeded in constant movement between the questions arising from biographies of particular technology, even individual devices, and what was learned about the broader-scale development of the class of technology and practices concerned. The datasets and methods are further discussed in the appendix to this volume.

CHAPTER DISCUSSION

The approach of longitudinally following the "biographies of technology"—taken to include related biographies of organizations, institutions, and participants—holds promise of gaining more unified and rich view to how design, use, and regulatory actions relate during the (early) evolution of a technology. The approach entails multiple data sources and scales of inquiry: biographies of classes of technology span decades, particular projects several years, while many of their most interesting events happen in dense processes that last only hours and weeks.

An innovation does not take place in isolation but is influenced by—and tries to actively influence—the socio-technical practices in design, use, and regulatory organizations. These collectives, often more obdurate and slowly changing than the technology under scrutiny, need to be studied in more depth than just in their immediate relations to the technology in question. To this aim, we turned to practice theorizing, particularly activity theory and symbolic interactionism, that provide means for studying work and collective action across the asymmetries in collectives that develop and use new technology.

The questions of how to relate different scales of inquiry hark back to how we should understand context and change and their interrelations. We proceeded by first examining the dilemmas inherent in sanitized notions of change, then proceeded to those that arose in thinking context through placing a phenomenon into its "surrounding context," and possibilities that open up when one takes obduracy—"speed of change"—as a defining criterion of contextual elements. In steering clear of the problems that arise with attempts to write "total history" or deploy a structuralist multilevel perspective, the present study deploys analyses on the biographies of technology in multiple foci and loci—"cases within case"—that are chosen such that they are likely to be located at the junctures where more pervasive and slowly changing ways of conduct have the most impact on the local unfolding of action and vice versa.

In practice, our studies did at some point produce an in-depth outline of the whole biography of each of the innovations studied. Such monologue narrative "truth" about the process on one scale of inquiry was not the final aim but merely one of the patterns under interest. The different time spans, foci, and environments of inquiry on the same biography by the same investigators and theory-methods approach are likely to shed light on how different inquiries relate *qua* their grain size and foci. In modernist terms, such a setup is likely to reveal biases, neglected areas of inquiry, and points of discontent. In a more postmodern register, this sort of inquiry is prone to reveal complexities and uncertainties underlying the taken-for-granted assumptions in studies of socio-technical change, as well as partialities that actors face with both ICT solutions-in-the-making and with the accompanying rationales, norms, and procedures.

Part II
Grounding and Theorizing

3   The Birth of the User
Community and Imagination

Having articulated the theoretical and methodological starting points for our inquiry, let us turn to empirical analyses. In the next five chapters, we shall examine the Vivago-Wristcare alarm and monitoring system for the elderly from its very inception to early stabilization of its uses. In this chapter, we shall focus on the birth of the invention and its conceptions of users and uses. In doing so, we elaborate theoretically how to conceptualize the role of professional practices in guiding imagination and in binding practitioners to some rather than other solutions. To understand the rise of this innovation, however, we need to depart from a wider development in elderly care and elderly technologies, and this is where we turn to now.

THE CHANGING ARENA OF ICT AND ELDERLY PEOPLE

In the past 20 or so years, the future of elderly care has been increasingly colonized by new groups of actors. The business analysts have joined the welfare economists, the heads of strategy of prominent high-techs have joined the small prosthesis manufacturers, and the private programs for housing and nursing the elderly have risen next to the state-run rest homes. Research, news, and the experts interviewed emphasize that there is an ongoing transition in the way the elderly live and are taken care of in Western industrialized countries.

Behind these changes is the aging of society. The relative number of the elderly to the workforce shall increase significantly during the next 30 years because of the longer life expectancy, the retirement of the baby boomers, and changes in family structures. The costs of care will also rise, as the longer life is partially achieved through better but more expensive medication and hospital facilities. There is also likely to be less "free" care from within the family since the future elderly will have fewer offspring, who, in turn, will tend to live further away from their elders (e.g., Kaakinen and Törmä 1999; Tornstam 1992; Valkonen and Nikander 1987; Hempel 1994). Politicians, caregivers, and the current and future elderly alike are faced with the same question: how to manage this transition economically and socially.

Many place faith in new technology. It has, however, remained less clear what the technical transformation would consist of. Studies in the homes of the elderly reveal anything but aging supported by the latest smart technologies. For instance, Östlund pointed out that there were only four "new" technologies actively used by the elderly: TV, radios, telephones, and safety phones (Östlund 1995). A Finnish study noted that "the residents ... typically had a television, a phone and a microwave oven" (Törmä et al. 2001, 55).

There are several partial explanations given for the phenomena. Mainstream products are designed for younger users and do not match the sensory and tactile limitations of the elderly (e.g., Harrington and Harrington 2000). Limited eyesight and hearing make exploratory learning, finding instruction, and recovering from the mistakes harder. These hindrances are paired with patterns of usage. With less exposure to the latest technology, the features, interfaces, and analogies used in new devices are less familiar (e.g., Cullen 1998; Östlund 1994; Hempel 1994). Just as importantly, many technologies for the elderly are technical aids designed for the various handicaps or for nursing the weak and the disabled. These are associated with one's capacity to act, and people tend to postpone getting an aid until it is plainly visible (for themselves as well as for people around them) that they suffer from a stigmatizing condition, such as loss of hearing or eyesight. At this point, technical assistance no longer compensates effectively for the lost abilities and is prone to remain useless or simply unused (Mollenkopf 1994). Moreover, many technologies imposed on the elderly answer someone else's needs: those of relatives, home-care workers, technology developers, taxpayers, etc. (Östlund 1994).

Finally, there is a cluster of explanations that center on the elderly having a fundamentally different technology relation than younger generations. There is some evidence that the elderly stick with the types of technology that were available during their active years. The pre–World War II generation is also seen to buy technology less whimsically than later generations do (cf. Harrington and Harrington 2000). Also, in general, values and time perspectives may change in the later years. Improving or developing one's life, or buying new things for oneself, may come to have less priority than orienting to the past and the coming end of life (Tornstam 1986). In effect, all these issues offer some explanation as to why "the gap between actual and potential use of technical aids by the elderly is substantial, due to a lack of knowledge, financial aspects, fear, and a need for individual instruction even with rather simple aids" (Klerk and Hijsman 1994, 117). This goes beyond assistive technologies to ICTs in general.

On the supply side, the "gray panthers" have only recently become anything like a business case for the technologists (Mollenkopf 1994; Roe 2001; Harrington and Harrington 2000). In 2006, a "Jitterbug dial" cell phone made the headlines as the first cell phone targeted at "tech-challenged older people," including only large number buttons and the call function (*BusinessWeek*, December 11, 2006). In all, the elderly and their care appear to aggravate the asymmetries that tend to exist in the relations of producers and users. Mainstream ICT products emerge from the aspirations, concerns, and design language of enthusiast ICT users and designers, who are typically young or middle-aged, predominantly male, technically oriented, educated, and enjoy good income. This sets elderly care in a double margin: not only are the majority of old people women and relatively low-income, but also the gross majority of their caregivers (both paid and relatives) are female, over 40 to 50 years old, and not fascinated by the (latest) gadgets. The low-income, "low-qualification," female field has not attracted technical investments but remained handicraft and service oriented (Wajcman 1991).[1] Correspondingly, the general experience and competence in using ICT is low among, for instance, the nursing staff in elderly care (Hyppönen 2004).

Attempts to change the technological mediation of elderly living and care present an interesting terrain at the present moment. Companies can appeal, and have begun to appeal, to various estimates of a very large and lucrative market among the elders. The gerontechnology movement (Harrington and Harrington 2000) and inclusive design (e.g., Hyppönen 1999) argue that technology can help and can make a difference, particularly now when ICT, in principle, allows easier customization for the needs of various users (Ekberg 2003). The technology design merely needs to be targeted to the needs of people with restricted mobility, fragility, weak senses and powers, and likelihood of accidents (e.g., Harrington and Harrington 2000). Alternatively, "mainstream" products can become inclusive by introducing guidelines and exemplary cases that industry can follow to broaden the range of users who might benefit from the products. On the demand side, governments have widely come to embrace home-based care extended for as long as humanly possible, and care facilities have come to seek labor-saving solutions. ICT is also a concern because of the fears of elderly people becoming "digitally divided," marginalized in a society running increasingly on IT (Kaakinen and Törmä 1999; Törmä et al. 2001; Harrington and Harrington 2000; Roe 2001).

To clarify this initial setting in elderly living and care and ICT production, let us turn to interactionist social worlds/arenas mapping (Clarke 2005). Figure 3.1 tentatively portrays the mutual relations of four large, fairly stabilized even if internally heterogeneous and evolving social worlds in the early 1990s. These are the closely related elderly living and elderly care and equally closely related "ICT production world" and "ICT delivery world." These have an interesting relation. The elderly population uses some of the technologies central to the "ICT delivery world" heavily, such as TV and radio programs and the telephone. These technologies are, however, fairly stabilized from the "ICT production world" perspective. Certainly the larger and clearer high-definition TV developments will find markets among the elderly, but on the whole new technology does not fare widely into active use by the elderly, nor is there much significant product development targeted specifically to elderly people or their care. Safety phones and more technology-reliant "service housing" and home care reside on overlapping terrain between the four social worlds.

The public discourse on the elderly, their care, and technology in Finnish magazines and newspapers at the turn of the millennium highlights the poles of attention quite well.[2]

> *The race to the Granny-market: we have heard all about the pension bomb, now the companies are figuring out how to exploit the grey panthers (Ylioppilaslehti, 5/2002).*

> *Helsinki forces the elderly from institutions to home care. Yet, they are no longer provided with help in daily tasks (Helsingin Sanomat, August 31, 2003).*

> *Technology does not remove loneliness (Kauneus ja Terveys, 12/2001).*

> *Billion markets in the wrist! (Tekniikka ja talous, 1998).*

> *The invention by IST Ltd. may save the aging society (Hyvä Suomi! S.a.).*

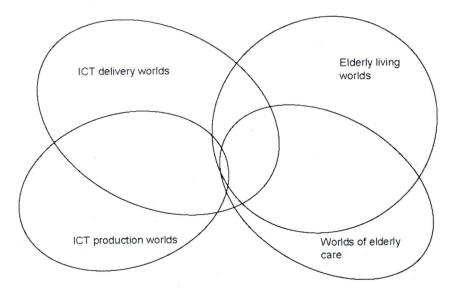

Figure 3.1 A schematic portrayal of the overlapping ICT and elderly worlds in the early 1990s.

The last two headings are related to a significant *class of technology* in the technological transformation of elderly care. This personal safety-alarm system—or, more colloquially, "safety phone"—is the only "new ICT" that is widespread and positively recognized among the elderly and their caretakers and designed specifically for them. What makes the headings particularly interesting is the particular project in this line of technology that is projected to have billion markets and "to save the aging society" called "Vivago-Wristcare."[3] It integrates sensors into a wrist-worn push button of safety phones to produce 24-hour, seven-day-a-week monitoring of the physiological state of the person. This monitoring and generation of automatic alarms may be seen as a welcome development where producers have taken seriously the needs of the elderly and responded with a serious product development project. Alternatively, it may be regarded as another instance of technologists trying to "push" overly complex, alien, and cost-inducing technology down the throats of the poor elderly.

Whichever the perspective, the project sits right in the middle of the arena formed by the four social worlds depicted in Figure 3.1. Should the Vivago-Wristcare project "hit the billion markets in the wrist," it would vitalize the existing connections and potentially open the door for more interchange and dependency between these social worlds. We could also argue further and note that its business and R&D case rests on a future where the connections between the actors in both pairs of social worlds become more active. Its R&D requires substantial funding, which its developers can only find in ICT-related venture capital; it also needs compatibility with various pieces of ICT infrastructure, rests on further technical developments around it, needs to be included in the sales repertoire of tele-operators, etc., etc. Its market reception rests on how the caretakers, policymakers, and the elderly perceive whatever potential for change it has: how much is invested; will it get subsidized, promoted, accepted as safe, etc., etc.?

Hence, regardless of the perspective, Vivago-Wristcare sits at the juncture in the technological transformation of elderly care in its attempts to renew the novelty safety phones and offers a good occasion for examining the relationships between telecommunications producers and the elderly and their caregivers. Let us now move to examining the early years of this project more closely.

THE BIRTH OF THE WRISTCARE TECHNOLOGY AND ITS USERS: RESOURCES FOR REALIGNING SAFETY-PHONE DEVELOPMENT

The impetus for launching the Vivago-Wristcare project lay in the estimate by its inventor, MM, that if physiological monitoring could be introduced into a safety-phone system, it not only would replace the existing devices but might also open up new market segments among younger users.[4] He established a small start-up company, International Security Technology Ltd. (Vivago Ltd.), in Helsinki, Finland, for this purpose in 1993. His estimate that this could factually be done was based on his knowledge of multiple practices that offered complementary solutions for a novel kind of approach to monitor the well-being of the user.

1. The most important of these practices was the inventor's and his associates' experience with safety-phone development and marketing. This provided the initial problem to be solved by Vivago-Wristcare: to create a better alternative to "passivity sensors" distributed around the house to detect whether a user had met with an accident such that she was not able to sound a manual alarm. Safety-phone development also provided several exemplary solutions—for instance, the importance of an easy-to-wear wrist-held device; emphasis on a low price; and, from passivity monitoring, the idea that combining relatively crude and cheap instrumentation could provide sufficient information about the users.[5]
2. The second source was the existing sensors and devices for physiological monitoring. After experimenting with simple pulse-measurement devices, the developers found out that movement, acceleration, body temperature, and the conductivity of the skin could potentially be sufficiently measured with available sensors fitting a wrist-held device.[6]
3. Experience in industrial automation added to these ideas. It would be easier to detect changes in the user's condition by focusing on secondary signs, reactions, and the overall state of the user than to detect these through precise measurement of any one parameter, thus allowing for lighter instrumentation that could be realized on the wrist, and with a competitive price.[7]
4. Fourth, discussions with first-aid personnel and a gerontologist suggested that the features to measure, principles for their measurement, and analogues for algorithms in Vivago-Wristcare could simulate the diagnostic practice of frontline helpers.[8]
5. Designers' experience in the technology business provided the means for achieving a viable design. Among the measures taken were: concentrating the company's effort only on R&D and outsourcing all else that was possible; adopting strict secrecy over key features to fend off competition; and defining the product as system independent, minimal, mass produced, and fully automated, to keep manufacturing, sales, and maintenance costs low.[9]
6. Finally, designers had acquired information about elderly care over the years in designing safety phones. This information convinced them that the extra security and possible proactive detection of the worsening state of the user could bring cost reductions by letting the elderly live longer in their own homes.[10]

The six professional practices provided the initial resources for trying to realign safety-phone development. But from where did the idea arise in the first place? Why embark on investigating how solutions from disparate fields could be crammed into a small wrist-held device and built into its associated alarm transmission and service concepts? To understand this, we first need to go back some time in safety-phone development, to where all the early developers of Vivago-Wristcare had their strongest professional commitments in, for it provides us insight for their view of the plausible and desirable development path.

The ancestors of safety phones were the various paging and nurse-call systems in hospitals, such as bedside bells, pull cords, and alarm buttons in toilets and wards. The first generation of safety-alarm systems consisted basically of a phone with an alarm button and a preprogrammed alarm path to a service provider. They started to proliferate in the 1970s, both in sheltered housing and in home use (Ihonen 1986). Gradually, a greater number of alarm buttons and cords were added to complement the phone that was usually located at the bedside (for instance, cords in the lavatory and kitchen). Some devices came to have an intercom system that could establish a speech connection between the alarm center and user, even if the user was lying on the floor unable to pick up the handset of the phone (Ihonen 1987; Wild and Kirschner 1994).

The 1980s saw the coming of wireless, wearable alarm buttons that made the "security" omnipresent inside the house. At the same time, there were attempts to use "passive alarms" to detect the instances when the

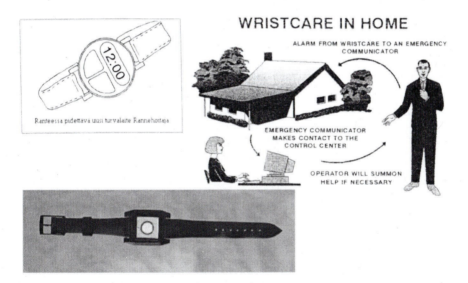

Figure 3.2 Early visions of Vivago-Wristcare. Top left: the earliest sketch; bottom left: the device launched on the market in 1997; top right: early graphical depiction of the system functions.

person was not able to sound an alarm manually. The solutions relied on finding indicators that would send an alarm if something had gone wrong with the person. Technologists reasoned that even "demented" humans normally do certain vital things, such as sleep, eat, and go to the toilet (cf. Björneby 1994). Sensors in doors, refrigerators, and beds were accompanied by wearable tags to which induction loops in the doors reacted. These accessories, however, had their own sets of constraints. Following the argumentation of the developers of Vivago-Wristcare, they were prone to false alarms, were too slow to react to problems, and required heavy wiring that was expensive and possibly intrusive.[11]

In the 30 years of safety-phone development, technical change has involved increasing complexity and changes in transmission media. It resembles the development of burglar alarms in that developers have advocated increasingly complex systems, marketing both the threat and their sophisticated remedies.[12] Changes in the artifacts have introduced more thorough and total monitoring within the limits set by unobtrusiveness and price, moving the devices away from the bedside to encompass spaces occupied by more mobile and healthy users. This change has been accompanied by exemplary artifacts (robot-phones, push buttons, radio-frequency receiver units), skills, and ways of working (mechanical and electrical engineering in signal transmission, sales strategies, ways to organize alarm centers, adopting solutions and people from other branches of telecommunications), instruments (changing tools to render circuit boards and manipulate plastics, changing software programming languages), marketing strategies and target customers (the caretakers and the elderly both at homes and in institutions), giving identity to technology (security as extension of phone, steering clear of medical devices and their requirements), *et cetera*.

Not many, if any, wholly new component technologies have been invented for safety phones, but most solutions used in them were first developed in other branches of telecommunications. Safety-phone development has followed advances in signal and voice transmission technology as part of the general development of telecommunications through the introductions of intercoms, wireless alarm buttons, and various sensors in passive alarms. By the same token, there are few people who have a career solely in the safety-phone business and engineering. Nonetheless, safety-phone development forms its own distinct branch, as it differs from the other telecommunication practices by its mix of instruments, markets, future prospects, and a sense of development from past to future—both in technology and in terms of changes in users' actions.

This observation that a class of technology and the related development practices can form a biography or a path is by no means novel. For instance, Pollock and Williams (2008) trace the complex trajectory of organizational software packages across decades, beginning with 1960s stock and inventory control systems in the aerospace and automobile sector. These were extended into Materials Requirements Planning (MRP) by including production scheduling, then capacity scheduling and yet further extensions leading to Manufacturing Resource Planning (MRP II), Computer-Aided Production Management (CAPM), and ERP systems by the mid-1990s. All these were built on the premise of integrating multifunctional and modular designs so that updating data in one module would result in all systems being updated. Important discontinuities mix with the striking continuities. The shift from mainframes to client-server architectures in the 1990s and to presently ongoing Web-based additions have been accompanied, for instance, by changing business prescriptions such as just-in-time in the 1980s and the presently ongoing value-network and supply-chain management emphases. Nonetheless, all the while the developers of these systems iteratively recycled previous software, design ideas, and organization of development effort and ideas for managing client relations so that there appears to be a line of expansion in the scope of these systems rather than distinct innovations in packaged software despite different names and descriptions.

In promising to introduce direct monitoring of the physiological condition of the elder and automated alarms, Wristcare addressed what was by many seen as the next step in the likely path of safety-phone development. The idea of integrating safety phones with more thorough surveillance of the user was "in the air" when Wristcare was invented and has continued to be since. Technical visions included radar, infrared detectors, and new kinds of distributed sensors around the house to extend the coverage to cases in which the user could no longer call for help herself (Zoche 1994; Berlo et al. 1994; Björneby 1994). Since then, intelligent robots have been proposed for the job and the development of GSM and GPS systems has led to attempts to create devices with safety-phone-like functions for outdoor use (such as EU-More project), which are likely to be incorporated more fully into safety phones in the future. These too were envisioned to be incorporated into Vivago-Wristcare from the outset once its first generation was out and making a profit.[13] And even though safety-phone producers have positioned their business within the alarm and security sector, they have been well informed about the development of medical instruments such as pagers, nurse-call buttons, and monitoring devices. This proximity to medical technologies as a potential source of new solutions for safety phones added to the argumentative power of the Vivago-Wristcare project.

Seen from this perspective, the key issue in launching a technically and commercially ambitious project like Vivago-Wristcare is not so much how well it caters to the identified needs of its targeted users but how it fits the visions and imaginations found in technical development and the business it seeks to become a part of.[14] Indeed, Vivago-Wristcare has received attention from competitors, distributors, and health care professionals ever since, and appears to have addressed the social imagination about one of the relevant directions of safety-phone system development. At the same time, many critical problems in the operation of extant safety phones have received producers' attention only when demanded by the state, including the large proportion of false alarms, the conduct of the often overburdened alarm centers, mistrust, and the unreliable logistics of alarm response (Ihonen 1986, 1987; Kokko and Ekberg 1993). The initial ideas for Vivago-Wristcare could be seen to aggravate rather than resolve these. This serves as a reminder that the social imagination about what kind of developments ought to happen in the future is not unanimously shared by all the different stakeholder groups.

EXPLAINING TECHNOLOGY DEVELOPMENT WITH TECHNOLOGICAL FRAMES

The depiction of Vivago-Wristcare development thus far suggests that if one acted within the safety-phone development in the early 1990s, an attempt to achieve more thoroughgoing monitoring would be seen as a direction to go in, and the particular developers in this project were fortunate enough to have additional experience that allowed them to envision how development could be realized—chance favoring a prepared mind, so to say.

The ways in which the construction of technology is embedded in scientific and engineering practices are an established concern for science and technology studies. Since Fleck's seminal work on thought collectives (Fleck 1979) and Kuhn's notions of paradigm and disciplinary matrix (Kuhn 1970), there have been a series of studies addressing the role of community, tradition, and imagination in the construction of technology (e.g., Bijker 1995; Constant II 1980; Bucciarelli 1994).

Wiebe Bijker's SCOT (see Chapter 2 of this volume) concept of technological frame (TF) builds upon previous conceptualizations of how traditions foster technology development. The idea is that humans relate to technologies through "frames" that govern the way in which they perceive and act with them. The frames give structure and resources for action but at the same time constrain the scope of possible ways to think and interact with technology. Bijker provides a sense of the heterogeneous but interconnected contextual elements at play in the practices of technology production by noting that a TF tentatively includes goals, key problems, problem-solving strategies, requirements to be met by problem solutions, current theories, tacit knowledge, testing procedures, design methods and criteria, (conceptions of) users' practices, perceived substitution functions, and exemplary artifacts (Bijker 1995).

Our analysis of Vivago-Wristcare is thus far largely compliant with Bijker's concept. We seem to have a "safety-phone development frame" that enables and constrains what people acting within it do with respect to developing these technologies. To surpass that frame, our developers had to draw from other frames to reframe the problem they sought to tackle. This is roughly analogous to how Bijker explains how *inclusion in* multiple *frames* allowed the invention of Bakelite and synthetic plastics (Bijker 1995). With this reasonable assumption, we could now move on to examine whether there are other relevant social groups and frames that later had bearing upon the Vivago-Wristcare project, as we have hinted at with our comment on future visions of safety phones not being shared by all stakeholder groups.

But explanations of socio-technical change that rest on enabling/constraining frames (or structures) have some shortcomings with regard to examining the biography of Vivago-Wristcare. These have to do with motivation, imagination, persistence, and multiplicity of influences on a technology project. It is evident that professional knowledge and skill rests on the ability to handle complex problems by treating them with (collectively) accumulated sets of methods, theories, instruments, materials, and criteria (and so on) and that expertise resting on such structures also constrains the way problems become handled; "all the world looks like nails when you have a hammer in your hand," as the parable goes. But this sort of portrayal of professionals' actions leaves out why people do what they do in the first place. Obviously, there can be a situation akin to Kuhnian normal science, when frames can be seen to have conditioned the actors operating within them so that they do not need to question why they are doing their tasks (Kuhn 1970). But this fits poorly when explaining an invention such as Wristcare—to go to the length of combining six different fields in a novel way is not exactly an exercise in compliance.

Moreover, the resources the inventor(s) drew from these fields do not yet imply much "inclusion in a frame," even as they do imply drawing material and imaginative resources for invention from these fields. In fact, solutions adopted from paramedical procedures, and from medical monitoring and elderly-care practices—as important as they were for the invention—were based on discussions, following of reports, and other quite liminal acquaintances in these fields. We shall document in the following how these solutions came to later require deeper participation in these practices; however, at this stage this clearly was not the case.

This implies a more formal concern. If we discuss the relation of people or social groups to technology through frames, a direction of causality also becomes set. There is a frame Y, typically resulting from past routines, models, materials, and ways of thinking, through which a technology X is oriented or related to enabling us to appreciate certain characteristics of technology that constrains our ability to appreciate it in other ways. This, in effect, is an assertion that the preexisting Y influences (in the sense of partly determining) our relation to X. However, as Flichy (2006) argues, following Baxandall, it would be rather inaccurate to say, for instance, that "Picasso was influenced by the works of Cézanne," as in Y influenced X; rather, the case was that, within the organization of artistic activity of that period, Cézanne's problems and solutions elaborated some of the pictorial problems Picasso chose to confront and gave parts of the solutions he chose to adopt. In this view, the agency lies in the agent X who reflexively engages with future-oriented yet preexisting Y "frames" or "social imagination" available to him. This way of reversing the direction of causality indeed seems also a more fitting way to describe how Wristcare was invented. The inventors were not just having stronger or lesser inclusion in a frame but were reflexively drawing from the resources available to them and positioning themselves and their project along contours of social imaginations.

Alas, this latter view would run a risk of "over-agentifying" the inventors. Clearly, some solutions and even some problems require years of education and devotion to grasp, and such participation in a practice leads to a competence and particular professional vision to issues within a field, not unlike what is often approximated with "frame," and there is some "X Y causation" involved, as in how Wristcare's inventors were influenced by their many years of experience in safety-phone development and the technology business. So we ought not to lapse wholesale into either explanatory register.

Finally, both registers can be—and tend to be—deployed in a manner that creates a "retrospective structures/prospective individuals split" (Lente and Rip 1998). The prospective element of humanity is bestowed in the agent whose multiple participations (and/or reflexive appropriation of material and imaginative resources) become the source of novelty, while broader social influences only enable or constrain his action and imagination. Such a split may appear natural for those of us who cling to the soul as an essence of humanity, but for the rest of us mortals, it should appear plain odd. Examine any given domain and you find not only collective views about how things are and how they have come to be but also a whole register of how they ought to be, could be, and may develop realistically, and how they should develop in wishful or utopian terms. Such social imagination forms a continually changing continuum from past to present to future and not only reinstates what there already is. It is prospective and not reducible to fantasies, visions, or utopias of any given person. Furthermore, we will come to argue that a central dynamic is that, while some resources—both material and imaginative—in social imagination are relatively loose and widely shared (as in imaginations of a future smartly sensing digital environment), some are more tightly anchored to particular practices and domain-specific solutions (as in how vital signals of the human body ought to be monitored) and from there are tied into sets from within which one may not be able to arbitrarily detach a single solution into a new combination that introduces deviation from how things are practiced and envisioned within that practice. We hence need more precision in addressing social imagination and the ways it gets conveyed into actions and technologies.

To address these considerations more fully, we now embark upon developing a more nuanced way to conceptualize how agency develops and is distributed among several "frames/structures" and "actors." To this aim, we next introduce the concept of the "practice-bound imaginary" and discuss how it differs from existing concepts devised for the job, such as technological frame.

PRACTICE-BOUND IMAGINARY: CONCEPTUALIZING TRADITION AND PRACTICE IN TECHNOLOGY DESIGN

The term "imaginary" has recently become more popular in, for instance, cultural studies (Marcus 1995), feminist theory (Stoetzler and Yuval-Davis 2002), and technology studies (Suchman and Bishop 2000; Gregory 2000; Verran 2001; Fujimura 2003). Like imagination, it evokes both vision and fantasy, while emphasizing the corporeality and specific cultural and historical resources present in imagining (Suchman and Bishop 2000; cf. Stoetzler and Yuval-Davis 2002). "Imaginary" is easily misunderstood as variously referring to image, imagination, imagery, or the colloquial meaning of imaginary as "existing only in the mind," associated with "free-floating imagination" (Gregory et al. 2003; Verran 2001). Verran further defines imaginary, in regard to land-right disputes in Australia, by saying that "an imaginary [is that] through which the land is meaningful and by which the primary categories of that meaningfulness are given" (Verran 1998 252). She refers to earlier work of Castoriadis, who defines imaginary as "the unceasing and essentially undetermined (social-historical and psychical) creation of figures/forms/images, on the basis of which alone there can ever be a question *of* 'something'. What we call 'reality' and 'rationality' are its works" (Castoriadis 1987, 3). The notion of imaginary encompasses its embodiment in action and artifacts; practices that take place through an imaginary and by which the imaginary is being recreated and reformed.

In *practice-bound imaginary* (PBI), "bound" underlines this connection among imagination, imaginary, practice, and materiality. While "bound imagination" is the topic at large, our use of "bound" in "practice-bound imaginary" acts to set a more specific meaning for the term. First, practice-bound imaginary denotes particular kinds of imaginaries, those *bound, in a sense of being restricted primarily to*, a specific practice. Hence "bound" denotes a particular sociocultural scope, that of a "practice," a sustained way of engaging in action and attributing meaning in a professional (or leisure) area of life, typically taking place in multiple different activity systems (see Chapter 2 of this volume). While resources for imagination (tools and concepts for imagining, envisioning, and play) that motivate and prefigure action are seldom restricted to any one particular practice (Wartofsky 1979; Gregory 2000), PBI also includes what Goodwin (1994) calls "professional vision": practice-specific ways of perceiving and acting, such as particular usages of models, tools, and conceptions for creating, maintaining, and reproducing artifacts and action (Wartofsky 1979; Engeström 1990; cf. Miettinen 1998; Gregory 2000).

The second specific sense of "bound" is that in a PBI, sets of tools, ways of doing and imagining, desires, expectations, models, procedures, and norms are *bound together* to form a relatively coherent whole. Such a coupling is one of the prime sources from which practices gain their continuity and potency in accomplishing their practical and ideological concerns within a specific area of life. This facet of PBI shall be discussed more thoroughly later in reference to how solutions and norms of ICT management reinforce one another.

The third sense of "bound" emphasizes change and expectation. Professional practices are imaginaries that are *bound for* a prospective state of that practice. Like other collective expectations, such as "guiding visions" (*leitbilder*; Dierkes et al. 1996), "prospective structure" (Lente and Rip 1998; Lente 2000), and "scenarios" (Law 1988), PBIs preadapt perceptions and evaluations and act as functional equivalents for rules, discourses, and imperatives that are not yet fully articulated within existing discourses. They mobilize people to think and act and stabilize interpersonal interactions (Dierkes et al. 1996).[15]

At the same time, practice and tradition form a springboard from which an imaginary *bounds* (leaps) *to* a prospected future. While the entire horizon of a practice is often unrealizable even in principle, the difference between fantastic imaginations and a practice-bound imaginary is that the latter appears partially realizable and desirable in the practical action of participants (Gregory 2000). This motivational power of expectations depends on their material embodiments: expected success of the artifacts embodying them, elaboration of visions, criteria for adequate solutions, prototypes, ways to organize work, and so on (Lente and Rip 1998; Lente 2000; Dierkes et al. 1996; Gregory 2000). A potent PBI thus animates tradition and current practice as if these were not only bound for a prospected future state, but also as if this state was *bound to be realized* in one way or another, making the practice appear as a durable and dependable continuation of change. It was owing to such boundness to futures prominent in safety-phone development and elderly-care discourses that Vivago-Wristcare's novel product concept won several innovation prizes and other public recognition during its early phases, before its eventual functioning was anywhere near reliable.

Thus, PBI refers not to imaginaries, expectations, *leitbilders*, scenarios, or traditions in general but to the relatively integrated sets of visions, concepts, objects, and relations that practitioners regarded as desirable, relevant, potentially realizable, and as having cognitive and motivational power for organizing their practice.

Such an understanding of professional practice and tradition offers conceptual and methodological advantages, which can be further elaborated by comparing PBI to the technological frame (TF) concept introduced earlier. The differences become visible with a closer examination of how we should understand what a "professional practice," "tradition," or "technological frame" consists of. What we have in mind are four interrelated questions.

Who holds a technological frame/PBI and how? How do people participate in and, by the same token, how do their actions depend on a TF/PBI? How does a TF/PBI change? How does it motivate and orient people acting within it?

In SCOT, frames are held by "relevant social groups," which were discussed in Chapter 2 of this volume. Different relevant social groups give different meanings to artifacts through technological frames. Yet, new technologies can also create new social groups by realigning the meanings attributed to technologies by creating new and changed technological frames, e.g., with respect to what the relevant characteristics of artifacts are (Bijker 1995). In Chapter 2 of this volume, SCOT was criticized for neglecting the actual interactions between participants. The methodological implication of this criticism is that an alternative (or at least complementary) sensitivity to the "relevant social group" should be developed from examining formations of joint action. As discussed in Chapter 2 of this volume, there are also readily available S&TS concepts for this purpose in symbolic interactionism (Hughes 1971; Clarke 1990) and in activity theory (Engeström 2000, 1987; Miettinen 1998).

This concern about the nature of communities that hold PBIs is related to the question of how PBIs are "had": how are they present in action and imagination? Bijker sees TF as a "hinge" between people and objects, and on this metaphoric point we agree, but we should further ask how different frames relate to one another. It is more a rule than an exception that technology projects are motivated by, and draw resources from, multiple practices and cultural sources (Law 1988; Miettinen 1998). Moreover, most modern design also takes place in teams and activities that are composed of representatives of different disciplines. In contrast to, for instance, Kuhn's notion of paradigm, Bijker recognizes that individuals and institutions in technology production may be influenced by a number of different frames (Bijker 1995). Bijker flags this by introducing the concept of "degree of inclusion in a frame" to explain how much a particular frame enables and constrains an actor operating within it as well as to explain differences between technologies influenced by one or more dominant frames (Bijker 1995).

But there tends to be more to multiple participation than the degree of inclusion. In joint action, individuals, teams, and activities interpret practices differently and combine them in novel ways with other practices. What follows is that instantiations of PBIs are often unique; both in terms of the combination of practices involved and in the way people and activities interpret and participate in those practices. Practice-bound imaginaries, in turn, may instantiate a unique recombination of more pervasive "incomplete utopian projects" (Gregory 2000), imaginaries (Flichy 2007; Suchman and Bishop 2000), ideographs (Lente 2000), and other cultural resources. Attention should therefore be paid to interanimation, layeredness, and conflicts between different PBIs from which a design team or an activity draws (see Gregory 2000). This is hard to do with the way "relevant social group" and "technological frame" have been conceptualized (see Figure 3.3 for further clarification).

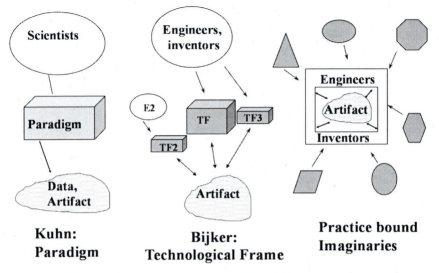

Kuhn:
Paradigm

Bijker:
Technological Frame

Practice bound
Imaginaries

Figure 3.3 While Kuhn sees scientists operating within a paradigm, Bijker recognizes that people may be members of more than one community (E, E2), and influenced by more than one frame (TF, TF2, TF3). Practice-bound imaginary sensitizes to the influences of a number of practices, which are mediated to action within the designers' joint doing in an activity.

This leads to the question about change. Bijker sees that "[a] technological frame is built up when interaction 'around' an artifact begins. Existing practice guides future practice, though without logical determination" (Bijker 1995, 123). Bijker implies that a cyclical movement then becomes: artifact–technological frame–relevant social group–new artifact–new technological frame–new relevant social group. However, as Klein and Kleinman (2002) point out, frames are not likely to emerge *de novo* in the case of each new technology but draw on existing practices and cultural resources. Parts within cultural formations typically change in different rhythms and have different durations (Braudel 1995; Hyysalo 2000). While particular technological projects affect practice-bound imaginary, they seldom create their own framing for technology but rather modify the existing practice-bound imaginaries. The concept thus sensitizes the analyst to pay attention to "stability in change and change in stability" as was done earlier in tracing the history of safety-phone development.

Finally, conceptions of change are further related to the question about how PBIs orient and influence the construction of technology. It is not only that frames structure, enable, and constrain action as retrospective structures, as Bijker sees it. Engineers and managers perceive the features of technology in relation to the changing collective expectations and "prospective structures" that create significance for current as well as expected events and findings (Lente and Rip 1998; Lente 2000; Dierkes et al. 1996;

Konrad 2006). Drawing from activity theory, our theorizing on practice-bound imaginaries regards that such prospective structures orient and motivate participants and align desires about the future that are necessary to launch and sustain complex and highly uncertain innovation processes. In fact, the characteristics of a particular artifact, or a frame in respect to it, may be superseded by more long-standing aspirations. Gregory has elaborated on how technology production is animated by pervasive practical and intellectual projects, "incomplete utopian projects," such as Taylorism in management and Evidence-Based Medicine. The scope of such a project is utopian, and its completeness is:

> not fully realizable as a practical achievement but whose partial realization—whether as instantiations of an idea or materialized as iteratively developed tools and forms of activity—engage actors in collaborative activities that produce and reproduce its instantiations over time. . . . They outlive any particular attempt at realization, nor is any particular failure sufficient to spell the end of a Utopian quest. (Gregory 2000, 176–177)

Hence, this facet of PBI emphasizes analyzing the dominant conceptions that guide a practice in addition to charting out the "frames" that enables and constrains action and thinking. This opens a new way of analyzing data and the evolvement of practices and technologies.

ILLUSTRATING KEY FACETS OF PBIS WITH PRACTICES THAT FED INTO WRISTCARE DEVELOPMENT

Let us return to safety-phone development with practice-bound imaginary now in our analytical repertoire, and in doing so elaborate further on the implications of theorizing professional traditions as practice-bound imaginaries. One of the issues that remained underconceptualized before was the various visions and motives that circled in the ICT and elderly-care social worlds, which had various impacts on safety-phone development and the Vivago-Wristcare project.

Some of these were firmly rooted in other practice-bound imaginaries, such as visions, aspirations, and imaginings in medical technologies and those in telecommunications. Just as importantly, many others were *not bound* in *this manner*. For instance, the development of safety phones and similar devices is animated by the long-standing desires in health care and technology production to rationalize the living and care of "problem groups," such as the disabled and elderly, by computer and communications technology, such as the "smart home" (Pantzar 2000). Likewise, safety phones are part of an increasing permeation of health care into the lives of the elderly in the form of home help, home care, frequent visits to doctors, and an increased amount of medication. There are a myriad of visions and aspirations driving this change in the long history of the human pursuit to enable variously disabled people to compensate for their lost abilities with technical means. It would be ludicrous to devise a narrative that portrayed the developers as working in a clearly bounded frame, and equally ludicrous to claim that our cultural aspirations are formed of *practice-bound* imaginaries alone. But the sociocultural makeup of human existence is not some representational soup either—formations such as activities and PBIs can be meaningfully discerned in empirical studies and used as conceptual devices to sensitize accounts on how cultural elements become ordered so that they can achieve productive force within particular domains.

Indeed, changes in the safety-phone systems have not only "introduced more thorough and total monitoring within the limits set by unobtrusiveness and price"; their development has rested on the premise that it would be *desirable* to be able to transmit help in all harmful incidents that a user might face. This has led to an (even in principle unending) pursuit of introducing more thorough and total monitoring within the limits set by unobtrusiveness and price, moving the devices away from the bedside and to encompass spaces occupied by more mobile and healthy users. There is more than frame: there is aspiration and there is persistence. As a developer maintained with Vivago-Wristcare after it had trodden eight years in the face of continued hardships:

> We shall see how well we manage to hold on, but it is certain that this won't fall as a concept. It might be that it has to be done with a different technology and in a different way . . . but even in the worst case [this company going out of business], some of us might be able to continue with this . . . [by now] it is certain that this kind of device will be made.[16]

This quote is not only about sunk economic and cognitive investment. Competitors to the company had not been disheartened by its difficulties but had taken the very existence of the project as indication of the potential in the idea. Neither is this quote a wishful self-assertion of the developer: Even as late as 2006, EU partner search described a practically identical new project to how Vivago-Wristcare had been envisioned in 1993 (Figure 3.4).

Through concretizing the idea of direct monitoring of the body to safety phones, Vivago-Wristcare was among the projects that added plausibility to the idea of aligning the future safety phones more with medical technologies (in contrast to safety phone's previous alignment with other forms of security telecommunications), regardless of the final fate of the project itself, which, as we see from the quote, was deeply uncertain for over a decade after its initial invention.

The practice-bound imaginary in safety-phone development would deserve to be elaborated on more fully, but as we have five other PBIs that

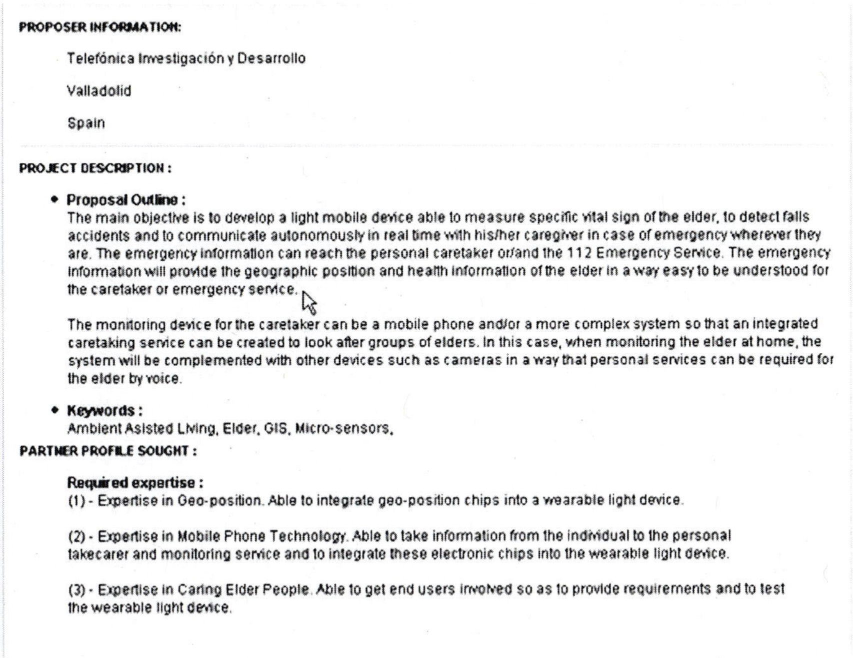

PROPOSER INFORMATION:

> Telefónica Investigación y Desarrollo
>
> Valladolid
>
> Spain

PROJECT DESCRIPTION:

- **Proposal Outline:**
  The main objective is to develop a light mobile device able to measure specific vital sign of the elder, to detect falls accidents and to communicate autonomously in real time with his/her caregiver in case of emergency wherever they are. The emergency information can reach the personal caretaker or/and the 112 Emergency Service. The emergency information will provide the geographic position and health information of the elder in a way easy to be understood for the caretaker or emergency service.

  The monitoring device for the caretaker can be a mobile phone and/or a more complex system so that an integrated caretaking service can be created to look after groups of elders. In this case, when monitoring the elder at home, the system will be complemented with other devices such as cameras in a way that personal services can be required for the elder by voice.

- **Keywords:**
  Ambient Asisted Living, Elder, GIS, Micro-sensors,

PARTNER PROFILE SOUGHT:

Required expertise:
(1) - Expertise in Geo-position. Able to integrate geo-position chips into a wearable light device.

(2) - Expertise in Mobile Phone Technology. Able to take information from the individual to the personal takecarer and monitoring service and to integrate these electronic chips into the wearable light device.

(3) - Expertise in Caring Elder People. Able to get end users involved so as to provide requirements and to test the wearable light device.

Figure 3.4 Screenshot of EU partner search announcement in 2006.

gave rise to Vivago-Wristcare and obvious limits of space, we need to turn to these other PBIs now. To make it easier to follow our two-threaded argument—about the PBIs relevant for the invention of Vivago-Wristcare and the characteristics of PBIs that we discuss through these empirical domains—let us pause to note that the discussion of safety-phone development has thus far been used to illustrate two key facets of PBIs, namely, how they are:

1. *bound for* and *bound to* future practice
2. *layered* and *interanimated* with other PBIs and cultural resources

What we do next is discuss the rest of the practices giving rise to Vivago-Wristcare but only in regard to particular facets of practice-bound imaginaries, namely:

1. PBIs are *bound together* from norms, solutions, projections, and so on (discussed with ICT-management).
2. PBIs are *restricted primarily to a specific practice* (discussed with medical monitoring practices, medical practice, and industrial automation).
3. PBIs have *varying memberships* and are *interpreted in communities of joint action* (discussed with elderly care).

PBIs are Bound Together from Norms, Solutions, Projections: ICT Management and Manufacturing

The third issue that the concept of PBI orients us to is the extent to which solutions, ways of thinking and calculating, and so on, are *bound together* and mutually reinforcing in professional practices. This point is first exemplified by expectations and exemplary solutions in ICT management and manufacturing that were adopted by Wristcare developers, and then deepened in examining the practices in medical technology evaluation.

Business practices in the telecommunications industry provided several solutions for the design of Vivago-Wristcare, such as maximal outsourcing and reliance on off-the-shelf components, strict secrecy, and aiming for a foolproof and stand-alone product. These concerned different aspects of the project but were closely coupled together by their background reasoning: each of these principles allows the producer to capitalize on the work of other providers (such as providers of subcomponents or maintenance) and to concentrate its own actions on a niche in the value-chain of the product. In particular, the crux of economies of scale was not having to deal with any context-specific configurations, installations, implementations, service, or maintenance. As a Vivago-Wristcare designer reflects on one of the company's previous products:

> A burglar-alarm . . . when delivered as mass goods to customers, also has to stay there . . . because if you even have to talk to a customer too much, you are bound to lose your overhead.[17]

While these solutions project a powerful way for a firm to diminish costs, they share an increased fragility of control (Toikka 2003). For foolproofing to succeed, the designers' prefiguration of users' actions has to suit their practice or be forced upon them. As access to reconfiguring the device is cut off from the users, errors or mismatches will easily render the technology unusable (cf. Akrich 1992; Engeström and Escalante 1996). The power of such projections may be furthered or diminished by the extent to which various solutions are bound with one another. If the calculations of the projected future state hold, the foolproof interface and the stand-alone character of the device will help in defining each other. But if the pre-configuring of users' actions fails, then the stand-alone nature of the product is easily compromised and vice versa. Other linkages may add to this source of power/error. Reliance on purchased parts and expertise would further reduce the cost of production and increase the resources and room that the company has for maneuvering. High secrecy was seen to fend off competitors as well as fend off users' modification of the product-in-use, providing the company with more control over its product and its price. It is therefore important to understand that the binding together does not necessarily form a balanced let alone neutral projection over the future.

PBIs are Restricted Primarily to a Specific Practice: Medical Monitoring Practices

Examining the tension that arose between the biomedical measurement tradition and the monitoring functions of Vivago-Wristcare derived from the actions of frontline helpers and industrial automation helps us further clarify how the *binding together* operates in regard to PBIs being *primarily restricted to a particular practice*.[18]

While Vivago-Wristcare seems an obvious step in safety-phone development, attempts to design such a device had stopped short because it had been impossible to combine a low price and easy-to-wear size with the reliability and accuracy demanded for medical monitoring devices. The Vivago-Wristcare project sought to overcome this by combining multiple sensors with principles derived from industrial automation and diagnostic practices of frontline helpers. In the words of the founder:

> When paramedics come to a person lying still on the ground, they want to know three things: does he react to external stimuli, does he breathe, and does he have a pulse? . . . So [our] device acts as a human would: if the person does not respond, we check the pulse and breathing. If these seem to be okay, then we just keep on observing [other signs]. There is no need for any mumbo jumbo when you look at the person slightly more all-inclusively, [laughs] [even] with these kinds of rather crude measures. . . . [It was my experience in] process control . . . [that] made the pieces fit together. . . . You can anticipate from small, secondary signs that now something is heading for the worse. Our system is primarily based on measuring the reactions and not the actual incidents, which is the case in basic medicine.[19]

This approach deviated, however, from established ways to monitor the human body in biomedicine and medical technology. The tension first became visible in the evaluation of Vivago-Wristcare's early prototypes by their collaboration partner, the medical technology laboratory of the State Technical Research Centre of Finland (STRC) in 1994. The STRC study pointed out that thus far the wrist had not been used for the measurement of bodily functions. There almost always seemed to be a better place for reliable and secure measurement of specific medical conditions or parameters. How should the results be interpreted even if the measurement worked well? The STRC also doubted that sufficiently reliable and precise measurements could be achieved by Vivago-Wristcare's prime sensors, or that the device could reliably cover all severe attacks of illness in different human physiologies, if it were to avoid excessive false alarms.[20] The STRC suggested adding extra sensors distributed around the body, attached to, for instance, the belt buckle, a chest belt, and a finger, to secure individual measurements, all difficult options for Vivago-Wristcare in terms of its wearability and feasibility.

In its evaluation, the STRC (and, in proceeding years, several other medical institutions) articulated the boundaries of acceptable medical technology by demonstrating what Goodwin (1994) calls "professional vision" for examining Vivago-Wristcare. In Goodwin's terms, the monitoring function of Vivago-Wristcare was evaluated against the *coding schemes* of established medical measurements. Its deviance was then *highlighted* as sets of differences and shortcomings that were further *articulated* into evaluations and suggestions about compliant *material representations*, such as the extra measurement points. Our way of conceptualizing professional practices as PBIs is largely convergent with Goodwin's way of examining professional vision. Yet, it further elaborates "vision" as not only a projection over a current domain of action but also one that orients to shaping the future of such a professional domain.

In the evaluation of Vivago-Wristcare, the STRC seemed to disregard the practical value, commercial potential, and other central concerns for safety-phone design and technology management. This evaluation involved more than the selective perception of medical technology professionals. The medical community had not shown any interest in passivity alarms in safety phones, but once the very same function was attempted (perhaps even more reliably) for direct monitoring of the body, it became interpreted as being relevant to the medical profession. The norms, ways of working, standards, and exemplary solutions central to a medical technology's PBIs were instrumental in maintaining the plausibility and future prospects of medical monitoring devices. As the design of Vivago-Wristcare potentially renegotiated these criteria, STRC evaluation also became related to the continuity of an articulated and pervasive tradition—with its established institutions, education, thousands of practitioners, and large companies—which in its entirety was vastly more important than a potentially valuable prototype. Part of this package was that representations of medically tested, reliable, and medically appropriate uses were accentuated. In a couple of pages, we shall find how these criteria were also effectively enforced for Vivago-Wristcare, even when the project sought to steer clear of being regarded as a medical technology.

PBIs Have Varying Memberships and Are Interpreted in Communities of Joint Action: Elderly Care

Another facet of PBIs around Vivago-Wristcare is illustrated with designers' acquaintance with the practices and requirements of elderly care. This is a matter of *membership* and illustrates the importance of *actual interactions in communities of joint action.*

Before the market launch of Vivago-Wristcare, the designers were acquainted with elderly care through safety-phone development, which provided them with various indirect contacts, such as reports, and contact with gerontologists and other people working with technologies for the elderly:

Even during the [early 1980s] Nokia period, we didn't have any people with firsthand knowledge [about elderly care], and the knowledge came to us through intermediaries. . . . [O]nly in Sostel [in the late 1980s] did we have some contact with elderly care. So it is all learned knowledge, learned in the hard way, I would say, to grasp the processes and problems of that area.[21]

Designers were initially content that their product was appropriately suited to the requirements of elderly care. Survey results showed that elderly people preferred staying home as long as possible, and the concern for the cost of care was leading to a trend to replace intramural care with cheaper extramural care, with the latter made still cheaper through technical appliances. Technology such as Vivago-Wristcare could detect, prevent, and mitigate the outcomes of accidents that would require immediate care in a more expensive setting (Vaarama 1995; Mäkitalo 2000).

These issues were mostly emphasized in what we call the managerial view of elder care, concerned with the cost of health care within acceptable moral standards (cf. Starr 1982). This view was strongly expressed in the newspapers and in the reports and by the specialists that Vivago-Wristcare designers encountered. However, it was not uniformly shared by frontline caregivers, older people, or their relatives. Caregivers' perspective or "caring-rationality" (Östlund 1994; Beck 2002) emphasized that the recipient of care should not be allowed to sink into a vortex of worsening conditions before receiving care (Heikkinen et al. 1992). This view emphasized breaking the isolation and solitude and building new ways of reorganizing patients' lives as fundamental factors in enabling prolonged living at home (Beck 2002). Cutting costs by offering technologically assisted security would need to be weighed against other solutions, such as enlisting volunteer groups or extra personnel who might assist elderly people to live more active lives, which would delay the point at which they require institutionalization (Beck 2002; Östlund 1994).

Moreover, both a managerial view and caring rationality share the aspiration to reach out to elderly people as potential or actual patients in order to prevent their conditions from worsening. The proactive warnings Vivago-Wristcare was designed to send about the worsening state of the end user fit nicely with these images. However, they fit much more poorly with how elderly people often preferred to organize their lives, with their lack of exercise, smoking, gaining weight, *et cetera*.

The fact that Vivago-Wristcare designers had only a peripheral membership in elderly care, and actual contacts mostly with people emphasizing a managerial view to it, effectively restricted their apprehension of the scope and variety of requirements relevant for designing their product. This highlights the importance of not restricting the analysis solely to the frames of shared meaning and of examining the actual communities in which design work is done.[22] Communities of joint action may be interanimated by a different set of PBIs, as well as have a different degree of inclusion in those PBIs. While designers are accustomed to dealing with multiple constraints, it is often the work of making the underlying positioning behind the given constraints visible that is at the root of the problem and calls for its own sets of means (cf. Greenbaum and Kyng 1991; Schuler and Namioka 1993). This is where we turn now.

PRACTICE-BOUND IMAGINARIES AS SOURCES FOR REPRESENTATIONS AND INSCRIPTIONS OF USE

This final section of the chapter addresses the question of how PBIs influenced the way the Vivago-Wristcare project ended up with the kind of prefiguration of its uses and users that it had at its initial market launch. As noted in Chapter 1 of this volume, "the user," as in the person out there, is not an obvious, let alone direct, referent for representations of use and user. Representations rather seek to "become productive" and (partially) create their own images and entities, shape discourses and modes of ordering reality, and suggest certain relations between peoples and things.

In discussing how "the user" of Vivago-Wristcare became conceived, we also deepen the discussion of what it means to say that particular projects can be interanimated by several practice-bound imaginaries. The analysis moves from clear representations towards more indirect ways by which PBIs affected the project.[23]

Some user-representations were emphasized over others in the PBIs influencing the design of Vivago-Wristcare. A first set of key representations of use were about *who the users will be*. For instance, the vision that the automatic monitoring should create a significant new market among still active "people of 60+ years under an increased risk of sudden fatal attacks of illness such as strokes and heart attacks" was prominent in the imaginaries in safety-phone development as well as the managerial view on elderly care.[24] But this vision was fairly vague and did not include detailed considerations of how this new group of users would be related to the customer base for current safety phones, or how these users would be related to the work practices of the secondary users, such as home-care nurses, relatives, and alarm centers.

These representations were intertwined with representations of *how the device will be used*. For instance, the managerial view of elderly care held that the major problems with the existing safety phones were the number (and price) of "talk-calls" and other alarms set off without immediate danger. The appropriate uses were seen as setting off an alarm when in acute danger and otherwise just wearing the device. Some of the users might suffer from dementia, and the ability of many other users to understand the new technology could be doubted.[25] While these assumptions could lead to various kinds of design approaches, the fool-proofing had desirable effects for cost and manufacturability. Fool-proofing was further supported by the assumption that, to be really useful, the device must account for all the situations for which it could provide help, and thus should be worn 24 hours a day, which increased the range of situations the device had to withstand.[26] This assumption of the necessity of maximum utility becomes understandable when we remember that it is central in the imaginary of the safety-phone development, backed up both by managerialist and by preventive imaginaries in elderly care.[27]

These representations were further related to the representations of *what kind of functionality would be appreciated by the users and buyers*. The device was seen to "surpass" the "alarm on/off logic" of safety phones and to provide accumulating data for care providers on the user's condition. If the user's condition began to grow worse, the device should signal first, for instance, "increased passivity," then "disruption in condition," and if the situation got out of hand an "acute disruption in condition" message. This way, the care providers could shift from reactive to proactive measures in ensuring the well-being of the end user. This representation of use was interanimated from multiple directions: safety-phone development, biomedical monitoring, and a managerial view to elderly care. In turn, these representations of the preferred functioning were accompanied by a set of representations of how the device was to be used: it should be worn on the weaker arm to keep the monitoring more reliable, the tightness of the connection to the wrist should be ensured, the device should be washed in the way instructed and at regular intervals and tested regularly.[28]

The price relative to that of earlier safety phones was an important characteristic. As noted, it lent support to one-for-all design that could then be mass-produced with a low unit cost.[29] The less the variation, the easier it is to automate and package. The remaining user actions could be seen as straightforward and simply definable, a question of training. These considerations further cross-fertilized the representations of the proper use of the device described earlier.

There were also more indirect ways PBIs affected the pre-configuration of use in Vivago-Wristcare. One of the most obvious ways was affecting what were seen as the key priorities and features in the technology. Nearly all the PBIs from which Vivago-Wristcare development drew suggested market success if only the device could be technically realized and economically feasible. The user-representations described earlier were mostly compatible with this view, contributing to developers not becoming very active in attempting to refine the initial user-representations over the early years.

Another indirect way of influencing which representations of use prevail in design is that PBIs give direction to and guide actions in a local activity, setting preconditions for the kind of user-representations developers shall encounter in the future. This includes seeking out and selecting collaboration partners, then preferring some ways of collaboration over others, and seeing some of the outcome representations of use as more vital. In the years following the initial 1992–1994 phase of invention, Vivago Ltd. not only worked internally with the technical development of Vivago-Wristcare but also launched some investigations with external consultants on the issues they found important for the device. We have already mentioned the collaborative investigations with the STRC on physiological monitoring, prompted by the STRC's authoritative position in it. The business concerns led to two marketing studies in Europe (SAI 1993; Leriche et al. 1995), later followed by more informal efforts to map out market dynamics in the targeted countries. The idea of establishing the 60-plus market segment led to a yearlong design study (Soosalu 1996).

The investigations that ensued matched the imaginaries of medical monitoring (modeling physiology) and business management (marketing studies and the design wrapping of the device), and similar investigations followed during the second round of development, in 1999–2003, further strengthening the role of these PBIs in designing Wristcare. It is also noteworthy that the way collaborations were organized did not bind the designers to any findings or decisions. Preexisting assumptions governed what was relevant knowledge in these investigations: while each of the studies identified some potentially critical representations of use, each one was, by and large, dismissed or not acted upon. A good example is that the results from the design study were used in 2000, for the second-generation Wristcare, only after they had been proven in actual use. Even then, only design details were adopted, though the study also revealed much broader implications for redesign, as we will discuss in detail in the next chapter.

Practice-bound imaginaries are also involved in formation of criteria for acceptable solutions and ways of conduct, even when a project participates only peripherally in a PBI, as Wristcare in medical monitoring. Until 1999, Vivago Ltd. systematically emphasized that Wristcare was a security device that was not intended to perform any medical functions.[30] There was a tangible commercial reason for this choice:

> It is a strategic choice, because if you go to the medical side you have to tell them everything; you are bound to be thoroughly tested. And we have made a decision that no matter how promising a market is, we will leave aside any country that requires complete clinical tests . . . until we are big enough [to protect ourselves against copycat products].[31]

However, it soon became evident that, even in Finland, the health care officials and their technical advisers not only had the regulative power in medical technologies but also had considerable informal influence on opinions about any new technology used in caregiving. By introducing the physiological monitoring, Vivago Ltd. had imposed on the medical officials' domain. In the clashes that followed, the company gradually realized that it had to generate biomedical evidence of the effectiveness of the device. Overall, there was a constant preoccupation with how Vivago-Wristcare really monitored human physiology. With regard to user-representations, this affected how the engineers inscribed normative user-scripts in the Vivago-Wristcare system to ensure adequacy and reliability of monitoring. Just as important, this preoccupation influenced what was regarded as important in how the devices worked:

> One of the best things in this [year-2000 redesign] process is that all the problems that have come up have been in one way or another connected to this nonsimulated border with users, whatever then [had been the particular reason for problems]: habits of use, attitudes, problems in communication.[32]

The "best" thing referred to here was that the initial design appeared "correct"; it measured the signals that physiological monitoring should monitor, according to the biomedical criteria. The not-so-harmful side effect was that the design did not fit very well into the life and work of the users. Medical criteria had become a passage point for Vivago-Wristcare developers that enforced compliance with their norms and interpretive schemes and, as a side effect, defined the subject matter in such a way that other practices were considered less significant.

Finally, PBIs are a source of legitimization for the representations of use. As noted, a central characteristic of a PBI is that it includes projected futures, which tend to make the assumptions and considerations appear a necessary part of a likely development. An expert participant in a PBI easily regards him- or herself as positioned to see "the change" more clearly than others do. In the case of Vivago-Wristcare, there was a continuing emphasis on designers being "ahead" of the "development." This was not restricted to the practices of elderly care (younger users, new ways to organize work). It also included physiological monitoring (bringing it to everyday life), the development of electrical appliances (into smart-home technology), and the performance of high-risk business moves. None of these projected states of affairs were only whimsical or hubristic expressions of a small start-up company; they were well in line with the PBIs in which designers participated. The outcome of this legitimization was the emphasis on training and communication instead of redesign when faced with users' resistance:

> About the problems, the first is that they [caregivers] have not understood the device right but have thought of it as if it were a traditional safety phone . . . so when they get an alarm, they respond to it as if it were acute and send in an ambulance. Our alarm might have been, for instance, caused by not taking medicine and should be understood as an initiation of conversation. So, obviously, these people have not been trained or have been poorly trained.[33]

In sum, then, we can identify several "direct" and indirect mechanisms by which the imaginaries bound to the professional practices of developers led to incorporating some rather than other representations of use. In the preceding analysis, the intricacies of local negotiations were sidelined to draw attention to how the "agency" of practice-bound imaginaries operated in motivating, offering, and enforcing some rather than other key representations of use.

A CLASH OF PRACTICES: WRISTCARE IN THE HANDS OF ITS USERS

Correlating closely with the preceding representations of use, the device launched to the market in 1997–1998 was, in short, a one-for-all, fully automated device (with the alarm button as the only manual feature) that had only an additional transmitter unit to accompany it. It was intended primarily for still-active people over 60 years living at home. Even though it aimed to be foolproof, it also had instructions for its optimal use that formed a seven-page pictorial manual, which grew quickly to 25 pages after the pilot use. For caregivers, the design provided 32 notices and degrees of alarm, which the caregivers could not disable or modify.

As in many other cases, it was not only up to the designers of Vivago-Wristcare to define an artifact. Even though their concept was commercially elegant and technically ambitious, the representations of use adopted from various practices came to clash with the practice and imaginary of frontline elderly care and elderly living. There were problems in how the device fitted the work practices of caregivers and the habits of

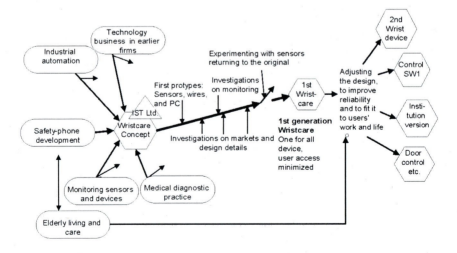

Figure 3.5 The development of Vivago-Wristcare from inception in 1992–1993 to the post-market-launch period in 1998–2000.

users, as well as how it monitored the physiology of many users. It fit poorly to the requirements of maintaining effective and efficient security service, on which the value of Vivago-Wristcare for its end users ultimately depended. Consequently the initial representations of use incorporated in the device were thoroughly questioned and redefined before the device started to win a market and trust among its users in the years 2001 to 2003. The device became used during the very last years of clients' life (just as the other safety phones did) and was used primarily in sheltered housing. The most ambitious alarms had to be removed from the product, and its software came to include the possibility of profiling alarms for each individual site and user. But all this we shall examine on a more fine-grained scale in the chapters to come.

CHAPTER DISCUSSION

Biography of Technology

These earliest years in the biography of Vivago-Wristcare shed light on the "gestation period" (Van de Ven et al. 1999) or "fuzzy front end" of innovation. As these names suggest, studies that have focused on the biography of particular innovation have faced formidable challenges in coming to terms with the seemingly dispersed resources, initiatives, and agency of various people involved in the preinitiation and initial conception of innovation. Intertwining the analysis of a particular development project with the biographies of the previous activities of its developers and practices from which they drew in these activities helps to remove the mysteries in how innovative ideas emerge (Miettinen et al. 1999). Further, the aspirations, visions, and argumentative power behind the innovative quest require drawing in the arena in which the development takes place, and social worlds (relatively stable and far-reaching social organizing in the fields involved in the arena) as well as those imaginaries that provide material and imaginative resources for the key actors.

The Vivago-Wristcare invention was achieved by creatively working together multiple practices, which provided the insights, knowledge, skill, and tools for conceiving and furthering the technological concept. The designers' deepest professional experience was in safety-phone development, but the limitations of this expertise were superseded by drawing solutions from other practices, including diagnostic practices of first-aid personnel, methods for monitoring physiological conditions, technology business and management practices, industrial automation, and elderly care. Instead of only straightforwardly adding to one another, the solutions were bound to further sets of instruments, expectations, skills, knowledge bases, and norms in the imaginary bound to each practice. In addition to particular solutions, some of their underpinnings needed to be aligned for a successful technology to emerge. The argumentative power of the project owed to how it furthered prevalent aspirations in safety-phone develop-ment and could be seen to strengthen its links with neighboring domains in telecommunications and medical technologies.

The concept of practice-bound imaginary was pursued here to refine the analytical possibilities offered by previously available concepts such as tech-nological frame in three respects. First, PBI was oriented to analyzing the continuities and conceptions of change in practices and between different types in a class of artifact. Second, it directed attention to the effects that multiple, sometimes peripheral, involvements in different practices had for the emerging artifact. There were many different kinds of participations involved. Developers came to be influenced by PBIs by personally participat-ing in them (as in safety-phone development, technology management, and industrial automation), in acquiring information about them for design (as in paramedics' procedures and managerial view of elderly care), and through collaborations and confrontations related to their product (as in biomedical monitoring). This underscores the third aspect, the need to attend to how frames/PBIs are mediated in actual communities of joint action, in which social mediation and interanimation of practices take place.

Design–Use Relations

Nearly all research on user requirements presumes that the referent of the user domain knowledge lies strictly outside the domain of design. Con-sequently, it proceeds on the premise that it needs to be brought into the sphere of design, requiring special means and arrangements. This is regard-less of whether the researchers propagate a highly rationalist approach to requirements (Ulrich and Eppinger 1995; Kotonya and Sommerville 1998; Pohl 1994), believe in market research (Kotler and Armstrong 2004), or advocate collaborative and participatory design (Schuler and Namioka 1993; Bødker et al. 2004; Beyer and Holtzblatt 1998).

Our analysis underscored the view that the "user" is a more complex issue. The (imaginaries bound to) practices of developers are rich with rep-resentations of use and users. Some of these can be primarily representa-tions about more technical or economic matters and implicate prospective use only as a side effect.

The analysis in this chapter suggested that both design and use are con-stituted and imagined beyond any given site or event of design. The innova-tion context for Vivago-Wristcare was more or less "linear" in nature and excluded any direct participation from users during these early years of development. Developers operated within a set of practice-bound imagi-naries that included various representations that became further articu-lated during their material inscription in the device. Some of these were clearly elaborated representations of use, such as who the users would be (for instance, healthy persons between 60 and 70 years of age), how the device would be used (worn only to trigger acute alarms), and what kind of functionality would be preferred (the most extensive coverage of physical injuries possible).

PBIs also emphasized other preoccupations. Some matters appeared urgent (maximal coverage of monitoring), and these held implications about use and users (for example, that users must be willing to wear the device firmly on their wrists 24 hours a day). These implications affected defining key problems and solutions (for instance, that the challenge with Vivago-Wristcare was first and foremost a matter of technical problem-solving), and means to seek and assess future collaborations (the end users did not meet the criteria for providers of relevant information). They also included attributions of quality and approval (medical practitioners could act as gatekeepers for distributing such devices, but elderly-care workers could not) and provided a privileged and self-legitimizing perspective on the future development of the practices at stake (the developers saw themselves as ahead at the cutting edge of developments in elderly care, home electronics, and physiological monitoring). Such implicated representations of use remained difficult to challenge, since they were connected to other priorities in design and entered into the design process in many different ways. These findings underscore the importance of implicit representations of use (Akrich 1992, 1995; Oudshoorn et al. 2004), but there is more at stake here than "I or Ego-design"—the professional tradition and imagination is equally a source of implicit user-representations.

Agency, or the Constitution of Developer, User, and Technology at this Moment of Biography

The analysis draws attention to the distribution of agency in the invention and in designing its usages. Clearly the developers, particularly the key inventor, showed extraordinary creativity, out-of-the-box thinking, authorship, and persistent efforts throughout the early biography of this technology. But the creative individual(s) did not work in a vacuum or without the resources created elsewhere and before this development work. It would be absurd not to recognize the importance of the arrays of components, extant solutions, instruments, and available materials in the work. To acknowledge the agency that accumulated material resources hold is fashionable in social sciences today (e.g., Latour 2005; Miller and Slater 2007; Hutchins 2005). This is, of course, only part of the story. Culture—or in this case professional practices—is not available through sheer materiality only. Interactions, doing, learning, teaching, and reasoning—in short, participating—are needed to make use of the materialities and instruments. We chose to argue further that participation hinges on (partially) shared aspirations and repertoires for imagining. Neither of these is somehow only "innate" or "abstract" capacity, but (in that they are bound together, for, and to) they are dependent on previous social, emotive, cognitive, and material realizations. In this capacity, they are able to animate practice and provide a sense of continuity to activities and actions that realize it. If "technology is society made durable," as Latour famously phrases it, imaginaries (both bound and not bound to specific practices) are "technology made durable." If in doubt, try to conjure up decent straw socks or splinter stones into actually workable axes without the long since waned PBIs of our forefathers.

Indeed, as Tomasello (1999) emphasizes, human culture relies on a "ratchet effect": materials, ideas, and skills for manipulating these are passed on and taken for granted, as opposed to each generation rediscovering most of the same features over again as happens in chimpanzee troops. PBIs include well-rehearsed solutions and well-articulated aspirations to be inspired by. But many of these working items come intertwined with other solutions and principles of relating these. People who enact practices need not be fully aware of how (let alone, why) all the connections work. Hence, when a person relies on practice-specific routines, PBIs can come to act behind his back, so to say. They too exert (accumulated, collective) agency.[34]

Learning

The analysis underscores the fact that the power of a technological development depends on difficult trade-offs between conflicting rationalities and the extent to which these can be (and end up) designed into an artifact. The analysis illustrated the empirical significance of (and difficulty designers face in dealing with) implicit representations of use. Many visions circled about in the arenas around the future telecommunications in health and elderly care with equally many representations of new kinds of users. After the implementation, the Vivago-Wristcare concept had to be redesigned because of the demands and daily care needs of elderly users, as well as the requirements of biomedical monitoring. These practices that forced the developers to reevaluate their original concepts were the ones with which they had the least direct contact to begin with. The trickiest learning challenge appears to lay in recognizing and being able to assess the relevance of different potential requirements among all the other practice-bound projections, predictions, and sanctions.

4 The Anticipation of Need
Investigations and Intermediaries

In addition to implicit representations of use, the designers of Vivago-Wristcare inquired into future use through user interviews, market studies, a design study, and pilot use. These investigations and their yield for design are examined in this chapter, and we position these inquiries in the interplay between the practices of the company that commissioned them, those of the people who conducted them, and the practices of potential users that were to be investigated. In doing so, we focus more closely on one part of the early development of Wristcare and take another angle of approach to how social imagination turns to characteristics of humans and nonhumans—namely, how "needs" for new technology emerge and how they can be explored.

Much of the industrial practice and literature on innovation presumes that explicit inquiries should be the prime source of information for anticipating the future use (Ulrich and Eppinger 1995; Mallard 2005). Indeed, in linear innovation contexts, developers will need to find ways to represent the future users and their requirements even years before the device will eventually be launched. The technical possibilities and restrictions, not to mention design details, are not yet fully known to the designers themselves at the time of inquiry.

The existing arsenals for investigating user needs could be grouped into three broad and historically layered families: quantitatively oriented preference elicitation methods, qualitative methods, and design-oriented methods. The first, and most established, of these families are approaches that seek to determine the consumer preferences. Common to these various methods is the fact that users' preferences for alternative product concepts must be gathered, ordered, measured, and transformed into (preferably measured) characteristics of the emerging product (Kotler 1988; Ulrich and Eppinger 1995). Emphasis on quantitative information, adequate sampling, and reliability is characteristic to these methods. Typical examples would be market studies based on comparisons with competing products. These approaches have dominated the scene of anticipating use in industry since the rise of customer research in the 1930s.

Advocates of the more recent entrants to anticipating prospective use, such as qualitatively and design-oriented research, have expressed growing criticism towards the elicitation approach. Practitioners of user-centered design and participatory design state that not only does the traditional marketing data fail to produce insight fine-grained enough for the actual design, but it also often misses that knowledge about use and environments of users that is most important for design. In contrast, these researchers emphasize direct *in situ* contact with users, as well as qualitative data, such as interviews, observations, and co-design with users (Schuler and Namioka 1993; Greenbaum and Kyng 1991; Kensing and Blomberg 1998; Karasti 2001). Accountability for these methods has been sought by claiming that they produce more valid information, while the reliability of the data is grounded on qualitative assessment and experience of the investigators.

The third family includes the radical design-oriented variants of the qualitative paradigm, which explicitly claim that the questions of reliability and (also to some extent validity) of the user data are in many senses secondary to the inspirational value and resources they provide for designers (Hemmings et al. 2002; Mattelmäki and Battarbee 2002; Kelley and Littman 2001). These approaches emphasize that the scientific ways to investigate use are inefficient in time and money, and, at the same time, falsely confident in how great an impact their results actually have in the design process. Product design is fundamentally seen to depend on the overall knowledge, insight, and experience of the designers, and the value of investigating use is only to inspire and provide resources for this work.

Even though the qualitative and designer-centered approaches have gained increasing recognition, the traditional elicitation methods are still the prevailing way of working in product design and human factors. In fact, the elicitation approaches are so entrenched in corporate structures and cultures that they are likely to prevail as the dominant ones in industry, even if user-centered design methods should proliferate in the future (Grudin 1993; Leonard 1995). It could be concluded that, rather than settling the case, the qualitative/design criticism has opened the door for questioning and improving the repertoires of methods used to incorporate understandings of user practices in design work.

Leonard has attempted to categorize the approaches according to their most powerful areas of application by differentiating between different conditions in product development projects. Her model rests on two axes, one being how well the technology and its possibilities are known, and the other how novel and well known the user groups and user practices are. Her claim is that the traditional elicitation methods are most adequate when both the technological possibilities and users are well known. Their adequacy decreases the less is known about either what the technology is going to be or who is going to use it, in which case the more "emphatic" qualitative and design-oriented methods generate more valid information (Leonard 1995).

While this is plausible, Leonard does not offer a real explanation why. More generally, it is difficult to make comparisons between the strengths and weaknesses of different approaches based on their successful or unsuccessful cases: different approaches are related to different ways of organizing the product development process as a whole, and also have different epistemological grounds (Leonard 1995; Boland 1978; Ives and Olson 1984; Edström 1977). However, given the persisting problems and debates over different methods and confusion over their applicability, some way of doing such comparisons would appear welcome.

This chapter attempts to use a more modest but perhaps more informative strategy in assessing the approaches to investigate future use. Vivago-Wristcare developers used user interviews, market surveys, a design study, and pilot projects in the very same project to investigate use, which allows us to contrast these to one another and their outcomes for the emerging design. While this strategy falls far from settling the disputes between different methods, it does give some assessment of the usefulness of some of the most common methods. Vivago also interestingly falls in the middle of Leonard's application-area mapping. It features some radically new technology as well as older elements and seeks to bring change to the existing user practices and to address a significant new group of users. After examining the investigations, we shall complement the comparison by examining in more depth some of the reasons for the clear differences there were in the yield of these methods from the vantage point that "user needs" for a given technology may not be a static preexisting entity or category.

MARKET SURVEYS AND USER INTERVIEWS

The market surveys and user interviews that Vivago Ltd. commissioned are typical methods within the family of preference elicitation. Soon after the birth of the initial concept, the company founder interviewed some potential users about the concept. Later the company commissioned two more structured expert surveys on Wristcare in Europe. The first one was done by a specialized consultancy company, in 1993, on the business opportunities in the UK, France, and Germany (SAI 1993), and the second one, in 1995, by a local university of technology (Leriche et al. 1995).

Investigations with individual users (mainly elderly relatives of the founder) consisted of unstructured conversations about the new concept and were held mainly on a one-to-one basis. All the relatives who participated were still in relatively good health and active.[1] The market surveys were based on documents such as existing regulations and technical specifications, and electronic publications. Both studies also conducted expert interviews. In the 1993 study, nearly 60 information sources are marked, but the exact number of interviews or the proportion of face-to-face and phone interviews remains obscure. The 1995 study is also not specific as to what its data consists of, but also here phone interviews were the dominant form of acquiring information. These studies aimed at positioning Vivago-Wristcare with existing technologies, service providers, and regulations.

Paging systems, patient monitoring systems, and nurse-call and alarm systems were taken as points for comparison in the 1993 study, while in 1995 only safety-phone markets were studied.

The primary message of the 1993 market study was that there was an overlapping area of application that none of the available technologies covered convincingly and that Vivago-Wristcare could fill. The study indicated some critical points such as a strong need for medical approval, nonexistence of current competitors, potential distribution partners, relevant regulations, and figures on market size and segments (SAI 1993). No investigation was carried out of the contradictory demands or prioritizations that had kept the three technological areas apart to date. Vivago-Wristcare was assumed to have all the possible dispositions and functionalities that were desired in the area between the existing technologies. No alternative scenarios or suggestions for customizing the technology were offered.

The 1995 expert survey extended the 1993 survey by examining care phones in England, Germany, France, and Sweden. It analyzed the competitors, prices and subsidies, service providers, and (in very general terms) the organization of the safety-phone services in these countries (Leriche et al. 1995). By and large, it followed the same level of analysis as the 1993 study and verified most of the latter's results: promising and expanding markets, no directly competing products, identifiable strong players in the safety-phone business in each of the countries, alliances with either a service provider or other manufacturer seeming necessary, the need to establish relations with home-care workers and doctors who recommend safety phones, and the differences in how the business is organized in the countries studied. Again, the technical concept was taken for granted, and the investigation did not probe the dynamics of how safety phones are actually purchased and used, or how the related service was organized (Leriche et al. 1995).

Combined with the investigation on technical regulations, the market studies and user interviews elicited important broad knowledge of the existing techno-economic environment (see Table 4.1). In terms of the design-relevant knowledge, the main contributions of the expert surveys were assertions on possible restrictions and conditions that the device must meet, such as drawing attention to the role of doctors and the medical community in recommending and evaluating this kind of technology (SAI 1993). Insights about the context of use and potential problems were mentioned only in the 1995 report regarding France, where the safety-phone service was still in its infancy, and the researcher had a difficult time gathering the preferred kind of data (Leriche et al. 1995). These two pages in a 40-page report are the only instance where crucial information on the age and condition of the safety-phone users, problems in organizing the alarm service, and complexities of buying dynamics are mentioned. These insights, however, were not reflected either in the conclusions or in

Table 4.1 The Main Conclusion of the Marketing Surveys and User Interviews and an Evaluation of its Critical Potential for Design

	Objective of the study	Key results for prime objective	Key information for design	Critical potential for changing the design
Market surveys	Competition analysis	- No directly competing products - Overview of regulations, markets, and key players in Europe - Positive support for the concept	- Need for medical approval of the device (- Safety phones have a stigma as prosthesis, appropriated late in life)	- Safety-phone markets and services differ in each country (- Safety-phone services can be complex and disorganized)[1]
User interviews	End-user evaluations of the concept	- Encouragement for the concept	- Target users: healthy 60+ year olds	

[1] The parentheses are here used to indicate passing findings that were potentially relevant but were not elaborated upon.

relation to the discussion of the findings from the other countries (Leriche et al. 1995).

The results provided by the interviews and market studies supported the existing assumptions of the designers and gave them reassurance of the market potential of the device (SAI 1993; Leriche et al. 1995). The few potentially critical remarks in the studies did not lead to questioning of the initial visions of the designers (see Chapter 3 of this volume) and the descriptions of Vivago-Wristcare remained the same as before.[2]

USER-CENTERED DESIGN STUDY

In 1995, Vivago Ltd. hired a designer to make a design and usability study for Vivago-Wristcare consisting of a literature survey and three rounds of interviews. The literature survey inquired into the design of safety phones and other wrist-worn devices (clocks, heart-rate monitors, etc.), and also into elderly living and use of safety phones (Soosalu 1996). Interviews were conducted with about 30 persons in a hospital day-care unit. The first round of interviews focused on safety-phone use in general and explained the Vivago-Wristcare concept in comparison. The second and third rounds centered on figures and mock-ups for the proposed new design alternatives.

Both parts of the study were restricted to safety-phone systems and their users.

While the market studies took the then loosely framed concept for granted, the design study set out to investigate how the concept was received and how it could be improved in detail. This approach yielded a number of direct improvements. The elderly disliked the "medical design language" of the existing devices and design interviews suggested that a rounder device, more color (instead of the existing beige, gray, and black), and perhaps fitting in a watch could be improvements. The analysis of used devices revealed that continuous use was prone to cause heavy soiling and unpleasant amounts of dirt. The indication for design was to minimize all seams and such textures as could gather dirt and find colors that would not be compromised even if the device became soiled (Soosalu 1996).

From a functional viewpoint, both the literature survey and the interviews clearly indicated problems with the alarm buttons of competing safety phones: accidental hitting of the button produced false alarms, yet at times the elderly users were not able to set off an alarm by pressing the button. Both problems indicated that the design of the alarm buttons needed to be thought through more carefully, particularly in relation to creating a sufficient tactile feel for finding the button, even during an attack of illness, and in determining both the correct size and appropriate stiffness of the button (Soosalu 1996).

Beyond the immediate design details, the study provided insights into the use, service, and infrastructure of the safety phones. Contrary to Vivago Ltd.'s and the market studies' assumptions, even the existing safety phones seemed to be far from being stand-alone devices or from being maintenance free. When devices were returned to the service providers, they were usually in poor condition. Moreover, almost all the maintenance had to be conducted by the service provider, because both the users and relatives usually refused even to change the batteries (Soosalu 1996). Finally, the literature review also challenged who the users were. Even if those in the 60-plus age-group had a positive perception of the safety-phone service, the current safety-phone users were considerably older. Older nonusers, in turn, were hesitant about safety phones: they were seen as a sign of helplessness and your last days of life. This piece of knowledge was potentially of the utmost importance for the company, since Vivago's measurements and modeling were based on the assumption of a relatively active person.

However, while all these insights had potentially crucial relevance for the design of the Vivago-Wristcare system, in the end the design study restricted itself to industrial design solutions and did not stress the critical points of the literature survey as something that could require further reengineering in the insides of the product or service associated with it. Table 4.2 provides an outline of the key results of the design study.

Table 4.2   The Main Conclusions of the Design Study, and the Evaluation of its Critical Potential for Design

	Objective of the study	Key results for prime objective	The main conclusions concerning design	Critical potential for changing the design
Design study	New mechanical design for the Wristcare device	- Models and mock-ups for the new design - Charting the key issues in the mechanical design, usability, hygiene, and appeal	- See results for prime objective - Questioned the assumptions of user groups and whether the device can truly stand alone	- The mechanical design should be renewed - The other features of the systems should be reconsidered (e.g., infrastructural fit, and assumptions of users)

PILOT USE AS A PROVIDER OF DESIGN-RELEVANT INFORMATION

The first on-site pilots started in 1997 and lasted until 1999. There were several sites that the company internally regarded as pilots, yet more formal evaluations were only carried out on three sites. In all, a few hundred units were in use at the end of 1999.

The company's primary aim in the pilots was to validate the technology and to find and fix any technical bugs there might be. But the pilots gradually also revealed an unexpectedly high number of false alarms and unreliabilities in alarm recognition. In addition to technical shortcomings, there seemed to be a mismatch in what the reliable use of the device required of the users and their condition and abilities in this respect. What the designers had mostly thought of as simple procedures in wearing, removing, and storing the device, canceling unwanted alarms, cleaning, and so on, seemed too demanding for many users.

In principle, the pilots provided a rather supportive environment for improving the technology. The staff and elderly residents in assisted living had time to explain and complain about their problems, and, as problems piled up for certain users, designers ended up having repeated contact with them. In addition, multiple instances fed back information to the company: the elderly themselves, home-care workers, alarm centers, and vendors that sold and assembled the devices. All this supported the possibility of gaining a more realistic picture of the use of the novel safety-phone concept. In practice, the engineers still had a hard time accurately tracing the situations in which false alarms or other problems had occurred. It was hard to judge what the problem was in the problem situations: failure in technical design, problems in wearing the device, misfit between the software algorithm and the user's actual activeness, problems in interpreting alarms (attributable either to suboptimal technology or, for instance, to the training and motivation of the helper), or simply some unusual action undertaken by the user, as we shall detail in Chapter 7 of this volume.

Between 1998 and 1999, the company launched multiple initiatives to fit the device into the social and technical environment. The monitoring algorithms were developed further, the instructions for using the device were crafted anew, and analysis software was developed. Even more substantial changes followed with the design of the second generation of the device in 1999–2000. The impact and information from the pilots were thus far greater than those of the prior investigations (Table 4.3).

Why did so many issues and needs for improvement surface only in the pilot use? An important reason was that the early studies did not provide this information, and the findings of the design study did not shake the assumptions developers had gained from the practice-bound imaginaries involved in the conception of Wristcare before the pilots verified the doubts expressed. An additional reason was that the pilot studies involved both users and designers, making it easier for the latter to gain firsthand experience of how users felt about their devices. Moreover, now that the product was in market use, any problems possibly affecting sales became more pressing for action.

Table 4.3   The Main Results of the Pilot Use and an Evaluation of its Critical Potential for Design

	Objective of the study	Key results for prime objective	Key information for design	Critical potential for changing the design
Pilot use	Eliminating technical problems in devices	- Many bugs were fixed - New instructions on how to wear the device were crafted	- Algorithms must be improved - The analysis software has to be developed - The number and variety of alarms must be reduced - Training must be emphasized - Mechanical design must be improved	- Questioned many of the previous assumptions on use and users - Expanded the scope that needed to be considered in design - Promoted the company changing its orientation to user practices

REPRESENTATIONS OF WHAT? THE CONSTITUTION OF THE NEED FOR WRISTCARE

Let us now deepen our analysis of these investigations by examining what they actually studied, that is, let us open up more what the users' preferences, or "user needs," consisted of for Vivago-Wristcare.

While "user need" has become an established term, it is mostly applied without a clear definition, being mixed with wants, preferences, requirements, and so on. It is perhaps best understood as a psychological metaphor translating the wider-scale notion of "market demand" into the complex behaviors of individual buyers and users (Ulrich and Eppinger 1995; Kotler 1988; Akrich 1995).

The traditional view of user needs tends to assume an individual user who has needs and wants regarding a singular piece of technology (Ulrich and Eppinger 1995; Kotler 1988; Akrich 1995). This has important limitations in understanding "user needs" in relation to new technology.

Drawing from activity theory, users' relationship to a technical concept is not something preexisting or given but evolves with the historical contexts, communities, and artifacts with which the people have grown and lived (Leontjev 1978; Valsiner 1998). "Needs" for new technology are only gradually elaborated for the users themselves. Miettinen and Hasu (2002) suggest that users' needs are first seen as unresolved problems, dilemmas, or contradictions in the users' activity. Needs are then defined as anticipations and desires in relation to the horizon of possible solutions that the new technological device might offer. Finally, the actual usefulness of the device, and the users' actual need for the device, is only realized when the device is made to work in collective activity with other artifacts and people.

To assess the investigations that Vivago Ltd. conducted to inform its product development, a deeper understanding needs to be created of what kinds of prevalent cultural representations mediated the way users apprehended a device like Vivago-Wristcare. This means a short excursion into the social history that has formed the representations and anticipations for the kind of technology that Vivago-Wristcare exemplifies.

In the most abstract, Vivago-Wristcare is based on a psychosocial need for the safety of those who feel vulnerable in their daily lives. Undoubtedly, such a need is both context sensitive and historically constructed. It would be absurd to claim that a granddad of the 1920s would have felt a need to have constant online body monitoring. He might have considered the possibility nice, but his view of a VCR and a personal moon rocket would have been on the same plane of relevancy. More likely, however, he would have regarded Wristcare as a rather miserable idea: the elderly lived in close relations to usually numerous offspring and neighbors; why on earth would someone need such a nuisance of a wristwatch? Since the 1920s, important social and technical changes have laid the ground for the "user needs" for a device like Vivago-Wristcare.

The beginning of Chapter 3 of this volume outlined how the demographic change in Western societies has shifted the balance of the responsibility of care from children to the elderly. At the same time, the elderly have become increasingly isolated by a number of factors including, but not limited to, higher pensions and standard of living that enable the elderly to manage their life on their own; increased mobility of people, making relatives and friends live further apart; women entering full-time work; and the state taking over care responsibilities with rest homes, home care, and so on (Tornstam 1992; Bleikie 1988; Philipsson 1988). In addition, in state-provided care, the material standard of care rose considerably until the late 1980s, accompanied by increasing medicalization of old age, as well as an increase in the institutionalization of care in sheltered housing (Vaarama 1995; Mäkitalo 2000). The recent trend, however, has been to seek out cost reductions by avoiding institutionalization and by supporting home care with technical appliances. In sum, societal change has created a growing number of independent but isolated elderly whose connections to relatives and friends have diminished. These connections have been patched up by home-care services, which the state, in turn, would like to patch up with cheaper technical aids.

As also noted earlier, the safety phone is one of the few applications that have an established position in elderly care (Wild and Kirschner 1994). One of the reasons for the popularity of the safety phone lies in elderly people's familiarity with telephones. By the 1960s, it was almost a norm to have a telephone in every household, and hence those who are currently elderly are quite accustomed to using telephone devices. The safety-phone service also resembles the operator-connected telephone of earlier days, which adds to the familiarity of the safety-phone service (Fischer 1992). The telephone is also one of the few applications that the elderly use daily, along with their TV, radio, refrigerator, and oven (Östlund 1995). This makes the strongly analogous safety-phone system natural and easily approachable, a key factor of success for technologies for the elderly (Östlund 1995; Harrington and Harrington 2000). User practices, infrastructure, government subsidies, and a good reputation mark some of the socially and technically relevant aspects of how the telephone and safety-phone services have influenced potential users, their relatives, care providers, and others. The need for, or rather the anticipation of the significance of, a kind of device like Vivago-Wristcare is grounded in this cultural history.

Further, while Vivago-Wristcare was not intended to achieve such precision and directness, its online monitoring fits the images of medical technologies that have come to mark the heightened care and reliability in the most vulnerable moments of life. Vivago's image as an advanced piece of transmission technology lends support for trust in that the company is up on the latest cellular and other telecommunications developments, and that this technology would be realizable and reliable.

In summary, the potential users and user-representatives anticipate the use and value of a device like Vivago-Wristcare mediated by a range of societal developments and cultural representations. These include representations of the increasing individualization and isolation of the elderly, representations of safety-phone services, and representations of medical monitoring and of the rapid development of telecommunications.

Also, when human cognition and action are seen as mediated by tools and signs (Vygotsky 1978), it becomes relevant what kinds of additional means and representations were available for users in situations when they made sense of their potential use of new technology, and how the social interaction in the investigations (the investigator, other informants) mediated informants' actions and cognition. Equipped with these insights, let us reexamine the investigations of Vivago-Wristcare user needs.

REEXAMINING THE INVESTIGATIONS
OF PROSPECTIVE "USER NEEDS"

Let us return to the two market studies. As noted, there was a noteworthy lack of anticipation of the shortcomings the Vivago-Wristcare concept faced later on. Three reasons in how these studies were organized resonate with our earlier discussion of the emergence and studying of user needs.

First, interviews with users and expert surveys did not cross-validate each other: experts commented on macro-scale issues of the market and service organization, while users related the technology to their personal lives. Neither inquired seriously into the systemic constellations, where Vivago-Wristcare would be purchased and used, that linked these two levels of description. Second, in the expert surveys there was a preplanned structure for the information that was deemed relevant, not encouraging finding unexpected information. This structure also effectively prevented any corrections and adjustments in the initial interpretative framework, even when the data suggested such change, as after the findings from the French investigation.

Third, and most importantly, all three studies described Vivago-Wristcare briefly and loosely as a safety phone monitoring health and issuing automatic alarms (SAI 1993; Leriche et al. 1995). No concrete restrictions on its functionality were offered when the studies related it technologically to pagers, safety phones, and monitoring technologies. This was emphasized by the decontextualized way of data-gathering, such as using phone interviews. Since the Wristcare concept was well aligned with the broad cultural representations outlined earlier, and hardly any of its particular functionalities were revealed to restrain imagination, the device was, rather unsurprisingly, received positively by all the interviewees as it appeared to answer all possible needs exactly because it was described in such vague terms.[3] At the same time, and not coincidentally, few significant suggestions for improvement or remarks on potential problems were found in these studies.

The design study generated more design-relevant knowledge, although little of it was incorporated in the technology at the time. In the design study, the contact with users was more extensive than in the earlier studies. The long and repeated face-to-face interviews allowed for unexpected information to come up (Soosalu 1996). The use of concrete representations, such as existing devices, pictures, and mock-ups, was reported as having enabled the users to comprehend and comment on the device (Soosalu 1996). These representations also created a middle ground between the users and the designer, where both could play their ideas out, and helped in obtaining critical and sufficiently fine-grained data for redesign. At the same time, this space might have detached the users somewhat from their actual daily living. This might have contributed to the failure to further develop the critical points the literature survey revealed: the setting of the design session, or the means and artifacts used in them, was not conducive to this kind of information being revealed.

Finally, the preceding theorizing on user needs helps to explain why pilot studies surfaced more design-relevant information. The pilots were the first contact with the real, not ideal-typical, represented, or representative, users. The technology was also now fully functional and incorporated into users' daily lives, so users could relate to it more comprehensively and gain long exposure to it. This was critical for Vivago-Wristcare, because both the downsides (e.g., false alarms and uncomfortable wear) and use-values (setting off the needed alarms) only became visible in sustained daily use. Finally, this was the first time the device was fitted into a whole social and technical environment that surrounded the safety-phone service. All these features could be summed up by saying that the pilots were the first occasions in which the users had sufficient access and exposure to the technical system to question how the device worked and how they were supposed to wear it and deal with it.

CHAPTER DISCUSSION

Biography of Technology

In this chapter we focused more in depth into one aspect of the early construction of the use of Vivago-Wristcare, namely explicit investigations on its use. This made us attend four intersecting biographies that factually intertwined in these events. First, the informational needs arose at specific moments in the innovation process. Some of these were partly due to chance, such as commissioning of the design study, others more carefully planned. Second, the practice-bound imaginaries within which the developers worked affected what inquiries were sought, what information was provided for the investigators, and how the findings were used. Third, the biographies of market research methods and user-centered design studies in industrial design affected how the studies were conducted. Fourth, the elderly and experts who responded to investigations oriented to their own historically formed experiences, representations, and practices.

Agency, or the Constitution of Developer, User, and Technology at this Moment of Biography

When informants in an investigation orient to a new kind of artifact, its actual characteristics and functions are compared to their previous experiences and images. Informants' often fairly contemplative representations of the technology can be articulated more concretely insofar as they are able to relate the technology to the fabric of their practical actions. Fully elaborated requirements and later a genuine "need" for technology should be expected only after a technology has been in use in the actual contexts for some time. The way people apprehend new technology develops in a triadic relationship between the instruments and cultural representations and their participations in the changing technical and social environment in which they live (Leontjev 1978; Miettinen and Hasu 2002; Valsiner 1998).

This dynamic view of the human–technology relation suggests that the methods of investigating prospective use are fundamentally "representation-hungry": the technology and its implications for users are, in most cases, underrepresented for users, who patch in the missing pieces from their own imagination, often drawing from broad social imagination, cultural images in popular media, or professional imaginaries (Miettinen and Hasu 2002; Dierkes et al. 1996; Gregory 2000; Pantzar 2000; Suominen 2003). Investigations for Vivago show how marked a difference there is for design, depending on whether the respondents' comments are broadly about this kind of device instead of this particular application.

Design–Use Relations

These investigations raise to the foreground two types of actors—intermediaries and proxy users—who act on the terrain between developers and eventual users. The informants in the studies were proxy users both in terms of it being uncertain how representative they were in relation to the eventual user-base and in regard to how representative the technological concepts presented to them were of the eventual functioning (cf. Williams et al. 2005). What the varying users and the varying representations of technology "proxied" varied from one study to another.

The people who conducted the studies bridged the information from developers to proxy users and back to developers. In this intermediary/ mediator position, their ability to generate design-relevant information in the studies depended equally on what information they were able to tease out from the developers as it was in their ability to tease information from users. It is important to recognize the lines of biography and their circulation here. All the studies were geared from the outset towards bringing credibility to the project in the eyes of potential investors and partners. Later, this was at least as important a usage as was informing the development work. Equally, the experts who were respondents did so *qua* having collected and ordered information that circled around safety-phone systems. They had concerns and professional stakes in how medical and alarm systems developed and how their expertise was represented. There was thus a circulation and shaping of interdependent representations: those of the technology, of the developer company, of users, of experts conducting and responding to inquiries. Each party (perhaps excluding the elderly interviewed) had multiple goals in presenting them to the other parties through their views and expressed findings.

Learning

A clear implication for learning about the evolving character of user needs is to take care when users are forced to apply guesswork in giving their opinions about a loosely framed technical concept: the technology would need to be represented adequately. This is a classic question of "double stimulus" in cultural psychology (Vygotsky 1987). The cognition and evaluation of people is mediated by the means and signs they have for orienting to their objects. Such "scaffolding" extends to the setting in which research is conducted. Here the key question is usages of mock-ups, full-scale prototypes, and narratives and how the designer/investigator can augment—and control how (s)he steers—informants' ability to transcend current conditions and their ability to question designers' solutions and principles. For instance, in cases like the early investigations of Vivago-Wristcare, technology could be presented not as a single concept but more widely as a horizon of possible alternatives. This could be created by adding potential shortcomings, problems, and new possibilities to the scenarios and use-cases depicting the technology, assisted by mock-ups or the like (cf. Ehn 1992; Hornyanszky Dalholm 1998; Säde 2001). The length and depth of exposure to novelty is obviously an issue, too. It remains open how far various methods—market surveys and expert interviews, but equally user panels, focus groups, future workshops, and scenario work—are able to incorporate enhanced ways to represent the technology for the users and, accordingly, how adequately they can be rendered as tools to investigate user needs for any more radically new technology.

5   Visions in Matter
Invention and Erosion

We now move down from an analytical scale of decades and years to one of weeks, days, and minutes of designing usage, and follow a series of design meetings in the mechanical design of second-generation Vivago in late 1999 and early 2000. We focus on how usage is shaped in a design process and, in particular, how, in situated action, user-representations enter into design, how they are worked on there, and how they depart from the process of design. To study the entry and transformation of user-representations in design, we examine four interrelated "micro-biographies" of central user-representations in the design of second-generation Vivago-Wristcare: inventing a new push-button solution, incorporating an LCD screen, creating auto-adjusting width of a bracelet, and that of an attempt to make the surfaces of the device anti-soiling.

The design process is predominantly presented as the primordial site where creativity of highly talented people flows into material form and results in novel solutions for human concerns (for variations in this line of thought see, e.g., Cross 2000; Schon 1983; Ulrich and Eppinger 1995). Design-critical views tend to question whether designers' intuition, creativity, and aesthetic sense is enough and, particularly, whether considerations of the implications of the new technology have sufficiently permeated the process and, through that, determined its outcomes (e.g., Papanek 1972; Schuler and Namioka 1993). This latter view has often been condensed into whether designers are guided by appropriate values and/or understandings in their work (Noble 1984; Woolgar 1991). While both discourses place the event of design equally on the pedestal (Stewart and Williams 2005), there is relatively little research on what actually does take place in the complex and uncertain considerations wherein "design decisions" are made or whatever "design values" are followed.

As we have discussed in previous chapters, the user-representations circling around an innovation project are many. Some of these are complementary and can have mutually reinforcing relations. Others have more conflicting relation and yet other representations of use concern such different areas in the product that they tend to remain unconnected: representations related to the visual image and marketing; those resulting from engineering details of, say, reliability considerations; and representations about adequate usability tend to fall into domains of different professionals, require different expertise, and also take shape in different ways (Norman 1999; Kotro 2005). The fascinating thing about design is that all these considerations have to be accommodated in the limited physical and cognitive space of the product and hence their mutual relations become more urgent.

Naturally, design and engineering do not stand helpless in the face of such difficult interdependencies; separation of concerns through compartmentalization, modularization, *et cetera*, is one of the principal activities involved. The micro-biographies we shall discuss in the following all entered design because of usage considerations. Yet their biographies invariably came to feature two other types of user-representations, ones developers recognized as affecting usage as a by-product and ones seen to affect only something very different, even as they factually did affect the design of usage. In addition, we shall note that when these features were designed into the limited physical and cognitive space of the artifact-in-the-making, they became further linked to issues that were effectively, often purposefully, separated off from affecting usage. Hence, four types of features in relation to designing of usage become salient:

1. ones explicitly brought to design because of usage (e.g., push-button functionality)
2. ones recognized to have bearing on usage or users but being primarily about something else (e.g., the hold of screws in the mold)
3. ones affecting usage but never discussed or considered from this vantage point during the design process (e.g., the layout of the circuit board inside the wrist unit)
4. features and solutions cut off from having much (if any) bearing on use (e.g., the molding channels built into the device to allow manufacturing)

This categorization emerging from the Vivago project, where no particular ambition to further research on user participation was present, interestingly parallels (Buscher et al. 2009) ways of stressing the type 3 and 4 issues as deeply consequential for how designing usage, user participation and choices available for envisioning uses can take place.

Furthermore, the range of issues that have bearing on use grows impressive even in the case of a small device such as Vivago-Wristcare. Table 5.1 sums up the main features that were considered as affecting usage in the design process of the second-generation Vivago. This complexity effectively waters down any attempt to describe "in full detail" how "The Usage" of even a small device like Vivago-Wristcare became designed, particularly if one wishes to draw connections to their sites of origin. Hence our focus on just four "mini-biographies" of features in the design process.

Table 5.1   Map of Features that Were Recognized to Affect Usage in the Second-Generation Design Process of Vivago-Wristcare

Main feature	Main attributes; minor attributes	Interlinkages to other key features concerning use
Push Button#	Securing intended alarm soundings, prevention of erroneous alarms; tactile findability, feel, feedback, look, height, placing, hole and button sizes.	Cleanability, look, area of interface taken, manufacturability, materials, watertightness, battery consumption, LCD-screen, etc.
Anti-soiling#	Dirt resistance, hygiene, conductivity problems, look; seamless surfaces, no dirt- gathering elements, ventilation in the arm, cleanability	Conductivity measurement, bracelet stretch, screw placement, materials, manufacturability, color, shape, battery replacability, robustness, etc.
Bracelet stretch#	Securing measurements, comfort, reducing skin irritations; stretching when arm swells	Conductivity measurement, anti-soiling, robustness, materials, look, feel
Watertightness#	Reliability, ease of wearing (showering, dish washing, etc.), standards and requirements	Battery life-time and replacement, robustness, screw placement, maintenance
Screws	Robustness, price, reliability; screw shape, placing, number, thickness, material, retightening	Look, feel, anti-soiling, conductivity contact, price of manufacturing, battery replacement, robustness, who does maintenance, etc.
Batteries#	Life-time, replacing, what all the device can send and display; size, placing, structure, etc.	Water tightness, robustness, maintenance, screen, measurements, antenna, sending, feedback, etc
Antenna*	Reach, energy consumption, usage areas	Forwards compatibility, battery lifetime, price, battery replacement, size, shape, etc.
Cover design#	Variation of looks, manufacturability	Water tightness, anti-soiling, robustness, forwards compatibility, etc.
Feedback#	Feedback on pressed and automatic alarms and battery life	Tactile feel, sound, screen/LED, battery lifetime, price
Robustness*	Robustness, sense of robustness for the user	Materials, all structural choices, price, etc., etc., etc.

Continued

Table 5.1   Continued

Robust-ness*	Robustness, sense of robustness for the user	Materials, all structural choices, price, etc., etc., etc.
Price#	Buyer acceptance, target markets, revenue	Manufacturing, materials, features, etc., etc., etc.
Forward compat-ibility*	Screen, size, measurements	
Sensor plate*	Measuring, secrecy, size	Robustness, battery life, screws, size, look, etc., etc., etc.
Screen/ LED#	Feedback, information for user, looks, image, interactivity, new functions	Manufacturability, push- button, size, looks, electricity consumption, compatibility with previous and coming electronics
Colors #	Pleasantness, soiling, signaling the need of cleaning, accept-ability	Push button, soiling
Looks/ shape#	Non-aid like, contemporary image	Price, monitoring plate, size, manufacturability, robustness, water tightness
Size#	Image, weight, fit to wrist, price	Push button, monitoring plate
Bracelet–device angle #	Fit to wrist, securing electrocon-ductivity sensor	Sensor plate, stretch of the band

Note: A # marks issues brought into design consideration because of usage, a *
marks issues developers recognized as affecting usage or users.
In addition *marked issues include ones such as manufacturability, regulation
compliance, hygiene, durability of materials . . .

The body of data for this chapter is a result from ethnography of all the
design meetings for Vivago-Wristcare mechanical design from September
1999 to June 2000. The process was conducted by outside industrial designers and company engineers in various specialties and a representative of the
contract manufacturer. We also attended the general R&D meetings of the
producer company at the time and conducted a series of interviews of the
participants in the mechanical design process. Hence, in addition to field
notes, over 60 hours of video recordings and close to 20 semi-structured
interviews form the primary body of data for this chapter. Together with
historical materials, and copies of the notes and sketches the participants

made during the process, this provides a rich view of the process, even though only small fractions of it are reported in detail in the following.

To accommodate analysis that hangs between interaction analysis and an ethnographic account, a simplified transcription has been opted for to ease the following of the interaction-analysis-wise lengthy sequences of up to five co-present interactants that span stretches of tens of minutes in design meetings within a series of meetings spanning months. There was no space to preserve both the Finnish original and English translation in this volume, and speech in the excerpts that follow has been translated from Finnish by the author. Translating Finnish utterances directly into English would make technical discussion extremely hard to follow, not least because Finnish is significantly further from English in terms of vocabulary, grammar, and idioms than any Indo-European language. Consequently, words have been translated into their literal English form, and whenever differing idioms are used, meaning has been preserved here rather than verbalization. A simplified "old" conversation analysis notation (Schegloff 2007) was then used, in which:

() marks inaudible speech or a long pause, without specifying length;

// marks the beginning of overlapping speech and * the end of overlap, with the overlapping speech delivered in the line below;

= symbols used in pairs, as in = =, connect talk that was broken into two lines to accommodate marking of overlapped speech;

((*text in italics*)) is used to mark action and objects when speech and action fully intertwine;

((text)) is used to clarify what is denoted in denotative expressions (including cases where the denotation is clear in Finnish but hard to translate adequately as well as anonymizations of the participants referred to in speech by name).

Some minor interruptions, orientation changes and gestures, and most aspects of speech delivery have not been preserved. Hence, it should be kept in mind that these simplifications create an overly orderly and skeletal depiction of recorded two-to-five-person design interactions and grossly overplay verbal exchange and its orderliness. Judging from the comments to the earlier drafts of this chapter, these simplifications were, however, necessary to convey the kind of relatively lengthy sequences of interactions we shall now move into.

THE SOURCES AND ACCUMULATION OF USER-REPRESENTATIONS: AN ERROR-FREE ALARM BUTTON

The official kickoff of the series of design meetings took place on a sunny, crisp October morning when the head of Vivago Ltd. (below "inventor") entered the studio of the industrial design consultancy hired to do the mechanical design. And, as is typical of design, much, if not most, of the communication took place through drawing, pointing, and gesturing accompanied by verbal descriptions (cf. Jordan and Henderson 1994). Figure 5.1 gives a sense of the setting: a group of people hunched over a table filled with materials, sketches, and notebooks, as well as previous and competitors' products.

Even though much of the action takes place outside talk, verbal descriptions are important carriers of information from the accumulated knowledge about use and related future desires—and, indeed, the entering and elaboration of user-representations is where we focus with the micro-biography we trace here: that of the error-free alarm button. Its elaboration begins right at the start of the design meeting series:

Designer 1:   Okay, I contacted ((the manufacturer)) yesterday and now, ((Inventor)), we have a structural idea, which we could // take as a starting point* =.
Inventor: Yeah.
Designer 1:   = that is, if you do not see any reason why it would not work. So the bracelet would act as unified surface ((*pointing to his drawing*)) here at the top.

Figure 5.1 Design setting. A clustering of artifacts, drawings, papers, and pens that are used to communicate and facilitate imagination. Note that even as the participants constantly talk with each other their bodily orientation and gaze rests mostly on drawings, material samples, and gestures, and (most importantly) sketching by others.

Designer 1: And it is entirely possible to do it that way and the furnishing, the components, would be dropped in through the bottom.

Inventor: Yeah.

Designer 1: And the principle is a bit like this here ((picking up the first-generation Vivago-Wristcare—Figure 5.2, right-hand side—turning it around)) apart from it all being entirely unitary. No sticker, no casing, all one. Structurally this would require ((*draws*)) that inside this elastomer, which is this one ((*draws, points*)), there would be a hard plastic frame placed there in the mold. And this frame-like part could continue as cover too, only leaving open the place for the ((alarm)) button, which would then stretch. And currently it apparently has this mechanical button, which is planned ((for remaining)) there?

Inventor: Yes.

Designer 1: And this would stretch down and there would be a clear click to be felt ((upon pressing it)). And think of the advantages for keeping it clean: all one surface.

From here, the discussion moves to hygiene, and we will return to this moment as we near the end of this chapter, but we now continue to follow the push-button elaboration, which is picked up at 28 minutes, where a set of user-representations about the alarm button is brought into consideration by the head of the company:

Inventor: () as real-life feedback: we have gone through different push buttons, competitors' buttons, and thought about that button. The button is going to be critical. We just had to deliver to Siilinjärvi hospital devices that do not have ((*pushes the button of his own wrist device unit*)) this click. Some of the people are in such poor shape that they do not have the strength to push ((even)) the 100-gram button—this one here ((on my wrist)) is a 250-gram button. Furthermore, when they seek the button, they cannot see. They search for it only by hand, somewhere there is some hole, and press that ().

Inventor: So let us think about it () hang on—how should I draw it? () ((*draws*)) that if the button is here, then in a way () I draw it ((*keeps on drawing*)) like this—just to give an idea—that this here is elastic ((*points to top right of his figure—akin to Figure 5.2's top left drawing, where the arrow is later drawn to indicate "elasticity"*)) and then it continues somewhere from there. If this here ((*keeps on drawing*)) is a nub and then this an even surface, then this one would need to be—this sheds a little new light on the requirements—such that if I press here it cannot tilt sideways ((and thus not make contact)).

Designer 1:   Sure, what about if it were made into a level, then if it would form a cup, the ideas we have had // but that is really that if you press it from the side it does not. Cup form*.

Inventor: It would need to be hard =

Inventor: = it would need to have a larger hard surface.

Designer 1:   Well, we can arrange that. But cup form might have that advantage that the finger is better guided onto the bottom. In that kind of even surface, just outlined, it's more laborious to find the center area, but it . . .

Inventor: Yeah the form there =

Inventor: = we had Telelarm's button for comparison ( ) no, sorry, Antenna's. Its shape is like this ((*draws, a level surface and a cup*)): it has the button as if finger-shaped. And they, as a matter of fact, have only a glued-in soft plastic and the pressing-hole around about there. It contains nothing else, just the soft plastic. When you press it, it too has the problem that if you press from the side, nothing happens, even as it suggests that you are in fact pushing that button. And we were just considering that the button () if you look at the prediction, not today, but prediction that people in increasingly poor condition will remain in home care and if you think about our devices // it

Figure 5.2 Early drawings and first-generation Vivago-Wristcare as an artifact used to envision the push-button functioning and shape.

was a total surprise for me that there are people in such a poor state in Siilinjärvi*.

Let us break out of the dialogue between the developer and designer in order to elaborate on some of the interesting issues in this discussion. What we find here are the four most common ways user-representations were brought forth in this series of design meetings: comparisons to existing products and their solutions, representations that are part of company visions about the future customer (who the target customer is and how the clientele is likely to change), implications about structural solutions to be adopted in the redesign of the device, and as anecdotes about users' identity, behaviors, and needs stemming from field-use experience. Let us return to the discussion where we left it:

Inventor: And if you think our devices // it was a total surprise for me that there are people in such a poor state in Siilinjärvi*.

Designer 1: This one ((*points to the first-generation device—Figure 5.2, right-hand side*)) only has integrated plastic there. Well, that is presently () a problem in nearly all ().

Inventor: = hence, I was left thinking on that surprise. Our ((developers)) visited Siilinjärvi and said that the patient material was, to begin with, in the terminal stage. You know those are not even our targeted customers, but, then again, it would be sensible for us to consider the needs of these more problematic users, in ((the design of)) this button.

Designer 1: Yes.

Inventor: For that reason () it became very clear to us through that Siilinjärvi case—when doing that comparative research—that we are no worse than competitors, but no better either.

Designer 1: n regard to the button?

Inventor: Yes, in terms of just the manual button.

Designer 1: Sure, sure.

Inventor: Really, if you want to put it this way, in Siilinjärvi we noted that for people in terminal stage our automatic monitoring is no longer a working solution—alarms are coming through all the time, as they are already at such a point in their life //that* =

Designer 1: Yes.

Inventor: = It's like () even the nurses are oriented a bit like, that they just wait for when they ((the patients)) die. They no longer even plan for acute care measures. But when that person wants help, then help, of course, has to come forth.

Designer 1: Of course, yes.

Inventor: And then it ((the calling for help)) has to be as easy as possible. So, in that respect I, we, back at work, pondered that if there had been the separate hard cover, it might have been beneficial to build different tactile feels for different user groups.

Let us again interrupt the dialogue, for this point is a "natural place" to do so, because of another common facet of this design discourse; now that some intial concerns and requirements have been elaborated on, the discussion shifts to related requirements, since any given feature tends to be rather complexly intertwined with solutions given for other features, as illustrated in Table 5.1. In this case, the discussion moves first into the different releases and versions of Vivago-Wristcare, then, from there, to other topics related to these. The ideas of how to realize the push button are returned to an hour later, at the end of the first meeting, when the structure of the device cover is again discussed:

Inventor: () and then it would just have a thin film, protective film on top of the ((mechanical button)), then it would be of the kind you showed, that you can press anywhere and you always score.

This then is taken up by the designers in the second meeting two weeks later, 30 minutes from the start, initiating a more focused sequence of considerations on how to realize the push button:

Designer 1:   Okay, the organization of the push button. It is now drawn ((*points to drawing*)) so as to have a small mechanical button underneath. And it would have the indentation, which would move under the finger so that it presses the button ((underneath)). The problem, then, is how to make it move so that it makes the connection in all cases. So () should the whole cup be elastic, or just an elastic rim, or what? This issue is really wide open as yet.
Inventor: One more thing, just a thought ( ) is that what they use in cell phones is a sort of nudging plastic.
Manufacturer: Silicone button or ().
Inventor: Sure, like a silicone button, but not made of silica // with a nudge. So, if here is the switch element ((*draws*)), which can ((even)) be of the conductive plastic so it does this "dok, dok, dok" ((*mimics the sound with his tongue*)).* =
Designer 2:   The whole thing can be a silicone layer, or . . . there are many alternatives, it really depends on the material, if it is . . .
Inventor   = for it doesn't need to be silicone, I've seen, there is one Swedish manufacturer who has done ().
Designer 2:   Here is an example ((*hands over a piece of material*)).
Inventor: Sure. But the Swedes have done the cover not out of silicon but out of plain polycarbonate.

The discussion now moves to details of materials and button elements for two minutes until the push-button shape is returned to:

Inventor: Further, some criticism we got from our bunch was that the hole should be bigger here ((*points to the drawing of competitor Antenna's device*)) so if we are dealing with () does anyone of us have big ((hands))? ((developer 1)) at our place is a big () he has even bigger fingers than you ((designer 1)).

Designer 1: My fingers are actually quite small.

Inventor: So somebody just remarked that if he is to push this one, it can be that ((the finger does not fit the hole)).

Designer 2: So it has got // to be*.

Manufacturer: Got to be bigger.

Inventor: Yes.

Designer 2: So there is a little bit of a dilemma there that it has to be big and easy, but then again it should not press down by itself.

At this point, there is again a shift to detail of materials for roughly two minutes that we fast-forward as it gets reiterated in the exchange that follows:

Designer 1: How is this part ((*points*)) here ((manufacturer))? It has this hard plastic cover and then the elastic part. Can it be made so that there is an elastic ring somehow and the intermediate part made of hard plastic?

Manufacturer: Yes, it can be done.

Designer 2: That ring has to be wide enough then, so it allows enough distance to be pressed.

Designer 1: Mm-hmm.

Manufacturer: ((*looking over the table and top-down on the drawing*)) I just cannot get my head around the shape of that cup that way around ((*snickers*)).

Inventor: So, in principle, it would be like this, in principle, if we think that it would be here.

Designer 1: It can be that way of course, so.

Manufacturer: I was thinking that last time when we spoke ((*draws—Figure 5.3, bottom left, figure in the lower part of the picture*)) that if this here would be hard, then we would ((*continues drawing the figure*)) put an elastic part here, but the mechanics itself would be underneath. Steady enough so it produces the movement, that mechanical switch. This ((elastic part)) just gives when you press.

Designer 1: Would this middle part ((*points—same drawing*)) then be elastic?

Manufacturer: Mm-hmm.

Inventor: It can be elastic if we opt for the other switch, the bigger switch. So, if we think, this one, it has roughly a square millimeter area in the switch, but the ones we've looked into are

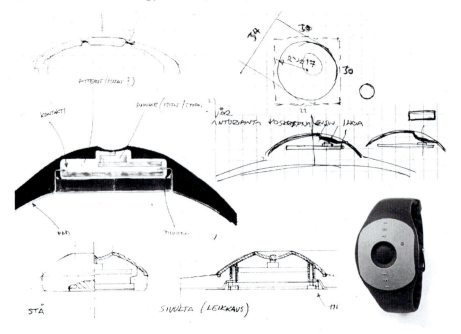

Figure 5.3 Progression of drawings for the push button.

roughly ((*draws*)) this size ((more than twice the area)). So then this ((elastic button)) would move in a directed channel, so that one can push wherever in the button, not just in the middle.

Designer 2:   Exactly.

Inventor: Hence, in a way, if we look at it sideways, and—let's draw this bigger ((*draws*))—it has this guidance in the button, so it goes ((always down)). I don't know how the spring structure underneath, which way it's been done, but at least one of those ((switches)) we looked at, which was a tad big for this purpose here, it was really good for one's finger ( ) We compared these two and this one then felt just plain odd.

Designer 2:   Then it does not require ((pushing)) in the middle but you can, in a way, press its side.

Inventor: And then this ((middle part)) could be soft. For then, what you planned as hard, it could be replaced by soft ().

Manufacturer: And the switch would give the mechanical movement, click, return, everything. And this // would just be* =

Inventor: A cap on top.

Manufacturer: = an elastic cap on top where you can press, and thin enough that you feel that switch. Then it's really () just two places that are pressed together.

Designer 1: Yes, yes, so it's all one // like*.
Manufacturer: All one except from two materials.

Upon revisiting the drafts drawn by designer 2 at the end of this meeting, the inventor exclaims, "So, in this structure we produced two solutions with one!" What happens in this episode is an inventive move from a simple button area on a level surface to one that is indented but raised to near the surface (and is therefore hard to press accidentally on surfaces, etc.), which rests on a switch element underneath that provides both "clicking" feedback upon pressing and support for structural guidance so that pressing anywhere within the finger hole will trigger an alarm.

The episode also reveals yet another set of user-representations; using designers' own physique as compared to that of elderly users (Akrich 1995; Kotro 2005), to be encountered several times later with other features. Finally, the episodes also reveal how initial ideas become elaborated in drawing and physically enacting different solutions, and how some of them establish their presence in more elaborate drawings that act as proxies for the future specification of the device.

Let us now rewind to near the beginning of the third design meeting, where the inventor reviews the design drawings of designer 2 (Figure 5.3, center left). The push-button solution has now been around a while, but it has been continuously challenged by other considerations, most visibly by the wish to incorporate an LCD screen into the device in its future versions. This issue is brought up in the first meeting, is reinforced in the second, and continues also after the initial eureka of the push button and much of the third meeting is spent on the screen:

Designer 1: So do you mean that the cover would have a ready-made place for the LCD, but when there is ((yet)) no screen there would be LEDs?
Inventor: For instance, so. Then there would be.
Designer 2: ((inaudible))
Inventor: What?
Designer 2: Underneath the glass or how?
Inventor: Yes, this brings to mind the message when we talk about—as in your investigation ((designer 2's study on elderly users and Vivago-Wristcare design in 1995))—many wished that it would not look like an alarm // device* =
Designer 2: Yeah, that is.
Inventor: = So it would have () even if it doesn't have a watch, it would look like a watch, that kind of message.
Designer 1: Um, yes.

Considerations continue about what there could be in terms of LCD content and LED content and how it could be realized, and at 32 minutes:

Designer 1:   Yes. It, of course, alters a bit that basic thought. In my mind, well, if we hold on to having LEDs in the place of the screen when there is no screen, so it would // use the same spot* =

Inventor: Yes.

Designer 1:   = where the screen comes into for LEDs or displaying LEDs, then I think that situation needs to be considered right from the beginning. That is, build the design so that it has a clear space somewhere for it. This ((button in the center)) here is, for example, a bit unfavorable for it has little room at many edges, but not much anywhere. So, that push-button would then need to be somehow dragged into the other corner right at the start ((as is done in the drawing in Figure 5.3, center right)).

The push-button solution, designed into the middle of the device, seems now to require reiteration. Its suggested place and the related shape are now contested by a feature supported by a set of strong complementary representations of use. The 1995 inquiry on design and users (see Chapter 4 of this volume), to which the inventor drew attention earlier, had found that many users resented the "aid"-like appearance of safety-phone wrist units and rather wished these would look like watches. Experience from early field trials had confirmed this user-representation, and it resonated strongly with the user-representation in the company strategy about establishing a new market among the younger, "60+" age-group. Furthermore, to lure the younger users, added functionality was deemed important in the future versions, with the screen deemed vital for this, and the need to reiterate the push button appeared likely.

But much depends also on the place a particular feature has acquired in the limited physical (and digital) space of the device. If a feature has not found its way to the progressing series of elaborated drawings—and hence not yet been elaborated in respect to the myriad of other features and constraints—it has an uphill battle to fight its way there, particularly when time pressure is high, and, consequently, the design consultancy tends to veer away from any unnecessary complications. The following interchange takes place at 27 minutes from the start of the third meeting, preceded by many questions, suggestions, and doubts about the LCD installation:

Designer 1:   So. What size would that possible screen then possibly be? If we are now to prepare for it ().

Followed by an answer three minutes later:

Inventor: () that which ((designer 2)) had in her design specified for a screen. It would be sufficient for appearing as a clock.

Designer 2:   That was really small ((*gestures with fingers to show how small the screen was*)).

Inventor: It's a bit bigger. I was about to take it with me, but () ((*points to the slightly enlarged gesture*)) yes, it was; it was roughly that size! And it just had this shape on top. Had this *kind of // =

Designer 2:   Round.

Inventor   = Yes, a bit bigger. So I was // like* =

Designer 2:   // It had*.

Inventor: = Empty space.

Designer 2:   A little bit empty, it could be () that shape was transformed from a square. So it was about that ((*draws*)) size. Pretty tiny it was.

Designer 1:   Um, yes, exactly ().

The client hence forces the issue onto the agenda, and so, some minutes later:

Inventor: That button once more. Those new samples ((of switches)), as I said, have been ordered, so we can start trying this ((design)) out.

Designer 1:   Next, we create a form model and start measuring up. ((Inventor)) will give us the information on the screen: what we are to prepare in regard to space. When that is closed, we can measure that ((button)) precisely.

This appears as clear verbal consensus about taking both the push button and the space reservation for the LCD forward, hence a call to reiterate the push-button design once more. And indeed, as we can see in Figure 5.3, right at the center, during the preceding discussion some early sketches were already drawn showing how the button could then be realized. Yet, when the fourth meeting begins, the place for the LCD is nowhere to be seen in the drawings produced by the two designers. Only a small space is reserved for a small feedback LED (see Figure 5.3, lower right-hand corner, for the finished device, where a small LED is visible in the top center on the right-hand side). In contrast, the push button in its central location form has become elaborated in detail (Figure 5.3, bottom left and center left)—a clear expression of designers' opinion about the trade-off and urgency of these two features. As another two weeks have passed, the client yields, and the LCD gains reality only as far as words and sketches go.

Never becoming incorporated into the actual design drawings, the screen no longer appears in further verbal considerations either. In contrast, the push button receives much enthusiasm from all participants and stakeholders throughout spring 2000 and in the hands of the users afterwards. It becomes perhaps the most successfully realized feature in the mechanical design of the second-generation device.

Yet to understand its success, we must become aware that the conditions for its success were laid out long before. In fact, when one of the earliest safety phones, Helena, came to Finland in the early 1980s, designer 1 was commissioned to create a robust and well-functioning casing and alarm button for it.[1] The later inventor of Vivago-Wristcare was working with this project, and, after several events and updates, this casing was used in first-generation Wristcare. And it was designer 1 who introduced designer 2 to the inventor for doing a design study of Vivago-Wristcare (see Chapter 4 of this volume). As noted, parts of the study were a literature review, expert interviews, and systematic comparison of the soiling of the alarm-button feature in all available safety-phone models. In many respects, both the LCD and push-button solution discussions here reiterate the design rationales known for years—only now tied to a particular novel solution. Cast in these terms, the otherwise perhaps surprisingly swift invention and success of the new alarm button becomes more understandable. Let us examine the network of concerns and their origins that went into the push-button feature (Table 5.2).

Table 5.2   Origins for the Push-Button Solution, Goals for its Design and Specific Features Realizing These

Push-button alarm	Origins of rationales	Mission and goals	Features
Competing against extant safety-phone systems	- Buying time for R&D on automatic alarms (1992) - Eliminating false alarms (1995) - Serving users in very weak condition (1998) - Different pricing (1992) - Less "aid" stigma (1995)	- Serving emergencies that cannot be detected by instruments - Improved usability and reliability of operation - Serving the segmentation of the device for different groups of users - Only manual alarm-button version (= safety phone)	- Button that is hard to miss or press - Sheltering the button to a hole - Ensuring tactile finding - Extrasensitive button - Nudge upon pressing - Feedback LED
Secure working of manual alarm function	- Manual alarms that have not come through (1995, 1985) - Problems with feedback on pressing (1995, 1998) - Elderly to press electronics long and hard, push again if in doubt (1995, 1998)	- Achieving increased usability and reliability of alarm (see preceding)	- Directing the hand on device surface - Directing the finger to right pressing direction - Cap model

Continued

Table 5.2   Continued

Reliability of the device	- Integrity of structure (1998) - Water resistance (devices destroyed in shower and dish washing, requirements by large telecom pilots, some country regulations)	- Maintain shock proof - Maintain waterproof structure - Battery lifetime and replacability	- One red LED, disabled later. vs. LCD, vs. buzz feedback, vs. sound feedback
Manufacturability, steps	- Price of assembly and materials - Difficulty - Reliability	- As few assembly steps as possible - Modeling and molds within the limits of ease - Use of only tested material combinations	- Polyurethane all over, no silicone - Button as a cap, nudge underneath integrated to the circuit board
Backwards compatibility	- Quick release of the new version - Use of extant circuit board (1999)	- Button preferably in the middle, where it is in the previous model and present circuit board	- Button in the middle, fitting the circuit board - Button height adjustable by the board height
Forwards compatibility	- Changing cover element - LCD screen reservation (1993, 1995)	- Preparing for more informational devices without new cover design - Ability to produce design variations easily	- Place reservation for more information displayed on the cover vs. direction of push, vs. button at the center
Stigma as aid	- To make the device appear not as an aid - Avoid gathering dirt and soiling of the device - Reports on elderly and technology - Earlier safety phones (1987, 1995, 1998)	- Design elegance - Round shapes "non-aid likeness" - Unnoticeability - Small size - Changing colors - Hiding the push button	- No seam cover, rounding of button hole and ascension so it allows for cleaning (- Make the whole cover an analog watch) - Integrate LCD and digital watch - Vs. large size of the device - Vs. high visibility of the button
Target market	- From "85" to "65" - Round shapes - High-tech looks and feel (1992, 1995)	- To brand the device as high-tech - To design device as non aid	- Vs. push button and LCD next to each other on flat surface

There is indeed 20 years of history in fiddling with and designing the push buttons of the devices, thinking through their weaknesses and strengths, and gaining appraisals of them from here and there. In this view, the push-button micro-biography is one of *accumulation* of social learning within and between the practice-bound imaginaries related to it, culminating in a new, neat design that eventually worked (even without proper testing); during the design, it was able to *stabilize* against LCD-related user-representations that had strong interanimated sources as well. Important issues leading to this stabilization were the tight schedule that truncated the attempts to elaborate LCD further and the fact that the push-button solution came to offer a feedback mechanism, rendering weaker any need for any kind of LED or display in the second-generation model and turning these user-representations into a future compatibility issue.

EROSION OF FEATURES WITHIN AND BETWEEN DESIGN PROCESSES

It would be, however, rather erroneous to assert that stabilization or rejection of technology in design would result in it being carved in stone. The LCD screen's mini-biography *in this design process* ends up as one of increasing marginalization. As noted earlier, it first got reduced to a feedback LED and then was later fully disabled by a software change to save on battery life. However, even a quick look at the third-generation Vivago-Wristcare at 2009 probably tells all that needs to be told (Figure 5.4). When we compare this to the early 1995 design sketches (see Chapter 4, this volume, and Figure 5.4, right-hand side), the pendulum swings between different design features that are in trade-off become apparent. The third-generation device no longer has a similarly indented-raised alarm button (perhaps producing some more accidental alarms), and, like the 1995 sketch, it capitalizes on new added functionalities and far less aid-like appearance.

Let us, however, not limit our scrutiny to how accumulation and (de)stabilization take place between different product releases. We next examine the micro-biography of the auto-adjusting bracelet and then, more fully, the erosion of the anti-soiling device, for they give us further insight on interrelations between design features as well as on the journeys of features during a design process.

Shadowing Over of a Feature: Auto-Adjusting Width of the Wristband

The idea for auto-adjusting width of the wristband stemmed from the need to achieve reliable monitoring from the wrist and hence the imperative to have the wristband tightened so that the monitoring surface would press against the wrist and not dangle loose somewhere around it, yet still be comfortable to wear. Its elaboration begins at the end of the second meeting:

Inventor: One more thing, that stretching part: how do we build that?

Designer 1: Right. Yes. We haven't taken any position on that as yet.

Designer 2: How much does it have to stretch? Or what would be enough?

Inventor: As a matter of fact, we don't have absolute knowledge on that. One doctor just visited us and we discussed with him how much fluid is gathered in the human body. This doctor said it should not be much, that if it does then you have a wrong medication and //ought to see a doctor*.

Designer 2: Alarm is in order then.

Inventor: Mmm, yeah. So when we told about those cases we had had, that ((the device)) was loose in the evening and in the morning their skin was wrinkled inside ((the device)) no, sorry, the other way around.

Designer 2: Well, that is, when these swell () every one of us has sometimes had swelling, for instance, in the legs, and then this ((swollen skin)) gives; it's very liquid-like. So then if it ((the wristband made out of polycarbonate)) is stiff, it ((the skin)) will not stretch it.

This is interrupted by a question as to whether the issue is just whether people know how to adjust the band width and hence whether just numbering the holes of the bracelet would do. This one-minute exchange ends up in another anecdote about users:

Inventor: No. We had one example—I might have told some of you, probably ((designer 2))—that one granny suffering from dementia ((was)) visited by a home-care worker and ((she)) put the wrist device onto her wrist, and said that it is that third hole that is good then. Well, the granny then kept it there, and by the summer it was really, there was a deep skin fold, and

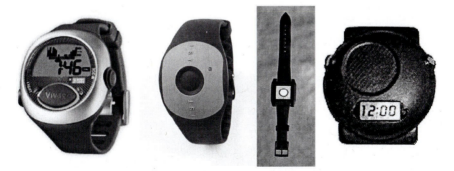

Figure 5.4 Third-generation Vivago in 2009, second-generation device in 2002, first-generation device in 1998, and 1995 design sketch.

all the skin here ((around the wrist device)) was fully broken. Because the nurse said it has to be there, so then it was.

Manufacturer: Mm-hmm. You see, it's the childish belief that it won't work otherwise than the way the nurse said ().

Inventor: So, it should; that little stretch would ((need to)) be created in any case. I know from myself, as I wear this for days on end, that particularly at night you start to feel it. Now ((in the morning)) it is like this, even has room here, but sometimes during the evening it starts to feel a bit uncomfortable. So even this much ((change during the day)) () I haven't visited the doctor for too much swelling but ().

Designer 2: Is that possible to make structurally so // that it* =

Manufacturer: It is possible to get. But we // have, for instance*.

Designer 2: = well, of course this stretches, but it won't stretch just when it ought to.

Designer 1: Mmm. It is ().

Manufacturer: For instance, for Suunto, we made a wristband for their watch, an extension band, which had a quite close ((wave structure)). It was surprisingly stiff. So it may be that it would work better with something more gentle ((sloping)). I don't know.

Designer 2: What we have here () this should be really tried, begin cutting it out. If this is what one wants to ().

Manufacturer: It is, of course, easy to make test molds with the final material. That's always the best indicator.

Designer 1: Could we try it somehow? If we had intact bands, ((we could)) just cut that form with some carpet knife or something.

Designer 2: Mm-hmm, just cutting a form like that.

Designer 1: I think we could test it to some length, yes. I've been thinking // exactly the same*.

Inventor: It could, sorry to interrupt but in principle =

Inventor: = I was thinking that it may be enough that this band would just have these cuts, cuts ((*laughs*)) like here. So that it looks intact from above but would be cut ((Figure 5.5, left center, a band cut in varying ways)).

What then follows is an exercise of trying out different bracelet shapes that would stretch automatically—the participants move from vertical winds into various horizontally cut or winding shapes (Figure 5.5, left-hand side) and realize that these too have to be tried out to see their various downsides, such as getting hair stuck between too close cuts, torque in horizontally wound bands, and serious dirt-gathering problems in any solutions watchmakers have used such as cloth or complex buckle structures (see the array of differently shaped bracelets in Figure 5.5, top middle section).

In doing so, they iteratively establish some key issues: that the materials can indeed be made to stretch the length needed, that a vertical leaf-spring structure would retain its shape, and that the structure needs to be open so as to prevent it from gathering dirt. One of the shapes cut out is a structure made of two rings (see Figure 5.5, center and right columns).

Inventor: Let me try that one ((two-ring solution—Figure 5.5, bottom middle)). And it retains its shape reasonably too. It does not ((exhibit torque)) as a point of fact, it retains its shape ( ) this, if you measure here, it stretches madly!
Designer 1:   Sure does.
Inventor: This goes already () easily—do we have lined paper anywhere? This stretches already over five millimeters and still retains its shape.
Designer 1:   And it still pulls all the time.
Manufacturer: We need to find an ((exact)) shape for that () continue this kind of cutting.

At the end of the third meeting, the slightly more advanced stretching rings have been built and are examined (Figure 5.5, centre right):

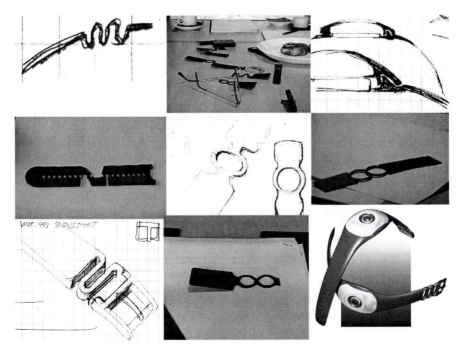

Figure 5.5 Different bracelet solutions, tests, and sketches.

Inventor: So, yes, the other issue ((the stretch)), which needs a bit more discussion.

Designer 1: Yes, right, we have done a bit //.

Manufacturer: As long as you don't make it too stringy, it will probably work.

Designer 2: This?

Inventor: This had a good feel () look at this ((Figure 5.5, center right)) it works ideally. This was () five millimeters' stretch here. I say this is the dream come true.

Designer 1: Yeah.

Designer 2: If you could make a bit more netlike one too. It would have four of those ((loops)) // or*.

Designer 1: ((Designer 2)) could investigate that. You did that one too; it's ((designer 2's)) idea.

Inventor: Yeah.

Manufacturer: Looks good, as long as it doesn't end up stringlike.

Designer 2: Yeah, but // doesn't it*.

Manufacturer: I mean the shape, the round shape there.

Designer 1: So that skin doesn't bulge from between.

Designer 2: Hence there shouldn't be too much // to make it* =

Manufacturer: And not too thin.

Designer 2: = Yes, not too thin, so they don't hurt, and if there is too much then it gathers all the dirt.

This is followed by another five minutes of testing and trying, which ends with the following interchange:

Designer 1: Yeah. We discussed with ((designer 2)) yesterday that what bothers me here is that, does it produce the feeling that it is about to break even when it doesn't? If those thin parts make one feel like, that it is no good. The material thickness there is sufficient as it is, right?

Manufacturer: Well, it is clearly the weakest spot there. It requires a bit of thinking which width.

Designer 2: And should it be oval, so it would not be necessarily ((round)) this.

Manufacturer: And it is also possible to, for example, take that detail into a mold shape and mold it in different materials.

Inventor: Yes, right, try it out.

Manufacturer: It's very // simple when* =

Inventor: You make it ((the mold)) out of aluminum?

Manufacturer: = Aluminum. That sort of detail is best done by really molding the samples.

In the bottom right of Figure 5.5, we see computer-modeled new versions of Vivago-Wristcare after the fifth design meeting. The stretch function—three oval rings—is visible in the corner at the right-hand side of the picture.

What we have here is a situated invention akin to the push-button solution. Its fate, however, was rather different. The structure was not challenged, and it worked well in the initial prototypes. But the first series with final production materials changed the situation:

Head of R&D on November 14, 2000:

> Well, no ((there are no alterations)). It is as it was originally planned and even thinned, and it certainly will not break. But then, of course, materially—because the injection molding material ((use)) now happens to be harder ((than that of the elastic one used in prototypes))— that stretch does not work . . . even if we thinned that to half, it remains so stiff that the stretch will not be enough () you know, we have chosen such manufacturing processes, chosen this kind of injection technique, that we mold two different materials together.[2] What it does is that it restricts the materials a lot—which these guys here had not figured out. () Because now we have () even though the material would be right otherwise, we cannot use it, because it won't attach to the casing. And if it attaches well, then it is just this ((present)) sort of iron bar.

The feature, hence, had remained in form as planned in its most elaborated phase, but it no longer could be trusted to carry through any of its intended functions after the urgency of changing the material overshadowed this function. The comparison to the push button is interesting also in regard to the situationality and prior background. While prior homework had been conducted also for the stretching wristband, there were fewer previous attempts to show the way and these developers had become alerted to the problem only one year prior to the episode. The only thing they knew for certain was that no cloth materials could be used because of dirt. In this regard, we could say that the design imagination was weakly bound to those practices where its reality and realizability came to be tested, such as the hands of users, various stretching structures, and polyurethane injection.

The Erosion of the Anti-Soiling Characteristic of the Device

The final micro-biography, that of the anti-soiling surfaces of the device, allows us to provide more flesh on how de-accumulation may happen. The elaboration of this feature began one minute from the kickoff of the design series, together with the push button, and continued through the tens of iterations related to how it could be realized in practice. Let us return to the discussion we began this chapter with:

Designer 1: So the bracelet would act as a unified surface ((*pointing to his drawing*)) here at the top. () And there would be a clear click to be felt ((upon pressing it)). And think of the advantages

	for keeping it clean: all one surface. I really got enthusiastic about the thought of "why should we have any separate cover structures?" as we discussed last time. For any and all separate covers inevitably include seams and that is always bad for cleaning.
Inventor:	() My only sort of objection here is that the device doesn't really soil from the top. It soils from the bottom.
Designer:	Yeah, well, there you have that one seam just as it presently has. That's unavoidable.
Inventor:	Yes, but just to add here that in this way this sensor coming from here would have been deep () if you turn this, and think about it the other way around, there would be a hole and this ((sensor plate)) would come to rest against the bottom crevice. So only one small, very narrow seam would be made, no holes for the screws. The screws form a problem of their own. Their material. As we talked about last time, we need to sink them in there somehow. They cannot stay at the surface, for they react chemically even if they were of a durable material as such.
Designer:	Sinking them in is no problem, but, of course, then the point of the screw is bad in terms of gathering dirt.
Inventor:	Yes, that's the problem in the present design () and then our ((sensor)) plate, it cannot be taken from the surface, and you cannot sink in ((the screws)) deeper than that screw head.
Designer:	Yes, the plate of yours, but we shall make that anew; it won't be the same plate, will it?
Inventor:	Yes, sure, but that material there won't allow it.
Designer:	Sure, but we can put more ((points to the sensor plate)) here; if we make it anew, let's make it thick enough to accommodate the sinking in of screws. ((It is)) the thickness of material there ((*points*)), or what determines that? What determines that thickness?
Inventor:	It is not that // ((the)) circuit board ((the sensor plate)) can in principle be thicker. It's not up to that* =
Designer:	So, // so this is*.
Inventor:	= the circuit board material can be thicker, but that eats up the exact same amount of space from the batteries ((inside the device)) ().

The anti-soiling presents particularly clearly how features become interlinked. Anti-soiling is now tied, on the one hand, to the screws, which had been one of the prime dirt-gathering spots in the previous design but that, as their main function, have to ensure many other things. In the course of the first six design meetings, the consideration of the screws and their various alternatives turned to considerations about compressing and locking the entire inner structure of the wrist device into place and, at that, ensuring its waterproofness, its endurance against dropping and collisions, changing of its batteries in such a reliable manner that nonspecialists could do it, *et cetera*. All together, this takes more than an eighth of the total time used in the meetings, in addition to the work done outside the meetings.

On the other hand, the anti-soiling becomes elaborated against other technical issues and user-representations. In the earlier passage, these are the sensor plate (and through it the reliability of monitoring); the space for the batteries when it two weeks later becomes connected to battery size and battery life; and back to the integrity of the structure—that is, the number, positioning, and material of screws and other locking principles. In some of these areas, usage is implicated, and retained, as a concern; others are seen and treated as technical and structural issues from which usage is purposefully one step removed. All these connections make anti-soiling almost an omnipresent concern, rather more a design-driver than a feature. The fourth design meeting, 92 minutes from the start, is illustrative here. The topic is how to connect conductive pads to the rest of the structure:

Developer 1: It ((the sensor plate)) has to be conical, to ensure ((*points*)) sealant ((structure)) here.

Designer 1: Yeah, yeah, the idea is that it would tighten there.

Inventor: As such, you know, it looks good in the sense that no trail can form there that even could gather dirt. In a way, that possibility has been cut out there.

Designer 1: You mean between the pad and the sensor?

Inventor: Yes, yes. In that alternative you've drawn, for the crack, it's not only the moisture but—regardless of how tiny the crack is—it can start gathering that dirt. And when you have a drop // of moisture*.

Designer 1: It is the combi // nation*.

Manufacturer: // It gathers*.

Inventor: Exactly! It gathers, yes that's clear as day. We've seen it. It's unavoidable.

Manufacturer: Horrible stuff. I just saw how a pulse meter that had been sent back from out there ((*laughter*)).

Designer 1: Yes.

Developer 1: Well, some of our bracelets too ((*laughter*)).

Manufacturer: Okay, well, let's try to find a solution, so that we can build a stop guard there ((to block dirt-and-water mixture moving into the device or forming a conductive pathway into it)). But I'm thinking that without testing you cannot say if it works.

Inventor: Well, can we go further here now? Well, no.

So again we find user-representations conveyed through anecdote and comparison to existing devices: both this technology and others. Yet even as the concerns have been clearly spelled out, their order of priority remains more open to qualification. As we come to see next, a somewhat soil-gathering device can be sold and used, but one disintegrating with the first collision cannot. Let's illustrate this with the fate of the screws. The third design meeting, 55 minutes from the start:

Inventor: () You cannot take it that far. You must () that there is the supporting structure. So if ((*draws*)) ((the screw support)) is here and there is plastic here, then all this is fluff—it will not hold, and even if taken all the way it won't seal or compress anything. The alternative is, as we pondered, that we have ((*draws*)) the polycarbonate here with a hole right here, and, and we accept that we must put the screw on top. Full stop. Then the polycarbonate acts pretty well as, as sealant.

Designer 1: How is that screw really, protruding from the sensor surface: does it hinder monitoring, really?

Inventor: No, not really, if it remains in the area we are about to place it.

Designer 1: It will, of course, look a bit funny, but then again.

Designer 1: So, screw here it is, either visible or if we can find low enough screw heads that we could patch it ().

Hence the screws end up at the surface. Similar trade-offs follow: to ensure that the conductivity measurement worked properly, diagonal entry of the pads to the device was eventually opted for, despite the crevice formed, since the "stop guard" discussed earlier was successfully designed such that dirt could not mess up the functioning of the device anymore. Yet the crevice as such became more accentuated when it turned out that the device had to be more watertight than expected and sealing was added. The ventilation principle and stretch solution for the bracelet introduced further channels for the dirt to cling to. Even as the top surface remained almost seamless as planned, the more difficult and more critical underside ended up disappointing the participants, as the CEO reflected in an interview, November 25, 2002, more than two years after the initial design process:

CEO: The device itself has now become conducting () and that problem is caused by the dirt () and it has caused a great number of brainteasers.

Interviewer: How have you solved it then?

CEO: We have now solved it by changing the mechanical structure of that wrist device and at the same time changing the electronics too. And it is in practice already solved.

Interviewer: Right. So there is going to be another round of iteration?

CEO: Yes, there will be. So the looks of the device are roughly the same, but when you look at the other side, now that is completely different.

We are today unsure who came up with the term *erosion* to describe the carving of channels, nooks, and crannies in the smooth, ideal, envisioned surface in the course of the advancing design both over and underneath it. Regardless of whether it started as a joke by our informants or as our own reflection, *erosion* captures this chain of events well: first an accumulation leading to a clearly identified feature in the topography of the design parameters, then its gradual waning. More generally, the term "erosion of user-representation" is appealing beyond this kind of literal case to describe a process where a particular user-representation is raised to prominence and held there yet subordinated to other pressing considerations such that its original form becomes gradually and partially, for lack of a better word, eroded. Erosion is also an apt metaphor because it can be extended to cases where a given function becomes further ignored, worked around, or physically altered after the technology has been taken into use, on the scale of individual devices as well as the scale of changing generic design as we come to see happening in Chapters 6 and 7 of this volume.

The erosion micro-biography clearly ends up in a less stable solution than, for instance, the accumulation biography of the push button. Yet open–closed dichotomy may be too limited to be useful here. The anti-soiling surface builds on equal history of accumulated experience from previous safety-phone models and their use. The repositories of this knowledge and its mediators to the Vivago-Wristcare project were the 1995 design study and the devices used in the 1997–1999 pilot studies, which revealed that both hygiene and monitoring reliability were affected by how the devices gathered dirt. The solutions for managing the dirt problem did become elaborated, as did the outcomes of this solution in the hands of the users, again leading to different solutions in the next design round of the device, in 2005–2007.

CHAPTER DISCUSSION

Biography of Technology

In all, design appears as a highly concentrated situational engagement between people and materials producing elegant new solutions, such as the novel structure of the push button and the stretching wristband. At the same time, the micro-biographies examined in this chapter situate design as just one moment in the evolution of technology, even when examined at the feature level. The features we followed in this chapter had origins in the original Wristcare functional description, in the 1995 design study on the interface design of the Vivago-Wristcare system (see Chapter 4, this volume), in the accumulated feedback from the users of the device during 1997–1999 (see Chapter 7, this volume), or in all of these. This was also reflected in the way they came to enter the design process as issues brought forward by the inventor (who had most contact with users at that time) or by the industrial designer who conducted the 1995 study. This design process was merely one, even if important, period in the biographies of these features.

These micro-biographies also document (some of) the evolution of design ideas and concepts during a design process. The gradual stabilization and erosion of features indicates how attributing user-unfriendly design to *values* or poor education of designers and planners (Winner 1980; Norman 1988; Woolgar 1991) appears rather daring if the eventual artifact is used as the sole evidence. Much happens in between the values of developers and the outcome artifact. Design decisions affecting users negatively can result from uncertainty about, and lack of, testing of the properties of materials (as in the fate of the stretching band feature); from competing "good" aimed at users (the best possible functioning of the push button versus equipping the device with a screen to make it look less like an aid) or from mechanisms such as the erosion in the anti-soiling feature, where waterproofing and integrity of structure were directly user-related overriding concerns. This parallels but goes beyond stressing "operational readiness" in gaining advantage of usage-related information in design processes (Voss et al. 2009b) in that indeed the value and possibilities to benefit from such information hinge on how the design process in general is organized, but also that even with the best intentions necessary trade-offs between competing "goods" can result in erosion of one or other requirement or design feature.

Design–Use Relations

The design process was exclusively conducted by developers, designers, and manufacturers. The only user involvement planned was user testing of the shape—and, later, colors—of the new device, but this was never realized because of time pressure. In stark contrast, users were very much present in the design discussion and a significant number of the redesigns originated from users' opinions or from problems they had voiced. These were represented in the process through the design brief's list of features and by anecdotes told by the company head and designer 2, acting as intermediaries between users and the rest of the team. Representation of use, users, and usages by no means stopped here. Sources of user-representation visible in the preceding material are:

- referencing one's own usage experience from actually wearing the device

  - using oneself as reference—for instance, when the size of the designers' fingers was used to determine the right size for the push button
  - reengineering previous push buttons, surfaces, and buckle solutions, providing the developers with representations of how these would respond to usage
  - business concerns, visions, and targets such as making the device appear less as an "aid" so as to make it appeal to younger users

The last two of these sources exemplify in more detail the ways practice-bound imaginaries were discussed to offer user-representations in Chapter 3 of this volume. The first two owe to the devices now being in actual use, but also blend with the third one, designers using their personal experience as fellow humans as representative to the physique and behaviors of users. "I-design" can take a whole range of different ways that deserve more careful inquiry (Akrich 1995; Oudshoorn et al. 2004; Kotro 2005).

Agency, or the Constitution of Developer, User, and Technology at this Moment of Biography

It is safe to say that "design is reflexive conversation with materials" (Schon 1983) as well as to note that these materials are, in fact, heterogeneous. Indeed, much of the discussion in the interactions in this chapter is about how materials are likely to respond to particular kinds of shaping and what implications these have for users, pricing, reliability, integrity, *et cetera*. The agency in designing appears distributed to the design team and the materials and means they have available for conducting the design. Let us go further and return to the observation that ideas and solutions for each feature were prefigured in earlier technologies and sites of usage. Nearly all alternative paths ever considered during these design episodes were equally bound to concrete events, artifacts, sites, materials, and images. Yet all the features were genuine shoots of invention: something humankind had not quite seen before. And the chain of imaginative actions (many of which were literally imaging actions) by which they came about was equally creative—devising clever solutions through analogues, creating new ways to use the available materials, and considering multiple outside-of-the-box avenues of design before choosing the eventual path to follow. Design was imaginative action, but the design imagination was very rarely unbound phantasma. Participants were quick to question the boundness of imagining, as in the case of incorporating the LCD screen.

  Returning to our theorizing about practice-bound imaginaries is in order also for methodological reasons. Examining design work in greater detail underlines how it does not do justice to the actual practice to represent designers or developers as acting within one or two dominating technological frames when they envision alternatives or make design decisions.

Naturally, each of the participants in the design process was (paid to be) there because of a specific professional background. But the design was accomplished within a group, and in acting in that group each designer drew from several practices (and imaginaries bound to them) and from their everyday experience.

Reflecting on the process of researching the initial invention of Vivago-Wristcare from historical materials and interviews (in Chapter 3 of this volume), one finds that the lack of attention to local and situated context in, for instance, "technological frame" could quite naturally follow from the historical materials used in the studies where it was developed. Such materials seldom include interactional detail and are usually more apt for describing longer time frames of analysis. Both characteristics invite cutting a corner in the level of detail in which one studies and conceptualizes the processes of technology development and use. Indeed, our own analysis in Chapter 3 of this volume remained somewhat vague as to how the developers arrived at their user-representations and how these became incorporated into the initial prototypes.

Conversely, should we have resorted only to the ethnography of the second-generation Vivago-Wristcare design process, its bindings to earlier events and more long-term features of practices of safety-phone development would have remained invisible.

Learning

The predominant kind of learning during the design sessions was conceptual and included material trials for how solutions would behave in foreseeable future situations and how they would relate to other considerations in the design. Interestingly, problems, not successes, posed easier targets to learning and remedying. Most problems that ensued after the second-generation design were due to issues that had remained hidden in first-generation Wristcare, and became visible only when the second-generation device was in the hands of users. And the hands of the users are where we turn next.

6   Nurturing Technology
Enactment and Impact

In this chapter, we move on to the adoption of Vivago-Wristcare in the life of elderly people and in the work of their caregivers in assisted living. We first examine the work and life projects of residents, nurses, and managers and the versions of technology in practice that each group came to enact. These projects, in turn, were affected by how the technology was deployed, and to this aim we compare two implementations of the Vivago-Wristcare system. After this, we fast-forward from the year 2001 to the years 2006–2009 to see how the impact of the technology has changed when it was used as a component to construct a new type of setting for the elderly.

As we discussed in the literature review concerning technology adoption in Chapter 1 of this volume, the move from design to use means a crucial transformation for a technology. Its actual functioning becomes visible, after all the visions and assumptions about how it should behave and how it is likely to be used. The technology is also literally passed from the hands of the designers to the hands of its users. It is no longer nurtured in a loving and technically competent environment, but expected to work in the practices of its users, who often do not share the enthusiasm, skills, or values of the designers (Engeström and Escalante 1996; Hasu 2001a). While designers build their sets of meanings and values into a technology, it finds new purposes, socio-technical configurations, and meanings in the hands of its users. The relevant characteristics of the technology are constructed within a different practice.

Appropriation of technology typically includes shaping both the technology and existing practice and this, in turn, hinges on how it comes to feature in the lives of its adopters (Berg 1997; Hasu 2001a; Lehoux 2006). To study this, we first turn to examining *personal and group projects* wherein Vivago-Wristcare came to feature in the rest homes studied. The term is adopted from McLaughlin et al. (1999), who used it to combine insights from consumption studies and workplace studies in examining the implementation of new technology. In their use, "project" is a relatively loosely defined term describing the fairly independent tasks and concerns that people strive for in their work. In this chapter, the term is made more specific. Projects are seen as reasonably independent and pervasive concerns that manifest themselves as tasks and strings of action that persist for years (in the sense of occurring regularly or frequently). Moreover, they are seen to do so within an activity, a relatively durable unit of technically, culturally, and socially mediated collective practice (see Chapter 2, this volume, and the following). Projects often do not have a definite goal or end point that can be met; rather, they are oriented to particular objects. The findings that follow indicate that such objects vary significantly, from managing one's life with reduced mobility to projects related to work routines, such as the nurses' socializing with residents of the rest home. Some of the projects we will outline were rather non-project-like in that they had no finite or pre-determined end point. Long-standing personal "projects" such as a cardiac condition or movement disabilities may last the remainder of the person's lifetime. Moreover "personal projects" always have collective aspects and are personal only in the sense that one key person "owns" or advocates the project. In this sense, group projects were instances wherein some people shared the aspiration and ownership of a project.

A further rationale for using the notion of project lies in the way McLaughlin et al. (1999) connect it to the process of "valuing" technology in a local setting. By *valuing* they mean the gradual construction of the utility of the technology by the end users; thus they reject seeing usability or utility as inherent qualities of technology but, just as importantly, as constituted by the practical achievement of creating work affording tech-nology-in-practice by its adopters (McLaughlin et al. 1999; McLaughlin and Skinner 2000).[1]

VIVAGO IN PERSONAL AND GROUP PROJECTS OF PEOPLE IN REST HOMES

Vivago-Wristcare and the Managers of Residential Homes

In 2000–2001 the device was mostly used in institutions for assisted living, in which the elderly residents lived in their own separate apartments but shared common areas, such as a dining room and lounges, and received help from the home-care workers and nurses if their condition deteriorated. These institutions were run by nonprofit organizations that gained their financing from the residents' monthly rent and from subsidies from the city. All the information that follows is from this kind of housing arrangement. For data used, see the Appendix, this volume.

The managers of residential homes were key figures in the purchasing and market success of Vivago-Wristcare. Managers perceived the utility of the Vivago-Wristcare system in the organizational development more broadly than did the designers, who regarded Vivago-Wristcare strictly as an alarming and monitoring device at this point of its development. By the managers, Vivago-Wristcare was unanimously perceived as a means for the organization and its residents and staff to get connected with technological development. It was employed in their pursuits to develop the external relations of the organization, and internally it became part of the reorganization of work, particularly in breaking down the rigid procedures in care rounds. The role of Vivago as a part of a wider organizational frame governed how its problems and the needs for redesign were addressed, and they addressed only in rather general terms the technical details and the concerns residents and staff had with the system, as general doubts about whether the device really worked as claimed and as concerns about how it affected social relations within the organization (see Table 6.1).

Vivago-Wristcare in the Projects of the Senior Residents

"Well, there would have been plenty of reclining to do [on the bathroom floor] before the morning meal would have arrived nine and half hours

Table 6.1 Vivago-Wristcare in the Work of Rest-Home Managers

People	Projects Wristcare featured in	Issue Wristcare was used for	Exemplifying quotes
Rest-home managers	Managing the external relations of the rest home	Building better appeal	*"This kind of high-tech can give the elderly as well as their care a status other than just being 'out of time.'"* (Manager, Espoo) *"Wristcare consolidates our good reputation, which gives us a number of direct and indirect benefits: better labor, the latest knowledge in the field, collaboration with schools and universities, partner organizations, visits by public-sector movers."* (Manager, Turku)
	Developing the organization	Keeping up with technical development	*"I see that this system raises the self-esteem of our staff, since they can use high-tech and show that they can do it."* (Manager, Turku) *"Its implementation and use lowers the threshold to implementing new technology in the future."* (Manager, Savitaipale)
		Work reorganization	*"This technology enables more natural communication between the nurses and residents than the scheduled rounds did. . . . And . . . maybe our residents have learned to want things a bit more than previously."* (Manager, Espoo)

later."[2] Similar grim humor about everyday life and concerns, and about the advantages of having Vivago-Wristcare, was often voiced by those who had problems with movement and faced the fear of falling on a daily basis. These residents were by and large extremely satisfied with their devices. Vivago-Wristcare had become their personal lifeline whenever they fell down or got stuck in some awkward position and could not get up. Some of them experienced these incidents several times a week. Even those who did not currently need the device were firmly convinced of its importance in light of their previous accidents.

This fundamental utility in one of their most important life projects—literally giving access to mobile living in the sense of getting out of bed in the morning—made these residents appreciate also the automatic alarms and overlook the inconveniences and discomfort felt in wearing the device: "I always try to rush from the shower within 15 minutes to get the bracelet back on so it won't generate an unnecessary alarm"[3] and "It's good to wear even though it presses my swollen and paralyzed arm."[4] Nor did these residents mind being woken up during the night or in the morning because of checking calls and visits for false alarms. The extra features of Vivago-Wristcare were perceived as enhanced care and the inconveniences as indications that they were being looked after continuously. No one complained about the price of the device or expressed doubts about whether the device actually worked the way it was said to.

Because the device was designed to be what its developers called "foolproof," the opportunities for shaping it were thought of as being very restricted.[5] Nonetheless, residents often opted for procedures that redefined the functionality of the device, such as wearing it on a paralyzed arm, or attaching it to a bedpost or a wheelchair to make the alarm button easier to press, even though this meant giving up all the monitoring functionality.

Another extreme in the relationship to the device was found among residents with a heightened risk of cardiac arrest and strokes. One resident had worn the device for over a year and there had not been any automatic alarms on occasions he had felt heart symptoms. "I don't know what generates these alarms in the first place, and the whole thing feels like humbug."[6] He was also annoyed by nurses having made several calls to him to check whether everything was all right when there were no symptoms at all. Similar doubts and concerns were voiced by other residents with cardiac risk. Uncertainty as to whether the device would be able to detect an emergency was accentuated by doubts about whether the help would arrive in time. The time required for the check-in call for confirmation of need and then for the ambulance to arrive added up to between 20 and 30 minutes, which was felt to be discomfortingly long.

The inconveniences of wearing the device irritated the cardiac patients more than, for example, people with reduced mobility. For instance, after being frustrated by having been woken up a couple of times in vain, one of the residents demanded that the staff not be allowed to react to any alarms from her during the nighttime. Cardiac patients also made more

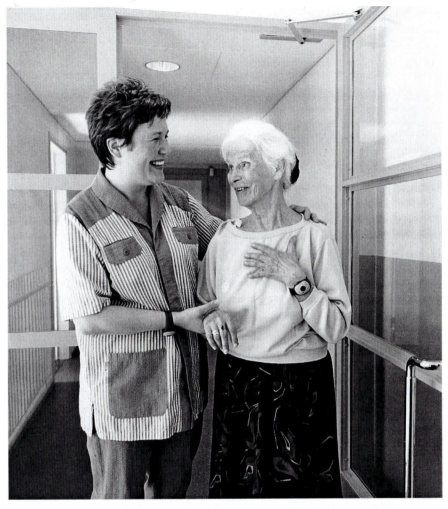

Figure 6.1 Vivago-Wristcare provided a new means for the interactions between residents and home-care workers, particularly appreciated by the people with reduced mobility. Vivago Ltd. marketing picture.

critical comments about the look and feel of the device: It had to be too tight, it looked clumsy and repulsive like an aid or prosthesis, or they wore it under their sleeve. Part of this difference came from the fact that cardiac patients generally had more active and mobile social lives and often did not have many other aids. While Vivago-Wristcare helped the people with reduced mobility to prevent major inconveniences as often as on a daily basis, the cardiac patients were protecting themselves against rare but potentially fatal incidents. The latter faced higher stakes, but their daily usage gave them less reassurance that the device could indeed be trusted in emergencies.

While the aforementioned two cases represent the extremes of the personal projects the device was incorporated into, the interviews also revealed an array of more subtle ways of utilizing the device. The first was pleasing caregivers and relatives: "I don't need the device for anything, but once it was put on my wrist, I did not have the heart to return it, because two others just did that."[7] These users were, by and large, not too concerned about how the device was worn or maintained. Two of them kept the device on the table by the bedside, and one wore it very loosely on her wrist, obviously more concerned about comfort than the fact that the device detected nothing when worn that way. The maintenance stories told by developers describe cases such as a user insulating the monitoring surface of the device with cotton to achieve more comfort. It seems, for some individuals, that just *having* the device was sufficient utilization, regardless of whether it could ever in principle be used for sending an alarm.

An overarching theme throughout the interviews was the sense of security. Even if there was no clearly identified physical threat, the device served as an assurance against threats: "I haven't really gotten any tangible benefits out of it yet, but I, rather, see it as a warning sign, as a reminder to watch my step."[8] However, the symbolism of security evoked by the design was not only positive. After giving away the device, one resident explained:

> The security I trust is in quite other hands . . . the span of our lifetime is decided elsewhere, and I have no need for this kind of device. If you can make it to the phone on your own, that is then a different story. . . . This is not like the real [safety] bracelet that my friend wore [an earlier-generation safety phone rented from the Red Cross], got help with it, and was taken to a hospital where she died a couple of days later. I didn't like the clumsiness and ugliness of the device either, not that I regarded it as a piece of jewelry, which one should not wear anyway.[9]

Vivago thus failed to match up to the sources of security—God, hospital, and technology established in her younger years—that she regarded as reliable. The religious frame of reference was employed also in relating to the appeal of the design but left room as well for evaluation stemming from everyday experience.

Roughly half of the residents in all four residential homes chose not to take up the device even when it was included as part of their rent. To these people, using the device meant legitimizing checkup visits; in some places an obligation to check out when leaving the building; and, on a more symbolic plane, sending out a signal that one was in need of increased nurturing and surveillance and could no longer manage an independent life. Agreeing to accept the device was a big step for the majority of residents, both symbolically and as a practical arrangement.

Table 6.2 Vivago-Wristcare and Elderly Residents' Lives: Projects and Purposes

People	Projects Wristcare featured in	Issue Wristcare was used for	Exemplifying quotes
Senior residents	Attending and maintaining mobile life	Recovering from the daily incidents caused by impaired mobility	*"Well, there would have been plenty of reclining to do [on the bathroom floor] before the morning meal would have arrived nine and a half hours later."* (Resident 1, Savitaipale)
	Guarding against cardiac problems	Getting help in the event of cardiac arrest or stroke	*"I'm not fully convinced about it. I would trust it more if it gave me alarms every now and then when I do have heart problems."* (Resident 4, Espoo)
	Pleasing the caregivers	Maintaining the significant social relations	*"I took the device when my son brought it, and a number of times he has insisted that I should have pressed the alarm button."* (Resident 5, Espoo)
	Refusing the device	Maintaining independence and sovereignty	*"Some residents feel they have lost some of their privacy, because of the checking visits for the false alarms and also because of having feelings of guilt for not wearing the device all the time, as well as having to check out every time they leave the building."* (Nurse, Espoo)

Technology in the Work of Nurses and Home-Care Workers

From the perspective of the designers the job of nurses and home-care workers, as users, was to respond to alarms and to ensure that the residents wore and used their devices correctly. When we observed their work, the reality was quite different. Wristcare entered an existing organization of work and a set of social relations that it somewhat reshaped. The most important of these collective projects of the caregivers was conducting daily tasks, such as care rounds, meals, washing, cleaning, and providing help with various requests. Intertwined with these tasks were the constant maintenance and activation of the (often impoverished) social relations of residents through chatting and small visits, frequently on the pretext of just checking that all was well, which the resident could turn into a conversation if (s)he wanted.

Nurses agreed that Vivago-Wristcare enabled a more flexible and efficient patient rounds' procedure and opened up new ways of gaining and maintaining control without engaging in time-consuming interactions with residents. One could just look at whether residents were present and how active they were. But since tasks and socializing were intertwined, this benefit was a mixed blessing (see Table 6.3).

The device provided a means to deal with reliability and responsibility, emphasized because the nurses worked within multiple commitments—to the relatives, the management, and the residents. Related to this, the increased control was expressed as a psychological improvement in their personal work. Reliability and responsibility were also emphasized because the nurses had to work for, and often on behalf of, patients who could no longer get by on their own. The system was legitimized as being "good for the elderly" since it gave them a greater "sense of security."

Yet the use of the device also interfered with other work tasks, particularly medical or sanitary operations carried out during the night shift. Nonetheless,

Figure 6.2 A nurse making a diagnosis with the help of activity-graph monitoring. Vivago Ltd. marketing picture.

nurses saw the most crucial drawback of the device as the occasional strain it caused to relations between staff and residents. A typical instance was that a resident would get irritated with the false alarms; complain about the extra cost (in all institutions, the cost of the device was included in the rent, notwithstanding whether the resident actually wore the device); and, most seriously, complain to other residents about the device.

The organizational structure did not allow the staff members to reject the technology without seriously disturbing their relations with the management and/or the residents. We find it telling that the management's prime concern, keeping up with the technological modernization of care, was voiced by only two young, technologically competent nurses . . . as being an important thing for the older staff members.

These group and personal projects guided the way the personnel made the device fit their work. Vivago-Wristcare design logic transferred much of the responsibility and diagnostic work to nurses. Designers had issued strict instructions on how to use, wear, strip, and store the device and how its various messages should be interpreted. Yet there were two main ways of altering the design logic in nurses' work procedures:

> The use of the program is based on knowing the personal rhythm of the residents. . . . To many of the problems in the device and in diagnosing [the alarms], there has emerged a solution in finding a personalized solution with the particular resident.[10]

Some of the alarms were ignored and were casually checked hours later to see whether they were typical for that particular resident. The recommendations, alarm histories, and activity curves offered by the machinery were replaced by firsthand experience with the resident and memorization of typical incidents.

The system was also realigned by receiving calls on nurses' cell phones. Some nurses and caretakers saw the cell phone connection as "the greatest benefit from the system, because it liberates us from the office, and we can go about our tasks more freely, since they can reach us all around the house or even from the neighborhood store."[11] At the same time, the cell phone enabled the nurses to bypass the diagnostics in the software. It often was quicker to visit the resident than to go to the computer in the control room. What grew out of this experience was that, on two of the sites, manual alarms were used as a nurse-call system.

The end result was that the design logic (which was restricted to alarms and tried to aid in the diagnostic tasks by providing information on the gradually changing state of the patient) was replaced by personal knowledge, by visits that were not differentiated according to the nature of the alarm, and by turning the system into an alarm–paging hybrid. This was taken as far as using the system as a personal emergency button for the nurse on duty.

Table 6.3   Vivago-Wristcare in the Work of the Nurses and Home-Care Workers

People	Projects Wristcare featured in	Issue Wrist-care was used for	Exemplifying quotes
Nurses and home-care workers	Carrying the daily tasks through	Making the care-round proce-duremore flexible Render-ing work more efficient (. . . but also inter-fering with work)	"*We have agreed that they press imme-diately if they feel at all worse . . . and that also makes them more active, when they have to evaluate when they want something and not just wait for the rounds.*" (Home care worker, Turku) "*We can skip some unnecessary check-ing rounds, since looking at the activity curve reveals that the resident is alive and breathing, and has not called for help.*" (Home-care worker 1, Espoo) "*If you are doing something else, espe-cially giving a treatment to a patient and the alarm goes off, it is not a pleasant situation. Just think of making stitches or of sanitary operations: you have to stop, take off the plastic gloves, reach for the device, sign in the alarm, and rush to the computer to see how acute a matter it is.*" (Nurse 2, Turku)
	Maintain-ing social relations with the residents	Managing time Managing responsi-bility Managing anxiety	"*We don't have to call to see whether people have made it in or are still outside. You know, when you call, you have to have a little chat, which easily takes 5–10 minutes, which adds up to a few hours a week.*" (Home-care worker 2, Espoo) "*We can better control the nightly movements in the wing for demented residents and compare the residents' explanations, events, and the details provided by the activity curve of the device.*" (Home care worker 3, Espoo) "*It gives you peace of mind when you know everything is OK right when you arrive in the morning.*" (Home care worker 4, Espoo)

Nurses also gradually created their own prescriptions for using the device. Some institutions dropped the obligation for residents to check out when leaving the building. In a similar vein, the staff did not react to information about the device not being worn on the wrist. Also, manual alarms from some residents were ignored because they had often "flicked" the alarm button unintentionally. With others, caregivers only reacted to

Figure 6.3 A nurse listening to an alarm message through her cell phone. Vivago Ltd. marketing picture.

alarms in the daytime and it was also common that caregivers encouraged their charges to wear the device however it was most comfortable (very loosely or on the more active arm) to ensure that it was worn at all, even when this completely contradicted the designers' prescriptions.

Overall, Vivago-Wristcare came to be appreciated by the personnel only when they were able to incorporate it fruitfully into their two intertwined major projects: delivering assistance and socializing with residents. Its functional capacities were explored and evaluated from the perspective of these projects. This meant ignoring some of the major capabilities of the control program in diagnosing physiological condition and led to the creation of work-arounds, and to local procedures and prescriptions that differed from those given by the manufacturer. This local process of valuing also affected

the general features of the product system, since the rest-home staff gradually convinced the designers that the technical system had to be redesigned
to better fit the procedures in which the device was actually being used.

VERSIONS OF TECHNOLOGY-IN-PRACTICE

As described earlier, the elderly and their caregivers reconfigured Vivago-
Wristcare in both material and nonmaterial ways. At the technical end,
there were demands for changes from the designers and working around
the system by using other technologies, using only some features of the
device, or expanding its uses. Less material mechanisms included replacing
the use of technical features by social knowledge and procedures, reducing
the technology largely to its symbolic value (such as a sign of modernization
of care), reducing it to its significance in social relations (such as in managing relations with relatives and personnel), or refusing the device because of
the associations the device had with dependency.

However, framing the findings in this way runs a risk of downplaying
the effects of these actions in the appropriation of the technology. The findings could be read as saying that the technology was interpreted differently,
that different meanings were ascribed to it, or that there were *also* minor
modifications and alternative uses of the technology. But both social con-
structionist and materially essentialist readings would miss the point. One
is warranted to ask "So what?" in response to the fact that there are minor
modifications of the technology. Minor modifications can quite sensibly
be regarded as a matter of better instructing the users to comply with the
design or maybe a matter of fixing some of the worst bugs as well. It is
equally inadequate to note that people interpret the same technology in different ways, because the technology can be seen to remain the same regardless of any ephemeral interpretations given to it.

A more full-bodied way to account for these findings of is to conceptualize that there emerged multiple versions of the technology-in-practice (Mol
2002; Sjögren and Helgesson 2007; Star 1989b, 1991). When we examined the projects in which users engaged with the technology, it became
clear that Vivago-Wristcare was never alone but was always enmeshed with
other artifacts (cell phones, notebooks, sanitary gloves, beds, wheelchairs,
etc.), procedures (care rounds, daily rhythms, etc.), conventions (in conversations, in conduct, in giving treatment, etc.), and people (nurses, residents,
neighbors, relatives, etc.), as well as frames of reference and participation
(daily habits and consumption rituals, prevailing narratives about new
technology, etc.), to name a few.

Vivago-in-practice was in effect an intertwinement of these elements,
which varied significantly from project to project. Users ignored and
removed characteristics of Vivago-Wristcare that conflicted with the version they preferred to enact into presence and that they preferred to allow

to have effects on their action and interaction. In this light, the various meanings ascribed to a technology or modifications to its material shape are symptoms or representations of the material–cultural–social hybrid (in other words, the version or socio-technical configuration in action) that was enacted into being (Cole 1996; Mol 2002).

But does not such practice-centered conceptualization run a risk of turning the phenomena examined into a "soup" in which different layers of practice, technical matters, and social phenomena become indistinguishable and thus risk losing explanatory power? Furthermore, is it not implausible to do away with differences between, for instance, things technical, procedural, and social? Such questions, often targeted at ANT, are indeed valid concerns. Where does the heterogeneous network comprising practice ever end, and how can it thus be analyzed (Miettinen 1999)?

Clearly, to gain insight into how Vivago-Wristcare became enacted, we need not, and should not, aim to understand *all* that is involved in a given practice. Midrange sensitizing concepts, such as that of project, allow patterns to be revealed from the practices examined so that we can approximate the minimal meaningful context relevant for the technology in question: in this case, relatively durable concerns and "strings of actions" within which versions of technology were enacted. This also reveals that, while practices may be soupy by their nature, they are far from run through a sieve. There are clearly bigger and smaller chunks of the technical, the social, and the organizational that do not dissolve into the texture or the "taste" of practice. However, these chunks do not exist in isolation and may not straightforwardly follow preexisting intuitions and assumptions of what must be technical, or what is social or, say, economic. These patterns must be revealed by inquiry.

Nor does talk about versions lead to seeing technology as utterly malleable or a matter of only social construction (Grint and Woolgar 1997). Accepting the notion of versions of technology means that there is no finite, predefinable list of functions to a given technology, while at the same time it points to the very concrete constraints to different versions of technology that can be enacted in any given concrete practice in a particular time. The 35 people using Vivago who were studied for this chapter enacted a relatively small number of significantly different versions of this technology. The stark differences in resources the various people had for dealing with, for instance, inconvenience and false alarms underscores the encounters, interdependencies, limits, and resources needed to meddle with "material," "organizational," "social," or "cognitive" aspects of technology in concrete settings.

ACTIVITIES AS SOURCES OF RESOURCES AND INTERESTS: COMPARING TWO IMPLEMENTATIONS OF VIVAGO-WRISTCARE

The projects of utilizers make sense only in relation to other projects and instrumentation in a rest home. Such a systemic whole may be discussed in terms of an activity system, another useful sensitizing concept for studying practices. As introduced in Chapter 2 of this volume, an activity is a formation of relatively long-lasting or durable collective action that often takes the shape of an institution. It is composed of a community of participants that have a social organization and the means to pursue their aims. Activities are animated by shared motives that are materialized in the objects the activity is engaged in transforming (Leontjev 1978; Engeström 1987). Rest homes can be characterized as this kind of relatively stable socio-material formation. A good example is the "Silverhair" rest home in Espoo. It was founded in the early 1990s as one of the many recent *palvelutalo* facilities (institution for assisted living) to fill the gap between independent living at home and the institutions for the elderly in rather weak conditions. The community consists of residents, home-care workers, nurses, and a manager. They have a set division of labor among them: care and assistance is provided by the staff and residents try to manage their life as well as they can while accepting some loss of self-responsibility. This division of labor is materialized in explicit and implicit rules about how people should behave in their homes, and while eating, bathing, giving and receiving treatment, and in socializing with others in public spaces.

Their actions are further socially mediated by, for instance, routines, social events, greetings, and conversations among members. Tools and signs, such as medications, telephones, safety phones, and instructions, also mediate the actions of all members. An important mediator is the special layout of seniors' apartments and the building in general. It provides each resident with his/her own apartment and private sphere but is equipped in such a way that the staff can provide help for those who need it. These aspects are connected by the social purpose for the activity: enabling a meaningful and safe aging for the residents who can no longer manage, or wish, to live in their original apartments. Its materialized outcome is the maintenance of the physical and social well-being of the residents. The

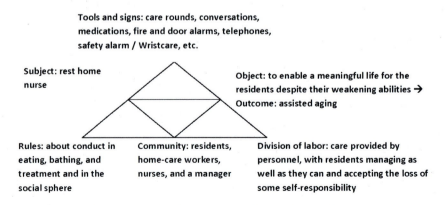

Figure 6.4 The elements of elderly care in a rest home depicted as an activity-system from a nurse's perspective.

state, the residents, and their relatives, who fund the institution, recognize this outcome (use-value). Such an activity system may be modeled as in Figure 6.4, here from a rest-home nurse's perspective (cf. Engeström 1987):

Vivago-Wristcare enters this activity as one of the new means of mediating the interaction between the staff and the residents. It does take on a variety of roles in the division of labor and rules of the community, yet, as we described earlier, its importance should not be overemphasized among the well-established routines, means, and identities of the home-care workers, nurses, and residents.

It is now time to put the introduced elements into action in comparing two implementations of Vivago-Wristcare in sheltered housing during the years 2000–2001. In the city of Espoo, the implementation turned into a struggle, while in Turku, the system was implemented with a rather high level of satisfaction among workers and relatively little worry for the rest home. The differences between these two cases in satisfaction with the system find some explanation when analyzed in terms of the resources and arrangements the two rest homes used in implementing this technology.

The two institutions were roughly identical: both were *palvelutalo* institutions for assisted living, built recently, and equipped with all the latest solutions for elderly care. Both were relatively large and included special facilities for housing demented residents and were staffed accordingly. They were clearly "flagships" of the foundations that ran them. Within them, the Wristcare system was worn by all those living in their own apartments wanting the device, and all those suffering from dementia. Alarms were routed to cell phones and the control software was in the nurses' office. Since both institutions were manned 24 hours a day, no outside alarm center was involved.

Espoo Implementation in Brief

The Espoo site was a brand-new institution, and Vivago-Wristcare was one of the many technologies that were installed. The technologies all came from different providers and it soon appeared that nobody had overall responsibility for the complex electronic and telecommunications systems, which kept on causing hassle. The difficulties were accentuated with the residents moving into the rest home before the construction of the building and its various technologies was completed.[12] At the same time, Vivago Ltd. was in the middle of a struggle to master the initial bugs in the second generation of the device and, as a consequence, could only provide devices from the first generation ridden with component problems.

In implementing the Vivago-Wristcare system, the rest home strictly followed Vivago Ltd.'s instructions on how the devices were to be worn and alarms responded to, to ensure maximally reliable monitoring. The advice offered on how to get started with the system, from another Espoo-based rest home, was turned down. The expectation was that all technical systems should function the way suppliers had promised or, more to the point, the way conveyed by their sales pitch. Inside the rest home, nobody was appointed to be specifically responsible for the implementation of the various technologies or working out appropriate procedures for how to deal with them.[13]

Some of the elderly residents had difficulties in understanding even the basic idea of the device, not to mention the technically oriented instructions that were quite removed from their daily life. The result was that residents then suffered, for example, from much too tight bracelets and false alarms, while the technology suffered, for instance, from being worn too loosely and being destroyed by water in the shower. Once it became clear that not all of the instructions could be followed as such, the staff faced the difficulty of determining which of the instructions in the many page technical manual really had to be enforced. With the recurring problems and changes in the instructions, some of the residents began to lose their confidence in the system.[14] The staff members, in turn, experienced this as having to listen to the residents' frustrations with the technology, and as their own growing frustrations in how they should go about diagnosing and responding to the alarms and managing the various technical systems.[15]

Amidst all the problems, the rest-home manager struggled also to find (and to retain) enough competent staff members for her new institution;

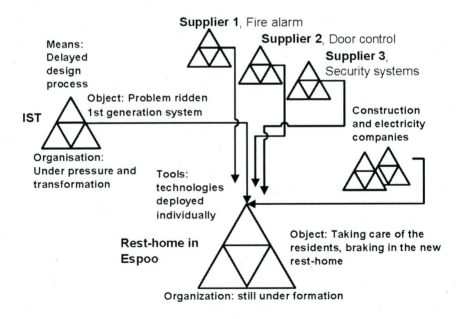

Figure 6.5 The network of activity systems around the rest home in the city of Espoo. All technologies were supplied and assembled by different companies and all implemented at once, while the rest home itself was amidst the last of the construction work.

the vendors had to deal with accumulating complaints; and, finally, Vivago Ltd. had to deal with frequent product replacements, extra training sessions, and ongoing complaints, and gained few ideas for improving the device in the future.[16] It took over a year before the rest home and the company managed to work out all the details to make the system work technically and to create appropriate procedures to fit the system to work practices. Put another way, while there ended up being plenty of company involvement, it was slow to yield the results hoped for by both parties.

Turku Implementation in Brief

In contrast, the rest home in Turku allied itself with a local telecommunications vendor who wanted to start selling Vivago-Wristcare and other rest-home telecommunications and electronics in the region. Even though the process in Turku and in Espoo began at roughly the same time, the Turku site rejected any temporary solutions and waited until Vivago Ltd. was able to provide the second-generation system ordered. The technical assembly was handled by the vendor, who faced the difficulties (not unlike those in Espoo) in making the system fit the rest home and its other technical systems. The deal with the vendor buffered the rest home against the economic losses associated with the initial difficulties.[17] The deal also provided a much stronger position to negotiate with the supplier company, since it

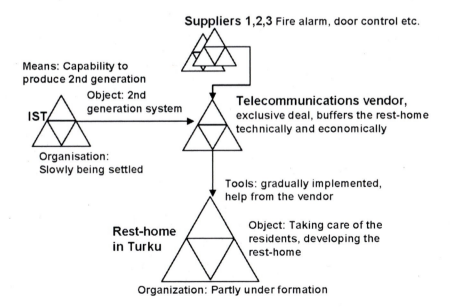

Figure 6.6 The network of activity systems around the rest home in the city of Turku. The telecommunications vendor buffered the rest home technically and economically, while Vivago Ltd. and the rest home itself could also devote sufficient resources to the implementation.

was expected by all parties that future sales would follow in the region if the Turku site proved successful.

In the rest home, the implementation and development of work procedures were discussed and customized on a weekly basis in a staff meeting, and, in addition, the process was assigned as the special responsibility of one technically more competent nurse.[18] As at the Espoo site, Turku initially strictly followed the producer's instructions and reacted to all alarms the system generated, and they also experienced this as burdening. But in Turku modification of the system began as soon as the facility had some experience of how it worked. For instance, the personnel ceased to react personally to "off/on the wrist" notices and extended the time by which the automated function in the system informed them about this. They also profiled the monitoring for those elderly who experienced inconvenient numbers of false alarms.[19] At the same time, the staff instructed the residents, who gradually learned how to wear and clean the device and what not to do with it, which reduced the number of false alarms and the inconvenience for the users.[20]

The better position of Vivago Ltd. and the alliance with the vendor seemed to have helped the Turku site in customizing the system for its needs. The people on the Turku site expressed that they truly benefited from the three occasions on which the Vivago Ltd. people came to upgrade the control software, to replace malfunctioning devices, to gather feedback about the system, and to give additional information about it. Around three months after the implementation, both residents and staff regarded the system as running fairly smoothly, even though the company had not met all their key requests for improvement.[21]

Comparing the Implementations

Some of the differences in these two cases may be attributed to the quite formidable changes that happened in the Vivago-Wristcare system between 2000 and 2001, but there seems to be more than that involved. The difficulties in Espoo and the success in Turku do not seem to be derived from any one part of the network; they were, rather, the sum of the interactions between the actors that further affected one another.

The examples point to the importance of the collective resources within the activity: people mediating each other's actions (other residents, other nurses, and a manager) and the practices that had been created to deal with technologies in general and the implementation of new systems in particular.[22] In Espoo, there were multiple technologies that needed to be implemented at the same time, while the personnel had no clear responsibilities or a strategy for dealing with the creation of appropriate procedures and the unexpected shortcomings of the technologies. In Turku, a more positive spiral was formed, since the personnel could focus more on the implementation of this particular technology. This enabled them to give clear and understandable instructions to residents, whose learning to wear the device turned out to be a major issue in reducing the drawbacks of the system. The site in Turku also had more previous experience with implementing new technology and thus may have been better prepared for the nature and demands of the implementation.

Second, these cases underscore the importance of appropriation intermediaries in implementing new ICT. While the Espoo site was left to grapple with the chaos generated by many partially working technologies, Turku was significantly helped by its vendor. The vendor helped to configure the technical system at the site in a specific way and to integrate it with other technologies, such as cell phones; helped to fix the bugs that ensued and apply the needed work-arounds; acted as a ready source of help and information about the system; and, finally, added power to request improvements from the supplier company, Vivago Ltd. Other important intermediary roles were that of the head nurse appointed at the Turku site and those played by the rest-home managers. The latter organized the deals; the relationship to vendors, various supplier companies, and funding bodies; and how the implementation process was handled inside their organization.

EVOLVING IMPACT: FROM INDUCED TRANSFORMATION TO DOMESTICATION TO CO-INFLUENCES

We shall now extend the time frame in analyzing technology adoption to examine how the anticipated and realized impacts of technology change in its early biography. At the market launch in 1997, Vivago-Wristcare's design prefigurations could have been seen as technologists imposing new and potentially foreign procedures and values on elderly care. Key design features such as introducing continuous monitoring of relatively healthy residents, allowing (and demanding) home-care workers to shift from reactive measures to proactive control of the residents' physical condition, and seeking cost savings through technically supported extramural care all appear to induce transformation of elderly care and living from the outside.

However, such a strong determining power of technology did not appear in the first years following Vivago-Wristcare's market launch. The technology of replacement and transformation was turned into a supporting tool within the preexisting models for services and institutions. Vivago mostly added a layer of technically mediated monitoring of residents and made some procedures, such as care rounds, more flexible. It neither replaced workforce nor diminished the personal care for residents in any of the four sites studied during 2000–2001. When writing the initial report on the case in 2002, we concluded that "in summary, the benefits and savings gained by using Vivago-Wristcare had to do more with developing care-practices and quality of service and less with any direct savings in staffing."

Indeed, the notion of domestication (Sorensen 2002; Pantzar 1996; Berger et al. 2006) appears well suited to characterizing the installations in 2000 and 2001 (two and three years from initial market launch) wherein it was mostly the technology that was adjusted in various ways to diminish nuisance to extant work practices, even though these evolved somewhat too. The wild and alien technology and its developers became tamed by the order of elderly living and care.

The follow-up studies we conducted in 2006–2007 at a new residential institution for the elderly (Gävert 2008) and at the producer company in 2009, however, reveal how the impact of the technology changed as more years passed. This facility was architecturally designed to make elderly living more comfortable and convenient and prided itself in several new kinds of housing and technological solutions. Within this context, some of the residents referred to Vivago as the "14th nurse." It really was. The rest home had fewer personnel, and with this staffing relying on care rounds for security was seen as too risky and burdensome. This housing facility had given up the traditional care-round procedure all together and relied intensively on the Vivago system for monitoring and detecting the condition of the residents. It also followed categorically the protocol of checking, by visit or calling, all manual and automatic alarms and had instructed the residents to wear the devices all the time (hence no longer conducting two of the major refigurations to the use of the system by earlier users).

There are several reasons for this change in the potential impact of the technology from an add-on back to a work- and procedure-replacing one. Follow-up interviews at the company revealed that it had indeed reverted back to more stringent instructions on how to operate the system as well as returned to emphasizing cost savings in the marketing, through staffing as well as through preventive care measures. This was partly made possible through diminishing problems with monitoring (for more on these points, see Chapter 7, this volume), and it was partly owing to the fact that Vivago Ltd. had to justify the higher price of their technology in comparison to push-button safety phones.[23]

Just as importantly, "technology as nurse" did not concern all elderly-care facilities; however, in this particular configuration the new type of security technology providing for proactive care measures and new visions of private, high-quality elderly-care facilities interanimated each other. As Gävert (2008) observes in her study, in terms of "domestication" it became rather unclear what was home and what was the wild to be domesticated. An important aspect of rest-home life is how residents experienced a disjunction with their previous lifestyle. Their new homes at the institution carried some elements from their decades of past life but at the same time were entirely new in many other respects, such as size, architecture, location, and neighbors, as well as their own weakened physical or mental abilities (or social setting) that had led the residents to move from their homes into residential housing.

The same applied to nurses and home-care workers who entered the new institution—with new kinds of care arrangements, new kind of instructions for charging for tasks done for the residents, and a new (somewhat more healthy) clientele—which presented a disjunction with some of the work practices in their previous workplaces. The setting and rules of the institution domesticated its inhabitants while the residents often did plenty to adapt their typically far smaller apartments to the image of the "real home" of their past life. Within this broader configuration, the Vivago-Wristcare technology did lead to new routines in wearing, storing, cleaning, and discussing well-being between residents and nurses, yet when it produced awkward and cumbersome situations it was worked around and its functioning adjusted in some of the ways we observed in 2000. Hence, rather than a straightforward "home" domesticating all else, a many-way adaptation between new setting, new work actions, homemaking practices, and new security technology took place. The "impact" of Vivago-Wristcare hence appears squarely dependent on the kinds of configurations within which it is deployed as well as on the manner in which it is deployed there.

CHAPTER DISCUSSION

Biography of Technology

It is not news that the technology, its uses, and its "impact" evolve over time. The telephone (Fischer 1992), the private car (Kline and Pinch 1996; Hoogma et al. 2002), organizational software packages (Pollock and Williams 2008; McLaughlin et al. 1999), and many other technologies show the intended, unintended, and second- and third-order consequences of technological systems coming into being (Fischer 1992; Rip et al. 1995). The question is rather *how* this happens during the early years of development and use of new technology. In Chapter 7 of this volume, we shall focus on the effects of learning between developers and users as one such mechanism, while this chapter elaborated on how the impact of technology depended on the changing configurations within which it was made useful and sellable. Initially, users domesticated the technology by creating various versions of the technology in practice and effectively turning it into an add-on to their work practice, but later, as part of a new type of elderly-care facility, the technology turned again into a work-replacing one. Such shifts in the impact of technologies have importance for health technology assessment; assessing the impact of given equipment depends on assessing the configurations and procedures wherein it is deployed, as well as the timing of the assessment in the biographies of the generic product and the biographies of the particular installations examined.

Design–Use Relations

People such as the elderly and their caregivers have received little attention in discourses related to the shaping of new technology. A closer look at their engagement with technology reveals that they can be active and inventive. The extent and importance of the elderly users' shaping, however, only become fully visible when findings from their work-arounds, minor improvements, complaints, redefinitions, symbolic uses, and interpersonal arrangements are examined as parts of different versions of technology-in-practice within their personal and life projects. Resources and efforts are needed to go into implementing, adjusting, and maintaining the technology to gain value from it. This "nurturing of technology" took place within personal and group projects that predated a given piece of equipment, and was further nested within activity systems, more encompassing and durable collective formations.

Agency, or the Constitution of Developer, User, and Technology at This Moment of Biography

If we analyzed the potential "readings" of the technical artifacts in, for instance, the first- and second-generation Vivago-Wristcare system in affinity with how many researchers analyze literature, images, and media (content) in cultural studies, we would gain a wealth of compiled representations and possible actor positions. Certainly (many of) these associations would be present in how its users perceive the technology and how it affects its users. It is significant, however, that the actual enactments and associations spelled out in the interviews and observations were far fewer. At that, many of these, particularly those related to interpersonal usages of the system, were such that as analysts we certainly would not have expected them. The trope of inferring readings from media may work better in the cases of cultural artifacts that have only highly defined coding literally resembling text.

The analysis of how technology was enacted here takes seriously that technology, as technology, does not exist in some independent sphere of its own. It is always part of practices, be these those of developers, regulators, purchasers, users, managers, museum curators, or garbage workers (Latour 1993; Engeström and Blackler 2005). Reducing technology to text that is then read by the analyst establishes a curious "commonality act," or put more bluntly, it examines cultural artifacts within the analysts' practice. For this to have any value presumes a reliable continuity from the analyst's reading to other interpreters and their interpretation process, and, if the analysis is making assertions about the design of the device, also to its developers and development process, without studying whether, let alone how, such commonalities exist outside the assumptions of the analyst. Naturally, really studying the actual development and use practices in detail can be practically overwhelming, as in, for instance, studies of mass media: movie production, analysis of the given film, its varying receptions, *et cetera*. However, the studies of Pollock and Williams (2008) on the biography of enterprise-wide software packages manages to do much of this with technology, which is arguably much more complex than a given mass media production. From their experience, these authors also argue that the question is really mostly about preference: do researchers settle in purposefully simplistic research designs or engage in rather more complex and time-consuming studies?

Attending both uses and development of the same technology highlights the importance of attending to the actual environments, practices, and enactments of users (as well as those of its developers). Another way of putting all this is that we hold a strong reservation towards the ecological validity of studies that resort to exploring and evaluating technology use on the analyst's desk, in laboratory settings, or at any given individual site, for this detaches the analysis from the resources, constraints, and rationales that play a key role in how people actually enact technology.

Learning

The ability of the elders and nurses to create the range of enactments they did was not a given. Learning efforts related to six aspects of being able to use technology in daily work and life in rest homes can be discerned.

1. Learning the instructions and how to put them in action, often involving producers' training sessions and more informal learning efforts. This included learning what kind of immediate changes and arrangements had to be created for operating the system and ascertaining its reliability.
2. Learning how to intertwine the system in daily work and life. For instance, at first, all sites reacted to all alarms by applying a categorical check-in visit, but most soon developed more differentiated responses that better fit the rhythm of the nurses' work. The implementation of the system also transformed some existing procedures, such as added flexibility to the regular "care rounds" nurses did among the residents mostly just to see that all was all right.
3. Learning what to do in typical cases of the system causing trouble or devices not working—for instance, learning how to test them against the most common problems.
4. Learning how to work around the system more permanently—for instance, writing down mnemonics on pieces of paper to remember what the codes for various alarms mean and how to best react to them or rigging the SW such that alarms would not come through at night from residents who demanded that they not be woken up.

5. Sharing insights and ways of dealing with technology with other nurses and residents—in other words, spreading and consolidating preferred ways of working with the system.

6. Learning how to involve and coordinate external actors such as maintenance people and company designers to solve problems that users themselves could not fix.

Although this is by no means a conclusive observation, some of these six aspects formed a rough sequence in the learning: there was a move from more formal instruction and compliant usages into more informal handling and learning the system and then into stabilizing these into recorded procedures that were shared both inside and outside the organization. These observations continue the theme of the emergence and anticipation of user needs we began in Chapter 4 of this volume. Only after this learning process and the (re)stabilization of routines that follow the implementation period can we truly say the users had genuine needs for Vivago—if taken away, it would have disrupted the way many of them organized their lives.

7 The Post-Launch Change
Learning and Reconfiguring

The central argument in this book is that usable and useful technology, particularly health technology, results from a markedly long interchange between suppliers, users, regulators, and various intermediary actors. In the previous chapter, we focused on the gradual construction of usages, usability, and utility of the Vivago-Wristcare technology by its adopter organizations. In Chapter 5, we examined how its developers handled some of the user requests in the frenzy of design interaction. We will now expand the analytical time frame to draw out connections between these two loci and foci of shaping the technology and give a more encompassing portrait of the six years (1998–2003) after the market launch of Vivago-Wristcare. The particular focus is on interactions and learning between the producer company, Vivago Ltd., and elderly-care organizations, since these had a significant impact on the ongoing development, usages, and "diffusion" of this technology.

The analysis taken on here stands in marked opposition to mainstream diffusion research yet offers new insight for the research on learning about post-market-launch improvements of new technology. Mainstream diffusion research has been most concerned with how "potential users become informed about the availability of new technology and are persuaded to adopt, through communication with prior users" (Attewell 1992, 2). In adopter studies, early and late adopters have been compared in regards to factors such as firm size (Davies 1979), perceived advantage to be gained from technology (von Hippel 1988), presence of innovation champions (Rothwell and Zegweld 1985), and various organizational and environmental attributes (Attewell 1992). In studies on macro-diffusion, the spread of innovation has been most prominently examined in terms of a gravity model of spatial spread, flowing from early adopter sites to later adopters and an S-shaped curve in the extent of adoption over time (Rogers 1995).

Yet diffusion is dependent not only on the signaling and learning about the availability and potential of the new technology but also on the learning required to explore and realize the potentials of the technology. Innovation typically results from accretion of multiple, often hundreds of, small improvements; emergence of associated technologies and services; and organizational redesign, which significantly enhance its value for the adopters (Rosenberg 1979; David 1990; Gardiner and Rothwell 1985).

The most examined learning process for post-launch improvements is "learning-by-doing," used to explain why the cost of manufactured goods tends to decline significantly due to the accumulation of skill in producing them (Wright 1936; Arrow 1962). Similar improvements and cost reductions have been suggested to result from "learning-by-using" capital goods: the users' increasing skill and/or understanding in using the product, leading to, for instance, less maintenance and new uses. The redesign of products due to feedback from users' problems and requests and locally made modifications by the users themselves lead to "embodied" learning (Rosenberg 1982). It is now regarded as more a rule than an exception that users of new technology modify it to better suit their work, culture, and priorities (von Hippel 1988; Suchman et al. 1999; Williams et al. 2005). Correspondingly, the importance of the flow of user-identified problems and solutions to the iteratively improving design have been emphasized (Freeman 1979; Gardiner and Rothwell 1985).

However, many studies have drawn attention to the lack of such interaction in actual corporate environments and the impediments to realizing it (Leonard 1995; Miettinen et al. 2003; Williams et al. 2005). For instance, the upsurge of user-centered design since the early 1990s (Greenbaum and Kyng 1991; Nielsen 1993; Preece et al. 2002) created initiatives to study designer–user collaboration in industry. In well over 30 in-depth case studies, direct collaboration, use of user-centered-design methods, or even efficient channeling of user problems and inventions to improvements in products happened on a more modest scale and in a more *ad hoc* fashion than ever expected by the researchers or by the managers of the firms studied (Williams et al. 2005; Oudshoorn et al. 2004; Miettinen et al. 2003; Hasu et al. 2004). On the other hand, a study on mediation between developers and users of a large social media site surfaced 23 distinct modes of engagement between them in less than a 10-year span (Johnson 2010).

These findings resonate with the assessment made by Eric von Hippel and Marcia Tyre:

> Although the economic significance of learning by doing and using has been made clear, the process by which these gains are achieved is still quite unclear. That is, we do not know the micro-level mechanisms by which learning by doing is actually done. (1995, 1)

Consequently, von Hippel and Tyre explored how learning-by-doing is actually tied to doing (von Hippel and Tyre 1995) and how the situatedness or "stickiness" of knowledge of designers and users affects diagnosing, answering to, and collaborating around solving problems in use (Tyre and von Hippel 1997; von Hippel 1994). This chapter seeks to add to this research on micro-level mechanisms of learning-by-using and comes to identify several learning dynamics that make up a more aggregate "learning-by-using" and provides an account of some of their preconditions and interrelations. To lay the ground for this discussion, we first outline a six-year post-launch improvement and interaction process, structured in three two-year phases that also roughly correspond to major changes in the product and interactions between designers and users.

CYCLES OF RECONFIGURATIONS: VIVAGO-WRISTCARE IN THE PLANS OF DESIGNERS AND IN THE HANDS OF ITS EARLIEST USERS, 1997–1999

As described in Chapter 3 of this volume, early Wristcare was, most importantly, based on its designers' visions and experience in the practices related to the technical and economic aspects of the technology. The pre-market-launch descriptions of Vivago-Wristcare emphasized rapid growth, internationalization, and a focus on core technical development. A conscious decision was made to avoid any product variation or drift into development of the infrastructure or services and to stay focused on recovering the research and development costs.[1] The device was to be made as automatic as possible and foolproof in its functions to suit all possible end users, even those suffering from dementia. Its correct use was to be further ascertained through short instructions on how to wear, remove, and store it.[2] As the founder of the company reflects:

> Any kind of programming to be done by the end user or home-care workers has traditionally been a problem in the safety devices. Whatever the case, it requires some technical know-how, and the things that can then be programmed are so childish and simple that we decided to make the device so that all—well, almost all—of its features can be programmed remotely.[3]

As noted in Chapter 4 of this volume, in the pilots and other early uses of the technology, the designers' primary objective was to validate the technology and find and fix the "bugs" inevitable in any hardware and software. The testing was to quickly pave the way to high-production volumes. But the outcome of the early pilots was ambiguous for the company: while users and partner organizations regarded the concept mostly in positive terms and the overall technical idea seemed to work by and large, there were an intolerable number of false alarms. The end users also turned out to be in much weaker physical shape than ever expected by the designers. The fluctuations in their conditions were harder to monitor and also differed from the assumptions developers had when building Vivago-Wristcare's monitoring algorithms. The technology was received most enthusiastically by rest homes and sheltered housing, whereas there was a fairly poor reception in the home-use sector, which was the market originally targeted. The home-use-sector sales remained low and, despite the developer company's efforts, began to rise only after six years (in 2003). These unexpected developments had further ramifications, as nurses and home-care workers then experienced problems in dealing with the various alarm signals the device generated:

> It gave too many of those "acute alarms," and we had to call in [the residents] all the time . . . when there was a rush, it was burdensome to attend such nonsense [checking in on acute automatic alarms, very few of which were for real].[4]

It also turned out that the kind of use presumed by the design was hard to enforce on the end users, who continued to "misuse" the device in various ways, creating problems for its automated functions. As elaborated in detail in Chapter 6 of this volume, users then generated an increasing number of work-arounds and site-specific procedures. Developers responded by making small, often site-specific, changes to meet the various new requirements. Determining the causes of problems often took considerable effort from the designers. As reflected by a designer:

> The original single home device turned out to be the most difficult to realize: if the alarm is for real, the device and help should respond quickly, but, then again, you don't want to send in an ambulance for nothing. And then you don't have a clear focus on what you are monitoring the person for; you know, different people have very different symptoms and fluctuations in health, different wrists, and daily rhythms. It's a lot easier if you know that the person suffers from, say, dementia or epilepsy, so the device could just watch the signs for those.[5]

Indeed, developers' categorizations of problems ranged from "bizarre" actions of the users (such as insulating the wrist unit with cotton) to slight alterations in the way the devices were worn, from incorrect technical assembly on a user site to bugs in the devices or transmitters or the unfit design of some part of the system and, finally, to deficiencies in product design. Even though this was the first time the developers faced the actual environments of use and the real end users, they preferred looking at the technical system directly, since most problems were simply technical bugs and users were mostly unable to provide accurate technical information about the problems (Tyre and von Hippel 1997). Any site visit was seen as a distraction from the designers' and marketing representatives' "real work," of which there was plenty in a start-up seeking rapid growth. This discouraged wider or more systematic inquiry into the needs to change the system. Users, in turn, expected the designers to fix the system so it would work in the way the users had understood it should.[6] Their involvement with the redesign of the product was restricted to complaints and occasional accounts of what had happened.

However, this cast of roles and responsibilities was not satisfactory for either party in the long run. A technician involved in implementing and maintaining the system reflected on the interaction around an early 1999 installation:

> The firm would benefit from placing emphasis on gathering extensive and systematic information about new kinds of sites with the staff, before building up the system. Now there were many difficulties in the Savitaipale health care center where the system was implemented in a bed ward. The company did not have much understanding about hospital environments, and the health care center sent unclear requests—for instance, parameters that could be interpreted in many ways. We got the system running only after I stepped in between the two and started to gather what is really needed here.[7]

Whatever interaction did occur was partly undermined by how the early sites were organized. The company could not afford to hold multiple free pilot trials, and most early user sites were, in fact, paying customers even if called "pilots." The tension was further aggravated by the sales talk that had generated unwarranted assumptions about the device. As a result, not only were the problems that occurred with devices setbacks for the company's technical project, but they also strained its customer relationships.

The mode of interaction and improvement of technology in this period is best characterized as *cycles of reconfiguring technology*. Users made their own alterations and filed some of their suggestions, complaints, and problem reports with developers. The developer company responded by creating both site-specific and more generic minor improvements yet did not consult users in any systematic way about these. Until late 1999, there had been several minor redesigns in the wrist device and transmitter unit, and a number of iterations of the software for handling the alarms. A new product variant was created for sheltered housing. The manual also grew from seven to 25 pages, with more illustrations and instructions. These additions had two primary goals: to avoid problems that had occurred in the actual use of the device and to make the monitoring more reliable as a response to the doubts expressed by representatives of the medical community and some user organizations.

COORDINATED IMPROVEMENT OF TECHNOLOGY:
THE SEARCH FOR COLLABORATION
AND MUTUAL BENEFIT, 1999–2002

In parallel with the early alterations, there was some rapprochement between developers and users. Gradually, developers started paying attention to people and to the spatial organization of the sheltered housing: its architecture, technological infrastructure, and social conduct. The users, in turn, entered the world of modern ICT in general—for example, learning to operate PCs and electronic mail (which were new to many), and how ICT people worked and approached problems.[8] Further rapprochement in designer–user relations took place during the design process of the second-generation Vivago-Wristcare, 2000–2001. Particularly in the redesign of its alarm reception "control software," the company started to actively seek design suggestions from its users instead of just passively waiting for problem reports.[9] Alongside a formal long-standing pilot test at one site, extended collaborations followed on six other sites to find any bugs or redesign suggestions. The company's new R&D manager reflected on one of these sites as follows:

> The best thing that came in this spring was the new rest home across the street, where they have 15 elderly ladies, and we can change our devices whenever we want. Of course, we should have had a place like this two years ago. People in this rest home are prepared for us to go and figure out the results together with them, and then tune our software further. This has shown itself to be indispensable. You know, we don't bring in any garbage but the best stuff we have available, but these are still test devices. . . . For us this reveals how the device works in real life, how it gathers dirt, how it wears on the arm, how they wear them, and what has actually happened [physiologically and behaviorally] when our device has sent a signal about, for instance, unusual passiveness.[10]

While this kind of beta-testing had been part of the company strategy before, the difference now was that the cycles of iterating the design were short (e.g., testing for a specific software change for a week) and that designers sought out improvements more broadly than merely finding bugs to be fixed. The user organization was explicitly made a development partner instead of being something in between a customer of ready products, a tester for further development, and a testing ground for the best available devices. This arrangement steered clear of the tensions that prevailed on previous user sites, which had expected the smoothly working devices for which they had paid.

The company also concentrated responsibility for all its assembly, maintenance, and customer training in a newly hired person who had many years of experience with safety phones.[11] This resulted in shaking the company's confidence in its assumedly reasonably working feedback mechanisms. In the words of the company founder:

> Since he started, it has come to light that our retailers, partners, and assemblers haven't really provided us with information about how the device works in actual use. Neither do they know how the device should function. . . . Here is the one employment that has most effectively paid for itself.[12]

Moreover, the company invested time and money to reprofile its brand, image, and sales arguments. It also changed its approach to instruction, partly because the new information and design changes allowed it to do so, partly because it had learned the limits of trying to control use through instruction:

> It was emphasized that it [the wrist unit] has to be placed firmly against the skin [to monitor properly]. . . . Now users wear the bracelets so tightly that it feels uncomfortable and they cease to wear it. Now we [have made it technically possible to] loosen it up so that it can be worn normally. It simply did not do the trick to write in huge letters that you have to wear it so it does not move around.[13]

The variety of alarm messages was dramatically cut from the peak of 50 (of which users actively responded to only seven and worked around the rest).[14] In doing so, the most ambitious quick-reaction alarms were removed from the device to reduce false alarms. The control software allowed users to time, route, enable/disable, and modify alarms specifically for each site and end user. The SW interface was redesigned to enable users to make these changes themselves. This was vital, because virtually every user site had different layouts and work routines. Also, physical differences and preferences of the elderly required local alterations to the system. The previous design logic (which emphasized fool-proofing and the stand-alone character of products) had great difficulties in accommodating such a scope of requirements and demanded designer intervention in most cases.

The tailoring continued in the form of creating accessories for different groups of the disabled (more sensitive alarm buttons, one-hand buttons, etc.) and by making the system better accommodate adjoining products, such as cell phones and the organization-specific portable phones via which nurses preferred to receive the alarms. Alarm messaging, through both text and talk, was further improved. The combined effect of these actions was appreciated by the users, not only in terms of engaging in collaboration but also in regard to evaluations of the devices, as voiced by a rest-home nurse in 2001:

It is ideal how I can tailor this system for each of my residents just by clicking buttons. This was absolutely a pain in the old version. We can now also change the codes by ourselves, which means, for instance, that I can do all the needed testing here [in the office] and don't have to involve the resident in it.[15]

The period from 1999 to roughly 2001 was characterized by intentional and active engagement between developers and several user partners in improving the technological system and its usages. It would, however, be an exaggeration to call this co-design, for no users were directly involved in final design decisions, nor did they have final say or ownership over how the features of the generic system came out. Yet it clearly is *coordinated improvement of technology* between developers and users. More theoretically speaking, these interactions come close to *innofusion*—a type of innovation context (see Chapter 1, this volume) where the development of technology takes the form of drawn-out give-and-take between developers and users (Fleck 1993b; Williams et al. 2005).

DISHARMONIOUS COORDINATION: TENSIONS BETWEEN USER-COLLABORATION AND COST-EFFICIENCY, 2001–2003

As a researcher following the project, I expected that the mutually beneficial collaboration between the designers and users of Vivago would have further intensified after 2001, following the strategic management literature (Victor and Boynton 1998; Prahalad and Ramaswamy 2004; Normann and Ramirez 1994). This turned out not to be the case. The resources of the small company were stretched in many directions, even as it doubled in size to nearly 20 people. The realities of the R&D department were described by one of the designers as follows:

Usually what happens is that we need some feature or version to do business. And usually it appears that we actually need the thing now, or, if it is a problem [in existing features], then we are already late when we begin to investigate it . . . this means the nature of the job is kind of firefighting . . . and this means that the [more long-term] projects have to be handled when there is time, and there is little hope of keeping the deadlines.[16]

After 2000, the newly appointed management sought to package product offerings and several product versions available. Stricter control was imposed over the R&D department to prevent work on any but the most vital projects. Similarly, marketing and sales personnel were to refrain from promising anything that would require further product development. These concerns reinstated the business imperatives that were spelled out prior to the 1997 market launch:

> In terms of the economics of production, the dream would be to have one device that would have all the functions. And then we would just open or close some features with software. Even though we now have only one gray bracelet, it is quite a nuisance with all its variations. What has happened is that we have promised or said that we can do such and such, and the customer has then bought it, and then we have made a customization for that particular customer, and that ties up our resources . . . and when you look at it as a whole, it ends up being no good. That particular deal may be sweet, but it disturbs everything else . . . and if we aim at hundreds of thousands of devices, the system just can't be this complex. Just the work that goes into selling and assembling now is too much.[17]

These business imperatives went against gradual improvement by working with customers. User-collaboration was actively practiced until late 2001, when major use sites of the then main product, the rest-home system, expressed few new requirements and previously unknown problems.[18]

In late 2001, a resolution of the tension between use and standardization was sought through a reconceptualization of the product and division of labor between the producer company and other actors. The producer defined its responsibility in technical terms only, as a matter of correlation between the specification provided and the actual behavior of its products. It is noteworthy that the details of this correlation took two years of on-site testing to establish and owed much to the "activity curve," which was itself one of the results of interactions with users. This feature—showing a visual graph of the client's overall movement and activeness on the monitoring PC—was first created by the company in 1998 as a showpiece illustration. However, nurses found that it helped in deciding whether or not to react to alarm messages because it provided information on how users' states had developed. Nurses further drew implications that had never occurred to designers, such as inferring the effects of sleep medication, customizing their care rounds so as not to awaken the residents, etc.[19] These findings led the company to seek collaboration with sleep researchers, which in turn, led to studies where the activity curve was used for comparisons with gold standard medical devices in sleep research. This provided the company with urgently needed scientific evidence about the adequacy of its measurement, and, as mentioned, a point of comparison in regard to whether individual devices worked appropriately.

The limiting of company responsibility only to technical functioning was balanced by forming alliances and encouraging user organizations to explore ways to apply the technology. This included the medical community in the form of sleep research, convalescent care, and use in bed wards, as well as elderly care in the form of various end user organizations.

These partners were given information and consulted on how to utilize the devices. This separation of product design from the application design put an end to the site-specific reconfigurations of Vivago:

> We emphasize that this is the product, this is what is now tested . . . we file the information, but we don't redesign on the basis of any singular wishes, only integrate our system into a local protocol. This is no longer a product development project but a commercial product . . . there is no more fine-tuning to be done in this platform, but it will come with the next platform.[20]

The fundamental aim was to separate mass production from the iteration and knowledge-gathering. The tensions in the company's agenda in reconciling gradual improvement and mass production draw attention to the cycles and timing of different aims in R&D. Iterating the product in co-coordinated partnerships with customers would take place when problems, lucrative new markets or regions, or new user practice required substantial changes in the product or the way it was to be deployed in use. When this was not the case, the product and commercial offering would be kept as standard as possible.

CLARIFYING THE CHANGES IN DESIGN, INTERACTION, AND LEARNING

Let us now revisit this post-launch development from the perspective of post-launch learning. Innovation processes, if anything, are processes of continuous learning and accumulation of expertise. At the same time, they evade attempts to think of learning in terms of the ability to produce more adequate reactions under similar conditions, which has been customary in laboratory settings (Bateson 2000). The context changes continuously, and the relevant knowledge shifts as the construction of technology progresses. Yet blind trials do not allow for the building of a complex technical system requiring high reproducibility, standardization, and the accumulation of results. The term "learning dynamics" is here used as shorthand for the various acts of searching, evaluating, and reconsidering the technology, oriented towards enhancing it. These processes denote (a) what typically gets reported as "learning": learning within given arrangements (in the discussion that follows, dynamics 1, 2, and 5); (b) preconditions for learning (dynamics 3, 4, and 6); and (c) managing of conflicting learning goals (dynamic 7). The following discussion is restricted to learning dynamics related to the development–use relation of technology.

The multifaceted and detailed data gathered in the case study proved vital in discerning the dynamics. Dynamics 1, 2, and 7 became visible during the field observations of design meetings and the product's usage. They were further confirmed through interviews. Dynamics 3–6 only became visible because of the longitudinal scope of the study: At the time of my entry, the changes in products and procedures so far were noted and then updated mappings were made throughout the study. The changes were first examined in each period with regard to six dimensions: the constitution of the product, designers' and users' orientation towards the product, the physical terrain of interaction, the temporal extent of interactions, the nature of contacts and their means, and contractual and normative assumptions of relationships. Data were then revisited for behaviors that had directly led to or acted as catalysts for these changes. In doing this analysis, it was vital to compare interview statements with my field notes on actual behaviors and to support inferences with the remaining documents, pictures, artifacts, etc. The discussion that follows moves from the market launch onwards to the present day, highlighting the most important learning dynamics in chronological order.

First Dynamic of Learning: Learning About Technical Problems in the Hardware and Software in Field Use.

The first dynamic of learning was that "bugs" and other technical shortcomings became visible and diagnosable after the device was implemented in its actual contexts of use, thus paralleling the findings of von Hippel and Tyre (1995). Many such shortcomings would have arguably been hard to prevent in the laboratory with simulations or other means of predicting field problems (von Hippel and Tyre 1995, 10–11). As in the cases examined by Tyre and von Hippel (1997), here also the diagnosing of problems involved engineers going to the field site to look at the problem personally, then moving the problem back to the laboratory, going back to the field site, *et cetera*.

Second Dynamic of Learning: Users' Learning How to Operate the Technology and Make it Work in Practice.

There was a rough sequence of learning efforts related to the use of technology in the daily work and life of rest-home nurses and residents (see Chapter 6 of this volume for more detail): (a) Learning the instructions and how to put them in action, often involving producers' training sessions and more informal learning efforts; (b) learning how to intertwine the system in daily work and life; (c) learning what to do in typical cases of the system causing trouble or devices not working; (d) learning how to work around the system more permanently; (e) sharing insights and ways of dealing with technology with other nurses and residents—in other words, spreading and consolidating preferred ways of working with the system; (f) learning how to involve and coordinate external actors such as alarm centers, maintenance personnel, and company designers to solve problems that users themselves could not fix. This last point is discussed further in the following, under the fourth dynamic.

Third Dynamic of Learning: Destabilization of and Unlearning the Existing Assumptions About the Product and its Use.

The third dynamic of learning has to do with prerequisites for further learning. While the definitions for learning are (perhaps forever) subject to debate, most researchers agree that learning is about adaptive change (Bateson 2000) and, at that, adaptive change that follows from improved knowledge and understanding (Fiol and Lyles 1985). The question of what is adaptive is far from trivial in innovations that take place in multiple overlapping contexts that set conflicting priorities for the project (Van de Ven et al. 1999). The designers working with the initial "bug-fixing orientation" presumed that only deviations from the expected technical performance were relevant. This had a very tangible rationale: an orientation to get quickly back to work from customer sites was vital for company profits and growth through new design projects, both crucial for the survival of the start-up. The third dynamic of learning visible in the case is designers' gradual and often collective questioning of how they diagnosed problems: what aspects of the physical form of the product needed changes, the purpose of designers' relationship to users, and the roles set for designers and users in gathering information about problems.

Fourth Dynamic of Learning: Opening New Cognitive Trails in the Multi-organizational Terrain.

The questioning did not take place in a vacuum, nor did it automatically lead to improved actions. Along with it, a gradual improvement in designers' orientation took place. At the market launch, the company entered terrain that was largely unknown to it. Who was to use the device? How could one reach them? Who were the relevant actors, and how one could deal and communicate with them? Nurses and the elderly alike were unsure of how to deal with this kind of high-tech device and how to relate to its designers. Along with the mundane operations of fixing bugs, assembly, training, etc., the parties gradually learned more about the constraints and possibilities of this technology in relation to rest homes, alarm centers, government agencies, vendors, and other players on the multi-organizational terrain. At first, this learning did not take the form of focused learning efforts and much of the learning remained "subterranean." It did not result in many visible changes but laid the ground for later advances (Engeström et al. 2003; Engeström 2001b). Together, learning the third and fourth dynamics contributed to expansion in what the designers paid attention to and how deeply they saw that user requests should affect the form and functioning of the device.

Fifth Dynamic of Learning: Forming Networks of Collaboration and Learning in Them.

Beginning in late 1999, the relationships formed in the interaction were gradually transformed into more formal and stabilized network relations, aimed at improving the product system. This transformation required changes in virtually all aspects of designer–user relations: marketing, training, field visits, way of interacting, processing of information in the company, *et cetera*. These initiatives were positively responded to by user organizations. The earlier means and tools for collaboration—error logs, conversations, collecting work-arounds, instructions, and assigning main users as links to each site—came to be used more systematically.

Sixth Dynamic of Learning: The Artifact as an Expanding Boundary Object.

The interaction and learning were significantly dependent on the means and tools available. The form and functioning of Vivago-Wristcare itself was perhaps the most important mediating means between designers and users. Star has examined how partially shared objects can be effective in augmenting interaction and collaboration between social worlds. Such boundary objects can take on robust meanings that allow interaction between social worlds, while they remain able to take on more specific meanings in individual site use (Star and Griesemer 1989; Star 1989b). The Vivago-Wristcare case draws attention to the trajectory of change related to a boundary object: an increase in the shared meaning and terrain related to the artifact during the process. In the beginning, the boundary between designers and users followed the outer shell of the product. Designers examined their devices as technical configurations while users kept to the functioning of the (back then, literally) black box in their hands and in their daily work. Relatively little was shared in the "same" object. When designers started to pay attention to how the technology was organized in use and users started to make remarks about the functioning of the system, the shared area in the object grew even as it remained marked by disagreements and divergent perceptions.

The expansion of the shared area of the object corresponded with the growth in the temporal extent of interaction (from bugs to partnerships), the contractual relationship (from transactions to reputation and collaboration), and more systematic usage of other mediating artifacts. Just as importantly, there was a change in the constitution of technology. While Vivago-Wristcare prevented most user access during its early development, it grew to encourage local modifications, which also allowed its utilizers to further elaborate their wishes. In terms of learning, attention should, thus, be paid to the expansive potential in boundary objects: they may remain as means to coordinate tangential concerns and the interactions of two social worlds, or they may be made to open gates for deeper collaboration and acquaintance (Bowker and Star 1999; Engeström 1987).[21]

Seventh Dynamic of Learning: Managing the Tension Between Co-coordinated Improvement with Users and the Pressure to Create a Standardized Mass Product.

Along with the challenge to achieve a product that sufficiently fits users' practices and requirements, there remained the economic imperative to achieve high-production volumes of standardized products. Hasu has characterized such tension as "critical transition": the producer has to learn a new way of working in design and customer relations in order to survive, but, at the same time, its original imperatives in competition and organizing the company have not disappeared (Hasu 2001a).

The analyzed period featured two approaches to resolve this tension that are arguably common practice in industry but that posed further learning challenges for the company. Firstly, the company sought to establish cycles between seeking coordinated improvements with users and seeking standardization. Challenges lay in recognizing and anticipating when and how standardization must give way to coordinated development with users, as well as in the extent to which a producer company must customize its stabilized products locally to keep its customers interested in the collaboration.

Secondly, the firm sought to stabilize its material product while it engaged in various collaborations to ensure that users could draw utility out of Vivago-Wristcare. This aim is close to the idea of coproduction of value (value star) in the interactions of the producer, users, and different instances having an interest in the coming configuration (Normann and Ramirez 1994). The challenge remained of which levels of design—ranging from components of the device to use in different practices—the company should engage in and what the most appropriate mechanisms for doing so in each setting are—ranging from further technical development to providing information and money for developing usages for the device.[22]

FAST-FORWARD SIX YEARS

In our follow-up study conducted in 2009, interviewees at the company reflected on what had happened during the last 10 years and what they had learned about their business and clients during this time. Technologically, Vivago had come to include a display and a watch, become waterproof, had rechargeable batteries incorporated, and been made in three different models for different clienteles. As noted in Chapter 6 of this volume, the company had come to emphasize possibilities for labor savings and also returned to providing preventive measures. However, while the initial 1990s ideas for accident prevention relied on automation and automated notices for nurses, these had been removed from the system and the case was now made through detection of sleep patterns—that is, providing nurses with means to diagnose their patients better via findings established through sleep research and through enhanced diagnostic software.[23] This also meant that added value to the system was being sought not from rapid detection but from the ability to scan monitoring data fluently in up to three-week sequences. It is worth reiterating that this solution continued developer–user–sleep researcher complementary inputs to innovation and the added value the system could provide.

Further, these changes owed much to the attempts to justify Vivago's higher price in comparison to other safety phones, which, in turn, was related to the company's understanding of its market and competitive position. The company's CEO was straightforward about the twofold change in European discourses on elderly care.[24] On the one hand, the amount of cost induced by the growing number of elderly had only begun really to sink in during the last couple of years. On the other hand, the discourse on telecare and monitoring technologies for enabling the elderly to live longer at home and for receiving more proactive care measures had been overly optimistic in regard to the actual reception of these technologies in elderly care. The marketing manager specified further the learning related to both of these conditions from the company's perspective:[25]

- Even as there is much talk about elderly care, it remains treated as an expense to be minimized, and this affects what kinds of subsidy and pricing models are in place.
- A push-button safety phone is the cheapest option and meets the criteria that a security aid has been provided for. Moreover, safety phones tend to be given to people only after an accident has happened.
- Since most safety-alarm schemes are subsidized, relatives expect society to cover much of the cost and seldom seek proactive monitoring measures.
- These practices enforce the negative image of the devices as "death watches" among the elderly, because they are used only when things are already in a poor state: "You know, even if one is slightly demented, putting on your wrist something you did not need before is a sign of 'things probably not going too well with me here' . . . which is further aggravated by most of these devices being designed ugly and cheap."
- The call centers equally resent any added information flow from each of their patients. It not only would add work as such but could "double the work from the existing clientele because there is a common

policy of understaffing the centers in proportion to clientele in an expectation (wish) to never hear from half of their subscribers."

- In addition, the company had gradually grown to understand how substantial "variation there is in different nations and regions in how residential and institutional care and markets are organized—while the needs of the elderly and even their caregivers are roughly similar, *how* that caregiving works differs greatly between particular histori-cal development of regulations, subsidies, organizations, extant tech-nologies, fiscal relations, and responsibilities."
- More extensive monitoring is hard to sell for many intermediary orga-nizations, for they, in turn, would face immense difficulties in selling it to their clients when municipal subsidies hardly even cover the costs of cheaper push-button safety alarms.
- Finally, the cost savings business case of Vivago-Wristcare, showing that monitoring of activity, particularly sleep patterns, leads to sav-ings through detecting people who begin to suffer from dementia or other slowly progressing medical conditions that prevent them from expensive hospitalization, tends to be hampered by fiscal divisions. Hospital beds, home care, alarm centers, and rest homes are typically handled by different departments in cities and districts and hence a proposal to achieve savings in one with increased cost in another tends not to fare well except in small municipalities where all these are treated within the same department.

In all, the company staff had come to regard the successful form of the technology and its sales arguments as hinging on the more general evolu-tion of technologies for the elderly. The value and impact of the technology (and ultimately its sales) depended squarely on the future shape of broader configuration of technologies, actors, policies, and stances by intermediary organizations (resellers, health care authorities, alarm centers, *et cetera*). In 2009, the company followed attempts to introduce "residential gateways" and telecare into homes by large telecom and software houses particularly closely. Such initiatives were seen to potentially help in rebranding Viva-go's monitoring functions as well as to provide them with interfaces to widespread standard software platforms for handling the monitoring and alarm information. This would be instrumental in opening a new market alongside the extant safety-phone scene, ease interfacing to third-party sys-tems internationally, and save some work in devising routing and alarm-handling software. At the same time, however, the company was aware that it had hoped for this development to happen already twice before and consequentially had gone to-and-fro between focusing on just the wrist devices and building a more extensive solution.[26] Evolution of configura-tions was known to be tricky to foresee both in the user domain and in technical fields, yet the evolution of business potential and societal impact of the particular technology were tied to it.

CHAPTER DISCUSSION

Biography of Technology

The analysis supports earlier findings on the importance of learning-by-using in the development of new technology. Far from straightforward diffusion, the shape of Vivago-Wristcare evolved significantly during the first years after its market launch. The phase was no minor add-on to the innovation process. It took five years (1992–1997) to develop the technology to the point of launch and another five years (1997–2003) before the system had been redesigned to a point where it could even start to redeem its commercial and societal promise.

Together with Chapters 3 and 6 of this volume, the analysis draws attention to the various venues of shaping involved. The developers and users did not merely respond to each other's actions as in "inscribing" and "de-inscribing" technology (Akrich 1992). They were, in parallel, affected by more pervasive concerns about the right way to conduct business and to develop and maintain technology, and about the appropriate standards of elderly care, etc. (cf. Williams et al. 2005; Konrad 2008). Indeed, most of the interaction and learning between designers and users took place alongside bug fixing, assembling, maintaining, and struggling to operate the technology. The return to some of the original agendas in developing the technology is witness to the interplay of "newly acquired" ways of working, such as developer–user collaboration, and more persisting concerns, which is likely to affect the evolution of this technology also in the future.

Designer–User Relations

While companies routinely channel user feedback into improvements in next-generation products, the analysis shows the difference this has from identifying and capitalizing on the knowledge that is vital for the future of a technology. Gaining high-quality input from users is not self-evident, requires "gardening," and can be easily undermined. Active collaboration with users may be almost inherently fragile in a producer organization: it exists in tension with more established priorities such as cost-efficiency in production, which requires large standard volumes. Tough customers may lead to good designs simply because they keep the active contact with users from disappearing from the company's top priorities (cf. Gardiner and Rothwell 1985).

The analysis provides evidence for three distinct modes of innofusion-type improvement of technology (see Chapter 2, this volume). These are, in chronological order of appearance in the case:

> *Cycles of reconfiguring technology*, where users first reconfigured their existing practices and the new artifact into a technological

configuration; the developers then refigured their initial product anew after discovering that the technology does not function
(and is not being used) according to their wishes; and the users
responded to new changes, etc.

Coordinated improvement of technology, where developers and a
number of user organizations jointly create and improve arrangements within which they can learn how to shape the technology to
their mutual benefit.

Disharmonious coordination, where the producer seeks to gain feedback from users but translates it to the product only with delay and
strictly within the limits of its own interests.

It is noteworthy that all three modes can be effective in improving the
technology, and all are likely to include divergent interests, even conflicts,
between developers and users as well as amongst different users.

Agency and the Constitution of Technology

The six-year span of analysis witnessed significant changes in the Vivago-
Wristcare technology, as a generic offer as well as in terms of the makeup of
its particular installations and their further evolution. It also featured a multiplication and then a decreasing of the different *versions* of the technology
both as a generic offer and as a technological-configuration-in-practice.

Throughout this time, this technology (in its various versions) was the
most important mediating artifact between developers and users. It could
be further characterized as a gradually expanding boundary object mediating the disparate activities of the developers and users (Star and Griesemer
1989). Indeed, this scale of analysis shows how the technology clearly had
a capacity to act—to facilitate, to allow, and to prohibit certain kinds of
exchanges and interactions between people—yet this capacity was nothing
inherent but changed throughout the period and was equally dependent on
the capacities of the other actors it formed a network with (cf. Latour 2005;
Yaneva 2008). An important part of this were the roles played by the various
intermediaries—technicians, assemblers, the resale staff, industrial partners,
pilot test evaluators in other organizations, rest-home managers inside user
organizations, maintenance and user training people inside the developer
company—that configured systems; facilitated usages; and brokered information about the problems, requests, and suggestions for improvement.

Learning

Learning was discussed at length earlier, and hence we make only a brief
further remark about it here. On closer examination, post-launch learning
between designers and users does not appear to be an issue of "flow of user
feedback," as Rosenberg originally conceptualized it. The "flow" required

learning *for* interaction: learning how to create necessary preconditions for beneficial interactions and learning, and questioning and seeking resolution between the available models for thinking and action. The process also consisted of learning *in* interaction—the more commonly recognized processes of acquiring information about issues identified in the product and in regard to users' needs for further design. The learning processes here hark directly back to changing distribution of agency among the actors in the post-launch networks of Vivago-Wristcare.

Part III

Comparisons and Implications

8 Diabetes Databases
Co-Design, Its Evolution, and Power Relations

Written together with Janne Lehenkari

Part II of this book operated on a rather detailed level of presentation to give flesh to what kinds of findings the biography of technologies and practices approach can provide. In the third part of the book, we move on to documenting other innovation processes, and, even though the fieldwork was done with the same level of detail and quantities of data, we now present the material in a more terse manner because of limits of space. Safety-phone systems were developed in a mostly linear innovation context, dominated by the producer company. In this chapter, we proceed to examine the biography of a user-initiated innovation that soon moved into the "evolutionary co-design" innovation context. The particular project we shall focus on is called the ProWellness Diabetes Management Database (PDMS), but, as we exercise the biographies approach, this innovation process is looked at via multiple loci and several time frames of analysis. At the level of "class of technology," Finnish diabetes databases provide over 20 years of material about the biographies of collaboration between users, user-developers, in-house coders, and outside software firms.

Some forms of user–designer collaboration are common in medical technologies. In such branches as the development and manufacturing of medical instruments, most of the new technological innovations are initiated by users. The most likely reason for this is the restricted access and the privacy of medical settings. Designers often do not have sufficient knowledge of the needs of the medical practitioners to develop products for these settings (von Hippel 1988, 2005). As a result, it is common, on one hand, that medical practitioners search for an industrial partner to implement their ideas. On the other hand, technology companies hire medical experts to assist with their product development work. However, the collaborative design in the PDMS project is exceptional in the sense that it involved an extended network of collaboration between a software company and a number of users from various institutions and professions. The collaboration was born out of the complementary interests of the participants and involved no specialized skill, staffing, or research involvement in collaborative design methods. The project thus presents a "participatory design in the wild": intense and long-standing collaboration, yet oblivious of any methods and means developed in participatory design and in user-centered design for these purposes over the decades. The project also interestingly predates the enthusiasm about user-innovation that followed open source, open innovation models and Web 2.0 peer content production after the turn of the millennium. Yet the project was built on many of the same ingredients; combining of complementary expertise, egalitarian organization, rapid quick-and-dirty prototyping, usage of digital media to facilitate collaboration, "smart pricing" models, *et cetera.*

Just as importantly, the project features shifts in the relationships between developers and users, which gives us purchase to examine the evolution of developer–user collaborations—a topic in need of more empirical and theoretical attention. There is work on evolution of user-innovations at the level of social practice and industry development in some of the extreme sports wherein it has played a major role (e.g., Baldwin et al. 2006; Luthje et al. 2005). In regard to shorter time spans, trajectories of collaboration in co-design and open source projects have been documented in, for instance, various transportation and ICT experiments (Hoogma et al. 2002; van Lieshout et al. 2001; Williams et al. 2005).

There are two dominant portrayals of the evolution of co-design. The first is the broadening of collaboration that involves an increasing circle of participants, scope of the project, and societal impact; it is also exemplified by the technology experiment model in SLTI (see Chapter 1, this volume). The development of the technology and building the market go hand in hand: these are continuing activities and there is no clear boundary between technology development and diffusion. There can be progressive broadening of the socio-technical constituency of players involved as barriers between technology developers and users are eroded and the boundaries of the project expanded. The second dominant portrayal is that of co-design that wanes, developers strategically moving out of collaboration, or an experiment that was from the outset geared to merely verify the chosen technology model negotiated early on in the process (van Lieshout et al. 2001; Williams et al. 2005; Hoogma et al. 2002).

Yet the shifts in the biographies of collaboration can factually be significantly more complex, as suggested by the studies on the biographies of enterprise-wide software. Periods of collaboration to achieve site-specific customization are in these studies shown to alternate with "generifying" the software for wider audiences. Collaborative, coordinated, and arm's-length relationships typically coexist with different users simultaneously, and varying kinds of deployments of the systems take place (Cornford and Pollock 2003; Pollock and Williams 2008; Wang 2007). These studies point to an important area for further research. The tensions between generic and particularized configurations were examined in the previous chapter, on Vivago-Wristcare, within a momentary innofusion-type context. The group-work applications for diabetes differ dramatically from organizational software and Vivago-Wristcare's technological configuration in terms of technology characteristics as well as characteristics of their users' practices. Moreover, the mechanisms that shape generification efforts in particular projects merit more inquiry. In this chapter, we focus on how collaborative relations intertwine with power relations and endeavors to reorganize work, research, and administration.

ISSUES OF POWER IN COLLABORATIVE DESIGN

Ever since its outset, participatory design literature has stressed that empowerment may turn out to be nothing else than a rhetorical tool that disguises economic motives and aims at easing users' resistance to new technology (Bjerknes and Bratteteig 1995; cf. Howcroft and Wilson 2003). Participatory design studies have sought countermeasures against the influence and domination of management (or manufacturers) over employees in design work, such as arranging separate design sessions with different stakeholder groups and openly aligning with the workers (Bødker et al. 2004; Ehn 1993).

However, we will argue that the complexity of patterns of power and dominance in health care settings poses challenges for any predefined rule set of empowerment and participation. In the science and technology studies literature, actor-network theory (ANT) has concentrated on the issues of power in technological projects since its origin (Callon and Latour 1981; Law and Callon 1992). ANT stresses how power relations are to be studied in terms of activities that lead to the production of knowledge, artifacts, work practices, and institutional elements. An information system may form an essential component in furthering an actor network some party is attempting to build. For instance, the content and structure of a health care information system can substantially shape the possible actions and work routines in patient reception and make this practice serve their interests better in, say, the way diabetes treatment is organized or in selling more encompassing information systems for this work in the future. Tactics, alliances, strategic development, and conflicts feature prominently in such network-building, implying that using only producer–user or employer–employee dichotomies as the starting points of analysis may conceal the dynamics in the actor network in which positions are more temporary and open to change (Latour 1987; Callon 1992). These dichotomies may also conceal diverse conflicts between actors, such as enactment of power and resistance between different user groups.[1]

We need, however, to look at not only the central network builders, but also pay attention to the margins of technological projects and systems (Star 1991; Gherardi and Nicolini 2006). We are further interested in whether participants' better awareness of power dynamics that appear potentially mutually detrimental could facilitate a collaborative design project. To do so, we turn to the activity-theoretical idea of "re-mediation" or "re-instrumentation" and its relation to researcher-driven interventions in terms of collectively constructing a "zone of proximal development." The idea is that researchers can provide potentially useful means for the people studied, such as new conceptualizations or tools, which may help them to become aware of, reframe, or even solve dilemmas that had affected their practices. For the researcher, the eventual usages of these means presents an opportunity to deepen his or her understanding of the constraints, underlying potentials, wishes, and needs present in the practices (s)he studies (Y. Engeström 1995, 1999).

In practice, activity-theoretical interventions have taken many forms, such as a user seminar in which different user groups and producers of technology reflect on their activities and mutual relationships (Miettinen and Hasu 2002). Analysis of power relationships between stakeholders could also be used as an effective means of helping stakeholders reflect and reconstruct their mutual relationships. Such an attempt also holds some novelty value for AT, since the studies within this theory have had a relative de-emphasis on power that has continued to the present day but probably stems from its long history in the former USSR before its diffusion to Western countries (Engeström 1999). How to better address power is thus an ongoing concern in recent studies of AT that address complex interrelations of multiple activities (Engeström et al. 1999a; Kontinen 2007).

In terms of overall research setup, these concerns are discussed within the methodological maxims outlined in Chapter 2 of this volume. Four scales of analysis were deployed also here, but in a more strategic order, since the diabetes study allowed us to use the project and two practice-level biographies in choosing the sites and times for focused ethnographic inquiry as well as for researcher-driven interventions. Hence, a particular biography, that of the PDMS, is examined first as (a) a part of the local design process, then as (b) a part of a set of similar design efforts within a class of technology, and then as (c) a part of the societal development of user activities. Following these, the use of this technology is examined as (d) part of situated action. Our emphasis on intervention and analysis of power relations took us as far as comparing local and "meso-level" analyses to inform the project about the limits and possibilities it was likely to have.

THE DESIGN PROCESS OF THE PROWELLNESS DIABETES MANAGEMENT DATABASE

From User-Innovation to Innovation Community

The database was initiated by medical researchers of the Department of Public Health and General Practice at the University of Oulu. They manually analyzed over 100,000 patient sheets for diabetic retinopathy at the turn of the 1990s. As a follow-up study loomed in the future, they were eager to computerize the patient records. A municipal diabetes clinic joined the pursuit because it wanted to have a statistical tool that would make it easier to follow the treatment balance of its patients.[2] With the help of a programmer from Oulu University Hospital, these users created a preliminary database with Microsoft Access.

In 1996, a small software company, ProWellness Ltd., was founded in Oulu to create an Internet-based archive for medical records. As a condition for providing seed funding, the city of Oulu recommended that the parties engage in collaboration. ProWellness saw diabetes as a good starting point while the users saw promise in the expertise of the cutting-edge programming firm. While users provided the details of diabetes care and practice, the company brought in its programming skills and experience in designing programs and databases for time-pressured work.

In the first phase of the collaboration, both parties came to an understanding of what information should be included in the database and how it should be handled. The contents were solely specified by the users, who also spent time in educating the designers about diabetes treatment and the details of their work. The collaboration quickly refined the goals of both parties. The company realized that its original archive idea had been too ambitious and too difficult to realize. The business idea was refined into creating PDMS-like expert systems for other long-term illnesses. Users appreciated the idea that, using Internet technology, the database could be used by all key personnel and would facilitate coordination between the various physicians, nurses, and auxiliary nurses, as well as the specialized care given in the local hospital. Additionally, the company envisioned an additional module for patients' home use. In this way, the database program grew to encompass most of the data generated in the treatment and monitoring of diabetes. The first parts of the program to grow into prototypes were the physician's and nurse's screens that were piloted and further improved in the Oulu diabetic clinic, beginning in 1998.

In this early period of collaboration, the main form of collaboration was ordinary, albeit intensive, communication with users and software developers. Ideas were exchanged in face-to-face discussions and e-mail, as well as in simple handwritten notes and drawings about the data contents and potential interface solutions. The ideas were iterated on paper first and then worked into prototypes that were tested and developed further. The interactions were made easier by the fact that some users had also previously tried to create their own applications and thus had experience in attempts to computerize their work practice. The designers made the final decisions about how to incorporate the various features; however, their decisions were wholly dependent on the expertise of the medical participants. All in all, the parties were mutually dependent on the complementary resources of their counterparts.

When the first version was up and running, the collaboration network was extended with the help of the professional contacts of the users. The new participants were physicians and nurses in the diabetes clinics in the central hospitals of Tampere and Kajaani, who were giving specialized care to diabetics. This extended collaboration proved successful, and, again, it was facilitated by several of the participants being clear lead-users: esteemed experts who had also previously been involved in (their own) attempts to build database systems for recording diabetes data. In two years, most wishes of the personnel in specialist care were incorporated, and the usability and statistical functions of the program were significantly improved. By the year 2001, the program was bought and put to use in most of the major hospital districts in Finland and the new user sites were incorporated into the development team. As a result, the database became a *de facto* standard for recording information about diabetes in Finland, even though it was not yet being used in any regular health care center in these districts. The local lead-user prototype had grown into an application used nationwide and its small development group had grown into an innovation community that included a software provider and representatives from most settings specializing in diabetes treatment.

The benefits of user–producer collaboration appeared significant for the producer and user participants:

- *It enabled the designing of a genuinely useful and usable system.* On one hand, it would have been quite a challenge for designers to achieve the appropriate content and form of the database, and, on the other hand, the users' preliminary designs showed that they had a rather restricted sense of the technical possibilities.
- *The designers gained a strong position for learning about the restrictions of their product concept and the environments of its use.* The collaboration rapidly showed that the designers' original idea for building a new kind of database for all illnesses was unrealistic. Moreover, the collaboration enabled them to move forward with the design without an extended period of learning about diabetes care in practice.
- *The collaboration proved valuable in the marketing of the product.* The user partners took an active role in recommending and proliferating PDMS. They were also a valuable reference and a source of credibility for the program.
- *Broad collaboration allowed for the tailoring of the system to the needs of different medical professionals.* Employing individual experts at the company would not have provided the required understanding of the work of different professional groups. Also, the patterns of interpersonal and interorganizational collaboration would have likely remained biased, at best.

However, the collaboration also had its challenges. The interactions, organization of collaboration, analysis of data, and appropriation of new knowledge required time and resources from the company and medical

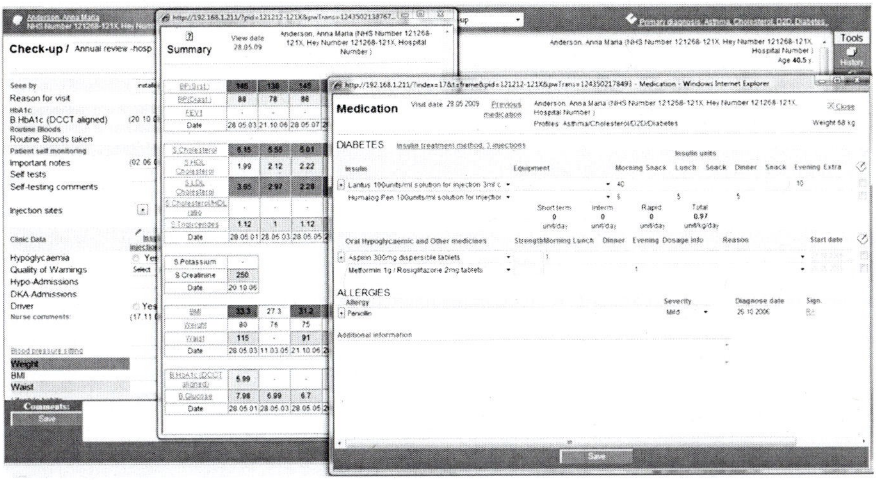

Figure 8.1 PDMS diabetes database program in its late second generation. Several interface sheets are typically open during patient reception. All differences in shade are in reality bright color differences designed to help in assessing the information.

practitioners alike. Achieving a shared language and creating an appropriate means for interaction took significant effort. Furthermore, the company had to learn to give away some control over the outcomes and schedule of the project. During these early years, however, these challenges did not seem to pose any crucial difficulties for the participants, who were wedded to each other's complementary competencies in furthering the project.

From Harmonious Collaboration to Tensioned Cooperation

At the point when the co-design work had been going on for four years and the program had gained a promising market share in Finland, tensions and significant problems arose in the network of collaboration. First, the expert-network developing PDMS saw the use of PDMS in health care centers as a matter of motivation and training. The collaboration was not extended to regular medical general practitioners (GPs) and nurses, since the users in the innovation community believed they knew what "has to be in the program." Yet primary health care seemed to shun this conviction: the program was not taken into use in health care centers.

Second, instead of the previously swift action to incorporate new ideas for improvement from users, the company took a reserved stance towards the various wishes for customization and new features that were voiced, particularly by new user sites. It wished to see the program as an essentially ready packaged product that incorporated enough configuration options for different user sites in different hospitals. This was not unlike the situation we observed with Vivago-Wristcare towards the end of its most intense user-collaboration period. The ProWellness producer company also became frustrated with what it termed "cacophony management" in its user-collaboration. Different user sites had conflicting wishes and views on what ought to be in the system and what features would just make it more burdensome to use. This finding parallels observations made of the development of ERP systems (Pollock and Williams 2008; Wang 2007): after an early period of accumulating functionality in a *product* (in opposition to a dedicated system), it becomes increasingly difficult to keep its development clear and coherent in the midst of further requests and options wished for by clients in different settings. Cacophony management and more frequent usage of techniques such as inviting the PDMS user group into seminars in order to create consensus within the innovation community can be seen as forms of what Pollock et al. (2007) call "generification work," work that goes into detaching a product from the idiosyncrasies of its early user sites to make it more robust and easier to move to new users.

Indeed, the autonomous collaborative design, in which a wide range of diabetes professionals were involved, proved to be a limited period in the company's collaboration strategy. As the firm incorporated more and more of users' hands-on knowledge about the medical treatment relevant for the database, it became less dependent on the incoming flux of this expertise. This, in turn, freed the company from some of its dependency on individual users and made it an increasingly central actor in the innovation community. When the firm ceased to incorporate the wishes of individual user partners, their involvement in the innovation community waned as well.

In the PDMS project, the generification work by the producer was motivated not only by the internal necessities in managing the project but at least as strongly by its changing business strategy. The company decided to seek overseas markets and diversified into making end user programs for patients with long-term illnesses.[3] Also, having now accumulated several years of skill with programs for long-term illnesses, the company began to regard itself as the entity that knew how to develop these systems. It consequently started to recruit, exclusively, the leading domestic and foreign medical professionals as collaboration partners for convincing the buyers of medical databases.

However, the development of PDMS did not freeze at this point, even as the producer more or less wished that to be so. The company wasted five years in a merger and demonstration projects in the UK and eventually decided to collaborate with the UK physicians in redesigning the system more to their requirements in 2006 (Miettinen et al. 2008). Cooperation with some of the Finnish user partners continued in regard to some less developed features of the system, some new customers demanded new development as the condition for their purchase, and the primary care units stubbornly overlooked the efforts to persuade or pressurize them into using the program. This led the company to recruit some primary care doctors into tailoring the system for these settings, albeit rather slowly and in relatively modest intensity in comparison to early co-design phases of the project.

The period from roughly 2002 to 2006 in the development of PDMS hence appears to have shifted from an evolutionary co-design type of innovation context to one of innofusion and domestication where innovation factually continues at the user sites, leading into opportunities and demands for improvements in the generic product (see Chapter 1, this volume). Meanwhile, many end users who adopted the package factually domesticated it into their reception work and in doing so relied on their own learning and the help of other user sites in deploying it effectively—as we shall document later, the procedures through which PDMS usage could be made fluent within the pace of reception work were not trivial achievements.

In sum, in the second and third stages of the collaboration the company seized the opportune moment to move into a more arm's-length relationship with its clientele. Even the early developers had to pay handsomely for the program they had been developing. The work that users had put into the development work was acknowledged only with a brief and anonymous referral, "developed in collaboration with users." In contrast, the firm had gained a significant amount of free expertise in diabetes care and care practices in general, co-design help in achieving a working program, thorough on-site testing in a number of locations, good references, and often direct help in marketing the program as well as good contacts with health care professionals and decision-makers in regard to its coming products. The asymmetry between the benefits for the partners appears simply stunning. Indeed, while formalized participatory design methods were not necessary in producing a successful co-design, the cautionary lessons about power relations in Scandinavian participatory projects appear more than adequate in this commercial context (Ehn 1993; Bødker et al. 2004).

TECHNOLOGICAL LINEAGE: BATTLE OVER DIABETES, OR A GRAVEYARD OF ABANDONED TECHNOLOGY

The rather grim picture of benefits of user-collaboration for users in the PDMS project appears almost incomprehensible in the sense of: "why would any user continue to participate in a project leading to such outcomes?" However, this observation would be to an important extent an artifact of limiting the analysis to the scale of the project and omit the socio-technical "meso-scale" that in many respects motivated and provided paradigms for the project.

At some point during our interviewing, we noticed that some of the user partners had also previously been developing diabetes databases. When we started to inquire about what had happened to these projects, we found ourselves unearthing a "graveyard of withdrawn diabetes databases." There had been numerous attempts to create diabetes databases in Finland and almost all had floundered.

This led us to map out all the hospital districts in Finland to find out how these projects came about and what had caused them to fail. Our interview round revealed that in 11 out of 20 hospital districts in Finland, a total of 21 programs had been created since the mid-1980s (excluding PDMS). Only four of those programs were still in use when we conducted our interview, and their use was not about to end in the near future. In none of the cases had the use proliferated beyond the district where the program was developed. However, these projects to develop and maintain a database were not futile, random, or without effort: in 13 cases, the program had been used for more than three years. Nevertheless, in practice, the patient information usually had to be entered tediously during patients' visits and it hence took several years to gain enough coverage and depth in the database to achieve significant benefits for patient work, research, or administration.

What had motivated these numerous attempts? In our interviews, it became clear that the doctors and nurses lacked tools to follow how their patients were responding to treatment. More specifically, it was unclear how the "treatment balance" of the patients, particularly the blood-sugar level, was being sustained in the longer run. This made it even more difficult to know how the patients responded to treatment, including diet and medication changes, that became necessary with the advancement of the disease. At the same time, the number of diabetics continued to increase in the aging and increasingly overweight population. In activity-theoretical terms, these attempts to develop database programs can be seen to derive from this prevailing contradiction between the demand to gain control over the complex, proliferating, and expensive disease and the insufficient tools to handle information that was crucial for its treatment.

Who then developed these programs? Out of the 21 units having a database, 17 had been involved in its development. In only two cases had an individual physician pieced the program together. All other projects were more or less collaborative, usually including a number of doctors and nurses from the unit where the development work was done. In roughly half the cases, the programming expertise was acquired from the computing department of the hospital. There were also two cases in which outside consultants or a software company had been involved in the development work. It is remarkable that in most cases the developers were not aware of the other database projects, even when some hospitals had hosted multiple projects in different clinics and periods. In only one case was the collaboration extended to multiple units in a district. All in all, one can characterize the projects as mainly collaborative and user initiated, yet they remained isolated attempts to come to terms with the same problem.

Why, then, had the attempts failed? To answer this question, two aspects have to be considered: the reasons for abandoning the programs and the dynamics that had led to the abandonment. Table 8.1 summarizes the main reasons our interviewees gave for abandoning the program.

In the same way, the reasons for continuing the use of the remaining seven programs are summarized in Table 8.2.

Table 8.1   Reasons Given for Abandoning the Use of Databases in the 14 Units in which Use Had Stopped Altogether (In Some Places, There Were Multiple Key Reasons)

Reasons given for abandoning the use of a program	
The active user-developer left the health care unit	2
Hardware or programs had become outdated	3
The database had been replaced by another program	1
Program use was not seen as useful or bringing benefits	3
Changes had occurred in the organization	2
There were problems with the usability of the program	8

Table 8.2   Reasons Given for the Continuation of Use of the Databases in the Seven Units in which a Database Was Still in Use (Including Those Three Units Where Use Was about to End or There Was Only One Active User)

Reasons given for continuation of use	
Enthusiastic user-developers	5
Waiting for a new program (saving the data)	1
Complementary use of the database and paper forms	3
Good usability	1

As illustrated by Tables 8.1 and 8.2, there are a number of common reasons for abandoning a program, such as organizational transformations and technical obsolescence. Nevertheless, by far the most usual reasons for the abandonment of the program were problems that we have classified under program usability:

- The program was too complex for daily use.
- Manual filing and updating of the patient data were slow and tedious.
- Logging into the program and simultaneous use of other programs was difficult.
- Operating the program was too slow and difficult, owing to the hectic pace of reception work.

In only one case was the ease of use at such a level that our interviewees regarded it as supporting the use of the program. When we inquired into the structure of the programs, we discovered that they were built to comply with care recommendations and to incorporate as much of the relevant data content as possible. These features were particularly desirable for the diabetes specialists and their interests in research and population-level management of the disease. The more exhaustive and accurate the information, the more could be inferred about the disease.

From the perspective of daily patient reception, however, the aim for exhaustive data led to complex structures and required more tedious operations in program use. Frequently, the information had to be filed in the database outside reception hours, often at the end of the day. Slowly, the problems in usability then led to declining interest in the program. While this led to the outright abandonment of the program in eight out of 14 cases, similar problems were reported also in a number of the other programs as well.

The dominant role of the enthusiastic user-developers was emphasized among the reasons for continuing the use of the program. By *user-developer* we refer to a doctor or a nurse who was active in the development of the database and then an enthusiast in its use. Their motivation in holding on to the program seemed to be a factor that made up for the mundane difficulties. With one positive exception, the programs still in use resemble the abandoned programs in regard to ease of use and their fit with the work routines. They require significant efforts from their users in the daily medical practice.

Indeed, one of the main motives for developing diabetes databases was to gain possibilities to make inquiries and to do diabetes research. However, this interest seems to have resulted in programs that do not suit the daily work in patient reception. Aiming for exhaustive information seems to hinder the use of the programs and has continuously prevented their proliferation. In many cases it has also led to their abandonment in the initial location. When we look at the PDMS project in the context of diabetes treatment and its database development, we come to perceive that its development was also animated by a persistent imaginary bound to practices of diabetes research and its specialist treatment. This imaginary motivated independent projects on several different sites and over a two-decade time span in Finland alone. The databases were developed and used as tools to control the quality of the care given and to aid in the production of care recommendations and research results. The graveyard of the abandoned databases bears witness to how these instruments in the battle over diabetes were also instruments that collided with practices of how to manage daily reception work.

In comparison with paper-based methods, electronic databases imposed significant constraints on the ways practitioners could act and register information in their patient work. They also improved the ability to monitor the work routines and arrangements in patient reception, which vary significantly from one location to another. Even if these facets may perhaps be agreed upon as positives by the practitioners, the resulting extra work and loss of flexibility could not. The decades of development of paper-based work in diabetes care is so firmly embedded in procedures, artifacts, division of labor, and coordination that computerization could not enter work routines as a simple replacement.

When we look at PDMS in light of its predecessors, we notice that the power dynamic among the users was very much the same as in the previous projects. PDMS was designed by the enthusiasts and was made (even more) far-reaching in coordinating and enforcing the specialists' way of treating the disease. The wide user participation and skilled programmers were key factors in negotiating and resolving the conflict between the care recommendations and work routines that is inherent in the program's functioning. Most professional groups and specialized wards were satisfied with the result. Yet, again, the battle line remained, only this time with local primary care health centers. The freedom negotiated for work routines by the advanced structure and interface design of the program was not enough for primary care. The benefits from the program's use did not compensate for its poor fit. Interestingly enough, it seems that the specialist participants in design were not consciously aware of the conflict and hence saw no reason to consult with people in the "lower"-level units of the medical hierarchy. Their resistance was seen as unfortunate and as showing somewhat irresponsible disinterest in the treatment of diabetes.

In addition, ProWellness joined the project unaware of the internal tension between the treatment guidelines and the practice of diabetes care. During the early design process, the company was subordinate to specialists' views of the program. Through the company, specialists gained a way to further a number of their interests. First of all, with its programming expertise the company provided a way to overcome local work routines by creating an attractive standard means of recording the data. The specialists, too, sought generification, albeit somewhat differently than the company. Moreover, the company provided outside expertise to maintain and update the program in the long run, thus securing and externalizing the standardization of work practices. The company's search for cost-efficiency pointed towards a single standard, which matched also the wishes of the specialists. At the same time, the resources of the company were needed to overcome the numerous problems that were bound to arise with the effort to transform the existing local information and bookkeeping systems. Most importantly, company resources for selling the program for primary care (primarily to the managers of primary care) was most welcome for the specialists. It should also be noted that even if the company did not formally acknowledge the users, their professional colleagues were well aware of who had been active in the PDMS project.

To conclude, when the project is seen in the context of practice-bound imaginaries and power dynamics in diabetes care, we notice that the user partners were far from being defenseless or deriving no benefits from it. Rather, we see a shift in the power relations during the project as the company gradually gained independence from the user partners by realigning itself with individual experts.[4] At the same time, it became ironically clear that the excluded parties, the nonenthusiastic and nonspecialist primary care GPs and nurses, were the ones whom the specialists factually were out to subjugate. From the perspective of nonspecialist GPs and nurses, the company sought to reallocate their tight resources to the expensive program, while the specialists sought to reorganize their work routines by adding procedures that mostly benefited the diabetes specialists.

GLIMPSES INTO THE BIOGRAPHY OF PRACTICES OF DIABETES CARE

Let us now turn to tracing the changes that have taken place in diabetes care since the mid-1980s to the present in order to further enrich the preceding picture. During the 1980s and 1990s, public diabetes care had been allocated to three sectors in Finland: first, to a special ward available in central hospitals for complicated cases such as acute juvenile-onset diabetes; second, to municipal diabetic clinics conducting the advice and treatment of acute adult-onset diabetes; and, third, to health centers engaged in the treatment of noncomplicated cases. Citizens sought treatment from the treatment facility specializing in their specific type of diabetes. By the turn of the millennium, this public health care structure had started to change. The GPs working in health centers were given "population responsibility," which meant that they had to manage all the illnesses of a certain population in their district. As a consequence, many routine tasks formerly conducted in diabetic clinics were now conducted in health centers. This indicated that in the treatment of diabetes, and especially in the recording the treatment data, the role of nonspecialized physicians and nurses in health centers was decisively increasing. This shift was accentuated by the change in the shape of the diabetic population. The most significant increase occurred in adult-onset diabetes, which was primarily handled by health care centers, while the number of juvenile-onset and difficult cases saw a more moderate increase. The imaginaries of organizing medical care in Finland hence added to specialists' motivations to build databases, since more and more of the treatment could only be monitored indirectly by them. At the same time, this development factually added to the power of health care centers as they became more important players in the medical field, yet it also burdened the health care centers further and made them increasingly resistant to any extra work piled over their extant duties.

Together, these changes made the requirements of nonspecialist doctors and nurses in regular health care facilities appear even more warranted at the time of PDMS project than they had been with earlier database projects. After years of a highly collaborative design project, the fate of the product depended on whether those excluded would accept these alignments or, alternatively, would turn their backs on the use of the program.

USING BIOGRAPHIES APPROACH TO TARGET
DETAILED ETHNOGRAPHY OF THE USE OF PDMS

Our initial research plan was to study the use of PDMS in multiple organizations and in the work of several professional groups. This plan reflected the traditional understanding of ethnography as a sustained acquainting to the life of the people under study. However, three problems arose that are arguably typical of multisite ethnography in studies concerning the use of technology:

- An extensive amount of research work would have ensued from a prolonged and relatively unfocused engagement in multiple sites and with multiple kinds of medical professionals.
- An even greater research effort would be required to analyze, in detail, the minutiae of video-recorded interactions between doctors, patients, and various artifacts such as PDMS.
- The timing of events was off. Although decisions relevant for the destiny of PDMS were taking place every day, by the time we would had completed an exhaustive study, the participants would have regarded our results as something that it would have been nice to have had "back then" when they were still relevant.

We decided to let our historical analysis inform the choice of field sites, and in November 2000 and March 2001, we conducted an ethnographic field study in two primary care settings: the diabetic clinic of the city of Oulu and the health care center of Paltamo. In 2001, the Paltamo health care center was the first nonspecialized unit to begin to use PDMS. The use of PDMS could be compared with that at our Oulu site, a diabetes treatment unit that had been an active development partner and user of the program for over three years.

All together, we observed and videotaped some 30 patient receptions in which PDMS was available or used by physicians, nurses, and assisting nurses. The most important findings regarding the work routines can be summarized as follows. First, PDMS was used together with a wide range of mediating artifacts, such as laboratory and appointment databases, electronic health records, paper documents, diabetes sheets, and patients' own notebooks. Each staff member used this repertoire in a different manner and order. While some physicians filled in the PDMS data first and then various other papers, others filled in the papers first and entered the data in the computer only after the reception. Nonetheless, all the people we observed struggled to get the mass of reading and recording done during the reception. They had developed clever routines for handling the data during intervals allowed by, for instance, blood-pressure measurements, but it was still common that data had to be filled in at the end of the reception or even at the end of the day.

Contrary to our expectation, the PDMS software did not ease the interaction between humans and artifacts but made it more difficult. Not only was the use of highly sophisticated paper "diabetes sheets" faster than the software, *per se*, but, in addition, in the transition to computerized tools, most of the data had to be booked twice, either in PDMS and the other papers or in PDMS and some other electronic health record. We also learned that, because individual patients are treated at a number of locations, this double booking would persist at least until all the units within a hospital district had moved their existing records into the software. This would take years.

Our second surprise was the extent to which the patients participated in the entering and interpreting of medical data about themselves. This PDMS facilitated, since patients were able to discuss the graphical illustrations of their treatment balance and manipulate the data variables on the screen. The patients were, on some occasions, the only ones who had the complete record of their treatment, for there were numerous breakdowns in the information flow between the care units in the hospital and primary care.

The key differences between the two sites were not so much in the way the reception of a diabetic patient was carried out as, rather, in the relative importance of the disease for the organization. While PDMS created extra work in both settings, only the staff in Oulu's diabetes-dedicated unit expected that future benefits would justify the use of the program. In contrast, the Paltamo staff clearly expressed the opinion that the promise of the future benefits would not compensate for the inconveniences of its current use, since only a small minority of the patients was diabetic. Moreover, the devotion that had to go into learning and maintaining skill in the use of the program was significantly stronger in Oulu, where the program was used in all the receptions. In Paltamo, a diabetic might not appear even once a week.

These results confirmed and added details to the findings of our historical analysis, and they also provided some clear suggestions for further design improvements. In the health center practice, the database should be simpler and more closely incorporated into existing databases, whereas in a diabetes clinic, the database could be more complex, comprehensive, and autonomous. Since the double registration seemed to last a relatively long period of time, PDMS should diminish this hindrance by offering compact and comprehensive printing options (replacing paper documents) and enhancing connections to existing databases, such as laboratory databases (diminishing typing). In general, any measures to ease the work in filing and reading of the PDMS data in health centers appeared crucial, including the extensive use of defaults, etc. It seemed clear that as long as the system remained untailored for the use of health center personnel, its expansion into those user environments would prove difficult. This problem could even conceal the potential of the program to function as an information channel between primary and specialized health care.

Our instrument-oriented and historically informed on-site observation, while much lighter than in the Vivago case or in traditional ethnographies, gave us a relatively rich and multifaceted understanding of the work practices of those professionals who were crucially situated in regard to diabetes databases and of their environments and collaboration, and, in doing so, provided some unexpected findings, such as the extent of the patients' active role in treatment and documentation. Furthermore, the research setup would have allowed for an expansion in both our fieldwork and analysis if necessary. Had further field studies seemed necessary, they could have been easily arranged. In conducting the observations, we had two cameras running: one capturing interactions and the other the details of instrument use. This would have allowed for more in-depth analysis, for instance, of doctor–patient interactions. In practice, the setup provided sufficiently rich results without going into these further measures and provided these findings in time for them to still be potentially relevant in practice.

INTERVENTIONS TO FACILITATE LEARNING

Along with targeting ethnographic work, we used our historical analyses to purposefully intervene in the directions in which the innovation community was moving in September 2000. We organized a user seminar jointly with the ProWellness Ltd. PDMS user group day. Our aim was to make the participants aware that their assumption that the proliferation of the program was a matter of coordinating the implementation of PDMS from specialized care to primary care may turn out to be inappropriate. After all, the reliance on coordination, implying reliance on assumedly routine scripts for how new technology is deployed, had proved to be an explanatory factor for failures in other diabetes projects. Hence, we wished to alert the innovation community to the possibility that more thoroughgoing cooperation or reflexive communication (Fichtner 1984, 216–218) might be needed, including attempts to involve primary care staff in further design of the program to ensure the suitability of PDMS within the work practices of health care centers—as had been done with all other occupational groups. Drawing from activity theory, we tried to involve the innovation community in constructing a shared zone of proximal development (ZPD) for its joint efforts (Vygotsky 1989; Engeström

1999). The idea in ZPD is to identify the zone to which the people involved could be moving in the near future from their present starting points and historically formed resources and identities. It is, hence, a more concrete and elaborated vision than those in standard use in scenario-building and backcasting experiments. Moreover, the core of ZPD is to realistically view this zone for near-future action as internally tensioned and involving learning challenges, including the management of conflicting priorities of different actors (Engeström 2000). The proximal development can indeed be viewed as a zone wherein different pathways for change can be identified and actively constructed. Some alternatives are likely to continue business as usual; some lead to stagnation or retrograding; and yet others lead to potentially expansive pathways for the actors, their objects of work, and/or their collaborations.

In regard to PDMS, our analysis suggested that its multiparty design collaboration had opened and capitalized on a series of expansive ZPDs in fitting the project to practical concerns of patient work, in contrast to earlier failed specialist database projects that had overemphasized encompassing data recording and suffocated due to the complexity this introduced to daily work. Yet in the year 2000 the project's ZPD again included three significantly different paths, the first of which could be characterized as increasing specialist emphasis, leading to incorporation of ever-more recorded items and handling options but running a risk of reproducing the patterns that had led the previous databases to the graveyard. This type was indeed a very real possibility, because ideas for how to fortify the system further were not lacking among the user-developers. The second path would be a business-as-usual scenario, wherein the practical usability of the system remained a top priority in its further development yet its spread to primary care would be handled as a matter of coordination. This path could lead to a successful system but one that remained successful only in specialized care.

The third path was the potentially most cumbersome but also most expansive one, where renewed effort would be placed on ensuring that the system would become well suited also to primary care practitioners, where the bulk of the diabetics were actually treated, hence seeking the largest possible market and social impact. This expansive path—meaning efforts to prioritize learnability, speed, and ease of recording of the system above all else—was in potential tension with specialists' interests in the quality and quantity of data recorded, as well as with the company's interest in reducing the programmer hours used in the project, as well as in tension with the present makeup of the innovation community as the primary care staff, not the specialists, would take the leading role in the further development.

In the user seminar, all the PDMS user sites and some potential new users were represented. We gave a presentation of the preliminary findings

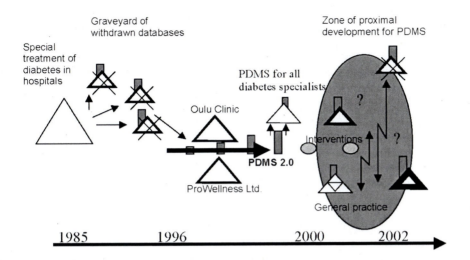

Figure 8.2 Potential ZPD for the PDMS project in autumn 2000. Three internally contradictory paths appeared likely, one leading to a more encompassing system not unlike previous programs, a business-as-usual product and success at least within specialized care, and an expansive effort to ensure its spread to primary care.

of our historical analysis and emphasized the risk that the GPs and nurses at health centers were perhaps not interested in becoming users of the current program. We then asked the participants to comment and make suggestions on the actions that should be taken.

The discussion was dominated by the users who had been active in the design process. Their comments tended to focus on how to convince the GPs, educate them, or enroll them in using the system. The comments took, on one hand, a normative stance: the GPs should use the database, owing to the obvious advantages to the patients, and hence in their view "no more simplifications can be made, since all these things should be checked, anyway."[5] The participants were hopeful about the attitude of the GPs: "I think they will see the benefits" and "now that the computers are coming into more general use in the city of Oulu, I believe that the health centers will start using the system."[6] On the other hand, the participants commented on the constraints of the system, which hindered the GPs' use of such programs: "Only 5 to 10 percent of their patients are diabetics, and the GPs already have other medical records to keep. So it is critical that they don't need to maintain two different databases."[7] These issues, however, were discussed only on a general level.

Overall, the seminar participants avoided the question of what would happen if the health centers did not use the system the way specialized diabetes care hoped. The only direct reaction in this matter came from the two users who expressed their support for our suggestion to enroll the GPs and nurses of health centers in development work. The company, in turn, wanted to see our concerns as already incorporated. It claimed that the simplification of the program had been going on ever since the early prototypes, and that the company was currently building links between the existing electronic patient records and PDMS.

For us, the user seminar confirmed that the participants seemed locked into the mode of coordination in regard to primary care. Moreover, it became clear that the company or major user-developers did not possess firsthand know-how about the needs and daily practices of health centers. Suggestions for possible incentives to health center personnel, such as shared care and screening of patients at risk, arose primarily from the interests of the specialists. In all, the seminar discussions verified some of our previous findings about the hold of the imaginary of encompassing recording and control over diabetes (and practitioners treating it) among the user-developers involved in the project.

The user seminar further motivated our field research in health centers and these, in turn, led to further interventions. In spring 2001, the results of our field research were discussed in two small meetings with the representatives from our user site, the diabetic clinic of the city of Oulu, and from ProWellness Ltd. We discussed the practical findings of the ethnography with the personnel of the diabetic clinic. We also discussed the upcoming use of PDMS in other health centers of the city. Proper training in the use of the program was, again, seen as the crucial issue in the expansion of its implementation in the city district. In the meeting with ProWellness Ltd. its representative drew the same conclusion: the health center practice was not thought to be demanding any major changes in the program content or involvement of the health center practitioners in the design.

Why did both the medical practitioners and the designer company shun our convergent results from historical and ethnographic analysis? A major reason lies in the network dynamics of the PDMS project. Our interventions coincided with a phase wherein the company sought to generify its product, factually wishing to regard it as more or less ready and reduce the time it spent in collaborating with user partners. This short-circuited our attempts to broaden the collaboration network at the time. At the same time, the power of practice-bound imaginaries in medical care should not be underestimated. The database graveyard and user-developer reactions seem to us to be indications of the same repeating patterns in what is imagined desirable in a future database application and how its usages and relationships between medical experts and regular health care staff were conceived. The concept helps to connect the biographies of diabetes treatment and database design to the prevailing orientations on how to construe their future both as practical and as imaginative enterprises.

CHAPTER DISCUSSION

Biography of Technology

Collaborative design can have a complex biography and many shifts in shape. The PDMS project started as a typical (lead-)user invention, when a group of users faced new technical challenges and responded by developing a prototype. The next phase of the project resembled an intensive participatory design effort where complementary competencies of the developer company and the user-developers were combined and some of their roles and responsibilities became blurred. In its next phase, an extended innovation community emerged in the wake of the first functional prototypes. After the company acquired a central position in the innovation network, the intensity of the community effort lessened. Even as the company sought to package its product as one generic offer, an innofusion-domestication-type constellation between developers and users ensued, leading to further, even if slower, development of the generic product and particularized user configurations of it.

Many of these changes are owing to contingent events such as the city of Oulu uniting the two projects or the dot-com bubble affecting company visions. Yet the contingencies appear rooted in more general issues about resourcing and managing the project. Programming expertise was urgently needed in the early stages. An extended innovation community was perhaps one of the only ways to adequately and effectively determine the requirements of the system, and it would have been hard to sustain without a functioning prototype into which many parallel changes could be incorporated. Similarly, the urge to package the program was spurred by both increasing difficulty in handling of development requests and the company's strategic and commercial interests.

The biographical view of collaborative development clearly suggests that a particular design phase, say, in concept design is insufficient, even misleading scope of analysis to the "nature" or "democratization" of technology. More generally this holds for any single scale of analysis, including the biography of an innovation project. Previous diabetes databases had mostly waned, regardless of their location or how participatory their development had been. There was enduring conflict between the care recommendations and requirements of patient work. This contradiction was based on practice-bound imaginaries and the power relations between the specialists and local health care personnel and was crystallized in the structure of the database programs. This was the case also in the PDMS project, which, despite the broad and democratic user participation, ended up disregarding the perspective of nonspecialists. Hence, we need to look at the biographies in an encompassing manner to understand their dynamics. This, in turn, demands attention to their details and acknowledging that multiple biographies and relevant time scales are involved.

Designer–User Relations

It is not news that co-design effectively steers clear of many difficulties associated with more linear development models (von Hippel 2005; Bødker et al. 2004; Williams et al. 2005). Diabetes reception work presents almost an incarnation of an ideal type here, where building a successful application requires much user domain knowledge and developers can only have restricted and burdensome access to it on their own. The benefits from developer–user collaboration for the company should be expected. From the users' side, the company–user partnership helped to incorporate and tease out more inventive ideas as well as to break beyond its initial local confines. However, when the company withdrew from collaboration, also users' innovativeness and learning-by-using lost their potency, they were no longer being encouraged and rewarded through improvements in their work instrument. The company hence came to play facilitating and configuring roles typically played by intermediary organizations, effectively coming to co-constitute users' ability to contribute to the innovation. Likewise, users facilitated software engineers learning about the contents and organization of the system and brokered contacts with other users and stakeholders. Indeed, there is a notable lack of influence from any typical innovation intermediaries in the project. These typical intermediating roles in facilitating, configuring, and brokering (Stewart and Hyysalo 2008) played by the user consortium and the developer company covered the terrain more effectively than any outsider intermediary players could.

The changes in the relevance of intermediary roles for the project also contributed to the projects' asymmetrical power relations. It became easy for the company to acquire a strong brokering role in regard to the technical configuration once much of the user domain knowledge was already incorporated. Users came to have fewer means to bargain for changes or to renegotiate the price of the program. More generally, the hope to achieve harmony among the different worker groups, producers, and users (or management for that matter) may indeed be misleading as a guiding principle for collaborative design (cf. Bansler 1989). While participatory design approaches have long underscored the power relations between different users and companies, it may be difficult for the participants in cooperative projects to recognize the complex contextual dynamics that are at play within particular constellations between different users, organizations, and technology producers.

Agency, or the Constitution of Developer, User, and Technology

Diabetes databases underscore our insistence on technologies being foremost configurations that have dynamic stability in time and space, being composed of distributed capacities to act in elements traditionally regarded as technical, social, emotional, infrastructural, or organizational. Another way to phrase this issue is in terms of what is sufficient and usable technology. The earlier diabetes databases were not somehow destined to fail, insufficient, or bad. In the hands of highly specialized enthusiastic user-developers, they were sufficient and adequate. The problems arose when the same systems needed to be used by other staff members, less enthusiastic, less skilled, and less willing to invest extra hours in keeping the record up-to-date. PDMS inherited the majority of its contents and much of its preferred usage procedures from these earlier systems, but its more advanced structure and interface design allowed other staff in units specialized in diabetes to use it without excessive burdens compared to its benefits. And, as noted, this was not enough for staff in regular health care centers.

One of the interesting issues here resides in who would be likely to indicate what would need to change in the technology to make it spread to new kinds of users. Indeed, diffusion of innovations can be discontinuous, and the lead-users who lead the development of technique and equipment do not lead all developments in all areas of any given practice. This in mind, we came to term those members of staff in health centers positively disposed towards PDMS *crucial users* for the success of this product. Even though these suggestions are only tentative, the more precise attributes of these users are:

- These are users who must be enrolled in order for the user-base to grow to a point where some economies of scale in production and delivery can bring the price of the technology down and allow other positive network externalities.
- These users do not receive extraordinary benefits from the technology. Their relative lack of enthusiasm makes them require clear value and smooth and relatively carefree operation from the innovation before they adopt it.
- These users are not only burdened by the technology in question, such that they do adopt innovation if it has benefits (versus Laggards in diffusion theory). Thus if these people do not adopt the innovation, there are some clear barriers to adoption or continuation of usage for most users.
- These users are not intimidated by technology and are likely to file reasoned complaints or simply balk at the novelty if it is not easy enough to install and use, too expensive, or poorly suits their ecology of tasks. This means they are articulate enough to be useful for a manufacturer.

In terms of diffusion theory (Rogers 1995), crucial users can be located as following the edge of the "chasm" between early adopters and early majority (Moore 2002).

Learning

Lack of specialized co-design methods did not pose the trickiest challenge for the collaborative design. The project was able to mediate the transmission of expertise between the participants with relatively simple communication and co-design tools. It was the power and interest issues that ultimately posed problems to the success of the project. Constructing a ZPD for a project appears as one potential means to clarify and subject to collective scrutiny the tensions and conflicting desires that prevail within the innovation community and/or between the project and its (future) implicated actors. It has potential to foreground the particular concerns of different actors and connect these to past experience and envisioned (or probable) future developments. What then happens is eventually up to participants themselves. A "schoolmastery" approach to consulting an innovation community may have its moments and functions, such as educating the participants about techniques or common dynamics in collaborative design projects. However, when it comes to decisions over the future direction in relatively mature multipractice collaborations—featuring different traditions, concerns, interests, and future desires—any outside view can ultimately be but one of the voices in the dialogue, even when it is geared for fostering particular kinds of considerations among the participants.[8]

9 TeleChemistry
Radical Innovation, Deviance, and Path Formation

Written together with Maria Höyssä and Nina Janasik

The generally held image of innovation is that of a heroic quest for a break-through that can disrupt or create an industry and solve society-wide problems. Somewhat ironically, the vast majority of technology projects are relatively incremental, and it is towards these that the decades of accumulated managerial routines, instruments, and scholarly thinking are geared. Even as there exists a considerable amount of literature on breakthrough projects, "few empirical studies have identified the idiosyncrasies of the development process for radical and really new innovations" and there is "considerable anecdotal evidence that radical innovations require unique and sophisticated development strategies, but little empirical evidence to support these theories" (Garcia and Calantone 2002). Further, most innovation processes have been analyzed only when their outcomes and impact have been readily identifiable. Indeed, the first thing people wish to know about potential innovation—laymen and investors alike—is "what does it do; what impact will it have?" But what do we really know about how far inventors can specify such outcomes—the value, details, usages, and implications of the product—in an early, ongoing, and potentially discontinuous innovation process? Some recent research has begun to duly recognize these uncertainties (e.g., Duret et al. 1999; Colarelli O'Connor 1998) and underline the management challenge that lies in clarifying what kind of innovativeness—and, by the same token, deviance from existing solutions and markets—the innovation is likely to introduce, since decisions affecting innovativeness can have dramatic impacts on the ability to advance the project.

This chapter seeks to take such work further. Empirically, we follow the innovation journey of the "liquid microprocessor" (LMP) that has spanned from the 1960s to the present with various ups and downs. While the ambition behind the journey—to automate chemical analyses—has prevailed, the focus of the innovation has shifted many times, producing several technical, social, and business inventions. It is still an ongoing project that *intends* but has not yet succeeded to launch an innovation that in its present form would be discontinuous technologically, in terms of market as well as in terms of how its users—physicians, specialists, and nurses both in patient reception and at clinical laboratories—conduct their work. Indeed, this, the longest biography examined in this book, is also (after several turns and changes in the shape of the innovation) the one closest to its infancy in terms of use as it is just about to go into its first pilots. Theoretically the chapter focuses on the changing understanding about innovativeness and deviance during a potentially radical project. By *innovativeness* we refer to those characteristics of the product that an actor perceives as having novelty value and by *deviance* to such novelty an actor regards as providing negative value or just added burden and uncertainty. We argue that a problem with the existing frameworks for analyzing ongoing (potentially) radical or discontinuous innovation processes is that they treat the very nature of the innovation-to-be as too evident and stable. Looking at this theme in greater depth, we return to the notion of the practice-bound imaginary to examine the effects of expectations, trajectories, and bindings between these for a radical innovation project.

COMING TO TERMS WITH CHANGES IN THE INNOVATIVENESS AND DEVIANCE OF INNOVATION

The prevailing ambition in research that addresses the challenges of generating or managing technologically or commercially discontinuous innovation projects has been to find those organizational structures and practices that would best respond to the problems in idea generation, uncertain markets, competency management in unfamiliar territories, and personality types suitable for advancing uncertain projects in potentially hostile or indifferent environments (Benner and Tushman 2003; McDermott and Colarelli O'Connor 2002; Veryzer 1998). These approaches regard the challenges related to innovativeness as being mostly about ways to frame the appropriate *business* case (Christensen and Raynor 2003; Kim and Mauborgne 2005). The various sources of uncertainty and the methods of dealing with it have not been related to the inventions at the core of the project.

In a different line of research, approaches such as strategic niche management (Kemp et al. 1998) and transition management (Smith et al. 2005) stress accumulated capital, economies of scale in production, regulations, consumer habits, and often decades of cumulative improvements and additions that allow the widespread extant technologies to form "socio-technical regimes" and "entrench" against entrants. Targeting the innovation first to niches where selection pressure is felt less is suggested to allow potentially radical innovations to grow to a point where they can challenge the socio-technical regime (Hoogma et al. 2002; Smith et al. 2005; Geels and Schot 2007). In such studies related to breakthrough innovations—be they electric cars (Hoogma et al. 2002) or new forms of water management (Hegger et al. 2007), for example—it has been considered evident *that* the innovation is discontinuous; the crucial task then becomes to learn *which* discontinuous framing might lead to success and how to pursue it. Yet we argue that in the early stages of *potentially* discontinuous projects it may not be evident whether—let alone which—discontinuous framing would be most suitable. Some of the leading proponents of these approaches have started to give attention to the kind of problems that actors face; in the words of Geels (2004, 43):

> [T]he multi-level perspective is a structuralist process approach, which provides an overall framework to analyse transitions. The approach needs to be complemented, however, with an actor oriented approach working 'from the inside out'. Such an approach would look at how actors try to navigate transitions, how they develop visions and adapt them through searching and learning.

An emphasis on social, cultural, and regulatory (along with technical, organizational, and business) embeddedness is stressed also by technology studies (see Chapter 2, this volume) and has given rise to approaches of periodic proactive evaluation: for coaching, PROTEE (Duret et al. 1999; Hommels et al. 2007); for project managers, SOCROBUST (Laredo 2002); and for key stakeholders more broadly, ESTEEM (Jolivet et al. 2008). These approaches seek not only to identify the right people or determine the right framing but to provide tools for learning about the uncertainties in a project and the steps necessary to respond to these to make the project better accepted by society (Duret et al. 1999; Laredo 2002; Jolivet et al. 2008). These tools include mapping the project history and its critical moments, the present techno-economic network (Callon 1991), and the *de facto* scenarios of the future embedded in the project (Duret et al. 1999), and relating these to a future network and scenarios of the future working world. The tools lay the ground for contrasting the project's vision to external checks and clarifying the project's capacities for action in affecting the concerns that have been identified (Laredo 2002). While these analytics clarify the implications of the project well (Laredo 2002; Jolivet et al. 2008), the means provided "to de-script" the future remain surprisingly vague when it comes to the core of the project. In fact, only ESTEEM categorizes the novelty of each project, and, while it does this in six dimensions, the studies using the framework have resorted to doing so only once per project, neglecting possible later changes (Poti et al. 2006a, 2006b; Laredo 2002).

All in all, we suspect that the existing research might have skipped too confidently over a set of thorny issues concerning innovativeness and deviance, particularly related to uncertainty and expectations.

While the biographies approach provides means to follow innovation and discern the gradually changing visions and reevaluations, material realizations of R&D, organizational contexts, and scenarios of the future for the project (see Chapters 2 and 3 of this volume), we wish to elaborate a further analytic for characterizing the changes in different aspects of the core of the project. Findings from innovation studies and science and technology studies indicate four complementary facets of innovation that at least need to be paid attention to[1]:

1. The most rehearsed of these is the "degree" of novelty. As is common in innovation taxonomies, we see it as ranging from business as usual to incremental to discontinuous (e.g., Tushman and Anderson 1986; Benner and Tushman 2003; Leifer et al. 2000).

2. The degree of novelty appears different, depending on the perspective (Afuaf and Bahram 1995; Garcia and Calantone 2002): to whom and in what respect is innovation novel? Techno-economic networks (Callon 1991) address this issue by differentiating among four poles: technological/industry, science, regulation, and market/users, (Lettl et al. 2006) with four *dimensions*: technological, market, organizational, and "environmental and institutional." This is the terminology we follow here.[2]

3. Innovativeness may reside in more than one place or *locus* within and around the product. Changes can occur or be implied in the underlying technological, scientific, or organizing principles; in components; in the product architecture; in user practices; or even in the existing regime. Indeed, structural features have been shown to have bearing on the relative ease or difficulty of introducing an innovation (Henderson and Clark 1990; Gatignon et al. 2002). By dividing the product concept into these loci, we can pinpoint where the project's innovative activity—problem recognition, envisioning, inventing, and development work—was focused, and where no innovative activity took place.

4. Not all techno-economic networks and all their loci are even or alike. "The seamless web" (Hughes 1988b) is not fully seamless at all times, and we found it necessary to distinguish (a) how seamlessly related the dimensions of innovation appear for the developers and (b) how tightly or loosely coupled a system (or configuration) the invention's locus of application appears to be (Fleck 1993a; Sorensen and Williams 2002).

In following the shifting innovativeness and deviance in the LMP project, we further draw from the symbolic interactionist notion of "trajectory," stemming from Anselm Strauss's work on patient trajectories. A patient enters the hospital with some condition that gets diagnosed and treated, which has further effects that affect where the patient is transferred and how (s)he is treated. While some trajectories take the ideal shape of illness–diagnosis–treatment–recovery, many other shapes in the trajectory are equally likely. Reversals, fluctuations, complications, even death can feature in the trajectory of the patient and illness in the hospital (e.g., Strauss 1993; Timmermans 1999; Bowker and Star 1999). Hence, trajectory is here understood as the varying flying path taking its shape because of how it is intertwined with other trajectories, those of drugs, diagnoses, doctors, relatives, insurance policies, etc. While cumulation is acknowledged, contingency and mutual influences between different trajectories are given equally great emphasis. Phrased in terms of our theorizing on practice-bound imaginaries, such a concept of trajectory provides us with means to examine how bindings between different trajectories and trajectory expectations become enforced, severed, and woven into more encompassing sets that could form new paths rather than present individual deviations from the dominant path (Lovio et al., forthcoming; Garud and Karnoe 2001).

As a means to discuss the deviance and often fragile early path formation efforts, the interactionist concept of trajectory also offers a conceptual corollary to the evolutionary economics trajectory concept (Nelson and Winter 1982). The latter departs from the observation that classes of technology and technological systems seem to have a "natural trajectory" on which these proceed on the basis of the techno-economic criteria for feasible development direction. Particular natural trajectories are seen to be affected by complementary trajectories such as those of jet engine power and aircraft streamlining and more generic trajectories such as exploiting latent economies of scale and mechanization of operations that had been previously done by hand. Also generic technologies such as electricity and the transistor have been regarded as driving industries and individual projects towards certain kinds of solutions, leading to the formation macro-trajectories in techno-economic change (Freeman and Louçã 2001; Perez 2003). In this usage, "trajectory" resembles a "ballistic trajectory": continuing to fly on the thrust it has managed to attain.

While "better technology" may appeal to technologists as presenting sufficient thrust even during the earliest development phases of new technology, the interactionist view of trajectories as contingent and intertwined helps to position these hopes with other considerations, not least those made by other stakeholders to the emerging technology.

These conceptual issues and resources now at hand, let us move into the case history. For clarity, we have divided it into three periods, and at the end of the description of each period we assume an analyst's perspective on the developers' understanding of the innovation-to-be, trying to keep simultaneously in sight the four facets of innovation described earlier, illustrating the changing loci of innovative activity further in Tables 9.1, 9.2, and 9.3, as well as the changing trajectory expectations and bindings.

FROM A TECHNICALLY DISCONTINUOUS NICHE INNOVATION TO A POTENTIAL BREAKTHROUGH

Here, in the first empirical section, we describe the origins of the technological discontinuity. At the end of the section, we analyze how the locus of the innovative activity moved from one application to another and we diagnose the developers' perception of the meaning of the shift.

The line of inventions began with frustration with human errors. The inventor, while doing laboratory rat tests in 1966 at the University of Turku in Finland, discovered that the method of manual sample preparation severely compromised the accuracy of measurements. He invented a metallic microstructure that enabled a hundredfold improvement in accuracy and also held promises of the automation of sample handling. This invention by a scientist turned inventor in the face of equipment shortcomings in his new experiments is in many respects a typical lead-user invention (von Hippel 1988). But while it allowed a whole new set of scientific questions to be studied, his fellow university researchers were interested in advancing their basic research, not in further studies on how cold metal tubes performed and could be further developed.

The first shift in the context and audience of the invention then ensued: from basic research to equipment development. Negotiations with local company Wallac led nowhere, but a representative of Packard Instruments happened to visit the lab and, on understanding the situation, provided a small grant to build a decent prototype. This led to further development, culminating in three generations of "Sample Oxidizers,"[3] which formed a technically discontinuous but market-wise continuous innovation for Packard and came to dominate the market in sample preparation soon after the introduction of the first generation in 1969. As the development was done abroad, Packard never integrated the project into its internal R&D department but funded a small Advanced Instruments Research Group (AIRG) in Finland wherein know-how of the new technology remained. Neither did Packard patent the Oxidizers in Finland, which spurred several successful careers in Finnish laboratories—at both universities and pharma companies—which would become important later.

While Oxidizers became a success, the group dreamed of a further all-purpose automated method that could provide unforeseen accuracy in chemical analyses. The solution was to be a miniaturized closed system akin to the Oxidizers. The problem was to find a suitable valve for controlling the liquids on a micro-scale after all the mechanical ports, tested in the Oxidizers, had turned out to leak or retain dead volumes of liquid. Then chance did favor a prepared mind: an Oxidizer blew up an entire laboratory in the US in 1972. Troubleshooting revealed that users' alterations had caused one of the tiny tubes (1 mm in diameter) to freeze. Melting such a clog required 2,000 bar of pressure in its below -20-degree centigrade state, or great amounts of energy and time if done by heating the whole system. The damned clog was an incredible plug! Yet very little energy would be needed if there were a way of applying heat directly to the clog. The idea of an ice valve dawned: whereas existing technology used gravity to keep liquids in open vessels during analytical steps, liquids could be controlled through freezing and thawing of ice plugs in the closed microfluidic environment.[4] With this radical invention, the group's dead end was conceptually resolved in 1973, and by 1977 the group had concluded that it would be possible to build a generic LMP for the automatic processing of extremely small liquid volumes.

Enthusiasm was high. The LMP seemed to offer significant advantages by removing manual errors from analytical steps "[i]n [a] clinical chemistry laboratory [on account of]:

1. Greatly reduced costs/test, because [of the] microvolumes of the present reagents used. A huge gain in cost/speed. Ten times the speed of any present autoanalyzer.
2. Reduced general costs, because of less negative tests.
3. Better quality control, reliability.
4. Less laboratory manpower."[5]

Indeed, the LMP appeared to represent a leap in the long-standing attempts at reconciling "the two fundamental and inherent contradictions [of clinical chemistry]: (1) to use as small a sample as possible or available, without exceeding the limit of detection; and (2) to achieve speed without sacrificing precision of analysis" (Rosenfeld 1999).

These visions were closely bound to the dawning capabilities of the system—they were no fantastic leaps in this regard: "Every single important aspect of this functional system based on SVV [the LMP] has been shown or tested in bits and pieces in AIRG laboratories since 2nd September 1972."[6] However, the vision's relation to the constraints and requirements of the application domains remained unspecified. An enormous business opportunity was expected from a bundle of generic improvements: "[t]he number of hospital days per patient can be reduced . . . in emergencies very fast [diagnostic] action can be accomplished."[7] As recognized by the key innovator himself: "[t]his list [of potential applications] is endless but I have not put too much time in[to] systematically studying it."[8]

At this stage, we wish to take a more focused analytical look at the project. The developers had firsthand experience of the research laboratory, which formed the locus of user practice (see Table 9.1), where cumbersome manual sample preparation had emerged as the problem driving the Oxidizer development. In the LMP project, the relevant industrial field changed from scientific instruments to clinical diagnostic equipment. The motivation was to eliminate the sources of inaccuracy introduced by manual user practice in all (bio)chemical testing, but the locus of the respective product was unclear: it was first without elaboration, then conceived of as an artifact subsystem ("LMP system") and later an artifact ("LMP analyzer"). Table 9.1 presents the shift of innovative activity from the principles, components, and subsystems of Oxidizers to those of the LMP.

The nature of innovativeness the LMP product would introduce remained loosely elaborated. This was partly because the developers were not aware

Table 9.1 A Shift in Innovative Activity from Oxidizers to the LMP Project

Locus	Oxidizer in 1970	LMP by 1977	For comparison: Respective elements in conventional clinical testing
Regime/sector	(Biochemical scientific research)	(Health care and water management)	Health care/clinical diagnostic processes
User practice	* (Measurement of radioactive markers in research laboratories)	* (Any practice utilizing chemical analyses, esp. clinical laboratories)	Clinical laboratory
Artifact	◻ (Sample Oxidizer)	◻ (*Analyzer*)	Laboratory analyzer
Artifact subsystems	# Electroformed structure for processing liquids and gases	◻ *Liquid microprocessor*	Various mechanical subsystems for performing the analyzer functions
Components	# Commercially available, unsatisfactory valves	# *Electroformed structures for ice valves*	Test tubes and cuvettes (for containing and moving liquids)
Principles	Automation # Mechanical valves Closed system for liquid and gas processing	*Automation* # Phase-change valves *Closed hermetic system for liquid processing*	Mechanization Liquids kept in test tubes by gravity Nonhermetic system for liquid processing

Notes: The locus where the original problem was perceived to be is marked by *. The locus of the envisioned product is marked by ◻. The main loci of development work are marked by #. Italics indicate work envisioned but not realized; parentheses mark loci that were assumed not to require innovative work.

of the differences between scientific and clinical laboratories—neither had they developed instruments for clinical use. Regardless—or perhaps because of this—it was assumed that the LMP would turn into a generative innovation that would transform a much broader and more complex locus than the Oxidizers had.

The type of envisioning done in the LMP project is common in early stages of "promising technology" (e.g., Lente and Rip 1998; Russell 2006). A strong, even hyperbolic trust in the capabilities of the promised technology and capabilities to produce it are conveyed to enroll supporting actors.

The envisioning of applications is without much precision or certainty and builds on advances in other fields as well as yet-to-be-articulated requirements and constraints of particular business applications. Indeed, the *degree of novelty* of the LMP technology became elaborated only in the *technical dimension*, where its discontinuity was evident. The visions entailed innovativeness in other dimensions as well, but there was little consideration of the exact implications. Similarly, the choice of clinical chemistry as the primary application area—as opposed to water management, which was also considered—was partly due to the developers' view that an advance in clinical instrumentation could have far-reaching effects—in our analytical terms, the field was perceived as relatively *seamless*.

The trajectory envisioned for the LMP by the innovators at this stage holds great affinity to the ballistic curve view of trajectory. The generative innovation, *qua* its *revolutionizing technological potential*, is seen to transform the implicated field once it becomes coupled with further institutional and financial inventions (and potentially then moves on further to transform other fields).

Yet, the exact manner of how the LMP was fitted to clinical chemistry was shrouded in the mist. In fact, the next phase in the development work reveals that not even the tightness of couplings between the components *internal* to the LMP could be anticipated before they could be further tested together.

THE DAWNING OF BUSINESS, SCIENCE, MANUFACTURING, AND USAGE DISCONTINUITIES

In the second part of our case analysis, we show how the downside of the technological discontinuity gradually became evident for the developers as they learned that the innovativeness of the LMP was regarded as a valueless deviance in the wrong direction.

Packard's competition in sample preparation equipment, chemistry, and supplies evaporated during the 1970s. The firm had little interest in funding an uncertain, long-term innovation project for clinical use. Just as further development of the first metal tube structure had not fitted into the practices and institutional environment of the university within which it was invented, its offspring, the LMP, grew out of the business strategy of the company within which it had emerged.

The inventor left Packard, recovered his ice-valve patents, and started his own company, Electrofluidics Oy, in Finland in 1977. After a successful line of innovation, there was a strong sense that it would be Packard's loss not to jump on the emerging technology. Negotiations with several companies progressed frustratingly slowly until the marketing department of IBM made an offer of $5.5M[9]: the intention was to design "a blood chemistry analyzer."[10]

Instead, however, the inventor accepted a competing offer from the Finnish companies Kone and Nokia. They had been following the negotiations with IBM and, at the time, had stakes in diagnostic equipment. The joint venture was "to develop micro-electro-thermo-fluidic equipment products and sell sub-licenses."[11] The financiers' explicit agenda was cost savings. "The removing of mechanical parts was the advantage; [an analyzer] is cheaper to produce when there are no moving parts. . . . We did not see that it would differ from existing analyzers in other respects" (interview with the main inventor on April 5, 2008). Nevertheless, the inventor's "hidden agenda" was to improve the accuracy of chemical analysis by automation, as he had done in sample preparation already.

The development progressed through new problems and inventions. A novel reagent package was patented (filed in 1985), and a centrifuge was integrated into the apparatus in 1986. Then the ice valves needed improvement. Nokia had insisted on using its existing construction technology and materials, and Kone its own production methods. Only after Nokia withdrew from the venture in 1985 was it possible to return to developing the original Oxidizer-type materials and create operable channels by 1990. More precision was now needed in liquid dispensing, and it was gained by 1996; and once the opening of ice valves was reconfigured by 1999 through the use of by-then commercially available, cheap lasers, the inefficiency of the heating was resolved, too, clearing one of the final major technical hurdles.

All in all, it was gradually realized that for any benefit to be gained from the increased accuracy, an increasing number of the analyzer functions (such as dispensing, mixing, incubation, measurement, and washing) needed to be built anew just for the LMP. Towards the turn of the millennium, it became evident that the performance of the LMP was useless if samples and reagents came into contact with air *at any point* in the analysis. The gradual creation of an alternative, fully hermetically sealed system was slow, since all components related to liquid handling had to be developed in-house.[12]

However, difficulties in the business, organizational, and environmental dimensions of the innovation overshadowed technical advances. These began with incumbent patron company Kone early on, during the 1980s. The diminished use of reagents became an issue for the parent company, since reagents were its main income in the clinical equipment business. Later, it emerged that the hermetic, closed nature of the system made the role of the laboratory, the customer, somewhat questionable, because the LMP in effect attempted to black-box the work done in the laboratory. Besides, the LMP was incompatible with central laboratories, which used parallel processing of samples whereas the LMP could analyze just one sample at a time, even when it did so much faster.

Kone felt it was a small player in the diagnostic equipment market and that it therefore could not afford any long-term radical projects. Kone insisted in its monthly reviews that the LMP must be used to improve conventional technology. The interpretation Kone had of the practice-bound imaginary in the clinical diagnostic equipment field and of its own organization kept it handling the LMP within a competence-enhancing framework. The performance of the technology was considered too good and the investments already made too significant to discard lightly, however, even as the incremental initiatives did not pay off.

Continuation became possible since the development of the LMP was, for a time, paid for by other firms—first DuPont and then Wallac—that hoped to use the LMP in their analyzers. But, eventually, there emerged a sense that integrating the LMP into the existing systems of the clinical laboratory would produce endless technical solutions without a marketable application. Eventually the company got a new majority owner, the LMP was shelved, and work was focused instead on an add-on innovation to the LMP, the "bellows dispenser," which had resulted from the efforts at hydraulic dispensing.[13]

Another disappointment came from scientific audiences. The technological commitments defined the range of questions that were scientifically or otherwise interesting for conference audiences: scientists in microfluidics dismissed the LMP for not being based on silicon (the evolution of this line of microfluidics is described in Robinson and Propp 2008), while experts in laboratory automation considered the LMP a hoax. The claim of negligible, 0.001 percent carry-over (from one liquid batch to another) was deemed outrageous, since the laboratory experts knew that (all other) microfluidic structures were flat (rather than round) and absolutely not cleanable. The inventor failed to communicate that cleaning became possible through the hydraulic principle, there being zero dead volume, etc.:

> The problem was that there had emerged phenomena for which there were no words, no concepts. When explained with old concepts, those phenomena appeared to be lies. They didn't fit. They were impossible. There was a whole chain of phenomena and operations that one should have been able to communicate, but at the time we hadn't yet formed those concepts, so everyone thought that we must be cheating.[14]

The LMP hence again appeared merely deviant and suspect within the PBIs of the potential scientific fields. The full scope of the disjunctive features of the LMP began become apparent when the owners wanted to sell the LMP patents in 2000 and failed miserably. The inventor, together with an outside consultant, met representatives from various diagnostics companies. These were often initially interested but invariably changed their opinion, some explicitly claiming that the invention would destroy their business and expressing rationales close to those already encountered with patron company Kone about reagent sales and changing client and industry relations, hence suggesting that the difficulty was not in Kone's interpretation of its own position but at the core in the more overarching PBI within the diagnostic equipment industry.

Let us again clarify the changes in the innovativeness and deviance the project was perceived to introduce. Throughout the 1980s and 1990s, technical incompatibility caused more and more of the analyzer functions to be incorporated into the LMP (see Table 9.2). This, in turn, revealed that the LMP might turn out to be business-destroying in the *market dimension* for the patron company, Kone, by undermining its sales of reagents and other equipment. Further, the LMP's serial rather than parallel drive was incompatible with how the clientele (clinical laboratories) organized its practices, which might, in turn, demand seeking new clients. The LMP also threatened to become competence-destroying in the *organizational dimension* by making Kone's competencies in other clinical products such as reagents and disposables obsolete. In the *environmental dimension*, other incumbents and potential patrons, as well as scientific communities connected with clinical chemistry, remained doubtful of the innovation.

Table 9.2 illustrates how the technical novelties accumulated while the product concept came to a dead end. The gradual work with developing artifact subsystems and components for "airless" analyzer functions was only enabled by the innovative broadening of the principles on which the system was based. The net result was that the hermetic solutions began to form their own development pathway increasingly separated from conventional clinical chemistry equipment. Meanwhile, despite accumulating inventions, the LMP project partners lost consensus about what problem the LMP was out to solve, the contexts it implicated in user practices, and expectations regarding the product.

Finally, these dimensions of innovation (and the stakeholders involved) at the targeted locus of application, the clinical laboratory, turned out to be more *tightly related* with regard to entrants like the LMP than was expected: the market and distribution of analyzers and supplements was divided among few large incumbents, and the scientific knowledge in producing and using the equipment had changed along an incremental path for a long time (Rosenfeld 1999). Even when a whole bundle of additional clever inventions was in place, the LMP's promises lost their potency when it became evident that it would have to challenge, even replace, the well-serving arrangements in existing instrumentation and business. The potentially increased innovativeness turned into mere increased deviance for all the expected audiences. The trajectory of the LMP hence became intertwined with several other trajectories and in this process appeared to suffer setbacks and even (near) death in infancy. Indeed, to maintain the kind of ballistic trajectory envisioned in the late 1970s, the project should have been able to wield formidable capacity and resourcing to transform the more entrenched and far more widely spread expectations and trajectories of how business, science, institutions, and organization of user practice proceeded. Within the auspices of its patron company, plausible promises of coming to wield such power were organizationally undesired, since they would, as we see next, entail a significantly more radical framing of the whole project and its targets.

Table 9.2 The Rise of a "Hermetic Pathway"—The Fall of a Product Concept

Locus	LMP by 1980	LMP by 1990	LMP by 2000	For comparison: Conventional clinical testing
Regime/ sector	(Health care and clinical diagnostics)	(Health care)	?	Health care
User practice	*(Clinical laboratory)	* (Clinical laboratory)	?	Clinical laboratory
Artifact	¤ (*Analyzer*)	¤ (*Analyzer*)	*Integrated analyzer*→ ¤ bellows dispenser	Analyzer
Artifact subsystems	*Liquid microprocessor* with extant analyzer functions	# ¤ *Liquid microprocessor* with some novel and some extant analyzer functions	*Liquid microprocessor* with all novel analyzer functions but reaction measurement	Various mechanical subsystems for performing the analyzer functions
Components	# Electroformed structures for ice valves	# As before + other capillary structures, reagent bags, syringe dispenser, *better heating method,* and *bellows dispenser*	As before + laser heating, incubation chambers, and digital bellows dispenser	Syringe dispenser, test tube, rotating plates, plastic cuvettes, etc.
Principles	*Automatic, hermetic system* for liquid processing, based on phase changes	# *Automatic,* hermetic, *and hydraulic system* for liquid processing, based *on phase changes and pressure changes*	As before + based on *digitally controlled* pressure changes	Liquids kept in test tubes by gravity and moved between vessels mechanically Open system for liquid processing

Notes: The locus where the original problem was perceived to be is marked by *.
The locus of the envisioned product is marked by ¤. The main loci of development work are marked by #. Italics indicate work envisioned but not realized; parentheses mark loci that were assumed not to require innovative work.

DISRUPTIVE FRAMINGS OF INNOVATION

In the final section of our case analysis, we focus on how the previous experience enabled the developers to conceive the innovation-to-be from a perspective that expanded its value-enhancing innovativeness and enabled them to better handle the deviance that the system needed to introduce.

Since the patent rights were commercially useless, the inventor was allowed to buy them back. But to what purpose? He decided to focus on all of the technology's strengths: what customer-related issues *could* it solve?

The one taken-for-granted assumption covering the entirety of clinical diagnostics was that the *laboratory* was *the* place for extracting information from patient samples. Even the existing point-of-care (POC) applications were only *add-ons* to the laboratory, never replacements. But the LMP as a near-patient system might go further. Technically, real-time analyses for one patient at a time at the health care site would not require the parallel drive that the LMP lacked. The LMP system could generate results in just a few minutes and with greater, not less, accuracy than the laboratory. Enough reagents for six months' use could be stored hermetically within the PC-sized device, since consumption was extremely low. The digital pressure and temperature signals of the analyzer would make remote monitoring of service needs and quality control possible via the Internet. The end-customer benefits would include the possibility of using the same blood sample in follow-up tests, which would, in turn, reduce the need for patients to return for new sample taking. Neither would samples need to be transported possibly dozens of kilometers to a central laboratory. These benefits were significant to the entire health care system.[15] The real revelation, however, was the business idea: the apparently impenetrable value network of incumbents could be bypassed if the use of the technology was offered as a *service*. The customer would pay only for the tests, not for the device. No laboratory, no incumbent business, no entrenched science or technology would be needed![16]

The inventor registered the trademark TeleChemistry in 2000, patented the respective—potentially disruptive—system invention,[17] and convinced two of his brothers to join in to purchase the patent rights and production technology.

But from these assets it was a long way to a functioning diagnostic system with working and appropriate testing servers; ICT interfaces; and the functions of a central operator, service provider, and so on. A few million euros would be needed for prototype development; one needed to set up and tune the serial production method for high-quality core LMP components that would fit seamlessly together as a system and prove the novel liquid processing concept beyond any doubt.

In 2000, the inventor approached the telemedicine department of a Finnish tele-operator. There was enthusiasm, but there were also delays and eventually no deal, because the operator dismantled its telemedicine department in a merger in 2004. There were numerous other partnering efforts; for instance, a German reagent company, IBM, Nokia, Ericsson, a representative of clinical research organizations, and an Indian company were approached, along with Finnish and EU funding bodies, programs, and research institutes.

Most partner and investor candidates wished for more evidence of the TeleChemistry concept or wanted full control over it, only to be turned down—the developers perceived them as lacking the hard-won lessons of the 1980s and 1990s. The partner candidates outside clinical chemistry regarded the terms as too poor or the concept as too alien to justify entering a new venture. No longer surprisingly, the incumbents were not keen to disrupt their own field. At best, Roche considered using LMP technology to calibrate its lab-on-a-chip products but did not want other applications. By 2007, only the EU's EUREKA, the Finnish Funding Agency for Technology and Innovation, and one reagent manufacturer remained as prospects that regarded the innovation as potentially valuable with respect to their goals *and* would not hinder the management of one or another of the dimensions of innovation. To its good fortune, the project received EUREKA funding in July 2008, covering the design and building of prototypes and the initial validation of the system crucial for gaining further rounds of investments.

While this funding was being sought, the project survived for eight years with modest resources, mostly mobilized from the regional innovation environment. In 2005, facilities were found within the bio-incubator of the Turku Science Park, also enabling collaboration with a local polytechnic through student theses and providing consultants to aid with, for instance, the creation of business plans. A manufacturing company allowed the developers to use its know-how and facilities in the hopes of later producing TeleChemistry servers and components. A professional CEO, a project leader, a laboratory leader, and an expert in clinical and laboratory work (who became the next CEO) joined in because they were familiar with either the LMP project or Oxidizers. The users' motivation was to "advance one's own field," as one of them put it, being deeply uncomfortable with the host of logistics and reliability problems—for example, being "tired of the stupid guarding to ensure that lab assistants don't leave the reagent packages too close to the back of the refrigerator for the night."[18] These kinds of local resources allowed the innovation project to inch closer to the building of a prototype and clarifying the business case and customer value of the concept.

An important aspect of this work was the emergence of technical, conceptual, and business "add-on" inventions that, again, altered the possible ways of framing the concept. To give a better idea of the contingencies involved, let us examine a development path that opened up a new possibility for framing the innovation as a quality control system. This began as a realization that the service concept might not work: while there were reagents that remained stable for months, human control serum did not.

Refilling servers every few weeks at user sites would have been unfeasible. It was known that the hermetic ice valve would keep the serum "virtually unopened," extending its life. And it became apparent that the serum did not even need to stay perfectly stable, as long as one would know precisely how it changed. Such subtle changes could not have been measured by other means, but the LMP excelled at that.

One problem remained, however: where to find an independent point of comparison. To the present day, quality control has been laboratory specific. The same sample, tested in two laboratories with identical methods, was not likely to produce precisely identical results. There was only the indirect, labor-intensive standard method for ensuring that control test results were close to reality. However, in the distributed TeleChemistry system, several servers could be loaded with small amounts of control serum taken from the same lot, hence jointly revealing any deviating daily control test value before the deviation could grow biologically significant. No one had conceived of the idea of grid-type networking and the use of an identical control serum before, since it was not practically realizable.[19]

The innovation network was increasingly confident and optimistic. The optimism was supported by a prominent diagnostic market research report predicting that:

> the future of the IVD [in vitro diagnostic] industry hinges on developing point of care decentralized laboratory testing. POC technologies still need to improve to the point that performance is comparable to central-lab test results. . . . Technology is stagnant. In order to jump to a new industry life cycle, new, relevant technologies will need to be brought to bear.[20]

Such appraisals confirmed the innovators' appraisal of the field—stagnant and hostile to novel and radical solutions—as well as elaborated that this previously impenetrable status quo could in fact be showing signs of destabilization in the wake of the spread of POC tests (even as their present technologies were still too unreliable) and increasing client and analyst frustrations.

But how could quality control be turned into a tangible asset? Guidelines and standards presented themselves as the prime place to turn. The inventor was an observing member of an international working group for guidelines on future quality assurance. While there were wishes for manufacturers to take responsibility for risk reduction, the work was actually focused on increasing the number of procedures for laboratory staff.[21] TeleChemistry's ambition to black-box and automate the procedures performed by people were, in theory, compatible with the aims of the standards, but the means obviously deviated from those required. Very robust demonstrations would be needed to counter the likely incredulity and resistance to such a solution. Thus, once again, the LMP's potential way forward was shrouded—this time by the proven techniques and the vested interests of the industrial and scientific experts who informed the regulators.

Let us again focus on the changes in the innovativeness. The disruptive framing resulted from accumulated experience from the domains the LMP concept was to face. When compared with the vision of the 1970s, the new vision elaborated far more precisely the innovation's immediate contexts and interface points. In Table 9.3, the actors' realization that quality control was a critical issue for TeleChemistry is analytically recognized as the added "system/ensemble" locus, situated between the artifacts and users controlling the artifacts. The table shows how, while there was only incremental improvement in the underlying LMP technology, its discontinuity with laboratory testing was resolved by *expanding the loci of the envisioned product* from artifact to service in the user practice locus, while it started to become evident that innovative activities might have to be expanded even further to prepare the ground for such a product. The laboratory in its present form would be realigned with location-independent networked testing, an unforeseen remote quality control method, and a new business logic—thoughts turned towards the diagnostic process at large.

The new inventions involved a relatively high *degree of novelty* along at least some *dimensions*: remote quality control was discontinuous in standard terms and organizationally, and the service business was discontinuous business-wise (yet location-independent testing was meant to be continuous, even incremental, from the point of view of the doctor who orders tests—the results would be similar but faster).

The changes in the degree of novelty in different dimensions also changed the expected relation between the actors in the field: this way of organizing routine testing would be free of pressures to centralize it, the customer could be either a laboratory or a health care facility directly—or a licensed TeleChemistry service provider, a role possible for both existing and emerging diagnostic companies.

These recent add-on inventions underline the problems that result from expanding the innovative concept in the wake of making it disruptive. The business credibility of TeleChemistry depends significantly on the new quality control method; advancing it requires demonstrating the technology in practice; to find funding and partners to demonstrate the technology is, in turn, difficult as long as the regulatory and business ambiguity remains; and the ways in which the faster testing would affect appointments at future user sites can be anticipated only to a limited extent before field trials. Indeed, when the dimensions of innovativeness turn out to be nearly seamlessly related in all available framings of the innovation, the number of interrelated issues grows, the targets become more and more ambitious, and the amount of work still needed to bring the product to success (or even to markets) grows rather than diminishes, even when the scope and appeal of the overall innovation may be enhanced. There is, hence, an obvious downside to framing the potential breakthrough innovation such that

Table 9.3 The Characteristics and Development of the TeleChemistry System Compared with the Characteristics of a Conventional Clinical Testing System

Locus	TeleChemistry in 2000	TeleChemistry in 2008	For comparison: Conventional clinical testing
Regime/sector	*(Health care: faster clinical diagnostic process)*	*Health care: faster clinical diagnostic process*	Health care: clinical diagnostic process
User practice	*¤# Location-independent testing service*	*¤# Location-independent testing service*	Clinical testing: centralized laboratories + point-of-care tests
System/ensemble	*(Automatic quality control)*	*# Quality control by online pooling and automatic performance and analysis of quality control test results*	Quality control by laboratory staff
Artifact	*Networked analyzers*	*# Networked analyzers*	Laboratory analyzer
Artifact subsystems	*Integrated liquid microprocessor*	*# Integrated* liquid microprocessor	Various mechanical subsystems for performing the analyzer functions
Components	Electroformed capillary structures where liquids move and ice valves operate, laser heating, reagent bags, digital bellows dispenser, and incubation chamber	*# As before +* prototypes for *the serial production of core components*, refrigerator, insulated cover, operation control software, and *nexus to local health information systems*	Syringe dispenser, test tubes, rotating plates, plastic cuvettes, etc.
Principles	*Automatic*, digitally controlled, hermetic, hydraulic, and networked system for liquid processing, based on phase changes and pressure changes	*# As before + based also on remote quality control*	Liquids kept in test tubes by gravity and moved between vessels mechanicallyOpen system for liquid processingLocal quality control

Notes: The locus where the original problem was perceived to be is marked by *. The locus of the envisioned product is marked by ¤. The main locus of work is marked by #. Italics mark work envisioned but not realized; parentheses indicate issues that were assumed not to require innovative work.

its locus would expand: this removes some uncertainties but introduces others. Anticipating and clarifying the likely changes in innovativeness and deviance in different configurations and framings of the project accordingly presents an unavoidable and continuous concern for an ongoing discontinuous innovation project at least throughout its gestation and early development phases.

Taking this challenge seriously means taking trajectory contingencies and divergence to the heart of management of radical innovation. Each of the preceding add-on innovations has its own trajectory, and developers presently expect that at least some unfavorable and confusing ricochets will follow whatever trajectory these form through the thicket of extant practices, institutions, and calculations of interests. The influences affecting the future shape of these trajectories are also better articulated, as are scenarios for what are acceptable outcomes for taking the TeleChemistry project forward, expanding its territory, and enrolling new support. This is in stark contrast to the early days of the project, when its initial thrust was expected to carry through as on a clean purified shooting range. The developers at present are prepared for the arduous work it takes to bend extant trajectories and sever their bindings to extant practices and institutions. Phrased in terms of practice-bound imaginaries, the project has moved from expecting a new imaginary being bound to be realized on its on accord to actively seeking to bind together different expectations, norms, and solutions into a set that would indeed appear as one bound to be realized for the stakeholder groups affecting its fate.

CHAPTER DISCUSSION

The Biography of Technology

The LMP development gradually moved on to an alternative technological pathway: from mechanization to automation, from an open to a closed system, from gravity-based to temperature-based liquid control, from analogue to digital pressure control, from local to networked solutions. All the while, the developers were able to reliably predict technical compatibility, the outcome, the interface points of the future configuration, and effects towards the intended environment *only some distance ahead*. Their view was further obscured by what could be called conceptual discontinuity—the lack of accurate terms, concepts, and traditions to elaborate and contextualize the work, the components, and especially the novel underlying principles.

While there is indeed an air of inevitability in the history of the LMP, it is not one of inevitable thrust but, rather, of the kind of inevitable otherness and deviance in the relations to the tightly interconnected and entrenched PBIs of stakeholders in the clinical chemistry arena (cf. Garud and Karnoe 2001; Hoogma et al. 2002). The hope in this arduous endeavor, in turn, rested on the project's compliance with long-standing desires in clinical chemistry for greater precision and lower reagent consumption. Its imaginative power grew also because several other socio-technical trajectories in the world around the project began to support it: lasers, increasing digitization, the increase in POC testing, distributed computing, *et cetera*. In effect, the clinical chemistry regime has grown less impenetrable in regards to this entrant.

The present form of the LMP has emerged through acknowledging the source and extent of its deviance and then gradually binding together different trajectories, imaginative resources, and new material and conceptual inventions. This horizontal expansion in the project network has been accompanied by the increasing materialization of objects and relations, adding to the "boundness" of the promises and imagination animating the project (even as these are yet far from forming a fully fledged practice-bound imaginary).

Design–Use Relations

The history of the LMP features several shifts in its developer–user relations. The initial Oxidizer invention adds to the list of technically entirely novel solutions invented by users (Lettl et al. 2006), casting doubt on the presumptions about users not engaging in more radical forms of innovation (Christensen and Raynor 2003). As is typical for lead-user inventions, a technical barrier to advancing their work further drove the scientist here to inventing, and, in doing so, was in no way wedded to previous materials or methods used (von Hippel 1988, 2005).

When it came to the development of the even more radical LMP concept, none of the developers had firsthand knowledge of the newly defined future user domain, the clinical laboratory. It does not seem coincidental that these years ended in a dead end. This reiterates the PDMS case finding about the limits of lead-user knowledge when the application area shifts beyond their actual domain of expertise. Equally, when the new disruptive concept has begun to rise from the ashes, it has done so only after the development group came to include people who have firsthand knowledge of clinical laboratories and medical reception practices. In-depth user domain knowledge has been crucial for elaborating plausible and realistic business case and development directions. This, in turn, reiterates the findings from the PDMS and Vivago-Wristcare cases about the value of user-collaboration not being limited to, as often tends to be expressed, user interfaces and "defining appropriate content" for the application but instead significantly affecting project's ability to make adequate decisions about key technical and business matters, too.

Agency, or the Constitution of Developer, User, and Technology

The case further indicates that knowledge about the way in which a particular invention is radical or competence-enhancing or competence-destroying *can only* accumulate gradually in some projects. In this light, analyses of projects whose outcome is already known—whether utilizing innovation typologies or the concept of disruptive innovation (Christensen and Raynor 2003), as well as SNM and transition analyses (Ende and Kemp 1999; Geels 2002)—by default portray breakthrough innovation projects with unrealistic clarity regarding what the project and its implications will turn out to be. This may appear a mere stylistic choice or a matter of convenience. To us, leaving this "fog of innovation" aside appears more consequential, akin to neglecting the "fog of war" in military strategy. This creates an "over-agentification" of the developers, the materials, users, and other stakeholders, making them appear to exert clearly observable and well-cognized influences on the project and its contexts. For instance, Christensen and Raynor (2003) prescribe an easy protocol, a "litmus test," for testing the disruptive potential of an idea. One would simply be a fool in failing to read the litmus paper correctly. However, in the case of technologically discontinuous inventions, it can be far from evident where the *locus* of substitution and disruption should be when the development is still ongoing—e.g., the disruptive idea of bypassing the central laboratory was close to science fiction before the Internet, inexpensive lasers, and a thorough understanding of present business logic and quality assurance practices were available. Reaching a point where a "litmus test" of disruptiveness can be reliably done can require years, even decades, as it did in the LMP case.

Learning

The case analysis underlines Geels's concern about the need to complement the multilevel perspective with "an actor-oriented approach working 'from the inside out' . . . look[ing] at how actors try to navigate transitions, how they develop visions and adapt them through searching and learning" (Geels, 2004, 43). Indeed, in this early period of the potentially radical innovations, frameworks such as PROTEE, SOCROBUST, and ESTEEM seem to provide more sophisticated ways to facilitate adequate learning about the relationship between the project and its contexts (Jolivet et al. 2008). Yet, even though "de-scripting" the project, including its core, can be considered a major original insight in PROTEE (Jolivet et al. 2003), its means have enjoyed little further development in SOCROBUST and ESTEEM in comparison to the other parts of the evaluation process. While we have here analyzed the ongoing case retrospectively, we argue that systematically exploring the innovativeness—here done through elaborating its degree, dimensions, locus, and tightness of connections—presents an approach that could be used to better characterize what is possible and what would be desirable in the nature of the system-to-be. This, in turn, helps to assess the implications of its alternative framings for different stakeholders and vice versa. Yet clarifying the innovativeness and its likely implications requires a great deal of domain knowledge that takes years to accumulate, and hence active network collaboration with, for instance, lead-users and other strategically positioned actors (as in the case studied) is vital in complementing whatever "innovation coaching" is to take place (cf. von Hippel 2005; Lettl et al. 2006; Poti et al. 2006a, 2006b).

In all, once one gives up the hope/fatalistic view that a natural trajectory will emerge from the initial inventive thrust of the project, it becomes pressing to figure out what kinds of entities and dynamics need to be taken into account upon firing human action into motion. These, too, offer a substantial amount of control, even if only through an arduous learning process. In Chapter 11 of this volume, we will return to the TeleChemistry project and show what more specific insight into the biographies framework and constructing a zone of proximal development can offer for envisioning the near future. Before moving into this, however, let us turn to summarizing and theoretically clarifying the lessons these biographies have taught us.

10 Conclusions
Findings and Theorizing

New information technology does not act like a bullet shot to a predictable trajectory. Neither does it behave like a tablet of dye dropped into a glass of water, bound to diffuse and color it to its own image. But it would be equally wrong to say that technology cannot diffuse into society, or that it makes no sense to try to track or anticipate its trajectory. The case analyses in this book have elaborated on the hard and varied work that accompanies whatever diffusion is to happen and whatever next turns are achieved in the trajectory of new technology. Indeed, these and many other registers need work, both in the sense that they need to be worked on further and in the sense that they need to better incorporate work done to orient ongoing technology projects and increase our academic understanding.

The strategy of showing the great relevance of various overlooked issues in economic, managerial, and engineering portrayals of technology and its relationship to society has been the bread and butter of critical and social studies of new information technology for over three decades. Historical and ethnographic case studies have excelled in foregrounding the shortcomings due to contingencies and uniqueness of local settings that are not easily amenable to prediction and instrumental control. The advancing of these studies and related lines of argumentation have, however, come to indicate that new edge and positive contribution could be gained through developing further the methodologies by which social studies of technology are conducted (e.g., Clarke 2005; Collins and Evans 2002; Pollock and Williams 2008). The biographies of technologies and practices approach is part of this pursuit to attend to the circulation of the ideas, aspirations, and information that go into the development and use of new technologies. Its core ideas can be expressed in terms of moving beyond truncated research designs in terms of *reach* (design, development, implementation, everyday use, intermediary activities); in terms of *scale* (beyond just one level of granularity of analysis, "zooming" in and out to bring contesting or enriching phenomena into view); in *balance* in that the theoretical framework should not unduly favor development, use, or any other practice involved (for instance, not defining stakeholders in terms of their relationship to the technology alone); and in the *shape of technology* in that the qualities of artifacts or systems and their effects should not be taken for granted but their change closely attended (without assuming technologies to be objects, black boxes, or "immutable mobiles").

Indeed, a clear finding from the cases in this book is that the choice of site and moment to be studied in the biography strongly prefigures the narrative that can emerge from the study. The "graveyard" of diabetes databases and the collaborative design of PDMS or its later difficulties in regular health centers would alone have yielded very different portrayals of developer–user relations. Similarly, the design episodes of Vivago-Wristcare, its enactments in rest homes, the interactions between its developers and users, and the emergence of the "14th nurse" suggest radically different capacities for the technology and the impacts developers and users can wield with it.

While this stands as a critique of most information systems, human–computer interaction, actor-network, structuration, ethnomethodological, and social construction studies of the 1990s, it resonates with many recent attempts to refine them. Let us move to examining in more detail what new insight the biographies of technology and practice framework provides for developing and using new health ICT.

REPRESENTATION OF USERS AND USAGES

How is usage anticipated and prefigured into new technology? The question can be phrased in terms of where the development project gains its representations of use, users, and contexts of use (Akrich 1995; Williams et al. 2005; Konrad 2008). So far widely different technologies and phases of development have been used to identify sources of user-representation. The biography approach has allowed us to scrutinize the same technologies at several loci and in multiple time frames of analysis, from design interactions to decades of accumulation. This proved indispensable. The Vivago-Wristcare case alone reveals representation of use and users from nearly all of the major directions identified to date (see Chapter 1, this volume). *Investigations to elicit user requirements*, ranging from market surveys to a user-centered design study, were conducted during the early years and generated a set of representations about users, usages, and preferred functionalities (see Chapter 4, this volume). *Extant systems and solutions* such as the previous safety phones, available sensors, robot phones, and elastic bands were a major source for representing usage and users throughout the innovation process (see Chapters 3 and 5, this volume). *Use of oneself and one's personal experience* as a reference took place from time to time, as in the feel of the push-button solution, the width of the wristband, and the pressure and soiling of the wristband. Moreover, in design discourse, common sense and folklore about specific groups of people (such as the elderly) accompanied—and filled gaps between—explicit requirements (see Chapter 5, this volume). *Cultural maturation* was effectively relied upon in the redesign of the control software in 2000 by means of the WIMP format and relying on its "logical" organization, as did the framing of the whole device as a new generation of safety phone (see Chapters 3 and 7, this volume). Interacting and *collaborating with users* (in various ways) provided the major thrust for many of the second-generation redesigns. Finally, developers' participation in their *professional traditions* gave the major thrust in how usage was designed in the earliest years (see Chapter 3, this volume). Examining these traditions as practice-bound imaginaries helped to clarify how they incorporated directly some representations of user and usages and also foregrounded certain ways to design usage over others. Issues such as technical functioning, regulatory demands, and the cost of manufacturing heavily influenced which features were seen as appropriate and desirable, what kind of user interface was sought, and what the criteria (and points of comparison) for principles and neatness of design and reliability were. All of these created *de facto* representations of use; representations that concern usage, even though only expressed in these terms when their implications became visible in the hands of the users (see Chapters 4, 6, and 7, this volume).

Similarly, the PDMS project featured representations of use and users arising from the designers' professional background in building quick-use software for phone ordering. The majority of its user-representations, however, were drawn from user partners who relied on their extensive knowledge of the practices of diabetes care and imaginaries of its future development and medical data handling (see Chapter 8, this volume). In PDMS, extant systems and standards and regulations also provided representations of use, but it is noteworthy that, because of the extensive user-collaboration, the few market investigations conducted had little bearing on design. Another interesting facet of both projects was that media views seemed not to find their way into design in any direct way even as both projects systematically tracked and stored media coverage of both the systems and the user domain.

Indeed, the previously identified sources of user-representation (see Chapter 1, this volume) yield six major source areas with subcategories (see Figure 10.1), and the biographic inquiries seem to suggest that this range of significant inputs for designing usage is not a matter of a range of different projects but a matter of variety even within single projects.

Such variety in major sources of user-representation provides us with a rather different portrait of how users and usages are arrived at during product design from that resulting from any of the endorsed scopes of research in requirement-gathering, marketing, user-centered design, participatory design, or sociology of technology. Indeed, giving each major source of user-representation an equal area in graphical representation provocatively suggests that future research on requirement-gathering should place relatively little emphasis on the most studied of explicit requirement-gathering techniques. Instead, it should take seriously the considerable advances in user involvement in areas such as participatory design (e.g., Bødker et al. 2004; Schuler and Namioka 1993) and innovation studies (e.g., von Hippel 2005),

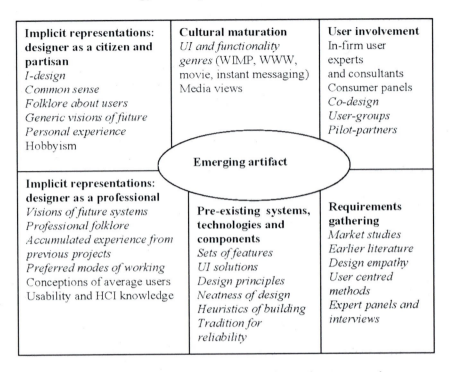

Implicit representations: designer as a citizen and partisan *I-design* *Common sense* *Folklore about users* *Generic visions of future* *Personal experience* Hobbyism	Cultural maturation *UI and functionality* *genres* (WIMP, WWW, movie, instant messaging) Media views	User involvement In-firm user experts and consultants Consumer panels *Co-design* *User-groups* *Pilot-partners*

Emerging artifact

Implicit representations: designer as a professional *Visions of future systems* *Professional folklore* *Accumulated experience from previous projects* *Preferred modes of working* Conceptions of average users Usability and HCI knowledge	Pre-existing systems, technologies and components *Sets of features* *UI solutions* *Design principles* *Neatness of design* *Heuristics of building* *Tradition for* *reliability*	Requirements gathering *Market studies* *Earlier literature* *Design empathy* *User centred methods* *Expert panels and interviews*

Figure 10.1 Major categories and illustrative subclasses for sources of representations of use in technology design. *Italics* indicate sources that were present in the Vivago-Wristcare and PDMS projects.

and help systemize the work that developers routinely do in regard to how they analyze and draw insight from preexisting technologies, components, and systems. But even this covers only half of the terrain to be explored. Implicit representations and cultural maturation present important domains that are actively used but neglected in terms of research, theory-building, and research-based advice for developers. Dismissing these altogether as unreliable appears escapist in regard to R&D realities and hence potentially misses an important source of methodological development. This message concerns equally "rational" development methodologies (e.g., Ulrich and Eppinger 1995) as well as participatory and user-centered approaches in, for instance, more systematically embracing cultural maturation.[1]

Relative Adequacy of User-Representations in Evolving Innovation Contexts

The relative merits and downsides to different sources of user-representation can be compared abstractly to only some extent (Hyysalo 2009b;

Kuniavsky 2003), since much depends on the particular project and innovation context. However, some clear findings emerge that are also backed up by the biographic studies of Hasu (2001a) and Hyppönen (2004).

First, the professional background and imaginaries of developers— including previous artifacts, ways of working, visions of the future, and assumptions about cultural maturation—provided initial but not sufficient grounds to represent use or users. In the Vivago-Wristcare project, early representations led to extensive redesigns after pilots ignored the improvements suggested by the design study. But these representations were close enough to the target that the project survived to this next round. Likewise, in the "graveyard of diabetes databases," both developers' and user-developers' representations of the systems had led to failures, and it is very likely that the two projects united into the PDMS project would have failed, too, had they proceeded on their own.

Second, none of the three projects prospered before sustained user–developer collaboration took place. This may be a more general dynamic. It certainly holds for four other biographic studies on health technology (Hasu 2001a; Hyppönen 2004, 2007; Kivisaari et al. 1998; Hyysalo 2000), and an in-depth look at innovation communities for other digital technologies has revealed surprising importance for producer–user linkages in close to 20 cases studied by the Finns. The collaboration provided a deeper understanding of users' contexts and priorities in their work, sharpened ideas about what would be possible and what required functionalities, and in the cases of PDMS and Vivago-Wristcare greatly contributed to the details of interface design. The interchange also called into question prior assumptions; for instance, in the PDMS co-design it turned out that the developers' vision to build an all-inclusive medical archive was unfeasible due to the complexity of data presentation that would have ensued.

Third, user requirements for new technology are seldom readily explicated, awaiting their collection (see Chapter 4, this volume). All sources of user-representation build on experiences and interpretations of design and appropriation of previous artifacts—be these everyday, professional learning, or scientific inquiry. The relative adequacy of a given source differs with regard to what kind of constellation between design and use has prevailed over time, how effective and extensive social learning processes have been to date, how much the development project at hand differs from earlier ones, and what kinds of instruments are available to facilitate the articulation. For instance, PDMS user-developers built on two decades of attempts to codify the information needs and information handling in patient reception. Small wonder that they could provide detailed design suggestions. In the Vivago-Wristcare project, the brief direct contact with users in the 1995 design study brought to the surface several user needs that pilot use later verified as important ones. But these were all of the kind that was *elaborated to the users themselves* through their use of earlier safety-phone systems to the extent that the mock-ups and drawings could tease them out (whereas market surveys did not). No elaboration emerged with regard to the new monitoring functions. It must be remembered that in both Vivago-Wristcare and the PDMS project the eventually beneficial interactions between engineers and users spanned several years and took place at a stage when there already was a first version or a previous proto-type to facilitate collaboration.

In addition, it is worth remembering that in the PDMS project not all users got well represented even by the extensive user-innovation commu-nity, and in the Vivago design process some of the user-representations val-ued by developers became *shadowed over* and faced *erosion* in contact with other use-related concerns. Managing user-representations in the course of design work as well as in the longer time frame of a progressing innova-tion project presents a challenge that goes far beyond correcting developer's values or priorities.

Ecologies of Intermediation and Circulation

The elaboration of user needs and developers' awareness of users' domain brings us to the intermediaries and circulation between development and use on the scale of a particular project as well as in a longer time frame. The Vivago-Wristcare project illustrates well the kinds of intermediaries that tend to be involved in mediating between development and use in a linear innovation context. Literature on the users' domain, two pieces of market research, a design study, pilot trials, and a branding company proffered representations of the user. After the launch of the product, intermediate users such as assembly workers from vendors and managers of rest homes became key user-side intermediaries. They helped to configure the system and reconfigure the associated work practices, facilitated the everyday uses and problems, and brokered contacts and information between the every-day usages and suppliers' ongoing development efforts. The component and platform providers were seemingly bracketed off "behind" the company building the health monitoring application, but in reality the configuration of the system brought issues surrounding platform and integration with other technologies back in, giving rise to intermediary activities by assem-blers and local small vendors (see Chapters 4, 6, and 7, this volume).

An evolving co-design innovation context can differ dramatically from the linear. In PDMS, there was a notable lack and irrelevance of interme-diaries, which one by default encounters in other innovation contexts such as market research, marketing and advertisement agencies, and usability consultants. In effect, the co-located design between users and developers bridged *the ecological niches of these actors* between development and use. In addition to design knowledge, users conveyed a very exact understand-ing of the markets, buying dynamics, and so on, and were active in market-ing the application. The user-designer community also held great depth and breadth in terms of addressing typical user-side intermediary activities: for instance, people in neighboring hospitals conveyed their expertise to newcomers to the use of the program. Indeed, in evolutionary co-design, informal intermediaries and local experts appear to be the key intermediaries.

The studies also show that over time a particular project, technology, or constituency can move between different innovation contexts—for example, when a technology moves from an exploratory phase to accumulation of functionality and onwards to being "generified" for a mass market (Hyysalo and Lehenkari 2003; Hasu 2001a; Hoogma et al. 2002; Williams et al. 2005; Pollock and Williams 2008). In the PDMS case, the IT company withdrew from evolutionary user involvement in 2001–2002 but later had to engage in innofusion-domestication-type further development (Chapter 8, this volume). Likewise, Vivago Ltd. moved from a linear to an innofusion-domestication-type constellation and back towards a more linear context (Chapter 7, this volume). As these kinds of shifts occur, some intermediaries tend to be sidelined in favor of others. Indeed, Vivago-Wristcare's developers bypassed the sales and maintenance organizations of their vendors and hired a seasoned technician to mediate information from user sites back to R&D . . . who then gradually moved out of this position to sales, because of his proficiency also there.

This hire brings us to the more sustained ecologies around different kinds of technologies and practices. The technician in question had been selling, assembling, training in, and maintaining safety-phone systems for over a decade and had worked for all major manufacturers in the region. In this facility, he was one of just three assembly and maintenance people who did the Y2K update for the whole stock of tens of thousands of Finnish safety phones, factually gaining an exhaustive survey of the deployment, the state of the problems, shoots for new procedures and features, *et cetera* (Hyysalo et al. 2003). In affinity, the PDMS project united many of the previous user-developers of diabetes databases in different hospitals around Finland. One of the problems in the LMP project was that it failed to fit the existing PBIs, and, because of its radical novelty, the existing ecologies had almost no connections geared towards intermediating its commercial and use-value claims, at least not ones with sufficient legitimacy. The sustained ecologies pre-domesticate both actors and novelties, but by the same token they predispose actors towards regarding novelty as mere deviance (Stewart and Hyysalo 2008; Höyssä and Hyysalo 2009).

These ecologies are further characterized by various *multilevel games*. On the one hand, multilevel games concern the *position* of the actors involved (Nicoll 2000; Stewart and Hyysalo 2008). Whatever investigations and evaluations were conducted in the three projects were from the outset positioned in terms of the eyes of partners, patrons, regulators, or potential investors. Adjusting these relations was at least as important a usage of the inquiry as was informing the development work. For instance, Vivago-Wristcare was evaluated in several pilots, which reported lacks or malfunctioning, but the very same appraisals were framed as positive demonstrations by the developers and actively used in the negotiations with investors and partners as witness to there being only minor hiccups. Such interpretive flexibility in trials for innovation has been well known ever since the days of Edison (Bazerman 1998), and the interesting issue here is the circulation and shaping of interdependent representations: those of the technology, of the development project and the developer company, and of users, as well as of experts conducting and responding to inquiries. Each party has multiple goals in presenting these to the other parties through responses, views, and findings. We can characterize these representations of future technology as forming one of the "currencies" that is being traded among stakeholders. Investment-hungry start-ups and intermediary agencies live on the money they establish through passing, modifying, and creating the representations and objects wherein these are embodied (evaluation reports, pieces of software, prototypes, repaired installations; cf. Nicoll 2000; Williams et al. 2005).

The second aspect of multilevel games is that power relations and *conflicts of interest are blended with mutually beneficial collaboration.*[2] In PDMS, the harmonious co-design of the diabetes software lasted only until the company had accumulated sufficient functionality. This functionality, in turn, had been furthering the subjugation of primary care physicians under the specialist. Similarly, in Vivago-Wristcare, introducing continuous monitoring of relatively healthy residents and seeking cost savings through technically supported extramural care were resisted by many in elderly care. The developers learned to differentiate their message for different audiences, to tone down their most unnerving ideas and introduce a set of changes to make the staff in elderly care more positively disposed. When the reputation and reliability of the technology increased, the developers returned to more stringent instructions on how to deploy the system and some of the new care facilities hired one fewer staff member because of the added technical security (Gävert 2008).

Third, "multilevel game" characterizes the complex epistemic situation. Whatever information there is, its reliability and validity hinge on side bets of the actors involved in its production and evaluation (Becker 1960). Commitments to recognized ways to produce knowledge (one practice-bound imaginary or a mix of several) are the closest thing for classifying the reliability and validity of a piece or source of information. Information becomes highly perspective based, as we've seen in the cases of diabetes experts, safety-phone producers, and elderly-care nurses. Information is at times also purposefully framed, made opaque, and strategically manipulated because the actors themselves are aware of the ties it has to their position and power and the competition they face.

There is a temptation to be fascinated by the indeed formidable mediating capabilities of such an ecology of intermediaries, and to portray it as a smoothly functioning machinery of qualification, resulting in an "economy of qualities" where the work of qualification is able to adjust the characteristics of products and tastes of the consumers into agreeable convergence. This may not be at all wrong when it comes to relatively stable products such as orange juice and pop music (Callon et al. 2002; Hennion 1989). But when it comes to innovative new products, the "economy of qualities" is rather a complex ecology of intermediation characterized by the disjunctions, indeterminacy, and learning that go into achieving trans-actions to do with qualities. Indeed there are constant shifts between the objects (characteristics of products), means (how to gain and convey infor-mation), subjects (creating, for instance, "transacting customers"), and the second-order learning (what goes into achieving information exchange for achieving transactional relations). In all, such a circulating ecology of things and knowledge between users, producers, and various intermediar-ies is far from systematic knowledge accumulation. Details about usages are unlikely to be attended if it does not happen to be in the interest of the person in question to attend to or record them; information from other, previous competitive projects trickles rather than flows into a new innova-tive quest; and the positions of intermediating people and other repositories in producer organizations and particularly informal help at user sites tend to be precarious (for extended discussion and examples see Stewart and Hyysalo 2008).

LEARNING IN AND BETWEEN DEVELOPMENT AND USE

The importance of the ecology and economy of circulating people, things, and information resonates with various attempts to view innovation in terms of learning. In Chapter 1 of this volume, we set out to provide more substance to conceptualizations of learning between developers and users in frameworks such as the SLTI and "learning economy" (LE). The concern is well voiced by Lehenkari, who notes that in the learning economy "the learning process remains a black box whose input consists of producers, users and their interactions and whose output for innovation is recognized, while what occurs between the input and output is obscure" (Lehenkari 2006, 45). What then *does* occur in between?

In the gestation and early development phase, two intertwined learn-ing processes were prominent in all three cases. The more straightforward one was learning about relevant matters, such as technical possibilities, adjoining technologies, user preferences, regulations, and so on, to deter-mine what could be built into the system. This knowledge was mediated by reports, standards, existing products, and (more or less chance) contacts with various practitioners and potential end users. The other side of the coin was learning what should not be in the product, what could be hazard-ous or detrimental to include, what issues could be left out or postponed for later releases, etc. In the analytic terminology adopted in this book, it was about *bindings* between the objects of heterogeneous engineering work: how relevant issues and objects were bound to others and which bindings were likely to be strictly enforced, hard to undo, or allowed more latitude. The difficulty in grasping the various bindings is that it requires more in-depth understanding of implicated practices than mere identification of relevant issues. This, in turn, sheds light on the (surprisingly) deep-seated difficulties developers had in anticipating the reception of their initial inventions.

Learning about issues and their bindings was further complicated because of the epistemic and positional multilevel games as well as the power relations potentially involved. By stressing "representation" of users, uses, and configurations rather than "knowledge" about these issues we have sought to underline how gathering, interpretation, assessment, and prioritization of the available information presented a complex and layered inferential environment (in contrast to viewing this as elicitation of objective and well-defined requirements for the new product, which is the way much of R&D management literature portrays this). But not necessarily and not always. Both the early PDMS project and Vivago-Wristcare project, around its second generation, feature periods of rather straightforward exchanges about what would need to be in the product and what would be feasible for the developers to incorporate.

This brings us to the importance of mediation and scaffolding, two concepts in cultural psychology. Particularly in the early years, much of learning about the user needs and possible technical configuration depends heavily on the mediating means people have at their disposal for elaborating and envisioning the future application. Such scaffolding includes *material and conceptual mediators* standing in for the future system and its context of use. Respondents' ability to appreciate, question, and contribute to design ideas hinges on how the technology is presented, as we discussed in the Chapter 4 of this volume. Literature on participatory and user-centered design has arrived at the same conclusion on account of experiments with scenarios, use cases, mock-ups, and functional prototypes by which designers can augment informants' ability to transcend current conditions (Greenbaum and Kyng 1991; Beyer and Holtzblatt 1998). However, sustained contact and communication appears to have been at least as important as mediation by signs and tools. Relatively crude material means such as pen, paper, problem listings, and later prototypes and working versions of the technology were accompanied by long discussions and acquainting the developers with users' contexts. These interchanges, not least because they were sustained over several years in PDMS and Vivago-Wristcare after the market launch, were crucial for the learning. It is safe to say that sufficient learning could take place in spite of sophisticated means, but, no matter how sophisticated the means, it could not have prospered without sustained contact. This is an important lesson in regard to the predominant "tool-orientation" in the user-innovation and user-centered design literature.[3] We can concretize this by revisiting the learning dynamics that went into establishing cooperative relationships between developers and users after the market launch of Vivago-Wristcare. Effective learning *in* their relations was tied to various forms of learning *for* their effective interactions (see Chapters 6 and 7, this volume):

1. *Learning about technical problems in field use* also had a by-product of making developers and users meet in users' settings.
2. *Users' learning how to operate the technology and make it work in practice* was pivotal for appraisals of shortcomings and how to improve it.
3. *Destabilization of and unlearning the existing assumptions of the product and its use* is another way to express the second-order learning from developers from early "bug-fixing orientation."
4. *Opening new cognitive trails on the multi-organizational terrain,* increasing acquaintance with who inhabited the producer–user arena, what they were willing to provide, how to interact with them, *et cetera.*
5. *The artifact as an expanding boundary object.* While the shell of the device black-boxed its inside/outside for the respective party, the increasing shared area in the object facilitated interactions greatly.
6. *Actively forming and sustaining networks of collaboration* through frequent visits and attention, deals geared towards development, creation of customized systems, devising of arrangement for reporting ideas, *et cetera*, was key to actually learning *in* these relationships.
7. *Managing tensions between learning and other priorities.* After the market launch, the company was desperate for cash flow, and three years later it was equally desperate to reduce the number of versions of the system that existed, in order to streamline its development and make it profitable. Segmenting customer and pilot sites, postponing features to larger version launches, and learning how to soothe disgruntled customers were all ways that gradually emerged for handling the tensions that prevailed between profitable sales and sufficiently satisfied customers and collaboration partners.

These dynamics sketch a varied topography of the learning that takes place in the ecology between production and consumption. On the one hand, much of the learning is simply a by-product of conducting other matters. It happens to some degree almost automatically in encounters and problematic situations. At the same time, however, important parts of the learning are precarious and require concentrated and continued efforts to come into fruition. Conflicts of interest, personal sacrifices of time and mental energy, disappointment, and unwillingness and failure to learn all feature significantly in the encounters and learning between developers and users. Collaborative relationships, openness about one's problems and goals, and willingness to do extra work for the benefit of the other party are easily undermined, even collapsed.

Learning in Developer–User Relations as an Object of Study

The preceding findings have implications for empirically studying and theorizing about the learning between developers and users. Clearly, the learning that occurs in design–use relations is not limited to the small-scale problem-solving tasks typical of behaviorist and cognitive learning research. To paraphrase Lave (1993), this learning is a part of substantial forms of action, spread over time and place, taking its meaning from its connections with and within other activity systems; it concerns multiple aspects of participation at once and tends to surpass any given problem or event. Neither is the learning reducible to firm-level or organizational learning, in that both the learning of individuals and groups and learning between organizations play an important part (Lehenkari 2006). This results in a need to orient to, conduct, and integrate findings from qualitatively different analyses:

1. Studying co-located interaction between developers and users is best captured by videotaped ethnographic material on actions and interactions and via careful interaction analysis, including scrutiny of the material means and interpretations of participants. Studies of "in the wild" interactions have been typical of studies in ethnomethodology, but few of them have addressed learning in this tradition (but see Melander and Sahlström 2009). Hasu's research on learning in developer–user encounters offers pathbreaking work in this regard (Hasu and Engeström 2000; Hasu 2001a; Miettinen and Hasu 2002).

2. Such analyses are vital for gaining a grasp of the situational specifics of interaction but leave much unattended: apart from technology experiments, developers and users are relatively seldom co-located. Interlinked episodes in developers' and users' activities need to be bridged in a principled way, even if the analyses then use similar data and analysis of directly observable behavior (Hyysalo and Lehenkari 2005; Hasu 2001b).

3. The preceding discussions on learning, however, predominantly describe strings of events distributed to both producer and user sites within which learning happens or fails to happen. These can only partially be ever directly observed and require inferences from multiple, more or less indirect sources of evidence. Some of their aspects became visible during field observations of design meetings and product usage, and they were further confirmed through interviews. Some only became visible because of the longitudinal scope of the study. In the biography approach here, historical and ethnographic inquiry were combined in order to zoom in on and out from the processes, a prerequisite to studying how individual and collective learning processes emerged and evolved over time (see Chapter 7 and the Data Appendix of this volume for exact data and methods used).

In all, the conceptual register for addressing learning in developer–user relations needs to cover situated learning episodes as well as slow changes in objects, practices, and participations. It further needs to link these in a principled manner. Owing to these reasons, activity theory's symmetrical terms for discussing development and use proved valuable.

With these findings, let us return to the learning economy (LE) and social learning in technological innovation (SLTI)frameworks. With regard to *learning as an empirical object of study*, learning by doing, using and interacting (DUI) denotes phenomena with economic significance, yet the learning processes involved may indeed be less clear. For instance, decades-long improvements in new airplanes have been characterized as learning-by-doing and learning-by-using (Gardiner and Rothwell 1985; cf. Rosenberg 1979). Even if learning is regarded as an unintentional outcome of processes that have a different aim from learning or increasing competence (Lundvall and Vinding 2005; Lehenkari 2006), glossing as learning—or taking learning as the side effect of—all the adjustments, calculations, competition, planning, tinkering, requests, complaints, etc., that went on for all this time in a number of large companies runs into serious over- and underdetermination problems. Many events that in hindsight have produced convergent or stabilizing outcomes visible in products and procedures may have had little to do with learning. At the same time, much of the learning in developer–user relations leads to divergent outcomes and trials that will not be identifiable as aggregate outcomes visible in the traditional data-sets or methods used by economists and economic historians (Miettinen 2002b, 45).

These problems concern both DUI and SLTI insofar as they resort to a "learning-by" register. To put it bluntly, such a register addresses learning in a sanitized social, behavioral, and objectual sense. Objects, domination, miscarried efforts, sacrifices, and unwillingness and failure to learn—all crucial parts of learning between developers and users we have witnessed in the course of this book—do not feature anywhere. Such a way of treating learning also fails to account for the objects of learning or the content and organization of relations within which it takes place. Issues such as users' gradual learning of their actual requirements, management of conflicting priorities in mundane encounters, difficulties in judging between competing representations of use, and multilevel games each characterize phenomena that practitioners struggle with but that fall through the cracks of learning-by conceptions. There is also a lack of concepts for discussing particularly the micro-level learning processes, and there has been little reporting on research designs for studying them in either framework.

There naturally are differences in what is represented through learning. In LE and DUI, learning foremost opposes neoclassical economics and assumptions of circular flow. It is used to emphasize the importance of continuously changing amount and kind of information as well as the interdependencies and organization of economic actors in an innovation system

(Lundvall 1988; Lundvall and Johnson 1994). In SLTI, learning is deployed to underscore the importance of trials, experiments, interactions between actors, and carry-over between projects in socioeconomic change (Sorensen 1996; Williams et al. 2005). The present book has also attempted to grasp the learning processes and dynamics of how developers and users interact and how this effects innovation processes (Hasu 2001b; Miettinen 2002b; Lehenkari 2006). Nonetheless, learning and interaction between producers and users—however these are treated—are key elements used to clarify socio-techno-economic change in all three approaches. In a positive vein, the partially shared referents between the three approaches to producer–user learning can support each other. Through LE, the significance of the case study findings can be argued to more aggregate and stylized economics models. Case studies, in turn, should make the claims to visible handshakes and interactive learning stronger. An implication here is that an integrative framework such as SLTI or LE—even if the framework does not aim to offer a nuanced conceptual repertoire for studying these learning processes—should treat learning in a manner that is compatible with frameworks that can do this adequately.

REFINING THE CONCEPTS FOR THE SHAPE AND SHAPING OF TECHNOLOGY: PRE-, DE-, RE-, AND CO-CONFIGURATION

The final section of this theoretical conclusion addresses our findings from the perspective of early evolution of technology, in conjunction to what they imply for our understanding of the shape and shaping of technology. In order to addresses these two themes introduced in Chapter 2 of this volume, we need to go somewhat deeper into technology studies theory than in the two previous sections of this chapter.

Social studies of technology have been a forerunner in conceptualizing the nature of technology. A significant outcome from the 1980s and 1990s studies was conceptualizing technology as heterogeneous ensembles or assemblages. Technologies were conceptualized as socio-techno-econo-cultural hybrids composed of various and even disparate elements that were assembled together to make "a technology" emerge (e.g., Bijker et al. 1987; Law 1991; Law and Bijker 1992). Rather than assuming that technology is composed of certain objects, researchers paid attention to what the sets of relations were that actually allowed something to act as technology in the settings of the actors studied. In effect, the question "who uses technology for what?" was reframed as one of what networks and association comprise technology, its design, use, and its users in a given moment (Baraldi 2009; Helgesson and Kjellberg 2009). Another outcome of these studies was a set of concepts for discussing how design, use, and technology are related. "Configuring the user" attempted to describe how designers built the user into computer hardware to favor enactment of only certain kinds of uses and user-ship (Woolgar 1991;

Grint and Woolgar 1997). Inscription, prescription, and users' subscription or de-inscription provided a more dynamic view of technology's temporal unfolding, akin to a script of a play (see Chapters 1 and 2, this volume).

The reach and scales used in the biographical studies in this book highlight some shortcomings in these conceptualizations. "Script" has a connotation of inscription resulting in *the* script in *the* artifact, one that is either weak or strong and then becomes subscribed to, contested, or subverted by its users (Latour 1991; Akrich 1992; Akrich and Latour 1992). Even though the notion of script can perhaps be made more robust by distinguishing developers' inscription from their ascription[4] and users' alignment from their compliance, building of nonconsequences of users' actions from developers' "respondance" and mutually held ignorance of the respective party's doings (Helgesson and Kjellberg 2006), the concept retains further deep-seated problems in describing design–materiality–usage relations. The "stage" of socio-technical encounters is almost never cleared to include only the designers' script (or "program for action") and users' response to it (e.g., possible anti-programs or "compliant nonalignment"). Further, many technologies indeed are heterogeneous ensembles that tend to have more complex affordances rather than clear scripts. While configuring is more compatible with ensemble, the idea that developers sought to configure users and other stakeholders who, in turn, configured designers (Johnson 2007; Mackay et al. 2000)[5] remains at the level of materialized interests and influences and does not reach into what happens in the encounters between materials and humans (Hennion 2007).

Finally, both configuring and scripts emphasize the "politicized" side of developer–technology–user relations and its military metaphors: the shifting battle line and negotiation on whose schemata will have the last word. The appropriation of technology is seldom a matter of wholesale subscription or de-inscription, and, as we have seen throughout this book, "de" and "re" are, almost necessarily, also productive, additive, and noncompeting aspects in the life of a technological configuration. They are also more sustained moments in the biography of technology, often blended with different forms of coordination and collaboration. Technologies and practices are simply more than politics by other means (and politics includes more than realpolitik power plays).

To avoid introducing yet more vocabulary to technology studies,[6] let us turn more deeply to configuring and configuration, since these notions could indeed help refine the vocabulary for describing the changing heterogeneous ensembles that constitute "a technology" and its "developers" and "users" in different times and places. Figuration (and its verb form "figuring"), the act of formation, is apt for drawing attention to the gradual and continuous shaping of technology that takes place in multiple arenas and modes in the life of a technology. This process of figurating technology is literally con-figuration, "figuring with," weaving things together into assemblies and capabilities for action.

The more technical usage of "configuration" retains the sense of the many elements being figured together, while resisting connotations of a unified and universal entity such as a system, object, or artifact. This is particularly relevant in characterization of ICT, especially in health settings. Vivago-Wristcare is a prime example, as was shown in Chapters 7 and 8 of this volume. While innovation taxonomies would be likely to classify it as a fairly linearly developed and self-sustained device (cf. Fleck 2002; Pavitt 1984), an in-depth look reveals that the "device" in fact consisted of an orchestration of multiple layers of configuration: The hardware of the device was, for the most part, composed of a novel arrangement of off-the-shelf components, and its functionality created by arranging PCs, cell phones, the telephone network, receiver units, and so on. Its value in use depended on the way it could be reconfigured to be intertwined with the fabric of actions and infrastructure in rest homes, alarm centers, vendor organizations, and the lives of the relatives. These configurations (what the technology is, what is part of it, and what is not) changed from one location to another.

Another way of phrasing this in design-oriented vocabulary is that "a technology" consists of various venues of material and symbolic design: (a) design of hardware and software components; (b) design of products and product systems; (c) design of local technical assemblage; (d) design of socio-technical procedures in using and utilizing new and old technologies; (e) (re)design of personal and collective projects of users as well as networks of using and securing, maintaining, and updating the technology; and (f) at the more slowly changing end of the spectrum, partial redesign of collective activities in which people work and spend their leisure.

While talking in terms of design may clarify what is meant, it also highlights why figuration–configuration is more apt terminology. To call all of the preceding "design" is to evoke a utopian "planning register" for how people's lives, hobbies, work, etc., are organized. In contrast, figuration has a more multifaceted figure, so to speak. While "to figure" means counting or calculating, it also means being included in the story, having a role. "Figure" also points to images made, such as drawings, which keeps open the question of whether the figuration stands for, or displaces, something else (Haraway 1997, 11). In this capacity, figuring draws attention to how different layers and different modes of configuration become embedded in an artifact. The previous markings constrain and suggest what is sensible to brush in or collage later but do not determine it. Many of these features reach (temporary) closures and are hard to reverse afterwards or by other people engaged with the technology (see the following and Chapters 6 and 8, this volume). At the same time, the figure of technology may be radically altered by placing it in yet another configuration or altering some layer in its constitution. Neither is technology a *mere* carrier of designers' intents or norms. As we learned from the mini-biographies in Chapter 5 of this volume, and from the added flexibility in customizing software in Chapters 7 and 8, it matters greatly how initial ideas are shaped in interactions among materials, other priorities, schedules, finances, *et cetera*, and what the users and usage contexts offer in further altering them.

The process of figuration can be analytically divided into four modes of shaping of technology—namely, pre-, de-, re-, and co-configuring. Let us first examine *pre-configuring* of the (sub)configurations that compose a functioning technology-in-use. An obvious mode of pre-configuring is what Woolgar describes in his study of configuring the user: designers' actions in trying to build in the ways they prefer users to be acting with an artifact. As Chapters 3 and 5 of this volume elaborate upon, we might contest the inferences from values to artifact, but such *pre-configuration* tends to reflect some closure of meaning and stabilization of form among its developers. However, as soon as this configuration leaves developers' lab and enters users' sites, it meets other prefigurations that will equally comprise the technology that may emerge. Such pre-configurations among users include, but are not limited to, procedures, routines, norms, conventions of artifact usage, and patterns in implementing new technologies. Other typical pre-configurations are those of regulators and institutions connected to a particular kind of technology or domain of users. The choice of the term "pre-configuring" thus emphasizes the fact that at least any closure or stabilization reached only among designers, only among users, or only among third parties tends to remain partial in time and in space.

The move from design to use means a crucial transformation for a technology. The technology is no longer nurtured in a loving and technically competent environment but becomes intertwined into the practices of users, who often do not share the skills, enthusiasm, and values of the designers (Engeström and Escalante 1996; Hasu 2001a). In figuration terms, there are two intertwined processes at stake. *De-configuring* marks altering and questioning of both the technology and existing ways of acting—and potentially contesting the prefigurations built in the technology or extant practice. These processes intertwine with *reconfiguring*: connecting, adding in, repurposing, omitting, and creating new solutions that change the shape of the socio-technical configuration. In other words, in making technology happen, in appreciation of its characteristics, the trajectories of artifacts become mingled with the trajectories of other artifacts, people, procedures, and so on. The scripts in the artifact become intertwined (added to, contested by) other scripts. As we saw in Chapter 6 of this volume, there tends to be an array of potential scripts but far fewer actual versions finally enacted by users, owing to historically formed prefigurations of materialities, imagining, and aspirations in their practices.

As the three biography studies show, some form of *active co-configuring* between designers and users was a prerequisite for survival for any of the innovations studied. The cases reveal several different modes of co-configuring. In the LMP case, the *developers were themselves lead-users* of Oxidizers, but they also interacted with other lead-users in their further development. In the LMP's pre-prototype phase, physicians and clinical laboratory experts again joined the development work. Similarly, the PDMS project grew out of *extended collaboration* with developers and users. In the Vivago-Wristcare case, there were *cycles of reconfiguring* technology, where users first reconfigured their existing practices and the new artifact into a technological configuration; the developers then refigured their initial product anew after discovering that the technology was not functioning (and was not being used) according to their wishes; and this was followed by users responding to new changes, etc. This intensified into *coordinated improvement of technology* where developers and a number of user organizations jointly created and improved arrangements within which they can learn how to shape the technology to their mutual benefit. The years 2001–2003 for both PDMS and Vivago-Wristcare also witnessed *disharmonious coordination*, where the producer sought to gain feedback from users but translated it to the product with delay and strictly within the limits of its own interests. Finally, the ecology between design and use reveals *dispersed co-configuration* of intermediaries, products, and user-representatives in the events in elaborating the properties of future product and its use. These forms of co-configuration underscore the need to further examine the forms and strategies of designer–user collaboration all too often lumped under "co-design" or even user-centered design.

In addition to active co-configuring, the more *passive forms of co-configuring* technology deserve due attention. Acceptance of a range of factual shortcomings in the early technological configuration took place in both the Vivago-Wristcare and PDMS projects. In the Vivago-Wristcare project, user and developer organizations regularly *silenced* some of the problems known to them in development practice (e.g., in the reliability of monitoring) and use (e.g., cases where users had run into problems when acting against instructions) so as not to unduly alarm or burden the other party. They further *refrained* from imposing on the other party ultimatums deemed impossible (e.g., on how to wear the device and, reciprocally, on reducing its false alarms and interface problems). Particularly important was that addressing most shortcomings was in mutual agreement *deferred* to later launches in PDMS as well as in Vivago-Wristcare, factually co-configuring these technologies as developments-in-progress and replacing certainty with confidence in their inadequacies becoming resolved. Supporting the observations of Helgesson and Kjellberg (2006), such aversions of oppositional actions ("anti-programs") were indeed key for the evolution of these technologies, not least because the survival of their financially tight technological development squarely depended on not facing the full pressure to get everything right from the outset.

Let us further clarify some of the key issues implied in the above configurational conceptualization of technology.

Why Configurations and Not Just Things or Objects?

Understanding technologies as configurations is motivated by the view that configuration, not object or artifact or thing or system, just may be the closest to a prototypical arrangement of materiality. What we mean here is well exemplified by the LMP. With the principles of its functioning and its components, artifact subsystems, the LMP analyzer started off as a set of component technologies and gradually worked into a configuration and then towards an increasingly integrated whole that in most respects could function as a black-boxed artifact. Should the TeleChemistry concept become what is presently intended, it would form a tightly coupled seamless web, but only if the particular configurations can be integrated can the system begin to have any system dynamic that covers its entirety and charts a clear path for sensible development directions. Both would be formidable achievements in turning the present configuration into an integrated and relatively "independent" whole. And, even then, some configurationality would still remain at the "useful ends" of the so rendered "artifact" and "system." For instance, in the physicians' patient reception, the LMP box and TC service would still constitute just one instrument among the many that need to be orchestrated. Indeed, configurations seem inescapable, while other forms of materiality may never appear and, when doing so, appear as refinements, deletions, integration, *et cetera*, of initial configuring.

Technology as an Evolving Mesh of Materialized Characteristics

There is abundant criticism of treating materiality as only objects of contemplation. Despite the elaborate turns to embodiment, transformation, and technological condition, the conceptions of technology have a great tendency to center on an individual (often the analyst) and his encounters with the technology in question. Even when it has become a truism to *note* that technologies *qua* technologies exist only as part of activities, the movement of technology both spatially and temporally has been treated as an *additional*, not definitive, issue of concern. The biographies approach makes evident the need to conceptualize technology in *spatially and temporally* more nuanced ways.

Technologies do not take place as individual encounters between the human and machine. Moreover, products, in contrast to custom-built systems, come to be constituted *simultaneously* by:

a) a myriad of particular installations of the technology, each having its own history of figuration, a biography of its change and intertwinement

b) the generic offering constituted by intertwined biographies of
   - a generic core/model that gets transformed relatively infrequently
   - several different "versions" for different clienteles

- additional modules and technologies
- attachable to any particular configuration
- a mesh of different "releases" and "customizations" of each version

c) the interactions and feedback that move between the generic offering and particular biographies: upgrades and instructions shape particulars and some changes in some particulars shape the generic offering

d) the "dispersion dynamics" by which particulars take more distance and which are retained in a closer bond to the generic offering (this includes segmenting the sites into pilot, consultative, and purely transactional customers)

e) the "congregation dynamics" by which both customers and the producer reconfigure new elements from neighboring fields into the configurations

A technology is hence not any single "product" or "artifact" but a bundle of capabilities, which evolve in parallel, on different sites, and at different rates. It has been customary to prioritize the "supplier's generic technology" as a stabilizing core. Exercising a balanced, non-artifact-or-supply-centered framework makes it evident that the kernel or other generic core is not the only stabilizing source in technology. Practices of users and other stakeholders have sets of orienting and organizing poles that persistently affect technology, as we have tried to emphasize through examining the activities and practice-bound imaginaries involved. Hence, the mesh of configurations weaves around several poles and yet retains an identity even though it is clearly one that has porous boundaries (Star 1989b; Bowker and Star 1999; de Laet and Mol 2000).

Apt conceptual means to address this temporally and spatially complex character of technology may indeed be lacking. Even in Antoine Hennion's beautiful elaborations of how taste emerges in attending the materialities and suspending one's identity and activity to make room for the respondance of objects, and how these attendances build on historically formed registers of cultivation, elaboration, and comparison involving the object, there is a register shift between momentary and sustained materiality. Whenever in the moment of appreciation the object—wine, pop song, or rock wall—is examined as an instantaneous respondent in the event. When it comes to the makeup of the event that has shaped particular objectivity, subjectivity, and tastings, the object is suddenly a general one, dispersed to practices, and at worst "taste effectively depends on everything," an infinitude of networks and attachments (Hennion 2007). Indeed, the configurational understanding of technology as an intertwined web of (socio) materializations spread through time and place introduced earlier could help in moving between the particulars and generics of technology in more nuanced manner.

Persistence by Temporally and Spatially Limited Closures, or, Evolution of "Impact" on Practice, Organization, and Imagination

Early technology studies revolved significantly around the concepts of closure of meaning and stabilization of form as adopted from sociology of science (Bijker and Pinch 1984; Latour 1987). When modalities such as time, place, arrangements, and doubts could be removed from a finding, its reality as representing nature grew, finally forming a universal scientific fact (Fleck 1979; Latour and Woolgar 1979). The success of technology was then equally treated as an outcome of efforts to enroll the relevant stakeholder groups in accepting what the appropriate form and meanings given to technology would be. If all the work—including standardization; black-boxing of functionality; integrating the technology into wider systems; and creating markets, practices, and distribution—achieved its mark, the network supporting the technology would be hard to reverse, making the success of the technology also appear inevitable in retrospect (Latour 1987; Callon 1991; Bijker 1995).

The present studies flag the generative nature of partial and failed closures and stabilizations. These appear equally requisite for "success" as representing a failure. In appropriation, de-configuration and reconfiguration was crucial to the spread of both Vivago-Wristcare and PDMS. In the development of the generic supplier offering, co-figurations were key. It seems that reopening and flexibly adjusting the technology is necessary to make products travel from one set of users to another. This observation finds support beyond health technology. For instance, Pollock and Williams (2008, 298) note in regard to organization wide software packages that "if supplier like SoftCo has succeeded in conquering the world, it did so one sector at a time, carefully, in a process characterized by setbacks and 'reversals.'"

On the scale of *kinds of technology*, it is noteworthy that the graveyard of withdrawn diabetes databases, the persistent problems with passiveness sensors in safety phones, and the stubborn attempts for decades to realize the failing LMP did not stop further iterations. Rather than being judged by their persistently failing outcomes, previous projects were taken to exemplify that there was a set of principles and plausible paths that could be realized.

Closing and opening processes (stabilizing, destabilizing, and restabilizing) hence tend to take in multiple scales of socio-technical organization: at episode level in design, at project level in implementations and design processes, in the biographies of particular innovations, and in the evolution of the kinds of technology and practice-bound imaginaries animating their development and appropriation.

Persistence draws attention to what else is taking place alongside the closing of modalities. We have argued that aspirations and imagination should be placed more firmly in theories of technological change. The dominant tendency is to treat aspiration and imagination as individualistic and intramental phenomena and divorce them from materialities. In contrast, we have tried to show how the motivational force of furthering, for instance, the data capture on diabetes is dependent on its partial materializations. Working solutions in neighboring practices as well as elaborated ideas, concepts, and prototypes in the same practice are crucial in the canalization and structuring of both imagination and aspiration. Materializations—computer hardware, database structures, and verbally expressed ideas alike—act, on the one hand, as handles that imaginative constructions of reality can grasp. As we saw in the design process in Chapter 5 of this volume, this grasping is equally constituted by grasping with a pen, with sample materials, by tactile feel, as it is grasping by "the mind's eye" (Ferguson 1992). On the other hand, materializations force ideas to congregate in limited spaces and expose them to resistances and complements thus emerging. Some bindings become strong and elaborated; some remain open, some contested, some fuzzy; and some remain (often purposefully) unelaborated and blurry (so as not to compromise bindings that can be better articulated). All resource imagination is somewhat different, creating uneven contours in imagined realities. Indeed, human culture is teeming with visions and phantasms, but in a given moment a relatively small part of these begins to be grasped as something potentially realizable, something that begins to propel sustained action. The "impact" of technology begins when imagination and aspiration begin to be shaped by it, often long before any "working" technology exists. Some technologies such as Vivago-Wristcare and PDMS build on relatively elaborate imaginaries bound to the practices of their developers and/or users. Still such projects add both new aspiration and ways to imagine solutions to the imaginations, and in so doing, shape the trajectories bound to realizing these imaginaries. In contrast, LMP, despite the early closure and stabilization of Oxidizers and the conquest of the radioactive sample preparation niche, is still presently aspiring to a mere handful of people. Without a demonstrated working prototype and ways to go around its patents, it has been sidetracked from the ways any of the stakeholders in clinical testing grasp the future of their fields.

"The end of impact" is equally elusive, because of the intertwining of diachronic and synchronic biographies. The rise of the 14th nurse gave new impetus to Vivago-Wristcare's "impact" in both development and user practices. However, had Vivago-Wristcare failed early on, or should it fail commercially in the future, it would be clear that its impact is hardly limited to transforming the present way of working on its adopter sites; rather, it reaches to elaborating the future potential and pitfalls in a particular route to automating security for the elderly for producers, various intermediaries, and political actors as well as for the caregivers of the elderly.

. . .

We have seen that the biographies of new health technology feature sharp contingencies as well as more stable elements. Anticipating the future trajectory of a given innovation is likely to be a fool's folly if pursued in terms of prediction of the events, dates, and outcomes that will follow in the years to come. To recapitulate a key theme in all three cases, the trajectories of new technologies resemble less a ballistic curve and more "shooting in a thicket," where the exact ricochets are hard to discern but the *kinds of* obstacles and course changes that affect the trajectory can be clarified to some extent, which this theoretical chapter has tried to do.

11 Implications
Policy, Evaluation, and Development Practice

In this chapter, we shall focus on implications of the book for three audiences—namely, those involved in devising new, more user-oriented innovation and technology policy actions; those pursuing health technology evaluation; and practitioners involved in technology development.

IMPLICATIONS FOR TECHNOLOGY POLICY ON USER INVOLVEMENT IN INNOVATION

A prevalent feature of policy documents related to technology, health technology in particular, is high optimism over how new technology will enhance productivity and improve citizens' lives.[1] The present volume stresses that techno-socio-economic transformation is a complex reconfiguration process that takes place gradually. It tends to feature painstaking difficulties in interweaving the novel with old technologies and work practices as well as developing new kinds of work, concerns, and arrangements that need to be iterated many times over before any actual productivity gains are achieved. This concerns both the form and functions of the emerging technologies, as well as the makeup of the work practices. In this view, too great a trust in the capacities of the latest technology is a dangerous artifact of far too simplified analysis of techno-socio-economic transformation.

The book's more in-depth view of technological transformation underscores the importance of users in innovation alongside producers. Users are crucial to the success of new technologies as reformers of their own work, as generators of new knowledge about the desired forms and functions of new technologies, as active creators of modifications and add-on inventions, and as innovators of new and improved generic designs. These are familiar themes from previous research that shows how users innovate significantly in many industries (von Hippel 2005) and that a long process of building eventual usability and utility is often required for reaping the benefits of new restructuring technologies in each adopter organization (e.g., Walsham 1992; McLaughlin et al. 1999; Orlikowski 2000). The eventual success of new technology, health ICT in particular, is predicated on how well the innovation project manages to accrue—or fails to accrue—insight into the eventual strongholds and constraints of the technology and incorporate these into the design of the products, services, and user actions.

This work, redesign, and learning involves many types of invention and adaptation by a range of relevant actors, and in doing so offers new targets also for policy action. In policy settings, these findings resonate with recent attempts to develop innovation policies that are more sensitive to user involvement in innovation. Denmark took a position as a forerunner in user-oriented innovation policy in the late 2000s, and Finland followed by launching an initiative on "demand- and user-driven innovation" at the time of finalization of the present volume in 2009. This provided an opportunity to reflect on the policy recommendations derived from this book in relation to some of the measures already tried and ones considered for the future. This is particularly fruitful because Finnish science, technology, and innovation policy initiatives, particularly its focused technology programs, have often been seen as advanced in international comparison.

User-Driven Innovation Policy: Eight Types of Policy Action, Eight Types of Challenges

In discussing policy measures for user-driven innovation, it is vital to keep in mind that these range from relatively conservative additions and reiterations of already tried policy measures to radical new forms of policy action. Let us begin with means where the question is how to support producers' gains from the added value users generate for their present and future products. Such value creation was vital even in the heyday of mass production of standard goods yet, as we have argued throughout the volume, was all too often taken for granted and/or regarded as insignificant. We shall discuss four types of "additive" policy measures that target the shortcomings of extant R&D and support measures and mostly do not require establishing any new kind of policy instrument. In these additive measures, the net beneficiary of actions remains the R&D firm. This said, the four types of policy action that Finns have experimented with in fostering better use–development relations are in many respects advanced attempts that hold potential.

Policy Measure Type 1: Encouraging user knowledge and user–developer collaboration in program formulation (in, for instance, how some program calls are worded in Finland, starting in the late 1990s and throughout the present millennium)

The present volume suggests that companies systematically underestimate the recalcitrance of practices and ways of imagining, both users' and their own. Mere encouragement is unlikely to be sufficient: as my interviewees put it after two decades of experience, "R&D companies tend to expect to know themselves what users want; users expect companies to deliver technology that is useful and usable in their settings at the outset."[2] Neither party tends to be prepared for the adaptations that innovative technologies tend to require, which leaves a yawning gap between the potential and actually realizable market and the envisioned utility and realizable usefulness.

Technology companies' engagement with users tends to be further hampered by a whole range of factors. Companies tend to lack understanding of techniques that can make developer–user collaboration more effective in various stages of development and on various sites of collaboration. Companies also lack knowledge, benchmark cases, and parallels to their own situation, and hence do not know how to manage knowledge about users and usages—gathering it, storing it, processing it—or how to support users' further engagement. In all projects studied for this book, many of the user suggestions have appeared trivial or unrealistic for the developers, but among their suggestions were gems that no less than saved the project. Companies also tend to be afraid to give away the control over content, releases, scheduling, and secrecy that tends to be needed when one is working in depth with a user-inclusive innovation community.

Improving This Type of Policy Measure

An obvious step would be to set a project's understanding of users and usages among the key criteria for public funding, akin to how market analysis is currently required. Indeed, perhaps one of the only ways to ensure that companies actually understand how to build and maintain sufficient user networks is to systematically request this as a condition for public funding. In light of the present volume, some key conditions emerge as pertinent markers for distinguishing how deep an engagement a producer company has with its prospective and/or actual users, here grouped roughly from more rudimentary to more advanced:

1. Does the project have a clear idea about who exactly would be using the product, where, and for what?
2. If so, has it established interactions with these people, and what has been the nature of these encounters (how sustained, how in depth)?
3. Has the project identified likely lead-users, key intermediary actors, and users who resemble the likely eventual user-base of the product?
4. Has it fostered an active network of different users to gain multiple perspectives—that is, as rich and objective a view as possible—on its innovation?
5. Has it developed strategies for sorting, storing, assessing, and prioritizing user ideas and requests, and are these used and developed actively (or just exist, e.g., as potential but unused functions in a company's quality management software)?

6. Does it enjoy the benefit of having an independent user community actively engaged with the project/company products and their improvement? How has it figured out the ways to support and collaborate with these users?
7. Does the project/company have a strategy outlined for shifting its user engagements in the foreseeable development path (through launch, product, and product family lifecycles)?

Policy measure type 2: Funding programs that span both developer and user-side projects in, e.g., health care to foster knowledge transfer and collaboration between developers and users (used in the Finnish Macro Pilot, FinnWell, and several other major programs)

One of the main problems with this type of policy measure has been that collaboration and interchange tend to remain too unspecific and short in duration to truly support particular innovation processes. Public actors and firms remain—for very good reasons—mostly focused on their own projects. As the present volume stresses, the issue is not in finding just any health care users or any health technology producers and having them interact. Sustained collaboration on specific objects of development is needed, and this requires people with complementary competencies and interests and motivation for collaboration. Moreover, the kind of relatively generic networking such policy measures easily introduce is likely to be useful in the very early stages of a development project, yet at this point it is most demanding to represent the new products and services in such a manner that potential partners in a complementary user/developer domain can fathom them fruitfully (see Chapter 4, this volume). This said, being united by a funding program could give the funding agency a legacy to force-feed the participating projects with consultative or networking exercises. However, any "one size fits all" measures are unlikely to work in large programs, since projects, their phases, usage contexts, and challenges differ substantially.

Improving This Type of Policy Measure

Consultancy and assessment packages could be targeted for each project or small project groups as educational measures. These should be based on solid expertise that allows tailoring for the needs of different projects. There are significant differences in innovation contexts and in any given project's locus within the value-chains (or value-stars) that can also vary in the biography of the project. These differences call for different measures and different depth of user–developer engagement (see Hyysalo 2009b). In addition, typical "networking within the program" should pay close attention also to identifying who would be ideally suited to be partners for each project outside the program; after all, finding highly suitable partners within the same funding program appears rather wishful.

*Policy measure type 3: Funding socioeconomic research
alongside scientific and technical research to steer clear of
societal problems that may be associated with projects in a
specific domain (in Finland, used in FEENIX and several other
technology programs, and used in some recent EU programs)*

While highly important, most research falling under this kind of measure does not address developer–user relations, nor should it. To alleviate problems in user–developer relations, these measures would apply mostly to cases where acceptability of innovations or the eventual utility and usability is crucial—e.g., in health and environmental technologies. When this takes place, connecting and timing of socioeconomic research in relation to innovation projects is a key issue. The standard procedure of having just one call for proposals results in socioeconomic research measures that study projects/issues outside the program as well as have their results ready only towards the end of the program.

Improving This Type of Policy Measure

It would make sense to designate some of the socioeconomic research for more direct service of the program. This could be achieved by employing some of the desk research to (a) identify those socioeconomic topics that are seen as most relevant for the program and (b) identify the patterns and challenges related to these topics. The ideal timing of this research would be *before* the program launch, since it could be used to facilitate its building. Similarly, designating further socioeconomic research, particularly if related to developer–user relations, works best if it actually studies and facilitates the actual projects in the program. The optimal timing of the bid, hence, would be *after* the program innovation projects have been selected, so that the applicants can cater for more specific actions already in their proposal.

As already actively used in, for instance, Denmark, co-funding or endowing dedicated chairs related to developer-user relation at relevant universities is likely to be the most apt way to ensure that there is long-term capacity and willingness to generate research, evaluation, and expert advice. Using consultancies or other rapidly changing research institutions for this purpose is unlikely to yield long-term capacity or building of expertise that is factually needed in the long run.

*Policy measure type 4: Supporting user-centered design
actions and new types of marketing research*

User-centered design, including design- and innovation-oriented ethnography, has become more mainstream in the last two decades. It certainly holds potential for gaining a better sense of users' actual practices and provides knowledge that can bridge customers, marketing, and design. However, there is a real danger of losing the potential in user-driven innovation policy if such funding gets channeled to mere add-ons to corporate marketing research. Market research is an established way to communicate about the demand for a product. Even though its shortcomings in regard to innovative products are well known (see Chapter 4, this volume), funding to conduct market research is a standard part of public R&D support in Finland, as in most industrialized countries.

Further, the new market research and user-centered design areas feature plenty of consultancy packages that are well suited for a particular type of technology and clientele but have limited potency elsewhere. In addition, single experiments detached from the company's core R&D concerns tend to have rather limited impact on products or company practices. At this, most "packaged" user-centered design and marketing research is best suited to relatively "designer-driven" innovation contexts (see Chapter 1, this volume), while less grandiose actions to support innofusion and evolutionary co-design types of development can be more far-reaching and effective in strategically supporting the company's renewal toward more sophisticated long-term engagement with users. On top of these concerns, most of these packages also propose new and revolutionary methods and outcomes but in fact mostly recombine extant methods and techniques (Hyysalo 2009b). Using "novelty" of market research or user-centred design approach as a funding criterion is hence likely to be elusive and unhelpful.

Improving This Type of Policy Measure

Experiments with novel market research are best supported within extant support mechanisms and by educating the offices (in Finland, local "technology support centers") granting funds for market research about what types of inquiries are available and suitable for different kinds of products. When funding novel market research, it would make sense to request educational components and a plan for knowledge transfer and knowledge integration in the recipient company.

If new market research is taken as part of user-innovation policy actions, support should be targeted to approaches that engage with users in sustained experiments or in-depth acquainting to user practices rather than approaches that merely continue to typify the buyers through, e.g., data mining or variations of well-rehearsed foresight exercises. The latter is mostly business as usual in new guises. When supporting living-lab- or test-bed-type experimentation settings, preference ought to be placed to ones set up in a "mode of experimentation," where users are actually engaged in developing the products and their usages further over a mere "test-bed" arrangement or reporting of bugs (cf. van Lieshout et al. 2001a; Hoogma et al. 2002).

More Radical User-Innovation Policy Actions

While the preceding types of policy action introduce add-ons to extant measures, benefactors, and types of funding, we should be clear that the viable user-driven policy initiatives clearly do not stop there. Some four decades ago, the finances and equipment needed in R&D and manufacturing prevented user-innovation from thriving without becoming channeled through manufacturing companies (von Hippel 2005; Benkler 2006). This is no longer the case. Open source and peer-creation communities and research on user-innovation show that users can make innovations independently (and directly even when in conjunction with producer company efforts). Let us now move to discussing what the present volume offers to four types of policy measures that feature prominently in current discussions.

Policy Measure Type 5: Supporting and Removing Barriers from User-innovation and User-innovation Communities

Targeting innovation policy to innovation by users is one of the most important as well as most radical policy directions that has come forth in recent years. The thus far suggested policy measures for supporting user-innovation reside mostly on regulatory level and aim to counter problems the present intellectual property regime creates for more egalitarian participation in innovation and shared creativity (e.g., von Hippel 2005; Benkler 2006).

While the present book is in full agreement with research that emphasizes the need to address the regulatory-level concerns, there are additional challenges to user-innovation projects to which policy action could be targeted. Obtaining funding for user-innovation is at present far more difficult than it is to gain funding for R&D firms, which enjoy a range of support mechanisms.

Many societally beneficial user-innovations are nonprofit oriented. The lack of profit and reservoir funds tends to make them vulnerable even to minor financial setbacks. Traditional funding bodies for research and technology such as foundations are well placed to handle one-time funding needs of some user-innovation projects but ill placed to finance anything that needs to span many years or for funding needs that are hard to present as clear projects and outcomes.

Some user-innovation projects are closely tied to promoting or opposing particular political objectives (e.g., opposing global warming or fostering active citizen forums in the Internet) and cannot always appeal to just neutral monetary gain or creation of new employment and still be publicly desirable. This said, some user-innovation projects have little value beyond the innovator seeking an opportunist gain or any mechanism by which the public investment could be returned through, e.g., increased tax revenue. As with all innovation projects, the vast majority probably should never be publicly funded, since they would be inferior to other projects or targets of public spending.

Improving This Type of Policy Measure

The present volume suggests a range of paths that may be worth experimenting with both as part of targeted technology programs in specific areas and, particularly, as the core of specific user-innovation policy actions. First, support for coordination of growing user-community innovations should be experimented with. To work adequately, user-inclusive innovation communities need to have some key actor(s) that store ideas coming from others and refine them into product characteristics (for more on these, see Ratto 2003; Heiskanen et al., forthcoming; Miettinen et al. 2003). User-innovation communities are often volunteer-based organizations, where people participate as an add-on to their main job or as a sidetrack to it. Particularly in "evolutionary co-design" contexts such as open source and peer-production-based projects, success may lead to difficulties in maintaining sufficient coordination, which, in turn, may lead to waning participation by others. Funding to allow somebody to work on the project coordination as full-time employment could boost projects at such a precarious point. The timing here is for the point when the project is growing rapidly.

A second issue worth experimenting with is fostering networking and collaboration between projects, particularly if no proprietary interests are at stake. The "graveyard of diabetes databases" shows how a sprawl of insufficiently staffed and resourced projects can be far less desirable than a larger joint effort. This type of educational action can be targeted from very early on, yet it must be kept in mind that refusal to collaborate (even as a condition for funding) might make perfect sense for a user-innovation project so as not to, e.g., jeopardize volunteer motivation.

Third, experiment with support for purchasing of technical development for user-innovators/user-innovation communities. User-innovators tend to be knowledgeable about the utility and markets of their inventive ideas and designs but may lack particular technical capabilities. Joint applications with a firm providing the needed technical research or development should be considered as well. This action is likely to be efficient in technically oriented projects already some distance from their start.

In evaluation of user-innovation projects (as well as manufacturer-driven projects), emphasis should be placed on requiring a clear explanation of the public good the project offers and a plan for how its outcomes will be diffused beyond the project to redeem this utility. Here, the technical and economic expertise typically found in science, technology and innovation-administrations ought to be complemented with specific domain expertise, not least to assess what common good the project offers and hence why it should receive public funding—after all, the market and utility knowledge should be the expected stronghold of user-innovation.

Policy Measure Type 6: From Techniques and Lead-users to Supporting Shifting Ecologies and User-producer Experiments

Current discussions of user-driven innovation policy follow closely the mainstream research on user-innovation that emphasizes various techniques of user involvement and mixing and matching the right ingredients of user-innovation communities (Heiskanen et al., forthcoming). Users are seen to innovate to find solutions to their own problems or to problems stated by their peers and forming innovation communities through communication links, often freely sharing their innovations with other users. Electronic fora, innovation toolkits, prototyping means, prices for solved problems, *et cetera*, are expected to facilitate this and to resolve the transfer of "sticky information" about users' needs and manufacturers' capabilities that is often highly contextual and tacit (von Hippel 1994, 2005).

The present volume and the related work in studying user involvement in nearly 20 projects in Finland suggests that collaboration and interaction are not simply outcomes of "the right techniques" or "mixing the right ingredients" but more contextual and dynamic processes (Heiskanen et al., forthcoming). The length of interaction between developers and users tends to be as important as the tools and means used. In this light, various "creativity exercises," quick ethnographies, and design trials can be expected to merely provide initiating or supporting conditions for innovation.

Neither automatic win-win situation between users and producers can be presumed. The collaborating parties tend to have divergent interests, cultures, perspectives, and resources for participating in innovation. We need to distinguish between innovation communities and the indigenous practices (activity systems, communities of practice) of product developers and users. While an *ad hoc* clustering of people or even a shoot for a user-inclusive innovation network can be fostered or even created through generic "recipes," these background communities are not amenable to similar purposeful alignment (see Chapters 2, 3, 6, and 8, this volume).

Emergence of successful collaboration involves a component of contingency in that a mutually beneficial alignment of resources and interests falls into place.[3] What the successful arrangement happens to be depends greatly upon the content and form of the innovation network at the time. Hence, rather than neatly functioning "systems" or "communities," user inclusion in innovation forms rather more complex "innovation contexts" (see Chapter 1, this volume) that entail different interactions and collaboration possibilities. Indeed, user involvement was at least a partial success in all cases in this volume and in the 20 Finnish cases studied elsewhere, but it was never a "silver bullet" to permanently transform the way the company worked. The form of user–developer collaboration as well as its rationales, and hence the most apt partnerships and forms of collaboration, shifted in the course of the evolution of the innovation. Also company interests tend to evolve with the maturation of the project (see Chapters 7 and 8, this volume), as do participation motivations in the course of the project and participation history (Heiskanen et al., forthcoming; Freeman 2007).

Finally, much user-innovativeness is a vital complementary to producer outputs. For instance, in new health technologies the activities of users in developing applications, procedures, reference data, data storage, and new practices are necessary complements to producer offerings.

Improving This Type of Policy Measure

These findings add to policy measures that could be used both as part of targeted technology programs in specific areas and, particularly, as the core of specific user-innovation policy actions. It is worth experimenting with support mechanisms for innovative activities of user groups. Even as the generic product is produced by the manufacturer, activities of users in developing further applications, procedures, reference materials, *et cetera*, can be crucially important complements and/or highly beneficial in their own right. Such funding could be applied for either by joint application with the producer (in which case the indirect support for the producer would be clear) or separately by users in cases where the user community is using the product as a mere platform for its own further development (particularly if the producer happens to be located in a place that is clearly detached from the given country's taxpayer money). These kinds of established user groups typically function in connection with an innovative product already on the market or, in the best case, in relation to a more general class of product.

The second issue is establishing support for longevity of societally valuable projects and their outcomes. The innovation biographies show the utter unrealism in one-to-three-year innovation project proposals. One of the major problems in, e.g., Finnish health innovation projects has been their project form and time frame—even when outcomes are promising, many efforts dry out at the end of the initial funding period, which is often a good distance from redeeming the eventual gain the project hopes to establish. The idea to have targeted funding from different instruments for different "phases," such as "basic research—applied research—innovation-related research," presumes a linear model, which does not fit how many user-innovation-active projects progress.

Third, establish mechanisms for supporting the continued availability of project outcomes as public goods. On the one hand, public-serving outcomes such as many informational Web pages and services quickly fall dysfunctional without any maintenance but can be made to run for years with meager update and maintenance funding. On the other hand, experimental project outcomes with major citizen contributions should not be given to firms only to be scrapped in cases where public funding has played a role; instead, the product and/or code should be made publicly available for further development. This type of action targets the post-launch support of innovative projects, the importance of which the present volume has strongly emphasized as crucial for eventual gaining of societally useful technologies.

Policy Measure Type 7: Inviting Stakeholders into Developing Policy Action Repertoires

An interesting feature of devising new user-driven innovation policies has been an often voiced uncertainty over what kinds of funding should be made available and where public innovation support would be beneficial and where dysfunctional. On the one hand, this reflects the major shift there is from moving beyond supporting firms and public research organizations in terms of competencies of the policymakers and policy experts consulted. On the other hand, it reflects the tradition wherein policy-setting and ideas must come from the established (techno-economic) elite.

The reason many of the earlier suggestions for improvements are labeled "experiment with" is to underscore the point that, eventually, the most functional ways to publicly support (as well as to refrain from public support for) user-innovation are likely to arise from, and be complemented by, the users themselves. Forming an advisory group convened from user-innovation community representatives, researchers dedicated to the area, and firms engaged with active users would facilitate the setup phase.

There is likely to be need to iterate the instruments for some time to come, and hence a need to gather feedback on how the instruments work in actual practice. Again, to ensure long-term capacity and willingness to generate research, evaluation, and expert advice as well as knowledge of relevant projects and their realities, it would be worth co-funding or donating dedicated chairs to relevant universities. Consultancies or rapidly shifting research institutions for this purpose are unlikely to provide long-term capacity and building of expertise.

Policy Measure Type 8: Supporting specific innovation coaching and/or niche formation activities in areas where a market failure is clearly present

While breakthrough innovation tends to be portrayed as what everybody wants, our research on the radical TeleChemistry innovation supports the view that standard technology support and finance is geared to supporting more incremental types of innovation and may indeed be ill suited to potential breakthrough innovation. The viability of breakthrough projects is hard to judge once and for all; their development paths tend to feature severe setbacks and hindrances as well as unexpected new possibilities in technical, economic, and social aspects of the project. Evaluating and funding the project's potential and its viability in reaching the next foreseeable development stage differs significantly from the usual cost-benefit instruments in evaluation of R&D projects. Assessing, coaching, and supporting breakthrough-potential projects requires its own instruments and expertise (see Chapter 9, this volume). However, such expertise is not readily available, nor can it be expected in agencies making routine innovation funding decisions. Further, breakthrough projects are rare, and hence policy experience as well as in-depth research concerning them accumulates rather painstakingly.

Improving This Type of Policy Measure

Experiment with educating funding personnel in identifying projects that do not fit conventional criteria but could hold breakthrough potential with societal benefits that warrant using tax money, and focus the assessment of such projects to a unit or network of experts that has appropriate expertise and could further accumulate it over time to support both research and policy action.

With regard to user involvement, our research supports the view that potential breakthrough projects benefit significantly from in-depth understanding of their user domain, which in health technology by default requires specialist medical expertise in the domain in question. Such expertise helps to concretize the exact value promise as well as the resistance and obstacles the project is likely to face. Involving such users in evaluation alongside technical/scientific and socioeconomic expertise is likely to be fruitful in terms of reaching decisions about funding as well as informing the future directions of the project (see Chapter 9, this volume).

Overall, these considerations about the eight technology policy types entail an ideal of more reasoned policy action that is grounded in the use of appropriate expertise and measures to select and support different technology projects. While new policy instruments need to be distinguishable, there is a clear need for governance competence and for broadening evaluation from narrowly technical and/or economic analysis into analysis that incorporates socioeconomic and user domain expertise where applicable.

(HEALTH) TECHNOLOGY ASSESSMENT

The biographies approach to health technology offers some critical insight for practices of technology project and product assessment. This book makes evident that health technologies are not composed of just the devices alone, and their appropriate evaluation cannot take place divorced from the other technologies and work arrangements wherein the technologies are to bring effects. However, when much depends on deploying and intertwining health ICT in extant practices and materialities, the effects are hard to evaluate objectively. As Lehoux (2006) argues, sorting the good technology from the bad or the cost-effective from waste of money becomes tricky and difficult to handle by rational calculations alone. Since much has been written on this topic on the whole, let us here focus on the core theme of the book: the evolving character of health technology and its development–use relations.

The close analysis of health technology biographies underlines that the findings from evaluating them are likely to depend significantly on the site and the moment in the biography at which the evaluation happens to be conducted. There appears to be an important temporal pattern, which resonates with other researchers' experience from various e-health projects in different Northern European countries. A health technology project first builds a business case by promising cost savings through reduction of labor, rationalization of care arrangements, or prevention of more expensive treatments. Such framing is needed to appeal to the expectations about health technology projects in the practice-bound imaginations of investors as well as health care decision-makers. However, this initial form of technology seldom performs exactly as intended. To make the technology work tends to require more attention and support from medical personnel; at least some of its features conflict with existing work arrangements, and some of its features offer new uses not anticipated by the developers. Indeed, both Wristcare and PDMS led to add-ons rather than (originally promised) transformations of earlier work arrangements throughout their first and second generations. In all, there tends to be shifts in:

- targets: what the technology is out to do
- features of technology, including their removal, redesign of problematic features, and enhancement to positively received ones
- usage instructions and recommended (re)arrangements of work
- configurations of adjacent systems and procedures wherein the technology is used
- criteria for judging the benefit of the technology that gets advocated

Interestingly, after the period of making the technology work and become acceptable, the business case again becomes more accentuated with the third-generation systems and their usages. Wristcare, for instance, reintroduced labor replacement as well as its case for preventive measures, but the crux of the matter here is that both value-promises were made somewhat differently technically and work-wise than those initially envisioned. For instance, in terms of preventive measures, Wristcare had fully removed its quickest reaction time alarms as well as the scaling of alarm types that could not be made to work in the practice of care. Instead, it had introduced preventive care through enhanced sleep monitoring functions (owing to user-initiated new uses that, in turn, led to collaboration with sleep researchers, further design, further user feedback, and further design enhancements).

This evolution in mind, we see that there are important sources of ambivalence in evaluations and appraisals conducted at the "typical evaluation time" of new health technology—that is, during the early field trials and in the first years of commercial usage. First, at this point the evaluations tend to witness a significant number of usability and reliability problems, and they concentrate on spelling these out. Yet these problems predominantly get clustered as "early hiccups" due to missing elements of the system or its technical shortcomings. What this hiccups register neglects is the fact that usability and "work affordability" are major issues in health ICT desirability (see Chapters 7 and 8, this volume). Second, at this point it is still hard to see the qualitative changes new technologies will introduce to work practices, since they tend to be deployed more in the way instructed by their manufacturers than in the manner most efficient within the overall techno-logical and organizational configurations of users' work (see Chapters 6, 7, and 8, this volume). Third, the evidence from eventual usage and utility of the systems in health organizations is rudimentary during the early field trials and evaluations tend to resort to supplier visions of what the technol-ogy will do (for instance, on Wristcare see Kaakinen and Törmä 1999; Törmä et al. 2001). These facets lead easily to something of an "evaluation of promise potential" rather than assessment of what the implications and form of the technology are likely to be. Together they also give a lot of lati-tude for evaluator sentiment concerning the particular technology because the envisioned usages or practical problems could equally be raised to the foreground.

One response to these problems would be to use periodic evaluation or constructive technology assessment methods that seek to shift technology assessment away from one-time evaluation to nudging the innovation pro-cess towards socially more desirable directions (Poti et al. 2006b; Rip et al. 1995). A less dramatic change to present technology evaluation practices would be to retain more caution in stating whether a technology will even-tually be suitable or not yet dare to offer more explicit assessments of the potentials it may have under different deployments and in adjacent systems. This would help to spell out more clearly the conditions under which the technology could drive for changes (often readily promoted by producers as well as its advocates within health care) as well as explicate some of its adverse effects in burdening work, subjecting professional groups or patients under undesirable measures of control, *et cetera*. Analytic effort should also be focused on evaluating usability and work affordability prob-lems: individual bugs differ from clusterings of problems, poor interfaces, misplaced design concepts, missing functionality, etc.

There are also several issues related to the recognition that assessments are likely to form parts of the circulation of representations in the ecol-ogy between development and use. They will not be used only as objective appraisals of—let alone the final word on—the technology; they are actively contested, reappropriated, and worked with as well as worked around. This took place in all technologies and trials studied for this volume. This observation adds to the critique of the health technology assessment view of technologies as neutral tools that can be sorted into good ones (to be sup-ported and diffused) and bad ones (to be limited) on the basis of their cost, efficiency, and safety—done preferably by accumulating rigorous evidence, such as that produced in randomized clinical trials (Lehoux 2006). On the other hand, however, such a "politicized" view of technology assessment—health technology assessment being used as just one resource in political decisions and industry actions—underscores, perhaps surprisingly, issues of objectivity even if from a perverse angle for many concerned. When diverse political interests and different sets of arguments and sets of information are contrasted, something that bears a resemblance to accumulating rigorous evidence, such as a randomized clinical trial, is a trump card in arguing for or against decisions. Strong appeal to objective and rigorous evaluation of health technology is hard, relatively, to debunk for politicians, laymen, and innovators as well as experts in health care. Thus, while recognizing the political connections of health technology assessment, we need to be aware of the complex commitments and interchanges between stakeholder groups wherein technology evaluation gains its value and set practical limits to the extent to which such broadening is sensible.

This politicized view of technology evaluation harks back to our earlier discussion about the evolution of new (health) technology and the timing of evaluation. It highlights the strategic choices different actors can deploy in regard to any one time trial: when to evaluate, what to evaluate, how to set evaluation criteria, and so on, all of which are likely to affect significantly whether the technology is going to appear beneficial or ill suited.

Finally, the multiple scales of analysis in the biographies and imaginaries framework provide an important yet grossly neglected facet of technology evaluation: shaping the imaginaries animating technological practice on the basis of actually realized projects (but see work on vision assessment, e.g., Dierkes et al. 1996). All the biographies examined in this book suggest taking seriously the fact that any evaluation is unlikely to spell a decisive end to a given development. Even when a particular project gets scrapped as too problematic or nonviable, the ideas tend to resurface. Shaping the imaginaries in developer and user communities could be seen as an important function for technology assessment. Assessment does provide a privileged occasion for spelling out why certain perceptions of the future of user practices and their technical mediation may be unreasonably simplistic (such as striving for complete coverage in imaginaries animating the safety phone and diabetes database development) and, conversely, why users' views of their own practices may overlook technical possibilities that are likely to open up. Part of facilitating such cross-practice learning should be raising to the fore issues related to cascading and "slippery slope" effects potentially associated with a *kind of technology*, for these may explain much of user resentment for projects and not be recognized by the supplier side.

IMPLICATIONS FOR PRACTITIONERS IN HEALTH TECHNOLOGY DEVELOPMENT

Facilitating and intervening in the innovation biographies studied has been a theme gradually developed in Chapters 2, 8, and 9 or this volume, suggesting that researchers may foster multiparty interaction and learn through the recognition of different stakeholders and the in-depth analysis of their practices, interests, and problems in relation to new technology (see also

Miettinen and Hasu 2002; Saari 2003; Engeström and Blackler 2005). We now move to describing how we harnessed the developed insights into more fully fledged recommendations for action in the case of the TeleChemistry (TC) Point-of-care (POC) application where we left it in Chapter 9 of this volume: the point when its first prototypes were being developed and strategies were being laid for how then to move to various pilot trials.

In doing so, we draw from some of the key findings and concepts in this book—namely, treating technology as an evolving set of configurations and practices and stressing the range of user inputs and variety of representations. We further tie these into actionable insight through the notion of zone of proximal development (ZPD) from activity theory.

One of the central themes of the present volume has been that we need to go beyond implementation or user-centered design "recipes" for practitioners in mastering developer–user relations. As a consequence, we do not aim at providing a generic pilot trial recipe but show how the insights can be adapted to the particularities of the project, objects, and practices at stake.

From History to Outlining the Zone of Proximal Development

As noted in Chapter 9 of this volume, the TeleChemistry project gained EU funding for building a production version of its networked POC testing application in the years 2009–2011. While technical realization of the core system was at center stage in the development work, this period is also key for piloting the technology in medical settings and gaining further funding for its further development. Indeed, when we elaborated the knowledge needs for TeleChemistry, we found a range of objectives for pilot studies. While this list is specific to TeleChemistry, most of the items resemble piloting objectives found in other health technologies, and most importantly, it illustrates well the often difficult to manage parallel and even conflicting goals that characterize the piloting phase.

1. Verify, validate, and develop the technical functioning of TeleChemistry POC units—both individual components and POC-unit performance as a whole.
2. Test the homogeneity of reagents in storage.
3. Verify, validate, and develop traceability of TC liquid handling.
   - digitizing pressure, temperature, and volume data and detection of changes in them; creating the parallel testing arrangement between the new digital and old manual procedures
4. Test and develop further network control and its reliability.
   - testing networked servers and cross-copying of data between them; determining the amount of data it is practicable to store in each POC unit
5. Develop and test real-time and remote (quality) controls.

- seeing what can be monitored/calibrated/fixed remotely and how to improve these with procedures or adjoining technologies; determining how many devices are needed for pooling and how cross-controlling (grid formation) progresses after the minimal device number
6. Create sufficient usability.
   - considering what functions should be incorporated into the POC unit and central server and what kinds of interfaces would be best suited to this; considering in detail issues such as whether the user interface screen should be integrated or the device should rely on a laptop on the side and whether a laptop should be used in prototypes even if integration is the final target
7. Arrange testing of whether and how TeleChemistry can bring benefits to running clinical tests and organizing of clinical laboratories.
   - seeing whether, where, and how it can be used to improve the reliability of clinical testing results; to diminish the costs of clinical testing; to simplify the technical support and expertise presently needed in clinical laboratories; and to simplify the supply-chain management of clinical laboratories with regard to devices, reagents, calibrators, storage, *et cetera*
8. Make arrangements to test whether and how the TeleChemistry system can bring clinical benefits.
   - determining whether and how it can be used to mitigate some clinical risk situations and to shorten waiting times for test results in different real-life contexts

The items placed early in this list are predominantly ones that call for relatively strong control over tests and experiments, "a mode of control" in running the pilots (van Lieshout et al. 2001), which are initially held exclusively on the premises of the company and its closest partners. Issues from the fourth item downward increasingly require inputs from users and require their sustained engagements with the system—that is, "a mode of experimentation" even if it involves risks in giving out devices that may feature problems in respects that the company would wish not to have out of its control. These considerations in mind, in our construction of a ZPD for the projects' producer–user relations we then focused on how to manage these two modes and the projects' underlying tensions through engagement with different user sites in a strategic way.

Clarifying the Possible Moves in the ZPD

The insights derived in the course of this volume support many facets of approaches such as PROTEE, SOCROBUST, and strategic niche management yet tend to advocate more detailed assessments and measures for handling developer–user relations. The first step in our work was to identify *different key usage settings* to approximate usage and market niches à la strategic niche management but in a more specific way that we came to call "micro-niche identification." In performing the initial assessments, we relied on combined researcher, developer, and lead-user expertise in joint meetings. As already noted in the discussion of Chapter 9 in this volume, this collaborative relation owes its existence to conviction that a few days of Web searches or desk research à la PROTEE is unlikely to provide more than starting points for fostering the kind in-depth understanding that would be needed.

In distinguishing these usage settings, we took seriously the findings from other case studies in this volume where, for a fruitful collaboration, "user" cannot be spelled s-u-c-k-e-r; mutually beneficial conditions must prevail for fruitful long-term collaboration. Along with scrutiny of what usages would be likely to emerge (see Chapter 6 and 8, this volume, for the kind of variations to be expected), this meant paying close attention to the value each targeted group of users would gain from TeleChemistry and to the prerequisites for that group getting this value in each state of TeleChemistry's likely technological development. We also considered what additional motivation there may be for (some) users in each setting for participating before a clear use-value promise could be delivered. In some affinity to the lead-user method (von Hippel 1988; Herstatt and von Hippel 1992), this was used for identifying particular actors within the type of user setting that would willingly bear the risks and burdens of engaging with TeleChemistry "ahead of time," that is, before tangible use-value could be offered for them. However, as the present volume spells out, lead-users and enthusiasts comprise only one of the actor groups that need to be identified in the "ecology" related to each usage setting. Key intermediaries and potential "crucial users" (nonenthusiast but well-informed users) were identified along with implicated users and other implicated or implicating actors.

Finally, emphasis was laid on the epistemic grounding of the view so developed by charting the sources of user-representation on which each of the assessments was based. This emphasis owes much to standpoint epistemology (e.g., Suchman 2002), as phrased by Miettinen, "Different actors have, owing to their social positions, a partial standpoint on the matter at hand. To maximize objectivity, that is, to achieve a valid, rich and workable conception of a thing (a product, for instance), a dialogue between the different standpoints is needed" (Miettinen, forthcoming). On the other hand, it owes much to the present volume's emphasis on innovation process and developer–user relations being fundamentally learning processes. Simple means of recording the sources and divergent opinions about assessments are key in refining these understandings as field trials progress and knowledge becomes tested and accumulated. In parallel with charting of sources, identified needs for further insight were suggested to be recorded and periodically reviewed in the course of the project. In all, the key issues considered were:

1. Why is the given setting possible for the project?
   - What problem or desire would the technology solve so that users would be interested in it?
2. What would the usage setting provide for the project?
   - What can be gained from piloting in this usage setting?
3. What is the ecology of key actors within the usage setting?
   - What are the key user groups?
   - Which are the likely main usages?
   - Are there lead-users?
   - Can crucial users be identified?
   - What are the key intermediaries—gatekeepers, brokers, facilitators, et cetera—within and around the setting?
4. What needs to be ready in the system and at the company before the system can be deployed in this usage setting?
5. What would be the added value the system could likely give for the setting in its first, second, and third phase of technical development?
6. What further bindings and path dependency issues may follow from engaging with a particular usage setting?
7. What sources of user-representation is the preceding assessment based on? What are the likely remaining biases or gaps?
8. Needs for further insight: are some of the assessments known to be based on scant information, educated guesses, or a one-sided perspective? Are there issues in need of more detailed understanding? What issues are such that trials are needed to clarify them?

As an example of the chartings we then made, let us compare (simplified and reduced versions of) three main types out of the 15 differing early micro-niches we identified: a private central lab doing tests for distributed clients, a night ward in a health care center, and a day ward in a health care center (Table 11.1).

Setting Out Guideposts for How to Handle the ZPD

What became evident in our comparative exercise was the different and varying value promises different user sites could hope to gain from TeleChemistry. It became equally clear that getting to actually deliver most of these value promises would take considerable further development in both the POC unit (in terms of the range of tests available) and the networked quality control and maintenance application. A key issue, then, for realizing many of the piloting goals (particularly goals 4–8) is to be prepared for simulating facets of the TeleChemistry system that the POC device and the available IT servers do not yet cover reliably at the time when it is sensible to start the first tentative experiments. This, in turn, calls for relatively organized piloting with sufficient developer and manager resourcing as well as engaging members from different user sites to work through emerging problems and to spread best practices.

Table 11.1 Comparison of Three Micro-Niches for TeleChemistry

Usage Setting Name	Why Possible for TC?	What Provides for TC?	Key User Groups	Main Usages	Ecology, Key Actors - Intermediaries (I) - Lead-Users (LU) - Crucial-Users CU)
Private central lab (PLC)	- PCL a share-holder in TC - PCL has three targets, see "main usages"	- Demonstrating that the system works - Demonstrates how quickly results come - Verifying the value-promise in logistics - Gaining some cash flow	- Lab doctors - Lab nurses - Managers of PCL - Client HCC doctors and nurses	- Digitally verifying quality control procedures at PCL - Processing samples in POC rather than transporting them - Remote monitoring of equipment	I: PCL partner, has a strong say in how piloting organized LU: ? CU: people handling samples from remote area HCCs
Health care center in-patient wards	Now use POC tests, but unreliable ones	- Establishing a usage concept for TC - References - Guaranteed volume of tests - Site for modeling on-site maintenance - Indications for how to ease laboratory purchasing and maintenance networks - An understanding what all (tests, equipment) is needed for minimum and maximal value promise of TC - Implementation support: extant equipment and personnel on-site	- Lab nurses - Ward nurses - Doctors (treatment and referral decisions) - Nurses (monitoring and recording patient info)	- Replacing extant POC tests in urgent cases and in home referrals - Doing most common central lab tests quicker as TC-POCs	I: Senior physicians, regional chemists LU: Found among doctors doing lab, GP, and clinical research - Nurses doing both ward and lab nursing (taking tests, lab rounds, ward work) CU: "surgery-oriented doctors" having to manage hours on-call
HCC outpatient wards	- Replacing POC tests - Quicker tests - Cheaper tests	See above, but less implementation support	See above	- Quicker referrals - Pacing lab and doctors appointments anew	See above for I and LU

Continued

Table 11.1 Continued

Usage Setting Name	What Requires from TC?	What is the TCValue Added for the Setting 1st, 2nd, 3rd Phase?	Further Bindings that May Follow?	Sources of User-Representations	Needs for Further Insight
Private central lab (PLC)	1. Phase 1–5 tests and parallel testing with extant instruments 2. Phase - Digital monitoring needed for logistic changes - Test range same as in HCC (flow cytometry)	1. Phase: inspiring and potentially profitable idea 2. Phase: Building the logistic alternative	In 2. Phase: Quality control and test pattern parts of the system must exist	LU 1 Dev 3	How much PCL is willing to invest in parallel testing and simulation? How early best to engage "halfway out of house"?
Health care center in-patient wards	1. PhaseSee above + arrangement for clinical implications if other tests had been available from TC 2. PhaseMax 40 analytes is likely to serve HCC-BW, but flow cytometry needed 3. Phase microbiology tests needed	1. Phase Replacing POCs. Quicker reactions to inefficient medication. Quicker home referrals 2. Phase- More reliable follow-on monitoring (--3.) Easier lab maintenance; less dispersion to different technology processes and quality control methods (---4.)Possibilities to novel decision support through pattern detection	The system should be reliable enough to be kept in use	LU 1	How many and what tests are needed for plausibly simulating what TC could offer? How to best organize TC testing Validation with a central lab on medication, home referrals
HCC outpatient wards	See above + - New arrangements for phasing patient receptions or for taking lab tests	See above	See above + integrations to Lab SW	LU 1 Dev 1 Dev 2	How quicker test results affect diagnosis "buying time with tests"

While the tangible clinical value from the system appeared to reside only some years ahead, it became evident that some enthusiast sites could begin to use it parallel to extant systems far earlier, which, indeed, would also be a prerequisite for establishing the validity of the TeleChemistry testing methods. While health care centers are needed for the eventual business case of distributed POC testing, it is also evident that the first sensible outside piloting environment is probably a private central laboratory (PCL) that is also one of TeleChemistry's shareholders, because of it being motivated to run the parallel tests, dedicate manpower to it, and tolerate early shortcomings better than any health care center would.

In terms of health center environments, our chartings suggested (as a surprise in regard to how the TeleChemistry business cases had been written) that an outpatient setting is likely not to be as good a starting point as an inpatient ward. In the latter, comparisons to extant POC tests are likely to work better (used more and also can be used as a case for TeleChemistry allowing quicker home referrals); the staff can observe better correlation with patients' symptoms and lab results; and, since inpatient wards have more stability in staffing, parallel usage of TeleChemistry and extant testing instruments is likely to be easier to organize. This also facilitates devising and developing the workarounds and other alterations that are commonly needed to make a pilot-stage technology work.

In contrast, the outpatient piloting will inevitably have to engage with timing of patient reception and laboratory testing and the new reception procedures this could entail. These, in turn, relate to questions of division of labor within the ward as well as the use of several information systems in use there, including reception programs, lab programs, patient record systems, and reference databases. To master these demands and to gain full use of information the piloting in outpatient clinic will introduce, time and staffing need to be available for iterating the procedures, instruments, and practices.

With more careful consideration of different micro-niches within this sequence, it became increasingly clear that the inpatient ward pilot sites needed to be chosen with an eye to protection and the resourcing they could provide. This suggested moving from PCL and partner organizations to sites led by senior physicians with lead-user characteristics in regard to laboratory testing and equipment (having physician's and laboratory expert qualifications, having developed new procedures or equipment, and/or having previously participated in field trials for new equipment). It further suggested strategic consideration of at which point in development and where exactly to engage in *formal field trials* and research on verifying clinical benefits of new equipment and procedures. Experience from nonenthusiast pilot sites should be gained first, to ensure that the system and all its parts will be sufficiently reliable and that piloting and troubleshooting procedures will be up to formal evaluation.

This perspective taken here to the one-to-three-year pilot phase operates at the strategic level yet places greater attention on the details of the technology, ecologies of actors, differences in usage environments, and the interests of different users than is customary in R&D management. This recapitulates the key message of the book. Many of the issues we most urgently need to address in health technology development and use (and innovation more generally) reside in the difficult terrain between generic models and the typical nitty-gritty listings of things to consider in each specific aspect of their evolution. The issue is how to *retain a strategic view close enough to the particularities* of the specific set of issues at hand. This applies equally to the earlier discussions of user-innovation policy and health technology evaluation. Many policy instruments and evaluation methods currently in use need refinement in how they are matched to the realities of innovation projects or require complementary measures to redeem their value.

Data Appendix

The three case studies reported upon in this volume build on similar methodology, data-gathering, and analysis methods (see Chapter 2, this volume). The data available varied somewhat, because of various contingencies in each study, but in all of them included three main types: semi-structured interviews, field observations, and documents about the innovation and discourses around it. In the Vivago-Wristcare study, these three types of materials had roughly equal bearing on the analysis, whereas in the TeleChemistry study we made little use of our observation data. This variation is indicative of the approach more generally: parallel research conducted by Hyysalo (2000) and Hyppönen (2004) had roughly similar data distribution, while Hasu (2001a) and Saari (2003) relied more on field observations. Since the Vivago-Wristcare case is reported upon in the most depth in this volume, let us begin with discussion of its data types and then move on to discuss the two other studies in relation to it.

VIVAGO-WRISTCARE STUDY

The table that follows presents the numbers and lengths of the semi-structured interviews in the Vivago-Wristcare case. There were, all told, four rounds of interviews within the company over the years and two rounds of interviews with elderly persons and their caregivers. The first and second rounds in the development company and among its affiliates focused on the history and current affairs of the innovation project and the personnel's views about the use and users of the technology they were developing. The third and fourth rounds of interviews (in 2002–2003 and in 2009) focused on updates about what happened in the company and in its relationship with the clients and users. In both rounds of interviews with users (2000–2001 and 2006–2007), the interviews with managers and nurses focused on their work, their organization, and the use of Vivago-Wristcare and those with the elderly on their daily lives, past, and usage of technologies. All interviews, with the exception of some informal conversations, were audiotaped, and 31 of them were transcribed in full.

Table A.1   Interviews Conducted for the Vivago-Wristcare study. Some Interviews with Designers and Nurses had 2-3 People Present, and Some of them Were also Interviewed Repeatedly

Groups of interviewed people	Interviewees	Interviews	Typical length (approx.)	Years
Designers	8	10	1–2 hours	1999–2003
Company founder	1	7	1–2 hours	1999–2002
Marketing /customer people	6	8	1–2 hours	1999–2003
CEO	1	3	1–2 hours	1999–2003
People affiliated with the company, Wristcare maintenance or its sales	4	4	1 hour	2000–2003
Outside experts	7	7	1 hour	1999–2003
Rest-home managers	4	4	1–2 hours	2000–2001
Nurses, home-care workers, and alarm-center workers	16	17	40 min	2000–2001
Residents	17	17	40 min	2000–2001
Follow up study 1, Rest home	9	9	1–2 hours	2005–2007
Nurses	3	3	1–2 hours	2005–2007
Follow up study 2 Vivago Oy	6	6	1–3 hours	2009
Total	82	95		1999–2009

The ethnographic observation in Vivago Ltd. started right at the beginning of the project. The 10 meetings in the mechanical design process were observed from October 8, 1999, to July 5, 2000. Weekly R&D, marketing, and general company meetings were observed during 1999–2000. All these observations were audiotaped and, apart from the first two design meetings, also videotaped. All of my visits to the company were recorded as field notes, and the recordings of design meetings were later transcribed.

Observation related to the use of Vivago-Wristcare took place between spring 2000 and autumn 2001 and in 2006. These took the form of intense one-to-two-day sequences of interviews with observations of how the work was carried out in an alarm-service center and four nursing homes for the elderly (one of which was observed four times over two years). These observations were recorded mostly as only field notes as the possibilities to use of video recordings in these health care settings were limited.[1]

Document collection included *functional descriptions, business plans, business projections, and strategy presentations*, varying in length between seven and 50 pages and produced annually or biennially. Since each new plan had to account for the progress so far, these documents created a relational series that articulates the changing view of past and future in the innovation project. *Reports* of technology prestudy, market studies, a design study, theses, reports, and memos on formal and informal pilot studies were accompanied with informal memos from the company and its user partners. *User manuals, instructions, and assembly manuals*, updated yearly after the market launch, were a rich source for analyzing how the company wanted its device to be used and assembled, as well as of the representations it had of how users would relate to the device. *An archive of newspaper articles held by the company* included three full folders related to the products, competitors, and issues in elderly living and care. Since 2000, this archive has been comprehensive in regard to major Finnish media and compiled by a company specializing in press coverage. *The company's Web pages in* 1999–2009, updated annually, described the products, the company, and the story of the innovation for various stakeholder groups. *Internal documents*, such as memos of company meetings, to-do lists, R&D project plans, sketches, notebook entries, and e-mail, covered the interactions between developers and some of their clients. Just as importantly, *old versions* of Vivago-Wristcare and its associated products, pictures and descriptions of these, and charts describing the evolvement of product versions, as well as rest-home organizational charts, floor plans, and instructions on how to use Vivago-Wristcare locally, were actively used data sources.

DIABETES DATABASE STUDY

In the diabetes study, we first conducted one-to-three-hour-long interviews with four developers and five user-developers. In conjunction with these interviews, we gathered original documents on the development work, such as e-mail correspondence, participants' personal notes, earlier program screenshots, and screen and content sketches. In the second phase of the study, we conducted 21 interviews with professionals who had been involved in building diabetes software in different hospital districts in Finland. All interviews were recorded, but only the first nine interviews were fully transcribed. In our historical analysis of diabetes care, we relied mostly on secondary sources such as various reports and research literature. Field observations were conducted on two user sites and included video recordings of doctor–patient or nurse–patient reception interaction occasions. In addition, we participated in a consensus conference on diabetes care held in Finland, attended a user group meeting, and ran three intervention sessions with the participants (these sessions were also recorded, partly transcribed, and then analyzed).

TELECHEMISTRY STUDY

In the TeleChemistry case, there were more than 100 full folders of paper remaining from the project from 1960–2008 (if stacked atop each other, these make more than a 10-meter pile!) and in addition over 4,000 electronic entries on hard drives from the years 1994–2008. Typical items were patents, contracts, reports, inquiries, technical reports, various correspondence, and newspaper clippings. Not least because of the overwhelming amount of remaining documents, we chose to intertwine the document analysis with, all together, 18 semi-structured interviews of one to three hours' length, dozens of e-mail exchanges, more informal chats, and short conversations over the phone and face-to-face. The main innovator was formally interviewed eight times and other stakeholders formally once or twice. Since 2005, we could also use notes from direct observations of meetings, funding negotiations, technical work, *et cetera*, since Höyssä had been an observing and commenting participant in the process.

A NOTE ON DATA HANDLING

The early phases of the research were characterized by classic problems in reconstructing an innovation process. The historical documents were partial, scattered, and often permeated by rhetoric. Interviewees provided partial perspectives, different interpretations, and biased accounts (cf. Miettinen 1993). In the document analysis, we followed the principles of historiographic source criticism (e.g., Tosh 1991), in which we are formally trained: Hyysalo, Lehenkari, and Höyssä all have an M.A. in history. Open coding of content was used to sort interviews (Strauss and Corbin 1990; Silverman 1993). In the initial Vivago-Wristcare study, we used ATLAS.ti, which led to 758 entries in 132 categories.[2] These were further coded in regard to various topical areas that were to be analyzed in more detail. The source criticism of documents and the initial interview analyses were complemented by data triangulation and "across-method triangulation" (Denzin 1989), which took place when data-sets were constructed by means of different methods of data-gathering. Interview data, such as informants' accounts of the development process, and document sets, such as the series of business plans, were compared and cross-validated to complement one another. The series of business plans provided a changing horizon of vision and expectation but, more importantly, also a retrospective account of how and why the previous visions had been met or modified. The interviews provided interpretations of why and how events had unfolded, as well as new data not mentioned in the documents, while similar triangulation was conducted in relation to observations and interviews. Observations provided a detailed and firsthand view of the process while interviews linked the events to background events as well as to concerns and interpretations of the participants.

The triangulation between different sources continued as construction of chronologies of the innovation processes. The first ones were rough mappings of key events and turning points, growing into more detailed data-overview narratives, which connected different chronologies and data sources. Topics and periods of particular interest were then identified and the rest of the process; for instance, how to compare and refine analyses on different sites and scales of analysis is discussed in Chapter 2 of this volume.

References

Afuaf, N. A., and N. Bahram. 1995. The hypercube of innovation. *Research Policy* 24:51–76.

Agre, P. E. 1995. Conceptions of user in computer systems design. In *Social and Interactional Dimensions of Human–Computer Interfaces*, edited by P. J. Thomas. Cambridge: Cambridge University Press.

Akrich, M. 1992. The description of technological objects. In *Shaping Technology—Building Society: Studies in Sociotechnical Change*, edited by W. E. Bijker and J. Law. Cambridge, MA: MIT Press.

———. 1995. User representations: Practices, methods and sociology. In *Managing Technology in Society. The Approach of Constructive Technology Assessment*, edited by A. Rip, T. J. Misa, and J. Schot. London: Cassel Publishers.

Akrich, M., and B. Latour. 1992. A summary of a convenient vocabulary for the semiotics of human and nonhuman assemblies. In *Shaping Technology—Building Society: Studies in Sociotechnical Change*, edited by W. E. Bijker and J. Law. Cambridge, MA: MIT Press.

Andersen, E. S., and B.-Å. Lundvall. 1988. Small national systems of innovation facing technological revolutions: an analytical framework. In *Small Countries Facing the Technological Revolution*, edited by C. Freeman and B.-Å. Lundwall. London: Pinter.

Ankersmit, F., and H. Kellner, eds. 1995. *A New Philosophy of History*. London: Reaction Books.

Appadurai, A. 1986. Introduction: Commodities and the politics of value. In *The Social Life of Things: Commodities in Cultural Perspective*, edited by A. Appadurai. Cambridge: Cambridge University Press.

Arrow, K. 1962. The economic implications of learning by doing. *Review of Economic Studies* 29:155–173.

Attewell, P. 1992. Technology diffusion and organizational learning: The case of business computing. *Organization Science* 3 (1): 1–19.

Baldwin, C., C. Hienerth, and E. von Hippel. 2006. How user innovations become commercial products: A theoretical investigation and case study. *Research Policy* 35:1291–1313.

Bandura, A. 1977. *Social Learning Theory*. Englewood Cliffs, NJ: Prentice Hall.

Bansler, J. 1989. Systems development in Scandinavia. Three theoretical schools. *Scandinavian Journal of Information Systems* 1 (1): 3–20.

Baraldi, E. 2009. How does an industrial network use information technology? Or how interacting resources use IKEA's PIA and Edsbyn's Movex. In *Use of Science and Technology in Business: Exploring the Impact of Using Activity for Systems, Organizations and People*, edited by E. Baraldi, H. Håkansson, F. Prenkert, and A. Waluszewski. Bingley, UK: Emerald Publishing Group.

284 *References*

Bateson, G. 2000. *Steps to an Ecology of Mind: Collected Essays in Anthropology, Psychiatry, Evolution, and Epistemology.* 2nd ed. New York: Jason Aronson Inc.

Bazerman, C. 1998. *Languages of Edison's Light.* Cambridge, MA: MIT Press.

Beck, E. 2002. Mediation, non-Participation and technology in care giving work. In *PDC 2002, Participatory Design Conference 23.-25.6.2002*, edited by T. Binder, J. Gregory, and I. Wagner. Malmö, Sweden: Computer Professionals for Social Responsibility.

Becker, H. 1953. Some contingencies of the professional dance musician's career. *Human Organization* 12:22–26.

———. 1960. Notes on the concept of commitment. *American Journal of Sociology* 66 (1): 32–40.

Beirne, M., and H. Ramsay. 1988. Computer redesign and labour process theory. In *New Technology and the Labour Process*, edited by D. Kniths and H. Willmont. London: Macmillan.

Belk, R. W., and J. A. Costa. 1998. The mountain man myth: A contemporary consuming fantasy. *Journal of Consumer Research* 25:218–240.

Benkler, Y. 2006. *The Wealth of Networks: How Social Production Transforms Markets and Freedom.* New Haven and London: Yale University Press.

Benner, M. J., and M. L. Tushman. 2003. Exploitation, exploration, and process management: The productivity dilemma revisited. *Academy of Management* 28 (2): 238–256.

Benyon, D., P. Turner, and S. Turner. 2005. *Designing Interactive Systems—People, Activities, Contexts, Technologies.* London: Addison-Wesley.

Berg, M. 1997. *Rationalizing Medical Work.* Cambridge, MA: MIT Press.

Berg, M., and A. Mol, eds. 1998. *Differences in Medicine—Unraveling Practices, Techniques and Bodies.* Durham, NC, and London: Duke University Press.

Berger, T., M. Hartmann, Y. Punie, and K. Ward, eds. 2006. *Domestication of Media and Technology.* Maidenhead, UK: Open University Press.

Berlo, A. v., P. Vermijs, and T. Hermans. 1994. Experiences with safety alarms for the elderly in the Netherlands. In *Safety-Alarm Systems, Technical Aids and Smart Homes*, edited by C. Wild and A. Kirschner. Knegsel: Akontes Publishing.

Bernstein, R. J. 1999. *Praxis and Action. Contemporary Philosophies of Human Activity.* Philadelphia: University of Pennsylvania Press. Original edition, 1971.

Bessant, J., and H. Rush. 1995. Building bridges for innovation: The role of consultants in technology transfer. *Research Policy* 24 (1): 97–114.

Beyer, H., and K. Holtzblatt. 1998. *Contextual Design: Defining Customer Centered Systems.* San Francisco: Morgan Kaufmann Publishers.

Bijker, W. E. 1995. *Of Bicycles, Bakelites, and Bulbs: Toward a Theory of Sociotechnical Change.* Cambridge, MA: MIT Press.

Bijker, W. E., T. P. Hughes, and T. J. Pinch, eds. 1987. *The Social Construction of Technological Systems: New Directions in the Sociology and History of Technology.* Cambridge, MA: MIT Press.

Bijker, W. E., and T. Pinch. 1984. The social construction of facts and artefacts: Or how the sociology of science and the sociology of technology might benefit each other. *Social Studies of Science* 14:399–441.

———. 2002. Scot answers: Different questions. *Technology and Culture* 43 (2): 361–369.

Bjerknes, G., and T. Bratteteig. 1987. Florence in Wonderland: System development with nurses. In *Computers and Democracy—A Scandinavian Challenge*, edited by G. Bjerknes, P. Ehn, and M. Kyng. Aldershot, UK: Avebury.

———. 1995. User participation and democracy: A discussion of Scandinavian research on system development. *Scandinavian Journal of Information Systems* 7 (1): 72–97.

Bjerknes, G., P. Ehn, and M. Kyng, eds. 1987. *Computers and Democracy—A Scandinavian Challenge.* Aldershot, UK: Avebury.

Björneby, S. 1994. The needs of demented people in future "smart homes." In *Safety-Alarm Systems, Technical Aids and Smart Homes*, edited by C. Wild and A. Kirschner. Knegsel: Akontes Publishing.

Bleikie, A. 1988. Vanhenemisen ja hyvinvointivaltion tulevaisuus: brittiläinen näkökulma (Aging and the future of the welfare state, a British perspective). *Gerontologia* 2 (4): 273–287.

Blumer, H. 1969. *Symbolic Interactionism. Perspective and Method*. Berkeley: University of California Press.

Boeke, K. 1957. *COSMIC VIEW: The Universe in 40 Jumps*. New York: John Day Company.

Boland, R. 1978. The process of and product of system design. *Management Science* 24 (9): 887–898.

Bowker, G. C., and S. L. Star. 1999. *Sorting Things Out: Classification and its Consequences*. Cambridge, MA: MIT Press.

Braudel, F. 1995. *Mediterranean and the Mediterranean World at the Age of Philip 2.* Translated by S. Reynolds. 2nd revised ed. Berkeley: University of California Press.

Brown, H. S., P. Vergragt, K. Green, and L. Berchicci. 2003. Learning for sustainability transition through bounded socio-technical experiments in personal mobility. *Technology Analysis & Strategic Management* 15:291–315.

Brown, N., and A. Webster. 2004. *New Medical Technologies and Society: Reordering Life*. Cambridge, UK: Polity Press.

Bucciarelli, L. 1994. *Designing Engineers*. Cambridge, MA: MIT Press.

Burt, R. S. 2004. Structural holes and good ideas. *American Journal of Sociology* 110 (2): 349–399.

Buscher, M., M. Christensen, K. Hansen, P. Mogensen, and D. Shapiro. 2009. Bottom-up, top-down? Connecting software architecture design with use. In *Configuring User–Designer Relations—Interdisciplinary Perspectives*, edited by A. Voss, M. Hartswood, R. Procter, M. Rouncefield, R. S. Slack, and M. Büscher. London: Springer.

Bødker, S., P. Ehn, J. Kammersgaard, M. Kyng, and Y. Sundblad. 1987. A UTO-PIAN experience: On design of powerful computer-based tools for skilled graphical workers. In *Computers and Democracy—A Scandinavian Challenge*, edited by G. Bjerknes, P. Ehn, and M. Kyng. Aldershot, UK: Avebury..

Bødker, S., F. Kensing, and J. Simonsen. 2004. *Participatory IT Design—Designing for Business and Workplace Realities*. Cambridge, MA: MIT Press.

Callon, M. 1991. Techno-economic networks and irreversibility. In *A Sociology of Monsters: Essays on Power, Technology, and Domination*, edited by J. Law. London: Routledge.

———. 1992 The dynamics of techno-economic networks. In *Technological Change and Company Strategies*, edited by R. Coombs, P. Saviotti, and V. Walsh. London: Academic Press.

———. 1998. *The Laws of the Markets*. London: Blackwell Publishers.

Callon, M., and B. Latour. 1981. Unscrewing the big Leviathan: How actors macrostructure reality and how sociologists help them to do so. In *Advances in Social Theory and Methodology: Toward an Integration of Micro- and Macro Sociologies*, edited by K. Knorr Cetina and A. V. Cicourel. Boston: Routledge.

Callon, M., C. Méadel, and V. Rabeharisoa. 2002. The economy of qualities. *Economy and Society* 31 (2): 194–217.

Carlile, P. R. 2002. A pragmatic view of knowledge and boundaries: Boundary objects in new product development. *Organization Science* 13 (4): 442–455.

Castoriadis, C. 1987. *Imaginary Institution of Society*. Translated by K. Blamey. Cambridge, UK: Polity Press.

Chaiklin, S., and J. Lave. 1993. *Understanding Practice. Perspectives on Activity and Context*. Edited by R. Pea and J. S. Brown. Cambridge: Cambridge University Press.

Christensen, C. M., and M. E. Raynor. 2003. *Innovator's Solution—Creating and Sustaining Successful Growth.* Boston: Harvard Business School Press.

Clarke, A. E. 1990. A social worlds research adventure. The case of reproductive science. In *Theories of Science in Society*, edited by S. E. Cozzens and T. F. Gieryn. Bloomington: Indiana University Press.

———. 1998. *Disciplining Reproduction: Modernity, American Life and "The Problems of Sex."* Berkeley: University of California Press.

———. 2005. *Situational Analysis—Grounded Theory after the Postmodern Turn.* Thousand Oaks, CA: Sage.

Clarke, A. E., and E. M. Gerson. 1990. Symbolic interactionism in social studies of science. In *Symbolic Interaction and Cultural Studies*, edited by H. S. Becker and M. M. McCall. Chicago: University of Chicago Press.

Clarke, A. E., and S. L. Star. 2003. Symbolic interactionist science, technology, information and biomedicine studies. In *Handbook of Symbolic Interaction*, edited by L. T. Reynolds and N. J. Herman. Walnut Creek, CA: Alta Mira Press.

Colarelli O'Connor, G. 1998. Market learning and radical innovation: A cross-case comparison of 8 radical innovation projects. *Journal of Product Innovation Management* 15:151–166.

Cole, M. 1996. *Cultural Psychology: A Once and Future Discipline.* Cambridge, MA: Harvard University Press.

Collins, H. M., and R. Evans. 2002. The third wave of science studies: Studies of expertise and experience. *Social Studies of Science* 32 (2): 235–296.

Constant II, E. W. 1980. *The Origins of the Turbojet Revolution.* Baltimore, MD: The John Hopkins University Press.

Coombs, R., P. Saviotti, and V. Walsh, eds. 1987. *Economics and Technological Change.* New Jersey: Rowman and Littlefield.

Cooper, A. 2004. *Inmates Are Running the Asylum—Why High-Tech Products Drive Us Crazy and How to Restore the Sanity.* Indianapolis (IN): Sams.

Cooper, G., and J. Bowers. 1995. Representing the user—Notes on the disciplinary rhetoric of human–computer interaction. In *Social and Interactional Dimensions of Human–Computer Interfaces*, edited by P. J. Thomas. Cambridge: Cambridge University Press.

Cornford, J., and N. Pollock. 2003. *Putting the University Online: Information, Technology, and Organizational Change.* Buckingham: Open University Press.

Cross, N. 2000. *Engineering Design Methods—Strategies for Product Design.* Chichester: John Wiley and Sons.

Cullen, K., ed. 1998. *The Promise of the Information Society. Good Practice in Using the Information Society for the Benefit of Older People and Disabled People.* Helsinki: STAKES, the Finnish Center for Research and Development of Welfare and Health

D'Adderio, L. 2001. Crafting the virtual prototype: How firms integrate knowledge and capabilities across organisational boundaries. *Research Policy* 30:1409–1424.

Darking, M., and E. Whitley. 2007. Towards an understanding of FLOSS: Infrastructures, materiality and the digital business ecosystem. *Science Studies* 20 (2): 13–33.

David, P. A. 1990. The dynamo and the computer: An historical perspective on the modern productivity paradox. *American Journal of Economic Review* 80 (2): 355–361.

Davies, S. 1979. *Diffusion of Product Innovations.* Cambridge: Cambridge University Press.

De Laet, M., and A. Mol. 2000. The Zimbabwe bush pump: Mechanics of fluid technology. *Social Studies of Science* 30 (2): 225–263.

Denzin, N. K. 1989. *The Research Act. A Theoretical Introduction to Sociological Methods*. 3rd ed. Englewood Cliffs, NJ: Prentice Hall.

DeSanctis, G., and M. S. Poole. 1994. Capturing the complexity in advanced technology use: Adaptive structuration theory. *Organisation Science* 5 (2): 121–147.

Dierkes, M., U. Hoffmann, and L. Marz. 1996. *Visions of Technology*. Frankfurt and New York: Campus Verlag.

Dix, A., J. Finlay, G. D. Abowd, and R. Beale. 2004. *Human–Computer Interaction*. 3rd ed. Harlow, UK: Pearson Prentice Hall.

Duret et al. 1999. *PROTEE. Procedures for Transport Evaluation and Monitoring of Radical Innovations in Learning Experiments*. Final report of the project funded by the European Commission under the transport RTD programme of the 4th FP. http://www.transport-research.info/Upload/Documents/200310/protee.pdf (accessed 13 October 2009).

Eames, R., and C. Eames. 1977. *Powers of Ten*. Documentary short film. USA.

Edström, A. 1977. User influence and the success of MIS projects. *Human Relations* 30:589–606.

Ehn, P. 1992. Scandinavian design: On participation and skill. In *Usability: Turning Technologies into Tools*, edited by P. S. Adler and T. Winograd. New York: Oxford University Press.

———. 1993. Scandinavian design: On participation and skill. In *Participatory Design: Principles and Practices*, edited by D. Schuler and A. Namioka. Hillsdale, NJ: Lawrence Erlbaum Associates.

Ekberg, J. 2003. Will the interfaces be more human in the future? In *Universal Access in HCI: Inclusive Design in the Information Society, Vol. 4*, edited by C. Stephanidis. Hillsdale, NJ: Lawrence Erlbaum Associates.

Elzen, B., F. W. Geels, and K. Green, eds. 2004. *System Innovation and the Transition to Sustainability—Theory, Evidence and Policy*. Chaltenham, UK: Edward Algar.

Ende, J. v. d., and R. Kemp. 1999. Technological transformations in history: How the computer regime grew out of existing computing regimes. *Research Policy* 28:833–851.

Engeström, R. 1995. Voice as communicative action. *Mind, Culture, and Activity* 2 (3): 192–215.

Engeström, Y. 1987. *Learning by Expanding. An Activity-Theoretical Approach to Developmental Research*. Helsinki: Orienta-Konsultit Oy.

———. 1990. When is a tool? In *Learning, Working, Imagining: Twelve Studies in Activity Theory*. Helsinki: Orienta-Konsultit.

———. 1993. Developmental studies of work as a testbench of activity theory: The case of primary care medical practice. In *Understanding Practice. Perspectives on Activity and Context*, edited by J. Lave and S. Chaiklin. Cambridge: Cambridge University Press.

———. 1995. *Kehittävä työntutkimus. Perusteita, Tuloksia, ja Haasteita (Developmental Work Research. Foundations, Results, and Challenges)*. Helsinki: Hallinnon kehittämiskeskus.

———. 1996a. Developmental work research as educational research: Looking ten years back and into the zone of proximal development. *Nordisk Pedagogik* 16 (3): 131–143.

———. 1996b. Interobjectivity, ideality, and dialectics. *Mind, Culture, and Activity* 3 (4): 259–265.

———. 1999. Activity theory and individual and social transformation. In *Perspectives on Activity Theory*, edited by Y. Engeström, R. Miettinen, R.-L. Punamäki. Cambridge: Cambridge University Press.

———. 2000. Activity theory as a framework for analyzing and redesigning work. *Ergonomics* 43 (7): 960–974.

———. 2001a. Expansive learning at work: Toward an activity theoretical reconceptualization. *Journal of Education and Work* 14 (1): 129–152.

———. 2001b. The horizontal dimension of expansive learning: Weaving a texture of cognitive trails in the terrain of health care in Helsinki. Paper presented at New Challenges to Research on Learning, March 21–23, 2001.

Engeström, Y., and F. Blackler. 2005. On the life of the object. *Organization* 12 (3): 307–330.

Engeström, Y., R. Engeström, and T. Vähäaho. 1999a. When the center does not hold: The importance of knotworking. In *Activity Theory and Social Practice*, edited by S. Chaiklin, M. Hedegaard, and U. J. Jensen. Aarhus: Aarhus University Press.

Engeström, Y., and V. Escalante. 1996. Mundane tool or object of affection? The rise and fall of the postal buddy. In *Context and Consciousness. Activity Theory and Human–Computer Interaction*, edited by B. Nardi. Cambridge, MA: MIT Press.

Engeström, Y., R. Miettinen, and R.-L. Punamäki, eds. 1999b. *Perspectives on Activity Theory*. Cambridge: Cambridge University Press.

Engeström, Y., A. Puonti, and L. Seppänen. 2003. Spatial and temporal expansion of the object as a challenge for reorganizing work. In *Knowing in Organizations*, edited by D. Nicolini, S. Gherardi, and D. Yanow. New York: M. E. Sharpe Inc.

Eriksson, I., and M. I. Nurminen. 1991. Doing by learning: Embedded application systems. *Journal of Organizational Computing* 1 (4): 323–339.

Fagerberg, J. 2003. Schumpeter and the revival of evolutionary economics: An appraisal of the literature. *Journal of Evolutionary Economics* 13:125–159.

Fagerberg, J., D. C. Mowery, and R. Nelson, eds. 2005. *The Oxford Handbook of Innovation*. Oxford: Oxford University Press.

Ferguson, E. S. 1992. *Engineering and the Mind's Eye*. Cambridge, MA: MIT Press.

Fichtner, B. 1984. Co-ordination, co-operation and communication in the formation of theoretical concepts in instruction. In *Learning and Teaching on a Scientific Basis: Methodological and Epistemological Aspects of the Activity Theory of Learning and Teaching*, edited by M. Hedegaard, P. Hakkarainen, and Y. Engeström. Aarhus: Aarhus University, Psychology Department.

Fiol, M. C., and M. A. Lyles. 1985. Organizational learning. *Academy of Management Review* 10 (4): 803–813.

Fischer, C. S. 1992. *America Calling: A Social History of the Telephone to 1940*. Berkeley: University of California Press.

Fleck, J. 1988. Innofusion or diffusation? The nature of technological development in robotics. Edinburg PICT Working Paper 4.

———. 1993a. Configurations: Crystallizing contingency. *International Journal of Human Factors in Manufacturing* 3 (1): 15–36.

———. 1993b. Innofusion: Feedback in the innovation process. In *Systems Science: Addressing Global Issues*, edited byF. A. Stowell, D. West, and J. G. Howell. London: Plenum.

———. 1994. Learning by trying: The implementation of configurational technology. *Research Policy* 23:637–652.

———. 2002. The structure of technological evolutions: Linear models, configurations, and systems of development. Paper presented to Nobel Symposium on "Science and Industry in the 20th Century," Stockholm, November 21–23, 2002.

Fleck, L. 1979. *Genesis and Development of Scientific Fact*. Translated by F. Bradley and T. J. Trenn. Chicago: University of Chicago Press.

Flichy, P. 2006. *Understanding Technological Innovation.* Cheltenham, UK: Edgar Elgar.

———. 2007. *The Internet Imaginaire.* Cambridge, MA: MIT Press.

Flick, O. 1998. *An Introduction to Qualitative Research.* London: Sage.

Foot, K. 1999. *Writing Conflicts: An Activity Theory Analysis of the Development of the Network for Ethnological Monitoring and Early Warning.* Academic dissertation. San Diego: University of California San Diego, Department of Communication.

Foot, K. A., and S. M. Schneider. 2006. *Web Campaigning.* Cambridge, MA: MIT Press.

Foucault, M. 1995. *Discipline and Punish: The Birth of the Prison.* Translated by A. Sheridan. New York: Vintage Books.

Franke, N., and S. Shah. 2003. How communities support innovative activities: An exploration of assistance and sharing among end-users. *Research Policy* 32 (1): 157–178.

Freeman, C. 1979. The determinants of innovation—Market demand, technology, and the response to social problems. *Futures* 11 (3): 206–215.

———. 1994. Critical survey: The economics of technical change. *Cambridge Journal of Economics* 18:463–514.

Freeman, C., and F. Louçã. 2001. *As Time Goes By: From the Industrial Revolutions to the Information Revolution.* Oxford: Oxford University Press.

Freeman, S. 2007. The material and social dynamics of motivation: Contributions to open source language technology development. *Science Studies* 20 (2): 55–77.

Fujimura, J. H. 1996. *Crafting Science: A Sociohistory of the Quest for the Genetics of Cancer.* Cambridge, MA: Harvard University Press.

———. 2003. Future imaginaries, genome scientists as sociocultural entrepreneurs. In *Genetic Nature Culture*, edited by A. H. Goodman, D. Heath, and S. M. Lindee. Los Angeles: University of California Press.

Gävert, L. 2008. *"Niin kauan kun mä vaan jaksan!" Ikääntyneiden palvelutaloasukkaiden toimijuus ja mahdollisuudet vaikuttaa toimintaympäristöönsä* (*"As Long As I'm Able To!" Aging Residents' Agency and Possibilities to Affect Their Environment in Sheltered Housing*). Master's thesis. Helsinki: University of Helsinki, Department of Sociology.

Garcia, R., and R. Calantone. 2002. A critical look at technological innovation typology and innovativeness terminology: A literature review. *Journal of Product Innovation Management* 19:110–132.

Gardiner, P., and R. Rothwell. 1985. Tough customers: Good designs. *Design Studies* 6 (1): 7–17.

Garud, R., and P. Karnoe. 2001. *Path Dependence and Creation.* Mahwah, NJ: Lawrence Erlbaum Associates.

Gatignon, H., M. L. Tushman, W. Smith, and P. Anderson. 2002. A structural approach to assessing innovation: Construct development of innovation locus, type, and characteristics. *Management Science* 48 (9): 1103–1122.

Gedenryd, H. 1998. *How designers work: making sense of authentic cognitive activities.* Lund: Lund University Cognitive Studies 75.

Geels, F. W. 2002. Technological transitions as evolutionary reconfiguration processes: A multi-level perspective and a case study. *Research Policy* 31 (8): 1257–1274.

Geels, F. W., and J. Schot. 2007. Typology of sociotechnical transition pathways. *Research Policy* 36:399–417.

Geertz, C. 1973a. *The Interpretation of Cultures: Selected Essays.* New York: Basic Books.

———. 1973b. Thick description: Toward an interpretive theory of culture. In *The Interpretation of Cultures*, edited by C. Geertz. New York: Basic Books.

Gell, A. 1986. Newcomers to the world of goods: consumption among the Muria Gonds. In *The Social Life of Things: Commodities in Cultural Perspective*, edited by A. Appadurai. Cambridge: Cambridge University Press.

Gertler, M. S., and D. A. Wolfe. 2002. *Innovation and Social Learning: Institutional Adaptation in an Era of Technological Change*. New York: Palgrave MacMillan.

Gherardi, S., and D. Nicolini. 2006. Actor networks: Ecology and entrepreneurs. In *Actor Network Theory and Organizing*, edited by B. Czarniawska and T. Hernes. Malmö, Sweden: Elanders Berlings.

Gibbs, W. W. 1994. Software's chronic crisis. *Scientific American* 3:72–81.

Gingras, Y., and M. Trepanier. 1993. Constructing a Tokamak: Political, economic and technical factors as constraints and resources. *Social Studies of Science* 23 (1): 5–36.

Ginzburg, C. 1989. *Clues, Myths and the Historical Method*. Baltimore, MD: The Johns Hopkins University Press.

Goodwin, C. 1994. Professional vision. *American Anthropologist* 96 (3): 606–633.

Green, K. 1993. Shaping demand for biotechnology. In *Technological Change and Company Strategies*, edited by R. Coombs, P. Saviotti, and V. Walsh. London: Academic Press.

Greenbaum, J., and M. Kyng, eds. 1991. *Design at Work: Cooperative Design of Computer Systems*. Hillsdale, NJ: Lawrence Erlbaum Associates.

Gregory, J. 2000. *Sorcerer's Apprentice: Creating the Electronic Health Record, Re-Inventing Medical Records and Patient Care*. Academic dissertation. San Diego: University of California San Diego, Department of Communication.

Gregory, J., S. Hyysalo, and J. Kangasoja. 2003. Imaginaries at work: Conceptualizing technology beyond individual projects. Paper presented at the Annual meeting of the Society for Social Studies of Science, Atlanta, October 16–18.

Grint, K., and S. Woolgar. 1997. *The Machine at Work: Technology, Work, and Organization*. Cambridge, UK: Polity Press.

Grudin, J. 1993. Obstacles to participatory design in large product development organizations. In *Participatory Design: Principles and Practices*, edited by D. Schuler and A. Namioka. Hillsdale, NJ: Lawrence Erlbaum Associates.

Grønbæk, K., J. Grudin, S. Bødker, and L. Bannon. 1993. Achieving cooperative system design: Shifting from a product to a process focus. In *Participatory Design: Principles and Practices*, edited by D. Schuler and A. Namioka. Hillsdale, NJ: Lawrence Erlbaum Associates.

Haddon, L. 2004. *Information and Communication Technologies in Everyday Life*. Oxford: Berg Publishers.

Haraway, D. 1997. *Modest_Witness@Second_Millennium. FemaleMan_Meets_OncoMouse*. New York and London: Routledge.

Hargadon, A., and R. Sutton. 1997. Technology brokering and innovation in a product development firm. *Administrative Science Quarterly* 42:716–749.

Harrington, T., and M. Harrington. 2000. *Gerontechnology. Why and How*. Maastricht: Shaker Publishing.

Hartswood, M., R. Procter, R. Slack, A. Voß, M. Buscher, M. Rouncefield, and P. Rouchy. 2002. Co-realisation: Towards a principled synthesis of ethnomethodology and participatory design. *Scandinavian Journal of Information Systems* 14 (2): 9–30.

Hasu, M. 2000. Constructing clinical use: An activity-theorectical perspective on implementing new technology. *Technology Analysis & Strategic Management* 12:369–382.

———. 2001a. *Critical Transition from Developers to Users*. Academic dissertation. Helsinki: University of Helsinki, Department of Education.

———. 2001b. *Critical Transition from Developers to Users. Activity-Theoretical Studies of Interaction and Learning in the Innovation Process.* Helsinki: University of Helsinki. http://urn.fi/URN:ISBN:951-45-9881-4 (accessed 13 October 2009).

Hasu, M., and Y. Engeström. 2000. Measurement in action: An activity-theoretical perspective on producer–user interaction. *International Journal of Human-Computer Studies* 53 (1): 61–89.

Hasu, M., T. Keinonen, U.-M. Mutanen, A. Aaltonen, A. Hakatie, and E. Kurvinen. 2004. *Muotoilun muutos—Näkökulmia muotoilutyön organisoinnin ja johtamisen kehityshaasteisiin 2000-luvulla (Change of Design—Perspectives to Challenges in Organizing and Managing Design in 2000s).* Helsinki: Teknologiateollisuus.

Hegger, D. L. T., J. V. Vliet, and B. J. M. V. Vliet. 2007. Niche management and its contribution to regime change: The case of innovation in sanitation. *Technology Analysis & Strategic Management* 19 (6): 729–746.

Heikkilä, J., H. Vahtera, and P. Reijonen. 2003. Taking organizational implementation seriously: The case of IOS implementation. Paper read at IFIP 8.6. Working Conference: "The Diffusion and Adoption of Networked Information Technologies," Elsinore, Denmark.

Heikkinen, R.-L., V. Virtanen, E. Heikkinen, and M. Kauppinen. 1992. Sosiaalinen yhteisyys, yhteisöllinen toiminta ja terveys (Social connections, collective activity and health). *Gerontologia* 6 (3): 176–184.

Heiskanen, E., S. Hyysalo, T. Kotro, and P. Repo. Forthcoming. Constructing innovative users and user inclusive innovation communities. *Technology Analysis & Strategic Management.*

Helgesson, C.-F., and H. Kjellberg. 2006. Macro-actors and the sounds of the silenced. In *Actor Network Theory and Organizing*, edited by B. Czarniawska and T. Hernes. Malmö, Sweden: Elanders Berlings.

———. 2009. Practical use: On agency and the use of science and technology. In *Use of Science and Technology in Business: Exploring the Impact of Using Activity for Systems, Organizations and People*, edited by E. Baraldi, H. Håkanson, F. Prenkert, and A. Waluschewski. Bingley, UK: Emerald Publishing Group.

Hemmings, T., A. Crabtree, T. Rodden, C. Clarke, and M. Rouncefield. 2002. Probing the probes. In *PDC 2002 Participatory Design Conference, 23–25.6.2002*, edited by T. Binder, J. Gregory, and I. Wagner. Malmö, Sweden: Computer Professionals for Social Responsibility.

Hempel, J. 1994. Opportunities and limitations of technical aids for the elderly. In *Safety-Alarm Systems, Technical Aids and Smart Homes*, edited by C. Wild and A. Kirschner. Knegsel: Akontes Publishing.

Henderson, R., and K. B. Clark. 1990. Architectural innovation: The reconfiguration of existing product technologies and the failure of established firms. *Administrative Science Quarterly* 35:9–30.

Hennion, A. 1989. An intermediary between production and consumption: The producer of popular music. *Science, Technology & Human Values* 14 (4): 400–424.

———. 2007. Those things that hold us together: Taste and sociology. *Cultural Sociology* 1 (1): 97–114.

Herstatt, C., and E. von Hippel. 1992. From experience: Developing new product concepts via the lead user method, a case study in a "low tech" field. *Journal of Product Innovation Management* 9:213–221.

Hienerth, C. 2006. The development of the rodeo kayaking industry. *R&D Management* 36 (3): 273–294.

Hirschheim, R., and H. K. Klein. 1989. Four paradigms of information systems development. *Communications of the ACM* 32 (10): 1199–1216.

Holland, D., and J. R. Reeves. 1996. Activity theory and a view from somewhere: Team perspectives on the intellectual work of programming. In *Context and Consciousness. Activity Theory and Human Computer interaction*, edited by B. Nardi. Cambridge, MA: MIT Press.

Holt, D. B. 1995. How consumers consume: A typology of consumption practices. *Journal of Consumer Research* 22:1–16.

Hommels, A., P. Peters, and W. E. Bijker. 2007. Techno therapy or nurtured niches? Technology studies and the evaluation of radical innovation. *Research Policy* 36:1088–1099.

Hoogma, R., R. Kemp, J. Schot, and B. Truffer. 2002. *Experimenting for Sustainable Transport—The Approach of Strategic Niche Management*. Vol. 10. London: Spon Press.

Hornyanszky Dalholm, E. 1998. *Att Forma Sitt Rum. Fullskalemodellering i Participatoriska Designprocesser (To Design One's Room. Full-Scale Modeling in Participatory Design Processes)*. Lund: Lunds Tekniska Högskola.

Howcroft, D., and M. Wilson. 2003. Paradoxes of participatory practices: The Janus role of the systems developer. *Information and Organization* 13:1–24.

Howells, J. 2006. Intermediation and the role of intermediaries in innovation. *Research Policy* 35 (5): 715–728.

Hughes, E. C. 1971. *The Sociological Eye*. Chicago: Aldine Atherton.

Hughes, T. P. 1979. The electrification of America: The system builders. *Technology and Culture* 20 (1): 124–161.

———. 1988a. *Networks of Power. Electrification of Western World 1880–1930*. Baltimore, MD: The Johns Hopkins University Press.

———. 1988b. The seamless web: Technology, science, et cetera, et cetera. In *Technology and Social Process*, edited by B. Elliot. Edinburgh: Edinburgh University Press.

Hutchins, E. 1995. *Cognition in the Wild*. Cambridge, MA: MIT Press.

———. 2005. Material anchors for conceptual blends. *Journal of Pragmatics* 37:1555–1577.

Hyppönen, H. 1999. *Handbook for Inclusive Design of Telematics Applications*. Helsinki: STAKES, the Finnish Center for Research and Development of Welfare and Health.

———. 2004. *Tekniikka kehittyy, kehittyvätkö palvelut? Tapaustutkimus kotipalvelujen kehittymisestä teknologiahankkeessa (Technology Develops, Do the Services Develop? A Case Study about the Development of Home-Care Services in a Technology Project)*. Helsinki: STAKES, the Finnish Center for Research and Development of Welfare and Health.

———. 2007. eHealth services and technology: Challenges for co-development. *Human Technology: An Interdisciplinary Journal on Humans in ICT Environments* 3 (2): 188–213.

Hyysalo, S. 2000. *Yhteistyö ja ajallisuus PET-merkkiaineiden tuotekehityksessä (Collaboration and Temporality in Product Development of PET-Tracers)*. Turku: Turun yliopiston historian laitos.

———. 2004a. Technology nurtured—Collectives in maintaining and implementing technology for elderly care. *Science Studies* 17 (2): 23–43.

———. 2004b. Users, an emerging human resource for R&D? From preference elicitation towards the joint exploration of users' needs. *International Journal of Human Resource Development and Management* 4 (1): 22–38.

———. 2004c. *Uses of Innovation. Wristcare in the Practices of Engineers and Elderly*. Helsinki: Helsinki University Press.

———. 2006. Representations of use and practice-bound imaginaries in automating the safety of the elderly. *Social Studies of Science* 36 (4): 599–626.

———. 2009a. A break from novelty: Persistence and effects of structural tensions in designer–user relations. In *Configuring User–Designer Relations—Interdisciplinary*

Perspectives, edited by A. Voss, M. Hartswood, R. Procter, M. Roucefield, R. S. Slack, and M. Büscher. London: Springer-Verlag.

———. 2009b. *Käyttäjä tuotekehityksessä: Tieto, tutkimus, menetelmät (User in Product Development: Knowledge, Research, Methods)*. Helsinki: University of Art and Design Helsinki.

Hyysalo, S., and J. Lehenkari. 2002. Contextualizing power in collaborative design. In *PDC 2002, Participatory Design Conference 23.-25.6.2002*, edited by T. Binder, J. Gregory, and I. Wagner. Malmö, Sweden: Computer Professionals for Social Responsibility.

———. 2003. An activity-theoretical method for studying user-participation in IS design. *Methods of Information in Medicine* 42 (4): 398–405.

———. 2005. Instrument-oriented history, ethnography and interventions in studying IS design. In *Putting Activity Theory to Work—Developmental Work Research*, edited by Y. Engeström, G. Ruckriem, and J. Lompsher. Berlin: Lehmans Media.

Hyysalo, S., J. Lehenkari, and R. Miettinen. 2003. Informaatiokumous, tuottaja-käyttäjäsuhteet ja sosiaaliset innovaatiot (Information revolution, user–producer relations and social innovations). In *Innovaatiopolitiikka*, edited by T. Lemola and P. Honkanen. Helsinki: Gaudeamus.

Höyssä, M., and S. Hyysalo. 2009. The fog of innovation: Innovativeness and deviance in developing new clinical testing equipment. *Research Policy* 38 (6): 984–993.

Ihonen, M. 1986. *Vanhusten ja vammaisten turvapalvelussa käytettävät laitteet ja järjestelmät (Devices and Systems Used in the Security Services for the Elderly and the Disabled)*. Helsinki: Sosiaalihallitus.

———. 1987. *Turvapalvelut .Vanhusten ja vammaisten turvapuhelin kokeiluprojektin raportti (Safety Services. The Report of Pilot Study on Safety Phones for the Elderly and the Disabled)*. Helsinki: Sosiaalihallitus.

Ives, B., and M. H. Olson. 1984. User involvement and MIS success: A review of research. *Management Science* 30 (May): 586–603.

Joas, H. 1987. Symbolic interactionism. In *Social Theory Today*, edited by A. Giddens and J. H. Turner. Cambridge: Polity Press.

Joerges, B. 1999. Do politics have artefacts? *Social Studies of Science* 29 (3): 411–431.

Johnson, M. 2007. Unscrambling the "average user" of Habbo Hotel. *Human Technology* 3 (2): 127–153.

———. 2010. User involvement, social media, and service evolution: The case of Habbo. Paper presented at Hawaii International Conference for Systems Sciences 43, January 5–8, Koloa, Kauai, Hawaii.

Jolivet, E., P. Laredo, and E. Shove. 2003. Managing breakthrough innovations: theoretical implications from—and for—the sociology of science and technology. Paper presented at 2003 ASEAT Conference "Knowledge and Economic & Social Change: New Challenges to Innovation Studies," April 7–9, Manchester, UK.

Jolivet, E., R. M. Mourik, R. P. Raven, C. Feenstra, A. Alcantud Torrent, E. Heiskanen, M. Hodson, B. Brohmann, A. Oniszk-Poplawska, M. Difiori, U. Fritsche, J. Fucsko, K. Huenecke, B. M. Poti, G. Prasad, B. Schaeffer, and M. Maack. 2008. *General Manual for the Application of the ESTEEM Tool: Create Acceptance*. http://www.esteem-tool.eu/fileadmin/esteem-tool/docs/ESTEEMmanual.pdf (accessed 13 October 2009).

Jordan, B., and A. Henderson. 1994. *Interaction Analysis: Foundations and Practice*. Palo Alto, CA: Xerox Palo Alto Research Center and Institute for Research on Learning.

Kaakinen, J., and S. Törmä. 1999. *Esiselvitys gerontologiasta—Ikääntyvä väestö ja teknologian mahdollisuudet (Prestudy on Gerontechnology—The Aging*

Population and the Possibilities of Technology). Helsinki: Secreteriat of Parlament Finland.

Kalela, J. 2000. *Historiantutkimus ja historia (Historiography and History)*. Helsinki: Gaudeamus.

Kangasoja, J. 2002. Complex design problems—An impetus for learning and knotworking. In *Keeping Learning Complex: The Proceedings of the Fifth International Conference on the Learning Sciences (ICLS)*, edited by P. Bell, R. Stevens, and T. Satwicz. Mahwah, NJ: Erlbaum.

Kaptelinin, V. 2005. The object of activity: Making sense of the sense-maker. *Mind, Culture, and Activity* 12 (1): 4–18.

Karasti, H. 2001. *Increasing Sensitivity towards User Practice in Systems Design*. Academic dissertation. Oulu: University of Oulu, Department of informatics.

Kelley, T., and J. Littman. 2001. *The Art of Innovation—Lessons in Creativity from IDEO, America's Leading Design Firm*. New York: Doubleday, Random House.

Kemp, R., J. Schot, and R. Hoogma. 1998. Regime shifts to sustainability through processes of niche formation: The approach of strategic niche management. *Technology Analysis & Strategic Management* 10:175–195.

Kensing, F., and J. Blomberg. 1998. Participatory design: Issues and concerns. *CSCW: The Journal of Collaborative Computing* 7 (3–4): 167–185.

Kim, W. C., and R. Mauborgne. 2005. *Blue Ocean Strategy: How to Create Uncontested Market Space and Make Competition Irrelevant*. Boston: Harvard Business School Press.

Kivisaari, S., S. Kortelainen, and N. Saranummi. 1998. *Terveydenhuollon tekniikan innovaatiot: tuotekonseptista markkinoille (Health Technology Innovations: From Concept to Markets)*. Helsinki: TEKES, the Finnish Technological Development Centre.

Klein, H. K., and D. L. Kleinman. 2002. The social construction of technology: Structural considerations. *Science, Technology & Human Values* 27 (1): 28–52.

Klerk, M. d., and R. Hijsman. 1994. Actual and potential use of home care technology for the elderly. In *Safety-Alarm Systems, Technical Aids and Smart Homes*, edited by C. Wild and A. Kirschner. Knegsel: Akontes Publishing.

Kline, R., and T. Pinch. 1996. Users as agents of technological change: The social construction of the automobile in the rural United States. *Technology and Culture* 37:763–795.

Kline, S. J., and N. Rosenberg. 1986. An overview of innovation. In *The Positive Sum Strategy: Harnessing Technology for Economic Growth*, edited by R. Landau and N. Rosenberg. Washington, DC: National Academy Press.

Kokko, J., and J. Ekberg. 1993. *Turvapuhelinjärjestelmien leviäminen Suomessa (The Proliferation of Safety-Phone Systems in Finland)*. Helsinki: STAKES, the Finnish Center for Research and Development of Welfare and Health.

Konrad, K. 2006. The social dynamics of expectations: The interaction of collective and actor-specific expectations on electronic commerce and interactive television. *Technology Analysis & Strategic Management* 18 (3–4): 429–444.

———. 2008. Dynamics of type-based scenarios of use: Opening processes in early phases of interactive television and electronic marketplaces. *Science Studies* 21 (2): 3–26.

Kontinen, T. 2007. *Learning Challenges of NGOs in Development: Co-Operation of Finnish NGOs in Morogoro, Tanzania*. Helsinki: University of Helsinki.

Kopytoff, I. 1986. The cultural biography of things: Commoditization as process. In *The Social Life of Things: Commodities in Cultural Perspective*, edited by A. Appadurai. Cambridge: Cambridge University Press.

Kotler, P. 1988. *Marketing Management*. Englewood Cliffs, NJ: Prentice Hall.

Kotler, P., and G. Armstrong. 2004. *Principles of Marketing*. 10th ed. Upper Saddle River, NJ: Prentice Hall.

Kotonya, G., and I. Sommerville. 1998. *Requirements Engineering. Processes and Techniques*. Chichester: John Wiley and Sons.

Kotro, T. 2005. *Hobbyist Knowing in Product Development—Desirable Objects and Passion for Sports in Suunto Corporation*. Academic dissertation. Helsinki: National Consumer Research Center and University of Art and Design Helsinki.

Kuhn, T. 1970. *The Structure of Scientific Revolutions*. 2nd ed. Chicago: University of Chicago Press.

Kuitunen, S., and K. Haila. 2007. *Terveys-, elinkeino-, ja innovaatiopolitiikan rajapinnoilla: FinnWellin ja Tekesin asemoitumisen arviointi* (Between health, business and innovation policies: evaluation of FinnWell's and Tekes's position). Helsinki: TEKES, the Finnish Technological Development Centre.

Kuniavsky, M. 2003. *Observing the User Experience. A Practitioner's Guide to User Research*. San Francisco: Morgan Kaufman Publishers.

Kusch, M. 1991. *Foucault's Strata and Fields: An Investigation into Archaeological and Genealogical Science Studies*. Dordrecht: Kluwer.

Laredo, P. et al. 2002. Final report of the Socrobust project: Management tools and a management framework for assessing the potential long term science and technology options to become embedded in society. Project in the EU TSER program, project no. SOE 1981126, Paris, CSI-Armines.

Latour, B. 1983. Give me a laboratory and I will raise the world. In *Science Observed*, edited by K. Knorr-Cetina and M. Mulkay. London: Sage.

———. 1987. *Science in Action: How to Follow Scientists and Engineers through Society*. Cambridge, MA: Harvard University Press.

———. 1988. How to write "The Prince" for machines as well as machinations. In *Technology and Social Process*, edited by B. Elliott. Edinburgh: Edinburgh University Press.

———. 1991. Technology is society made durable. In *A Sociology of Monsters: Essays on Power, Technology, and Domination*, edited by J. Law. London: Routledge.

———. 1993. *We Have Never Been Modern*. Cambridge, MA: Harvard University Press.

———. 1996. *Aramis, or, The Love of Technology*. Cambridge, MA: Harvard University Press.

———. 1999. *Pandora's Hope: Essays on the Reality of Science Studies*. Cambridge, MA: Harvard University Press.

———. 2005. *Reassembling the Social*. Oxford: Oxford University Press.

Latour, B., and S. Woolgar. 1979. *Laboratory Life: The Social Construction of Scientific Facts*. Beverly Hills: Sage Publications.

Lave, J. 1988. *Cognition in Practice: Mind, Mathematics and Culture in Everyday Life*. Cambridge: Cambridge University Press.

———. 1993. The practice of learning. In *Understanding Practice. Perspectives on Activity and Context*, edited by S. Chaiklin and J. Lave. Cambridge: Cambridge University Press.

Law, J. 1988. The anatomy of a socio-technical struggle: The design of the TSR 2. In *Technology and Social Process*, edited by B. Elliot. Edinburgh: Edinburgh University Press.

———. 1991. *A Sociology of Monsters: Essays on Power, Technology, and Domination*. London: Routledge.

———. 2004. *After Method: Mess in Social Science Research*. London: Routledge.

Law, J., and W. E. Bijker, eds. 1992. *Shaping Technology/Building Society: Studies in Sociotechnical Change*. Cambridge, MA: MIT Press.

Law, J., and M. Callon. 1992. Life and death of an aircraft: A network analysis of technical change. In *Shaping Technology/Building Society: Studies in Sociotechnical Change*, edited by J. Law and W. E. Bijker. Cambridge, MA: MIT Press.

Law, J., and J. Hassard, eds. 1999. *Actor Network Theory and After*. Oxford: Blackwell.

Law, J., and V. Singleton. 2005. Object lessons. *Organization* 12 (3): 331–355.

Le Goff, J. 1988. *The Medieval Imagination*. Translated by A. Goldhammer. Chicago: University of Chicago Press.

Lehenkari, J. 2000. Studying innovation trajectories and networks: The case of benecol margarine. *Science Studies* 13 (1): 50–67.

———. 2006. *The Networks of Learning in Technological Innovation: The Emergence of Collaboration across Fields of Expertise*. Academic dissertation. Helsinki: University of Helsinki, Department of Education.

Lehoux, P. 2006. *The Problem of Health Technology—Policy Implications for Modern Health Care Systems*. London: Routledge.

Leifer, R., C. M. McDermott, G. Colarelli O'Connor, L. S. Peters, M. Rice, and R. W. Veryzer. 2000. *Radical Innovation. How Mature Companies Can Outsmart Upstarts*. Boston: Harvard Business School Press.

Lente, H. v. 2000. Forceful futures: From performativity to prehension. In *Contested Futures: A Sociology of Prospective Techno-Science*, edited by N. Brown, B. Rappert, and A. Webster. Aldershot, UK: Ashgate.

Lente, H. v., and A. Rip. 1998. Expectations in technological developments: An example of prospective structures to be filled in by agency. In *Getting New Technologies Together: Studies in Making Sociotechnical Order*, edited by C. Disco and B. v. d. Meulen. Berlin: Walter de Gruyter.

Leonard, D. 1995. *Wellsprings of Knowledge: Building and Sustaining the Sources of Innovation*. Boston: Harvard Business School Press.

Leonard-Barton, D. 1988. Implementation as mutual adaptation of technology and organization. *Research Policy* 17:251–267.

Leontjev, A. N. 1978. *Activity, Consciousness, and Personality*. Moscow: Progress.

Leriche, D., P. Johnsson, L. Caffu, and N. Fink. 1995. Wristcare in Europe. A study of the market for Wristcare an IST product in Sweden, Germany, France and the United Kingdom. In *Marketing, International business, Business strategy, Mat 91.144, 1995*, edited by I. K. M. Kaila, T. Ulftedt, M. Suomi. Espoo, Finland: Helsinki University of Technology.

Lettl, C., C. Herstatt, and H. Gemunden. 2006. Users' contributions to radical innovation: Evidence from four cases in the field of medical equipment technology. *R&D Management* 36 (3): 251–272.

Levi, G. 1988. *Inheriting Power. The Story of an Exorcist*. Chicago: University of Chicago Press.

Lie, M., and K. Sorensen, eds. 1996. *Making Technology Our Own? Domesticating Technology into Everyday Life*. Oslo: Scandinavian University Press.

Lovio, R., P. Mickwitz, and E. Heiskanen. Forthcoming. Path dependence, path creation and creative destruction in the evolution of energy systems. In *Handbook of Research on Energy Entrepreneurship*, edited by R. Wustenhagen and R. Wuebker. Northampton, UK: Edward Elgar.

Löwgren, J., and E. Stolterman. 2004. *Thoughtful Interaction Design. A Design Perspective on Information Technology*. Cambridge, MA: MIT Press.

Luethje, C., and C. Herstatt. 2004. The lead user method: An outline of empirical findings and issues for future research. *R&D Management* 34 (5): 553–568.

Lundvall, B.-Å. 1985. *Product Innovation and User-Producer Interaction, Industrial Development Research Series no 31*. Aalborg: Aalborg University Press.

————. 1988. Innovation as an interactive process: From user-producer interaction to the national system of innovation. In *Technical Change and Economic Theory*, edited by G. Dosi, C. Freeman, R. R. Nelson, G. Silverberg, and L. Soete. London: Printer Publishers.

————, ed. 1992. *National Systems of Innovation. Towards a Theory of Innovation and Interactive Learning*. London: Printer Publishers.

Lundvall, B.-Å., and B. Johnson. 1994. The learning economy. *Journal of Industry Studies* 1 (2): 23–42.

Lundvall, B.-Å., and A. L. Vinding. 2005. Product innovation and economic theory—user–producer interaction in the learning economy. In *Product Innovation, Interactive Learning and Economic Performance*, edited by J. L. Christensen. Amsterdam: Elsevier Science.

Luthje, C., and C. Herstatt. 2004. The lead user method: An outline of empirical findings and issues for future research. *R&D Management* 34 (5): 553–568.

Luthje, C., C. Herstatt, and E. von Hippel. 2005. User innovators and "local" information: The case of mountain biking. *Research Policy* 34 (6): 951–965.

Lynch, M. 1985. *Art and Artifact in Laboratory Science a Study of Shop Work and Shop Talk in a Research Laboratory*. London: Routledge and Kegan Paul.

Mackay, H., C. Carne, P. Beynon-Davies, and D. Tudhope. 2000. Reconfiguring the user: Using rapid application development. *Social Studies of Science* 30 (5): 737–757.

Mackay, H., and G. Gillespie. 1992. Extending the social shaping of technology approach: Ideology and appropriation. *Social Studies of Science* 22 (4): 685–716.

MacKenzie, D., and J. Wajcman, eds. 1998. *The Social Shaping of Technology*. 2nd ed. Buckingham: Open University Press.

Mäkeläinen, B., M. Nurminen, P. Reijonen, and V. Torvinen. 1996. Everyday use between success and failure: Making sense with ONION layers. Paper presented at 19th Information Systems Research Seminar in Scandinavia (IRIS) August 10–13, 1996.

Mäkitalo, J. 2000. *A Historical Analysis of the Development of the Institutional Care for the Elderly in Finland*. Unpublished manuscript. Helsinki: University of Helsinki.

Malhotra, N., and D. Birks. 2003. *Marketing Research: An Applied Approach, Second European Edition*. Harlow: Pearson Education.

Mallard, A. 2005. Following the emergence of unpredictable uses? New stakes and tasks for the social sciences understanding of ICT uses. In *Everyday innovators: researching the role of users in shaping ICT's*, edited by L. Haddon, E. Mante, B. Sapio, K. H. Kommonen, L. Fortunati, and A. Kant. Dordrecht: Springer.

Marcus, G., ed. 1995. *Technoscientific Imaginaries*. Chicago: University of Chicago Press.

Mattelmäki, T., and K. Battarbee. 2002. Empathy probes. In *PDC 2002 Participatory Design Conference 23–25.6.2002*, edited by T. Binder, J. Gregory and I. Wagner. Malmö, Sweden: Computer Professionals for Social Responsibility.

McDermott, C. M., and G. Colarelli O'Connor. 2002. Managing radical innovation: An overview of emergent strategy issues. *Journal of Product Innovation Management* 19:424–438.

McDermott, R. P. 1993. The acquisition of a child by a learning disability. In *Understanding Practice. Perspectives on Activity and Context*, edited by S. Chaiklin and J. Lave. Cambridge: Cambridge University Press.

McEvily, B., and A. Zaheer. 1999. Bridging ties: A source of firm heterogeneity in competitive capabilities. *Strategic Management Journal* 20:1133–1156.

McLaughlin, J., P. Rosen, D. Skinner, and A. Webster. 1999. *Valuing Technology: Organisations, Culture, and Change*. London: Routledge.

McLaughlin, J., and D. Skinner. 2000. Developing usability and utility: A comparative study of the use of new IT. *Technology Analysis & Strategic Management* 12:413–423.

Melander, H., and F. Sahlström. 2009. In the tow of the blue whale: Learning as interactional changes in topical orientation. *Pragmatics* 41 (8): 1519–1537.

Miettinen, R. 1993. Methodological issues of studying innovation related networks. *Working Papers of VTT Group for Technology Studies* 4.

———. 1998. Object construction and networks in research work: The case of research on cellulose-degrading enzymes. *Social Studies of Science* 28 (3): 423–463.

———. 1999. The riddle of things: Activity theory and actor-network theory as approaches to studying innovations. *Mind, Culture, and Activity* 6 (3): 170–195.

———. 2000. The problem of creativity in technology studies: Invention as artifact construction and culturally distributed work. In *Working Papers 23/2000 of Center for Activity Theory and Developmental Work Research, University of Helsinki*. Helsinki: University of Helsinki.

———. 2002a. Artifact mediation in Dewey and in cultural-historical activity theory. *Mind, Culture and Activity* 8 (4): 297–308.

———. 2002b. *National Innovation System: Scientific Concept or Political Rhetoric*. Helsinki: Edita.

———. Forthcoming. *Rhetoric and Practice in Innovation Policy: Lessons from Finland*.

Miettinen, R., S. Freeman, J. Lehenkari, J. Leminen, J. Siltala, K. Toikka, and J. Tuunainen. 2008. *Informaatiotekninen kumous, innovaatioverkostot ja luottamus (Information Revolution, Innovation Networks and Trust)*. Helsinki: TEKES, the Finnish Technological Development Centre.

Miettinen, R., and M. Hasu. 2002. Articulating user-needs in collaborative design. Towards activity-theoretical approach. *Computer Supported Collaborative Work* 11:129–151.

Miettinen, R., S. Hyysalo, J. Lehenkari, and M. Hasu. 2003. *Tuotteesta työvälineeksi? Uudet teknologiat terveydenhuollossa (From Product to a Tool? New Technologies in Health Care)*. Helsinki: STAKES, the Finnish Center for Research and Development of Welfare and Health.

Miettinen, R., J. Lehenkari, M. Hasu, and J. Hyvönen. 1999. *Osaaminen ja uuden luominen innovaatioverkoissa. Tutkimus kuudesta suomalaisesta innovaatiosta (Know-How and the Creation of New Innovation Networks. A Study of Six Finnish Innovations)*. Vantaa: Sitra, the Finnish Innovation Fund and Taloustieto Oy.

Miettinen, R., D. Samra-Fredericks, and D. Yanow. 2009. Re-turn to practice: An introductory essay. *Organisation Studies* 30 (12): 1309–1327.

Miller, D., and D. Slater. 2007. Moments and movements in the study of consumer culture: A discussion between Daniel Miller and Don Slater. *Journal of Consumer Culture* 7 (5): 5–23.

Mol, A. 2002. *The Body Multiple: Ontology in Medical Practice*. Durham, NC: Duke University Press.

Molina, A. 1995. Sociotechnical constituencies as processes of alignment: The rise of a large-scale European information technology initiative. *Technology in Society* 17 (4): 385–412.

Mollenkopf, H. 1994. Technical aids in old age—Between acceptance and rejection. In *Safety-Alarm Systems, Technical Aids and Smart Homes*, edited by C. Wild and A. Kirschner. Knegsel: Akontes Publishing.

Moore, G. A. 2002. *Crossing the Chasm—Marketing and Selling High-Tech Products to Mainstream Customers*. 2nd revised ed. New York: HarperCollins.

Morrison, P. D., J. H. Roberts, and E. von Hippel. 2000. Determinants of user innovation and innovation sharing in a local market. *Management Science* 46 (12): 1513–1527.

Nardi, B. A. 1996a. *Context and Consciousness: Activity Theory and Human–Computer Interaction.* Cambridge, MA: MIT Press.

———. 1996b. Studying context: A comparison of activity theory, situated action models, and distributed cognition. In *Context and Consciousness. Activity Theory and Human–Computer Interaction*, edited by B. A. Nardi. Cambridge: MIT Press.

Narducco, A., E. Rocco, and M. Warglien. 2000. Talking about routines in the field: The emergence of organizational capabilities in a new cellular phone network company. In *The Nature and Dynamics of Organizational Capabilities*, edited by G. Dosi, R. Nelson, and S. Winter. Oxford: Oxford University Press.

Nelson, R., and S. Winter. 1982. *An Evolutionary Theory of Economic Change.* Cambridge, MA: Harvard University Press.

Nicoll, D. W. 2000. Users as currency: Technology and marketing trials as naturalistic environments. *The Information Society* 16 (4): 303–310.

Nielsen, J. 1993. *Usability Engineering.* Boston: Morgan Kaufman.

Noble, D. F. 1984. *Forces of Production: A Social History of Machine Tool Automation.* New York: A. A. Knopf.

Norman, D. 1988. *Psychology of Everyday Things.* New York: Basic Books.

———. 1999. *The Invisible Computer: Why Good Products Can Fail, the Personal Computer is So Complex and Information Appliances are the Solution.* Cambridge, MA: MIT Press.

Norman, D., and S. Draper. 1986. *User Centered System Design: New Perspectives on Human–Computer Interaction.* Hillsdale, NJ: Lawrence Erlbaum.

Normann, R., and R. Ramirez. 1994. *Designing Interactive Strategy: From Value Chain to Value Constellation.* Chichester: John Wiley and Sons.

Nurminen, M. I., P. Reijonen, and A. Tuomisto. 1994. Whose work is software? In *Human Factors in Organizational Design and Management IV*, edited by G. E. Bradley and H. W. Hendrick. Amsterdam: Elsevier Science B. V.

Okamura, K., M. Fujimoto, W. Orlikowski, and J. Yates. 1994. Helping CSCW applications succeed: The role of mediators in the context of use. In *Proceedings of Computer Supported Collaborative Work Conference.* New York: ACM Press, NC.

Orlikowski, W. 2000. Using technology and constituting structures: A practice lens for studying technology in organisations. *Organisation Science* 11 (4): 404–428.

Orr, J. E. 1996. *Talking about Machines: An Ethnography of a Modern Job.* Ithaca, NY: IRL Press and Cornell University Press.

Östlund, B. 1994. Experiences with safety-alarms for the elderly in Sweden. In *Safety-Alarm Systems, Technical Aids and Smart Homes*, edited by C. Wild and A. Kirschner. Knegsel: Akontes Publishing.

———. 1995. *Gammal är älst. En studie om teknik i äldre människors liv (The Elderly Are the Oldest. A Study of Technology in the Lives of Elderly People).* Academic dissertation. Lindköping: University of Lindköping.

Oudshoorn, N. 2003. *The Male Pill: A Biography of a Technology in the Making.* Durham: Duke University Press.

Oudshoorn, N., E. Rommes, and M. Stienstra. 2004. Configuring the user as everybody: Gender and design in information and communication technologies. *Science, Technology & Human Values* 29 (1): 30–63.

Pantzar, M. 1996. *Kuinka teknologia kesytetään—kulutuksen tieteestä kulutuksen taiteeseen (How Is Technology Domesticated—From Consumption Science to the Art of Consumption).* Helsinki: Otava.

————. 2000. *Tulevaisuuden koti. Arjen tarpeita keksimässä (Future Home. Inventing the Needs of Everyday Living)*. Helsinki: Otava.

Pantzar, M., and E. Shove, eds. 2005. *Manufacturing Leisure. Innovations in Happiness, Well-Being and Fun*. Helsinki: National Consumer Research Centre.

Papanek, V. 1972. *Design for the Real World*. London: Thames and Hudson.

Pavitt, K. 1984. Sectoral patterns of technical change: Towards a taxonomy and a theory. *Research Policy* 13:343–373.

Perez, C. 2003. *Technological Revolutions and Financial Capital: The Dynamics of Bubbles and Golden Ages*. Cheltenham, UK: Edward Elgar.

Philipsson, C. 1988. Kriittisen gerontologian kehitys: brittiläinen näkökulma (Development of critical gerontology, a British perspective). *Gerontologia* 2 (3): 198–210.

Pihlainen, K. 1999. *Resisting History. On the Ethics of Narrative Representation*. Academic dissertation. Turku: University of Turku, Department of History.

Pinch, T. J., and W. E. Bijker. 1987. The social construction of facts and artifacts: Or how the sociology of science and the sociology of technology might benefit each other. In *The Social Construction of Technological Systems: New Directions in the Sociology and History of Technology*, edited by W. E. Bijker, T. P. Hughes, and T. J. Pinch. Cambridge, Ma: MIT Press.

Pinch, T., and N. Oudshoorn, eds. 2003a. *How Users Matter. The Co-Construction of Users and Technologies*. Cambridge: MIT Press.

————. 2003b. Introduction. In *How Users Matter. The Co-Construction of Users and Technologies*, edited by T. Pinch and N. Oudshoorn. Cambridge: MIT Press.

Pohl, K. 1994. Three dimensions of requirements engineering: Framework and its application. *Information systems* 19 (3): 243–258.

Pollock, N., and R. Williams. 2008. *Software and Organisations: The Biography of the Packaged Enterprise-Wide System, or, How SAP Conquered the World*. London: Routledge.

Pollock, N., R. Williams, and L. D'Adderio. 2007. Global software and its provenance: Generification work in the production of organizational software packages. *Social Studies of Science* 37:254–280.

Pollock, N., R. Williams, and R. Procter. 2003. Fitting standard software packages to non-standard organizations: The "biography" of an enterprise-wide system. *Technology Analysis & Strategic Management* 15 (3): 317–331.

Poti, B. M., R. M. Mourik, R. P. Raven, E. Jolivet, A. Alcantud Torrent, D. Bauknecht, B. Brothmann, M. Difiore, C. Feenstra, U. Fritsche, E. Heiskanen, M. Hodson, M. Maack, A. Oniszk-Poplawska, and B. Schaefer. 2006a. *An Overview of Gaps in the Socrobust Tool and Proposals on How to Integrate this Missing Information*. http://www.createacceptance.net/fileadmin/create-acceptance/user/docs/E07050.pdf (accessed 13 October 2010).

Poti, B. M., R. P. Raven, A. Alcantud Torrent, B. Brothmann, C. Feenstra, U. Fritsche, J. Fucsko, E. Heiskanen, M. Hodson, M. Maack, A. Oniszk-Poplawska, and B. Schaefer. 2006b. *Manual on the Socrobust Tool and Recent Experiences with Using Socrobust*. http://www.createacceptance.net/fileadmin/create-acceptance/user/docs/E07049.pdf (accessed 13 October 2010).

Prahalad, C. K., and V. Ramaswamy. 2004. *The Future of Competition: Co-Creating Unique Value with Customers*. Boston: Harvard Business School Press.

Preece, J., Y. Rogers, and H. Sharp. 2002. *Interaction Design—Beyond Human–Computer Interaction*. Hoboken, NJ: John Wiley and Sons.

Procter, R. N., and R. Williams. 1996. Beyond design: Social learning and computer-supported collaborative work: Some lessons from innovation studies. In *The Design of Computer-Supported Cooperative Work and Groupware Systems*, edited by D. Shapiro, M. Tauber, and R. Traunmueller. Amsterdam: North Holland.

Proctor, T. 2000. *Essentials of Marketing Research.* 2nd ed. Harlow: Prentice Hall.

Ratto, M. 2003. *The Pressure of Openness: The Hybrid Work of Linux Free/Open Source Kernel Developers.* Academic dissertation. San Diego: University of California San Diego, Department of Communication.

Renvall, P. 1983. *Nykyajan historiantutkimus (Modern Historiography).* Porvoo: WSOY.

Rip, A., and A. Groen, J. 2001. Many visible hands. In *Technology and the Market: Demand, Users and Innovation,* edited by R. Coombs, K. Green, A. Richards, and V. Walsh. Northampton (MA): Edward Elgar Publishing.

Rip, A., T. J. Misa, and J. Schot. 1995. *Managing Technology in Society. The Approach of Constructive Technology Assessment.* London: Cassel Publishers.

Robinson, D. K. R., and T. Propp. 2008. Multi-path mapping for alignment strategies in emerging science and technologies. *Technological Forecasting and Social Change* 75 (4): 517–538.

Roe, P. R. W., ed. 2001. *Bridging the Gap? Access to Telecommunications for All People.* Lausanne: Commission of European Communities.

Rogers, E. M. 1995. *Diffusion of Innovations.* 4th expanded ed. New York: Free Press.

Rohracher, H., ed. 2005. *User Involvement in Innovation Processes. Strategies and Limitations from a Socio-Technical Perspective.* Munich: Profil-Verlag.

Rosenberg, N. 1979. *Perspectives on Technology.* Cambridge: Cambridge University Press.

———. 1982. *Inside the Black Box: Technology and Economics.* Cambridge: Cambridge University Press.

Rosenfeld, L. 1999. *Four Centuries of Clinical Chemistry.* London and New York: Taylor and Francis.

Rothwell, R., C. Freeman, A. Horlsey, V. Jervis, A. B. Robertson, and J. Townsend. 1974. SAPPHO updated—Project SAPPHO phase 2. *Research Policy* 3:258–291.

Rothwell, R., and W. Zegweld. 1985. *Reindustrialization and Technology.* Armonk, NY: M. E. Sharpe.

Rush, H., and J. Bessant. 1992. Revolution in three-quarter time: Lessons from the diffusion of advanced manufacturing technologies. *Technology Analysis & Strategic Management* 4 (1): 3–19.

Russell, S. 2006. Representations of use and need in R&D: The field of conducting and "intelligent" polymers. In *Run Working Paper 3.* Wollongong: Wollongong University.

Russell, S., and R. Williams. 2002. Concepts, spaces and tools for action? Exploring the policy potential of the social shaping perspective. In *Shaping Technology, Guiding Policy: Concepts, Spaces and Tools,* edited by K. Sorensen and R. Williams. Cheltenham, UK: Edward Elgar.

Saari, E. 2003. *The Pulse of Change in Research Work.* Academic dissertation. Helsinki: University of Helsinki, Department of Education.

Saariluoma, P. 2004. *Käyttäjäpsykologia (User Psychology).* Helsinki: WSOY.

Säde, S. 2001. *Cardboard Mock-Ups and Conversations Studies on User-Centered Product Design.* Helsinki: University of Art and Design Helsinki.

SAI. 1993. *An Overview of the Business Opportunities for Wristcare in France, Germany, and United Kingdom, Draft for Discussion 21.9.1993.* Helsinki: Strategy Analysis International.

Schatzki, T. R., K. Knorr-Cetina, and E. v. Savigny, eds. 2001. *Practice Turn in Contemporary Theory*. London: Routledge.

Schegloff, E. A. 2007. *Sequence Organization in Interaction*. Cambridge: Cambridge University Press.

Schon, D. 1983. *The Reflective Practitioner: How Professionals Think in Action*. New York: Basic Books.

Schrage, M. 2000. *Serious Play—How the World's Best Companies Simulate to Innovate*. Boston: Harvard Business School Press.

Schuler, D., and A. Namioka, eds. 1993. *Participatory Design: Principles and Practices*. Hillsdale, NJ: Lawrence Erlbaum Associates.

Sherry, J. F. J. 1990. A sociocultural analysis of a Midwestern American flea market. *Journal of Consumer Research* 17:13–30.

Shibutani, T. 1955. Reference groups as perspectives. *American Journal of Sociology* 60 (6): 562–569.

———. 1962. Reference groups and social control. In *Human Behavior and Social Processes*, edited by A. Rose. Boston: Houghton Mifflin.

Silverman, D. 1993. *Interpreting Qualitative Data. Methods for Analyzing Talk, Text and Interaction*. London: Sage.

Silverstone, R., E. Hirsch, and D. Morley. 1992. Information and communication technologies and the moral economy of the household. In *Consuming Technologies: Media and Information in Domestic Spaces*, edited by R. Silverstone and E. Hirsch. London: Routledge.

Sjögren, E., and C.-F. Helgesson. 2007. The Q(u)ALYfying hand: Health economies and medicine in the shaping of Swedish markets for subsidised pharmaceuticals. in *Market Devices*, edited by M. Callon, Millo, and Muniesa. Oxford: Blackwell.

Simon, H. A. 1996. *The sciences of the artificial*. Cambridge, Mass. : MIT Press.

Smith, A., A. Stirling, and F. Berkhout. 2005. The governance of sustainable sociotechnical transitions. *Research Policy* 34 (10): 1491–1510.

Soosalu, M. 1996. *Turvaranneke (Safety Bracelet) Thesis, Department of Industrial Design*. Helsinki: University of Art and Design Helsinki.

Sorensen, K. H. 1996. Learning technology, constructing culture. Sociotechnical change as social learning. *STS Working Paper, University of Trondheim, Centre for Technology and Society* 18. http://www.rcss.ed.ac.uk/SLIM/public/phase1/knut.html (accessed 13 October 2009).

———. 2002. Social shaping on the move? On the policy relevance of the social shaping of technology perspective. In *Shaping Technology, Guiding Policy: Concepts, Spaces and Tools*, edited by K. Sorensen and R. Williams. Cheltenham, UK: Edward Elgar.

Sorensen, K., and R. Williams, eds. 2002. *Shaping Technology, Guiding Policy: Concepts, Spaces and Tools*. Cheltenham, UK: Edward Elgar.

Standish Group. 1995. *The Chaos Report*. http://www.projectsmart.co.uk/docs/chaos-report.pdf (accessed 13 October 2009).

Stankiewicz, R. 1995. The role of the science and technology infrastructure in the development and diffusion of industrial automation in Sweden. In *Technological Systems and Economic Performance: The Case of Factory Automation*, edited by B. Carlsson. Dordrecht: Kluwer.

Star, S. L. 1989a. *Regions of the Mind: Brain Research and the Quest for Scientific Certainty*. Stanford, CA: Stanford University Press.

———. 1989b. The structure of ill-structured solutions: Boundary objects and heterogeneous distributed problem solving. In *Distributed Artificial Intelligence*, edited by M. N. Huhns and Gasser. Menlo Park, CA: Morgan Kaufman.

———. 1991. Power, technology and the phenomenology of conventions: On being allergic to onions. In *A Sociology of Monsters: Essays on Power, Technology and Domination*, edited by J. Law. London: Routledge.

————. 1996. Working together: Symbolic interactionism, activity theory, and information systems. In *Cognition and Communication at Work*, edited by Y. Engeström and D. Middelton. Cambridge: Cambridge University Press.

Star, S. L., and J. Griesemer. 1989. Institutional ecology, "translations" and boundary objects: Amateurs and professionals in Berkeley's Museum of Vertebrate Zoology, 1907–1939. *Social Studies of Science* 19:387–420.

Starr, P. 1982. *The Social Transformation of American Medicine. The Rise of a Sovereign Profession and the Making of a Vast Industry*. New York: Basic Books.

Stewart, J. 2007. Local experts in the domestication of information and communication technologies. *Information, Communication and Society* 10:547–569.

Stewart, J., and S. Hyysalo. 2008. Intermediaries, users and social learning in technological innovation. *International Journal of Innovation Management* 12 (3): 295–325.

Stewart, J., and R. Williams. 2005. The wrong trousers? Beyond the design fallacy: Social learning and the user. In *User Involvement in Innovation Processes. Strategies and Limitations from a Socio-Technical Perspective*, edited by H. Rohracher. Munich: Profil-Verlag.

Stoetzler, M., and N. Yuval-Davis. 2002. Standpoint theory, situated knowledge and situated imagination. *Feminist Theory* 3 (3): 315–333.

Strathern, M. 1992. Foreword: The mirror of technology. In *Consuming Technologies. Media and Information in Domestic Spaces*. Eds. R. Silverstone and E. Hirch. London: Routledge.

Strauss, A. 1978. A social world perspective. In *Studies in Social Interaction 1*, edited by N. Denzin. Greenwich: JAI Press.

————. 1991. *Creating Sociological Awareness. Collective Images and Symbolic Representations*. New Brunswick: Transaction Publishers.

————. 1993. *Continual Permutations of Action*. New York: Aldine de Gruyter.

Strauss, A., and J. Corbin. 1990. *Basics of Qualitative Research*. London: Sage.

Suchman, L. 1987. *Plans and Situated Actions: The Problem of Human-Machine Communication*. Cambridge, England: Cambridge University Press.

————. 2002. Located accountabilities in technology production. *Scandinavian Journal of Information Systems* 14 (2): 91–105.

Suchman, L., and L. Bishop. 2000. Problematizing "innovation" as a critical project. *Technology Analysis & Strategic Management* 12 (3): 327–333.

Suchman, L., J. Blomberg, J. E. Orr, and R. Trigg. 1999. Reconstructing technologies as social practice. *American Behavioral Scientist* 43 (3): 392–408.

Suominen, J. 2003. *Koneen kokemus. Tietoteknistyvä kulttuuri modernisoituvassa Suomessa 1920-luvulta 1970-luvulle (The Machine Experience. The Increasingly Computerized Culture in the Modernizing Finland from 1920s to 1970s)*. Academic dissertation. Tampere: Vastapaino.

Tierney, M., and R. Williams. 1990. Issues in the black-boxing of technologies: What happens when the black box meets 40 shades of grey? In *Edinburgh PICT Working Paper*, no. 22, Edinburgh University.

Timmermans, S. 1999. *Sudden Death and the Myth of CPR*. Philadelphia: Temple University Press.

Toikka, K. 1984. *Kehittävä kvalifikaatiotutkimus (Developmental Qualifications Research)*. Helsinki: Finnish Institute of Public Management.

————. 2003. *Verkosto, markkina, hierarkia (Network, Market, and Hierarchy)*. Unpublished manuscript. Helsinki: University of Helsinki, Center for Activity Theory and Developmental Work Research.

Toiviainen, H. 2003. *Learning across Levels. Challenges of Collaboration in a Small-Firm Network*. Academic dissertation. Helsinki: University of Helsinki, Department of Education.

Tomasello, M. 1999. *The Cultural Origins of Human Cognition*. Cambridge, MA: Harvard University Press.

304   References

Törmä, S., J. Nieminen, and M. Hietikko. 2001. *Ikääntyneiden itsenäistä suoriutumista tukevan teknologian arviointi käyttäjänäkökulmasta, turvahälytysjärjestelmät* (*The Evaluation of Technology Supporting Independent Living of the Elderly from the User Perspective, Alarm Systems*). Helsinki: Secretariat of Parliament of Finland.

Tornstam, L. 1986. *Åldrandets socialpsykologi* (*The Social Psychology of Older Years*). Kristianstad: Kristianstads Boktryckeri.

———. 1992. Demografinen pommi ja omaisten antaman hoidon uudet vaatimukset—uhka vai myytti (Demographic bomb and the new demands for the care given by relatives—A threat or a myth). *Gerontologia* 6 (1): 53–63.

Törpel, B., A. Voss, M. Hartswood, and R. Procter. 2009. Participatory design: Issues and approaches in dynamic constellations of use, design, and research. In *Configuring User–Designer Relations—Interdisciplinary Perspectives*, edited by A Voss, M. Hartswood, R. Procter, M. Rouncefield, R. S. Slack, and M. Büscher. London: Springer.

Tosh, J. 1991. *The Pursuit of History. Aims, Methods & New Directions in the Study of Modern History.* 2nd ed. London: Longman.

Traweek, S. 1988. *Beamtimes and Lifetimes: The World of High Energy Physicists.* Cambridge, MA: Harvard University Press.

Trigg, R., and S. Bodger. 1994. From implementation to design: Tailoring and the emergence of systematization in CSCW. In *Proceedings of Computer Supported Collaborative Work Conference.* New York: ACM Press.

Tushman, M. L., and P. Anderson. 1986. Technological discontinuities and organizational environments. *Administrative Science Quarterly* 31:439–465.

Tyre, M., and E. von Hippel. 1997. The situated nature of adaptive learning in organizations. *Organization Science* 8 (1): 71–83.

Ulrich, K. T., and S. D. Eppinger. 1995. *Product design and development.* New York: McGraw-Hill.

Vaarama, M. 1995. *Vanhusten hoivapalvelun tuloksellisuus hyvinvoinnin tuotantonäkökulmasta.* Vol. 55, *Stakes tutkimuksia* (*The Affectivity of the Services for the Elderly from the Point of View of Production of Well-Being*). Helsinki: STAKES, the Finnish Center for Research and Development of Welfare and Health.

Valkonen, T., and T. Nikander. 1987. Vanhusväestön demografiset muutokset neljässä pohjoismaassa (Demographical changes in the elderly population in four Nordic countries). *Gerontologia* 2:21–31.

Valsiner, J. 1998. *The Guided Mind: A Sociogenetic Approach to Personality.* Cambridge, MA: Harvard University Press.

Van der Meulen, B., and A. Rip. 1998. Mediation in the Dutch science system. *Research Policy* 27 (8): 757–769.

Van de Ven, A. H., D. E. Polley, R. Garud, and S. Venkataraman. 1999. *The Innovation Journey.* Oxford: Oxford University Press.

Van Lieshout, M., T. M. Egyedi, and W. E. Bijker, eds. 2001. *Social Learning Technologies. The Introduction of Multimedia in Education.* Aldershot, UK: Ashgate Publishing.

Verran, H. 1998. Re-imagining land ownership in Australia. *Post Colonial Studies* 1 (2): 237–254.

———. 2001. *Science and an African Logic.* Chicago: University of Chicago Press.

Veryzer, R. W. 1998. Discontinuous innovation and the new product development process. *Journal of Product Innovation Management* 15 (4): 304–321.

Victor, B., and A. Boynton. 1998. *Invented Here: Maximizing Your Organization's Internal Growth and Profitability. A Practical Guide to Transforming Work.* Boston: Harvard Business School Press.

Von Hippel, E. 1988. *The Sources of Innovation.* New York: Oxford University Press.

———. 1994. "Sticky information" and the locus of problem solving: Implications for innovation. *Management Science* 40 (4): 429–439.

———. 2001. Innovation by user communities: Learning from open-source software. *MIT Sloan Management Review* 42 (4): 82–86.

———. 2005. *Democratizing Innovation*. Cambridge, MA: MIT Press.

Von Hippel, E., and R. Katz. 2002. Shifting innovation to users via toolkits. *Management Science* 48 (7): 821–833.

Von Hippel, E., and M. Tyre. 1995. How "learning by doing" is done: Problem identification in novel process equipment. *Research Policy* 24 (1): 1–12.

Voss, A., M. Hartswood, R. Procter, M. Rouncefield, R. S. Slack, and M. Büscher, eds. 2009a. *Configuring User–Designer Relations—Interdisciplinary Perspectives*. London: Springer.

Voss, A., R. Procter, R. S. Slack, M. Hartswood, R. Procter, and M. Rouncefield. 2009b. Design as and for collaboration: Making sense of and supporting practical action. In *Configuring User–Designer Relations—Interdisciplinary Perspectives*, edited by A. Voss, M. Hartswood, R. Procter, M. Rouncefield, R. S. Slack, and M. Büscher. London: Springer.

Vygotsky, L. 1978. *Mind in Society. The Development of Higher Psychological Processes*. Cambridge, MA: Harvard University Press.

———. 1987. Thinking and speech. In *The Collected Works of L. S. Vygotsky*, edited by R. W. Rieber and A. S. V. Carton. New York: Plenum Press. Original edition, 1934.

———. 1989. *Thought and Language. Newly Revised and Edited by Alex Kozulin*. Cambridge, MA: MIT Press.

Wajcman, J. 1991. *Feminism Confronts Technology*. University Park: Pennsylvania State University Press.

Wallendorf, M., and E. J. Arnould. 1991. "We gather together": Consumption rituals of Thanksgiving Day. *Journal of Consumer Research* 18 (1): 13–31.

Walsham, G. 1992. Management science and organisational change: A framework for analysis. *Omega, International Journal of Management Science* 20 (1): 1–9.

Wang, M. 2007. *Cultivating the "Generic Solution"—The Emergence of a Chinese Product Data Management (PDM) Software Package*. Academic dissertation. Edinburgh: University of Edinburgh, Research Centre for Social Sciences.

Wartofsky, M. F. 1979. *Models. Representation and the Scientific Understanding, Boston Studies in the Philosophy of Science*. Dordrecht: D. Reidel.

White, H. 1973. *Metahistory. The Historical Imagination in 19th Century Europe*. Baltimore, MD: The Johns Hopkins University Press.

Wild, C., and A. Kirschner, eds. 1994. *Safety-Alarm Systems, Technical Aids and Smart Homes. Vol. 8, Ageing in the Contemporary Society*. Knegsel: Akontes Publishing.

Williams, R., and D. Edge. 1996. The social shaping of technology. *Research Policy* 25 (6): 865–899.

Williams, R., R. Slack, and J. Stewart. 2005. *Social Learning in Technological Innovation—Experimenting with Information and Communication Technologies*. Cheltenham, UK: Edgar Elgar.

Winner, L. 1980. Do artifacts have politics? *Deadalus* 109 (1): 121–136.

Woolgar, S. 1991. Configuring the user: the case of usability trials. In *A Sociology of Monsters: Essays on Power, Technology, and Domination*, edited by J. Law. London: Routledge.

Wright, T. P. 1936. Factors affecting the cost of airplanes. *Journal of Aeronautical Science* 3 (February): 122–128.

Yaneva, A. 2008. How buildings "surprise." The renovation of Alte Aula in Vienna. *Science Studies* 21 (1): 8–28.

Zeiss, R., and P. Groenewegen. 2009. Engaging boundary objects in OMS and STS? Exploring the subtleties of layered engagement. *Organization* 16 (1): 81–100.

Zoche, P. 1994. Emergency aid: Private alarm systems in a social and organizational environment. Experiences and perspectives of the German "hausnotruf." In *Safety-Alarm Systems, Technical Aids and Smart Homes*, edited by C. Wild and A. Kirschner. Knegsel: Akontes Publishing.

Notes

NOTES TO THE INTRODUCTION

1. Different set of problems is associated with the plentiful literature and advice for making the right choices and taking the right actions in regard to *specifics* of new technologies. Numerous consumer and professional magazines appear monthly to help us keep in pace with the next health appliances, diets, digital cameras, *et cetera*. Thousands of books have been written even on the single topic of how to operate and gain advantage from the Internet. When one joins a committee to specify the requirements of a software package or workplace redesign, information specific to particular technologies becomes even more plentiful. But, again, this plentiful advice does not prepare us for what goes on in the real-life processes of adopting or developing new technology. To the contrary, in order to make good use of all the specific information, we need an adequate grasp of how new technology, work, and organization interrelate and how they change.

NOTES TO CHAPTER 1

1. SLTI draws on a range of research fields: cultural studies of artifacts and marketing, engaging with the consumption of goods and services; innovation studies stressing nonlinear and heterogeneous innovation processes; and work on organizational learning and the reflexive activities of players in the innovation process.
2. This section as well as the following section on SLTI work on innovation contexts have been jointly written with James Stewart and first appeared in Stewart and Hyysalo (2008).
3. But the differences are also important. Ethnographies of consumption build on social anthropology, where goods are seen primarily as carriers of meaning and mediators of social relations. While these studies may include detailed descriptions of how people shape the material qualities of consumed objects, these findings are by default suppressed in favor of explanations in terms of shared rituals, tradition, authentication, and symbols, which are perhaps seen as culturally deeper by the tradition (Belk and Costa 1998; Sherry 1990; Wallendorf and Arnould 1991). In contrast, ethnographies of work tend to emphasize how both work and technology are shaped, and have often accounted well for the organizational context of technology use (Karasti 2001; McLaughlin et al. 1999; Suchman et al. 1999). This emphasis is accentuated in innovation studies, which tend to focus solely on the modifications and additional inventions users have made, while saying precious

little about any social and cultural context within which these changes take place (Gardiner and Rothwell 1985; von Hippel 1988, 2005).

4. Although they have attracted more attention in marketing around opinion leaders, word of mouth, and viral marketing (Stewart 2007).

5. We come back to this point in Chapter 2 of this volume when we discuss the few studies that actually have done so (e.g., Pollock and Williams 2008; Wang 2007).

NOTES TO CHAPTER 2

1. Itself a reformulation of the work of anthropologists W. H. R. Rivers and Margaret Mead (Kopytoff 1986).

2. Clearly these ideas were spurred on by Kuhnian and post-Kuhnian philosophy of science, and the pioneering work by Fleck (1979 [1935]), but, just as importantly, from historians of technology such as Noble (1984) and Hughes (1979).

3. There have been various attempts to refine SCOT to better take into account, for instance, the shaping of technology in use. Kline and Pinch studied how early rural cars were "reconfigured" by their owners (1996) and McLaughlin et al. (1999) examine the "restabilization of socio-technology" in the deployment of management information systems. However, these improvements, mostly drawing from fields that conceptualize use in more depth, have not been used to alter the original SCOT concepts in a sufficient manner, and, perhaps consequently, several studies that claim to use SCOT in studying use, in fact, use very little of the conceptual framework in doing so (Pinch and Oudshoorn 2003b). For critiques of various aspects of SCOT over the years, see, for instance, Mackay and Gillespie (1992), Pinch and Oudshoorn (2003a), Beirne and Ramsay (1988, 217), Grint and Woolgar (1997, 18–25), Klein and Kleinman (2002).

4. There are, of course, some alluring, and rather dominant, modes by which the questions about the relationship between change and context can be made to evaporate by emphasizing context. In holistic and structuralist theories, in-depth structural properties of language, culture, or society are taken to govern the way in which individual realizations take place. The significant change, thus, happens only at the level of the aggregate system that is perceived as fairly stable. Changes in the level of instances and their potential mechanisms for affecting the aggregate level are of secondary importance and interest. Another strategy is that of asserting that there is a fundamental context such as economists' emphasis on rational self-interested calculation explaining all other forms of human action. However, the most common, even if less brave, strategy is to resort to a division of labor where the researcher focuses solely on some favorite scale of analysis as the primary and regards it as "contextualized" and "contentualized" by (the usually compliant reading of) data of sorts and granularities without any further problematization.

5. Change-oriented scholars equally have some alluring means at their disposal for effectively evaporating context from analysis. The dominant mode is taking one aspect of change as the privileged process or again simply shunning the possibility that alternative contexts could be relevant for the inquiry. Intellectual, particularly internalist disciplinary, histories are a prime case of such tradition: for instance, philosophical ideas are traced from thinker to thinker across centuries, at their wildest seeing the intellectual history as a straightforward line of descent of thinking from Aristotle and Cicero.

6. Some of the important roots to this way of building a research setup can be found in Geertz's famous and debated study of the Balinese cockfight, where he reversed the customary order of priority in understanding a culture in anthropology. By focusing closely on the common phenomenon of arranged cockfights, on which the natives placed significant emphasis but ethnographers had shunned, Geertz was able to move gradually more deeply into the patterning of significance in Balinese culture. Far from being only gambling, these events turned out to revolve around "deep play" of social clustering, relating to violence, hostility and animality, and a range of other patterning in that culture (Geertz 1973a, 412–453). The key issue was to move inferentially from the close and detailed examination of a particular phenomenon to broader cultural patterns. In close affinity, Italian historians deployed detailed case analysis to reveal knowledge about the wider processes instantiated in their cases of everyday beliefs and social structures in early modern Italy (Levi 1988; Ginzburg 1989). For Geertz's own meta-commentary, see (Geertz 1973b). For instance, on page 14 he notes, "Culture is not a power, something to which social events, behaviours, institutions, or processes can be causally attributed; it is a context, something within which they can be intelligibly—that is thickly—described." But the way he goes on inferring culture, however, goes hand in hand with inferring the phenomena he studies, in a mutually constitutive manner, not as something within any sort of *given entity.*

7. Perhaps the awkward definition of relevant social group has survived because in many SCOT studies membership and doing are closely matched with a shared meaning towards a particular technology, such as in engineering, entrepreneurship, or sports enthusiasm. And, indeed, good research practice may overcome the concepts on which it claims to utilize, but this is hardly an excuse for one's conceptual shortcomings: see Bijker and Pinch's own argumentation in (2002).

8. AT has been used and developed in different contexts and for different purposes, resulting in some variation within the theory. Here the focus is on the work research and technology studies branches of the theory, particularly in the tradition of developmental work research (Toikka 1984; Engeström, Y 1995).

9. AT's insistence on materiality of objects and symbols as deeply constitutive to human action is shared by interactionist science and technology studies (Clarke and Star 2003) but is in some contrast to some other strands of interactionism—for instance, Blumer's notion of object.

10. This is also very much a matter of the questions asked. If one aims to generate a theory about how the cognitive functions of human beings truly function in a situated action, then one surely needs highly detailed recordings and a highly detailed analysis of the specific situation (Hutchins 1995; Lynch 1985). Likewise, a cosmology of a culture of engineering is hardly grasped by following an occasional series of design meetings; rather, it requires years of immersion (cf. Traweek 1988).

NOTES TO CHAPTER 3

1. As is typical of most work with these kinds of characteristics, much of its organizing rests on the presumption that there is and will be an abundant supply of low-income and voluntary (female) work (cf. Wajcman 1991).

2. In claiming that these quotes indeed illustrate some of the key facets in public discourse, I rely on a comprehensive archived news feed of all major newspapers and magazines in Finland in 1999–2002 compiled by an agency spe-

cializing in the task for the company I was studying. There is also more sporadic news coverage and archival for 1992–1998 and 2002–2007, the latter conducted by the company staff and the former by the present author. The quotes are translated from Finnish by the author.

3. The name of the product was originally "Wristcare" but it was rebranded into "Vivago" in the middle of our study period. Hence we use Wristcare, Vivago and Vivago-Wristcare interchangeably, even though Wristcare was used more until 2000 and Vivago more after 2002. The start-up company developing this product was originally called "International Security Technology" but later was rebranded "Vivago Ltd." and this latter name is what we shall use throughout the book for consistency.

4. Wristcare functional description, 1993; project business plan, 1995.

5. Wristcare functional description, 1993; interviews with the company founder October 15, 1999, October 22, 1999.

6. Wristcare functional description, 1993; interviews with the company founder October 15, 1999, October 22, 1999.

7. Interview with the company founder, May 9, 2001.

8. Interview with the company founder, October 15, 1999; software designer, January 25, 2000.

9. Vivago Ltd. business plan, 1995; interview with electronics designer, November 25, 1999; founder, May 9, 2001.

10. Wristcare functional description, 1993; Vivago Ltd. business plan, 1995.

11. Vivago Ltd. functional description, 1993.

12. Interview with a manager of safety-phone service in the Finnish Red Cross on June 11, 2001.

13. Wristcare functional description, 1993; Vivago Ltd. business plan, 1995, 1998.

14. For similar findings on the development of e-commerce and interactive television see Konrad (2008).

15. Much of this discussion of the functions of collective expectations has been paralleled in the activity-theoretical discussion about the functions of objects of activity (Leontjev 1978; Engeström 1987; Engeström and Escalante 1996; Kaptelinin 2005).

16. Interview with Vivago Ltd. R&D manager on May 14, 2001.

17. Vivago Ltd. electronics designer, November 25, 1999.

18. Imaginations animating medical practices and biomedical research can not be discussed at length here, for those interested in further readings on the topic see, for example, Berg (1997), Gregory (2000), and Berg and Mol (1998).

19. Interviews with the company founder on October 15, 1999, and September 5, 2001.

20. STRC baseline research report, 1994.

21. Interview with the company founder on May 9, 2001.

22. This is not meant to suggest that peripheral relationships are undesirable. Indeed, designers typically inhabit several communities of practice and almost by default remain peripheral to some of them. Moreover, as was the case with elderly care, many PBIs do not have one authoritative center or would be uniformly held by different participants.

23. Direct in the sense that they visibly implied certain aspects of use and users.

24. Functional description, 1993; business plan, 1995.

25. Functional description, 1993; business plan, 1995.

26. Functional description, 1993.

27. The durability of this user-representation and of the corresponding design decisions is evident from the fact that even during the year-2000 effort to redesign the second generation of the device, it was considered an inconceiv-

able design option to drop requiring the 24-hour use for every user despite all the trouble this had caused in the hands of the users.
28. Wristcare users' manual, 1997.
29. Functional description, 1993; business plan, 1995.
30. Company business plans in 1995, 1997, and 1998.
31. Interview with the Vivago Ltd. export manager on November 25, 1999.
32. Interview with the company founder on May 9, 2001.
33. Vivago Ltd. customer manager on November 9, 1999.
34. Any mechanistic view of the distribution of this agency is unlikely to be fruitful. As our analysis illustrated, the persons always internalize only some version of a practice and the nature of their participation can vary greatly. This goes equally for how they then externalize their (reinterpreted) ideas in their locally formed activity systems.

NOTES TO CHAPTER 4

1. Interview with the company founder, October 15, 1999.
2. Interview with the company founder, October 15, 1999 and October 22, 1999.
3. This, of course, lent support to the innovation process, which certainly was one of the aims of these studies. Following Grønbæk et al. (1993), a vague description in a market study supported the desire to appeal to as large a market as possible.

NOTES TO CHAPTER 5

1. Interviews with designer 1 on October 30, 1999, and March 3, 2000.
2. On which, for instance, the push-button solution was based.

NOTES TO CHAPTER 6

1. The shift in defining usability and utility as functions of end users' work practice has also been made previously, for instance, in the evaluative studies of computer use in various organizations by the LaborIS group (Eriksson and Nurminen 1991; Mäkeläinen et al. 1996; Nurminen et al. 1994).
2. Resident 1, Savitaipale.
3. Resident 2, Savitaipale.
4. Resident 3, Savitaipale.
5. Interview with company electronics designer, November 25, 1999.
6. Resident 1, Espoo.
7. Resident 3, Espoo.
8. Resident 1, Turku.
9. Resident 4, Espoo.
10. Nurse 1, Espoo.
11. Home-care worker 1, Espoo.
12. Interviews with the manager on September 1, 2000, and the project manager on August 30, 2000, of the foundation owning the institution.
13. Interview with nurse M and the manager on September 1, 2000.
14. Interview with the manager and nurse M on September 1, 2000.

15. Observation and interviews with nurses M and P on September 1, 2000.
16. Recording of the Vivago Ltd. training session on September 6, 2000; discussions with Vivago Ltd. designers on September 12, 2000.
17. Interview with the rest-home manager on November 8, 2001.
18. Interview with the rest-home manager on November 8, 2001, and with nurse on November 12, 2001.
19. Interview with nurse on November 12, 2001.
20. Interview with nurse on November 12, 2001; interview with another nurse on November 8, 2001.
21. Interviews with nurses and managers on November 8 and 12, 2003.
22. The importance of people helping each other out with tasks and artifacts besides their main job is a common phenomenon. Such informal intermediaries point further to the importance of unrecognized and invisible work in organizations (Stewart and Hyysalo 2008; Clarke and Star 2003).
23. Interview with CEO, June 4, 2009.

NOTES TO CHAPTER 7

1. Company business plan, June 13, 1997, 6–15.
2. Company business plan, June 13, 1997, 1–15, esp. 13; Wristcare functional description of January 13, 1997; Wristcare users' manual, 1997.
3. Interview with the founder of the company in Helsinki, October 22, 1999.
4. Interview with a rest-home nurse in Espoo, December 19, 2000.
5. Interview with a designer in Helsinki, October 22, 1999.
6. Interview with home-care workers in a rest home in Espoo, February 29 and August 22, 2000.
7. Interview with a technician in Savitaipale, November 1, 2000.
8. Interview with home-care workers and the manager of a sheltered housing facility in Espoo, August 30, 2000.
9. Observations of the design and product development meetings of the company in Helsinki, August 1–October 1, 2000.
10. Interview with R&D manager in Helsinki, May 14, 2001.
11. During this time, the company also hired several other key personnel (CEO, R&D manager, product manager, and heads of marketing and production) with earlier careers in larger high-tech firms. The safety-phone expert aside, the newer hires initially paid less attention to seeking out user requests than the existing staff, but once its importance became evident, they went further in pursuing it. However, I would refrain from inferring that this was due to their experience from previous firms but, rather, infer that they were less confident with the existing design because they had not been involved in constructing it.
12. Interview with the company founder in Helsinki, September 17, 2001.
13. Interview with R&D manager in Helsinki, May 14, 2001.
14. Observations in Savitaipale on November 30, 2000, and Espoo on August 30, 2000, at nursing homes.
15. Interview with a home-care worker in Espoo, September 13, 2000.
16. Interview with a designer in Helsinki, November 25, 1999.
17. Interview with CEO in Helsinki, November 13, 2000.
18. Interview with product manager in Helsinki, November 25, 2002.
19. Interviews and observations in Espoo in August–September 2000 and in Turku in November 2001.
20. Interview with CEO in Helsinki, November 25, 2002.
21. Emphasis on the change in what is shared about boundary objects is congruent with the original work with the concept and their later reconceptualizations

(e.g., Star 1991; Bowker and Star 1999; Clarke and Star 2003). Our view remains uneasy with the common organization studies trope of suggesting that boundary objects lead to "shared understanding," seen as a fusion in (or disappearance of) divergent perspectives (e.g., Carlile 2002). For more general discussion about differences in the use of boundary objects in science and technology studies and in organization studies see, e.g., Zeiss and Groenewegen (2009).

22. Conversely, how do the mass-produced and mass-marketed devices need to be supported and remain configurable to optimize customer satisfaction and profit?

23. Interview with software developer, June 8, 2009, head of R&D, June 10, 2009, and CEO, June 4, 2009.

24. Interview with company CEO, June 4, 2009.

25. Interview with company marketing manager, June 7, 2009.

26. Interview with the head of R&D, June 10, 2009, and CEO, June 4, 2009.

NOTES TO CHAPTER 8

1. It is noteworthy how closely the ANT program comes here to Foucaultian ascending analysis of power (e.g., Foucault 1995; Kusch 1991).

2. Diabetes is an incurable long-term illness. In the longer run, it leads to, for instance, kidney failure, heart attacks, and blindness. These complications can be countered by maintaining a "good treatment balance," mainly the right blood-sugar level, with diet and medication. A large amount of documentation is produced and used to control the disease over the years. For this purpose, paper forms have been the main tool, while software could allow more powerful data handling and storage.

3. These changes in its business strategy were partly motivated by their appeal to investors at the turn-of-the-millennium dot-com bubble that was taking place at the time.

4. It is noteworthy that, even in its realignment from the locked-in partners, the firm was entrenched in the power dynamics of medical practice in other ways. The purchasing decisions in the medical settings rely on the experts' opinion, which undoubtedly contributed to the company's decision to realign itself with experts.

5. Diabetes clinician 1.

6. Diabetes clinician 2.

7. Diabetes clinician 3.

8. Clearly the time that is most sensible to treat as "proximal" can differ, as can the "extent" of collectivity and actions in the "zone" in ZPD. Also, the cross-practice learning required in deliberating what would be "development" within the potentially tensioned agendas of the actors involved can naturally take different forms. However, the understanding of development as a complex, collective, and contested path-construction that can meaningfully only take place within a range of a foreseeable actions remains a constant (Engeström et al. 1999b).

NOTES TO CHAPTER 9

1. Hence, we stress that the aspects outlined here are not an eclectic mix from different theoretical positions but reflect relatively well-established findings about different aspects of innovativeness. In discussing the "dimensions," we chose to leave visible some of the alternative ways in which this aspect has

been addressed, but in discussing the other three aspects we identify only the main sources because of limits of space. The sprawl of concepts describing closely similar empirical phenomena used in innovation and technology studies is well documented (for one of the best comparisons, see Russell and Williams 2002) and in the space of this chapter there is no possibility to properly compare along the range of terms via which these aspects have been dealt with in different studies.

2. Other classifications exist; for instance, the CreateAcceptance project expands this to seven dimensions: law and regulation, social, cultural, economic/market, institutional, infrastructural, and technological (Poti et al. 2006a, 2006b; Jolivet et al. 2008; for close affinity, see Hoogma et al. 2002).

3. US Patent 3,682,598.

4. US Patent 6,311,713. Later the same invention occurred to Hitachi, the Chinese Academy of Sciences, and the Aerospace Corporation, but none of them could proceed along this line of invention after encountering the original patents.

5. Document "Revolution in health care by SVV [LMP] systems," dated June 5, 1977 (beginning), and July 14, 1977 (end), written by the main inventor to convince Packard to fund more R&D.

6. Ibid.

7. Ibid.

8. Ibid.

9. IBM's Blood Cell Processor 2991 had been launched in 1976 and IBM wanted to explore the market further.

10. According to a contract proposed by IBM on March 1, 1979.

11. Contract between Nokia, Kone, and Electrofluidics, April 4, 1979.

12. For example, in the conventional dispensing method (syringe + flexible tube + probe) sample and reagent are separated by an air meniscus in the tube. But air compresses by six orders of magnitude more than liquid. The functionality of the LMP required the removal of air because the volume of liquid that enters the system had to be measured with much more precision. In theory, six more digits were possible in a hermetically sealed environment. But there was an even more fundamental reason: any presence of air in LMP channels whose diameter is measured in fractions of a millimeter introduces powerful surface tension and capillary forces—as a consequence liquids move erratically. A hydraulic, airless, dispensing method had to be invented.

13. The dispenser could also be used independently for accurate dosing of small amounts of liquids. The dispenser was highly durable, which meant that it would have reduced Kone's after-sales of disposable syringes and was only commercialized under the next majority owner—in close affinity to the fate of some other LMP parts.

14. Discussion with the inventor, January 23, 2009.

15. Many of these ideas were envisioned informally and already in a draft of the inventor's unpursued research plan at the University of Turku, dated April 25, 1994, but rejected in the LMP company context, leaving little point in pursuing them further at the time.

16. The service concept was, in fact, a necessity since the analyzers would need a professional refill of hermetically packaged reagents every six to 24 months.

17. Published US Patent application 20040115829, first filed in Finland on February 1, 2001.

18. Interview with the laboratory leader, March 8, 2006.

19. The International Searching Authority of the Patent Cooperation Treaty found nothing to compromise the novelty of the quality control patent in its

response of December 12, 2006—meaning that no one had filed comparable claims before.

20. *Point of care diagnostic testing world markets: Trends, industry participants, product overviews and market drivers.* TriMark Publications, April 2007. Volume TMRPOC07–0416, p. 187.

21. Clinical and Laboratory Standards Institute, *Proceedings from the QC for the Future Workshop; A Report.* CLSI document X6-R. Clinical and Laboratory Standards Institute, Pennsylvania, 2005.

NOTES TO CHAPTER 10

1. For examples of approaches that build on a systemic way to articulate implicit understandings of designers, see Löwgren and Stolterman (2004) and Cooper (2004). It is noteworthy that most such approaches emerge from design research rather than, say, information system research, which still appears wedded to custom systems wherein requirements determination established a relation between the client and the SW builder—an increasingly rare situation.

2. Here it should be noted that none of the health technology projects were very "controversial" health technologies in contrast to, for instance, new contraceptive pills, genetic screening, or decision support software.

3. More apt tools and improved skills, however, could have made the exchange more efficient. This would have been likely in the PDMS project and certainly so in the Wristcare case. This said, the mediation capacity of sophisticated means such as repertoires of paper prototyping lies not only in enhancing users' and designers' ability to raise issues but equally in steering attention by highlighting some issues and hiding others—the home-brewed lists and screen drawings did this equally but were arguably more user initiated. For more extensive comparisons between different projects and constellations between developers and users, see Heiskanen et al. (forthcoming).

4. It is noteworthy that "ascription" bears substantial resemblance to the notion of "spirit" of technology in adaptive structuration theory (DeSanctis and Poole 1994). And just like spirit, ascription introduces significant methodological problems in how it can be read from the artifact by analysts, or alternatively, how exactly, e.g., designers' accounts of their design intents ought to be related to the actual script in the artifact.

5. This is also how Woolgar has continued to apply his notion; competing configurations by various stakeholders are contested and negotiated (e.g., in his keynote to the Nordic Consumer Research Conference, October 3, 2007, Helsinki, Finland).

6. For an excellent review of the wealth of slightly different terms and comparisons, see Russell and Williams (2002). All key analytical concepts in this book are iterations or variations of earlier concepts and vocabulary. This is a conscious choice and a position statement. STS scholars' infatuation with introducing new lingo has in many cases hampered rather than facilitated conceptual development.

NOTES TO CHAPTER 11

1. This goes for OECD, EU, and national contexts alike, Finland being a good case in point. For instance, 80 percent of stakeholders in policy-setting insti-

tutions involved in the recent major, €150m FinnWell program indicated that it would bring substantial change to Finnish health care and 90 percent of them believed the program had decisive influence on Finnish health technology companies. Few outside experts interviewed during program evaluation, however, shared this conviction. Despite the program's engagement with supporting public health care actors (as the first ever in Finnish innovation policy), its resources were seen as scattered to too many company R&D projects, which, in turn, were limited to the development phase. In all, only 28 percent of the interviewees felt that firm and development-phase support should be increased in the future (Kuitunen and Haila 2007).

2. The marketing manager of Suunto Ltd. and Vivago Ltd. and the R&D manager of both.
3. See, e.g., Heiskanen et al. (forthcoming); Miettinen et al. (2008); Miettinen et al. (2003); and Hyysalo (2009b).

NOTES TO THE APPENDIX

1. During these visits, I was typically led to meet a number of people, whose comings and goings depended on their work tasks. Trust in my study and a sense of its rationale had to be established anew each time, which restricted the use of video recording.
2. In addition, some of the earliest interviews were only coded manually.

Index

A

activity theory (AT), 26–27, 40–41, 54–60, 75–79, 103, 152–160, 201, 243, 269

actor network theory (ANT), 37–40, 52, 187, 244–245

agency, xxvi, xxx, 36, 73–74, 90–94, 107, 137–138, 160, 180–181, 206–207, 228–229

anticipation (of need), 95–108

appropriation, 10–18, 42, 139, 150–157, 245

arenas, 49–50, 65–67

artifacts, 12–16, 35–43, 90–94, 103–110, 175–176, 246–254

artful integration, 15

articulation work, 15

B

bias, 26–27, 39–40

biography of technologies and practices, 30–60, 91–92, 106–107, 135–136, 159, 179, 205, 227–228

black box, black-boxing, 7, 28, 36, 175

boundary object, 57, 175–176, 180

boundness, bound, 74–86, 137–138, 240. *See also* practice bound imaginary

C

change, 44–52; post-launch, 163–184; socio-technical, 30–40; speeds of, 47–52; technological, 6, 30, 42–43; and context, 32, 44–52

co-design, 24–25, 185–208, 236–238, 259–261. *See also* collaborative design

cognition, 54–57, 105–108

collaborative design, 4, 185–208. *See also* co-design

community: innovation, 190–192, 201–208, 236; user-innovation, 264; user-inclusive innovation, 172–180, 189–204, 256; user-designer, 236; user, 257–263; medical, 84, 98, 167, 171

comparison, 95–99, 117, 124, 131–133, 171

complexity, 10–11, 18, 110, 187

configuration, 22–24, 38–39, 158–159, 178, 245–251; pre-, de-, re-, and co-, 244–248

constellations, 20–26

consultants, 17–24

consumption, 6, 15, 18, 35, 139, 150, 241

conventions, 13, 150, 247

coordination, 168–172, 180, 186, 189, 248, 261

credibility, 108, 190, 225

crucial users, 207, 271–272

cultural maturation, 13, 232–235

customization, 25, 65, 171, 186, 191, 250

D

demonstrations, 192, 224, 238

design, 3–4, 9–19, 22–32, 38, 41–43; design studies, 30, 88; Ego-design, 12, 93; redesign, 8, 17, 52, 88–89. *See also* co-design

designers, 3–29, 38–39, 52–53, 109, 165–180, 206, 231–253

design process, 4, 22, 93, 96

developer-user/development–use nexus, 5, 20, 58

developer-user/development–use/design-use/producer-user: relations/

interaction, 3–4, 7–9, 21, 26–29, 32, 44, 53, 57, 165–181, 189–191, 206, 241–244, 247–248, 262; collaboration, 186, 206
diabetes care in Finland, 198–199
diabetes database, 185–208
diffusion: of technology and innovation 19; research 16–17, 163
doctors, 185–230, 254–276
doing, using, and interacting (DUI), 8–10, 243–244
domestication, 15–16, 24–25, 157–159, 193, 205, 237

E

economics, 6–11, 213
economy of qualities, 17, 239
e-health, 36–230, 265–276
elderly care technology, 36–183
enterprise resource planning systems (ERP), 25, 71, 192
ESTEEM, 211, 229
ethnography: 10, 15–16, 38, 109–159, 199–201, 231, 242, 258, 278, 307, 309; of change, 32, 40–42, 58–59, 165–180; methods in innovation studies, 4, 10, 41, 258, 262
ethnomethodology, 74–75, 84, 113, 242
evaluation, 83–84, 99–102, 108, 169–170, 211, 237–238, 254–276
expectations, 76–78, 211–213, 266

F

fool-proof/fool-proofing, 86–87, 90, 142, 169
framing, 211–212, 223–233, 266
fluid, fluidity of objects. *See* plasticity of objects

G

general practitioners (GPs), 185–230, 254–276
gerontechnology movement, 65
going concern, 55–56

H

home-care workers, 145–150, 157–159, 165–166

I

imagination, imaginaries, 12, 73–78, 105–107, 114, 131, 137, 204, 227–228, 250–252 ; social, xvii, xxix, 73–78, 95, 250–252; practice-bound, xxix, 63–94, 102, 106–107, 131, 137–138, 196–198, 204–205, 213, 219, 227–228, 233–238, 250–252; shaping of, 250–252, 268
impact: of technology xxi, xxiii, xxvii, 14, 157–161, 177–179, 195–198, 202–205, 209, 215–217, 220, 227, 231–232, 251–253, 265–268; of methods, 102, 259
implementation, 15, 30, 34, 82, 139, 151–161, 254–276
information systems, 4, 187–207
innofusion, 24–25, 179–180
innovation: community, 190–192, 201–208, 236, 256; contexts, 25–26, 95; journey, 32–35; policy, 260–261; processes, 11, 22, 28, 172, 210; projects, 25–26, 228–229; studies, 6, 10
innovativeness, 209–230, 262–263
interaction: in design, 43, 112–135; in technology use, 140–151, 199–201; between design-use. *See* design use relations, *See* co-design, *See* collaboration
interface, 69, 169, 185–208
intermediaries; 17–26, 95–108, 157, 180, 206, 236–239
intermediate users, 20–26, 236
interventions: designer, 169; researcher-driven, 187–188, 204, 268–275

K

knowing/knowledge, 8–10, 14–19, 38, 72–78, 85–88, 91–92, 95–96, 98, 105, 135, 147, 150, 172–179, 190–194, 206, 211–230, 233–234, 237–240, 255–263, 271–273

L

lead-user, 5, 190, 228, 271–273
learning, xxvii, 8–11, 26–28, 56–57, 64, 94–95, 108, 138, 160–162, 180–181, 208, 229–230 ; 239–244 ; learning-by conceptions, 9, 243; -by-doing, 8–10, 164, 243; -by-interacting, 8; -by-regulating, 11; -by-searching, 8; -by-using, 8, 17, 164–165; dynamics, 172–176, 240; economy, 9–29,

239–244; post-launch, 172–
181; micro-level learning, 10,
164–165, 239–244

M

maintenance, 100–101, 144
management, 4, 84, 192, 209, 227
market research/study, 98, 256, 259
market launch, 5, 23, 163
markets, 4–29, 38, 66–67, 98–99, 172,
178, 209–210, 236, 261
materiality, 75, 93, 75–79, 249–252
micro-biography. *See* biography
modalities, 12, 251
models of innovation, 5, 18, 26, 32–44
multilevel perspective (MLP), 48–49

N

narrative, 13, 40, 47, 60, 80, 232
national innovation systems (NIS), 8–9
negotiation, 40–41, 245
networks, 17–19, 33–39, 58, 68–69,
151–156, 174–176, 185–207,
211–212, 222–228, 230,
241–251, 256–257, 261–262,
265, 269–273
new sociology of technology, 30, 36,
231–232
niche, 20, 48–49, 82, 210; ecological,
236; markets, 7–8, 23, 271,
innovation, 48
nurses, 139–184, 185–208, 252

O

obduracy, 32, 43–44, 60
objectivity, 250, 267, 271

P

participatory design (PD), 3–4, 24, 92,
96, 185–187, 195, 205–206,
233–234, 240
pilot: sites, 101, 275; use, 90, 101–102,
106, 165–168, 269–270, 275
physicians *See* doctors
plasticity (fluidity) of objects, 39
policy, 254–265
post-launch change, 163–184
post-launch learning. *See* learning
power dynamics/relations, 187–206,
238–240
practice-bound imaginaries, xxix,
63–94, 102, 106–107, 131,
137–138, 196–198, 204–205,
213, 219, 227–228, 233–238,

250–252; shaping of, 250–252,
268; *See also* imagination, imaginaries
practice (as a concept), 52–56, 75–79,
150–151. *See also* practice-
bound imaginary
producer–user interaction/relations. *See*
developer/user
professional traditions, 72–79, 233. *See
also* practice bound imaginary
PROTEE, 211, 229, 270–271
ProWellness Diabetes Management
Database (PDMS), 185–208
proxy users, 20–23, 107

R

re-innovation, 17, 34–35
relevant social group, 36, 52–54, 77–78
representation of use, users and systems. *See* user representation
risk, 6–7, 18, 142, 203, 210–211

S

safety phones, 63–184
script, inscription, 201, 245; critique of,
244–252
snapshot studies/inquiries, 26
social construction of technology
(SCOT), 36–37, 52–54, 72, 77
social imagination. *See* imagination
social learning in technological innovation (SLTI), 9–29, 243–244
social shaping of technology (SST), 10,
26, 40
social worlds, 56–57, 65–67, 175–176
socio-technical change. *See* change
sociology: of science, 30, 251; of scientific knowledge (SSK), 53; of
technology, 36, 233–234
SOCROBUST, 211, 229, 270
standardization, 171–172, 170, 197,
251
sticky information, 5, 10, 17, 164, 262
symbolic interactionism (SI), 54–58. *See*
arena, *See* boundary-objects, *See*
going concerns, *See* social world,
See trajectory

T

technical support. *See* maintenance
technological change. *See* change
technological frame (TF), 72–79,
137–138
technology assessment, 159, 265–268

technology: design, 3, 65, 75–79, 234; development, 23, 36, 72–75, 186, 268; experiment, 23–24; -in-practice, 140, 150–151; management, 19, 84; policy. *See* policy; production, 11, 72–79; studies, 4, 30–60, 72, 244–252
TeleChemistry (TC), 209–230, 268–276
trajectory, 43, 52, 70–71, 212–230, 252–253

U
usability, 14, 99, 110, 141–152, 195–196, 266–270; as a slow process 165–172, 188–198
usefulness/utility, 6, 87, 103, 140–142, 188–198, 261–267
user: data, 96; feedback, 179–181; group, 96, 263; needs, 95–108, 235–240, 262; interviews, 97–99
user-centered design (UCD), 22–23, 96–101, 240, 258–259
user-initiated innovation, 3–6, 185–208, 259–265

user-innovation communities. *See* communities
user-innovation research, 4–6
user-representations, 11–15, 86–89, 109–138, 232–240

V
value: -chains/-stars, 176, 257; coproduction of, 176; economic, 17; for users, 17, 160, 163–164, 178, 271; novelty, 210, of product/artifact, 82, 105; of user-collaboration, 228; practical, 84; symbolic, 150
values: changing of, 64; designer's, 109, 136–139, 229, 236, 247; user's, 64
valuing technology, 140–150
vendors, 155–157, 236–237
visions. *See* expectations, *See* imagination, imaginary
Vivago-Wristcare, 63–181, 231–253

Z
zone of proximal development (ZPD), 188, 201–203, 208, 269–276